Eternal Echoes

Exploring the Rituals, Beliefs, and Syncretism of Ancient Egyptian Religion

M L Ruscsak

Exploring the Rituals, Beliefs, and Syncretism of Ancient Egyptian Religion

Trient Press
3375 S Rainbow Blvd
#81710, SMB 13135
Las Vegas,NV 89180

Ordering Information:
Quantity sales. Special discounts are available on quantity purchases by corporations, associations, and others. For details, contact the publisher at the address above.
Orders by U.S. trade bookstores and wholesalers. Please contact Trient Press: Tel: (775) 996-3844; or visit www.trientpress.com.

Printed in the United States of America

Publisher's Cataloging-in-Publication data
Ruscsak, M.L.
A title of a book : Eternal Echoes: Exploring the Rituals, Beliefs, and Syncretism of Ancient Egyptian Religion

ISBN
Hard Cover   979-8-88990-032-0
Paper Back   979-8-88990-034-4
Ebook   979-8-88990-033-7

Exploring the Rituals, Beliefs, and Syncretism of Ancient Egyptian Religion

Part 1: Introduction

Religion holds a significant place in the history of humanity, providing a lens through which we can examine the beliefs, practices, and worldviews of ancient civilizations. Among these ancient societies, the civilization of ancient Egypt stands as a remarkable testament to the enduring power and complexity of religious traditions. The ancient Egyptians possessed a profound reverence for the divine, manifesting in an intricate tapestry of rituals, ceremonies, and spiritual practices.

In this comprehensive exploration of ancient Egyptian religion, we embark upon a captivating journey into the realm of prayers, hymns, chants, and spells. This book delves deep into the spiritual landscape of ancient Egypt, shedding light on the multifaceted nature of their religious expressions and their profound significance in the lives of the ancient Egyptians. Through a meticulous examination of textual sources, archaeological evidence, and scholarly interpretations, we aim to unravel the intricacies of ancient Egyptian religious practices, offering students a window into this fascinating world.

Chapter 1 provides a brief yet illuminating overview of ancient Egyptian religion. We delve into the fundamental concepts that shaped their spiritual worldview, exploring their beliefs regarding the afterlife, the divine hierarchy, and the concepts of Ma'at and Isfet. By understanding the foundational principles of ancient Egyptian religion, we lay a solid groundwork for the subsequent chapters.

Chapter 2 delves into the vital role of prayers, hymns, chants, and spells in the religious practices of ancient Egypt. We examine the significance of these rituals as conduits of communication with the divine, as well as the ways in which they were integrated into everyday life. Through the examination of textual sources, we analyze the structure, themes, and purposes of these religious expressions, providing students with a deeper understanding of their importance in ancient Egyptian culture.

Chapter 3 outlines the purpose and scope of this book, setting the stage for the ensuing exploration of ancient Egyptian religion. We elucidate the objectives of our study, highlighting the interdisciplinary nature of our approach, drawing upon insights from fields such as witchcraft, divination, herbalism, shamanism, ecospirituality, and magic in ancient Egypt. By exploring the connections and parallels between ancient Egyptian religion and various spiritual practices, we strive to present a comprehensive analysis that illuminates the complexities of this ancient civilization.

Throughout this book, students will encounter examples, problems, and exercises that stimulate critical thinking and encourage active engagement with the subject matter. By engaging with primary sources, scholarly interpretations, and thought-provoking exercises, students will develop a nuanced understanding of ancient Egyptian religion, its evolution over time, and its interactions with other cultural and religious traditions.

As we embark on this journey into the sacred world of ancient Egypt, let us delve deep into the rituals, beliefs, and practices that shaped the lives of the ancient Egyptians. Together, we will unravel the mysteries and complexities of their religious heritage, fostering a profound appreciation for the enduring legacy of this remarkable civilization.

Chapter 1: Brief Overview of Ancient Egyptian Religion

In the annals of human history, few civilizations have captured the imagination and fascination of scholars and enthusiasts as profoundly as ancient Egypt. Nestled along the banks of the Nile River, this civilization flourished for millennia, leaving behind a rich legacy that encompasses art, architecture, literature, and perhaps most significantly, religion. Ancient Egyptian religion permeated every aspect of life, providing a framework for understanding the cosmos, guiding social interactions, and offering solace in the face of uncertainty.

In this chapter, we embark on a captivating journey through the enigmatic world of ancient Egyptian religion. Drawing upon a wide range of sources, including inscriptions, papyri, tomb decorations, and temple reliefs, we strive to provide students with a concise yet comprehensive overview of this complex belief system. By exploring the fundamental tenets, key deities, and core rituals, we aim to unlock the mysteries of ancient Egyptian religion and lay a solid foundation for the subsequent chapters.

The Cosmological Framework:

To comprehend the intricacies of ancient Egyptian religion, one must first grasp the cosmological framework that underpinned their spiritual worldview. Ancient Egyptians perceived the universe as an ordered and interconnected realm, where harmony and balance were paramount. The concept of Ma'at, embodying notions of truth, justice, and cosmic balance, formed the bedrock of their religious and social fabric. We delve into the significance of Ma'at and its influence on the ancient Egyptians' ethical and moral principles.

Polytheism and Deities:

At the heart of ancient Egyptian religion lay a pantheon of deities, each with their unique attributes, functions, and mythological narratives. We explore the polytheistic nature of their belief system, examining the roles of major gods and goddesses such as Ra, Osiris, Isis, Horus, and Thoth. Through a careful analysis of their iconography, sacred texts, and cult practices, we elucidate the multifaceted relationships between the divine realm and human existence.

Rituals and Offerings:

Rituals served as a vital means of establishing and maintaining harmony between humanity and the divine. We delve into the intricate tapestry of religious ceremonies and offerings, ranging from the grandeur of temple rituals to the personal devotions performed by individuals in their homes. Through a close examination of textual sources and archaeological evidence, we shed light on the significance of rituals in ancient Egyptian religion and their role in cultivating a sense of communal identity.

Afterlife and Funerary Practices:

The ancient Egyptians' profound preoccupation with the afterlife shaped their funerary practices, which held paramount importance in their religious framework. We explore the beliefs surrounding death, the preservation of the body through mummification, and the journey of the soul in the afterlife. By delving into the enchanting realm of tomb art, funerary texts, and burial customs, we gain insight into the ancient Egyptians' quest for eternal life and their reverence for ancestors.

Throughout this chapter, students will encounter examples, problems, and exercises that foster critical thinking and facilitate a deeper understanding of ancient Egyptian religion. By engaging with primary sources, analyzing artistic representations, and contemplating thought-provoking questions, students will develop a nuanced appreciation for the complexities and nuances of this ancient belief system.

As we embark on this scholarly exploration, let us peel back the layers of time and immerse ourselves in the spiritual universe of ancient Egypt. By delving into the essence of their religious practices, we unravel the mysteries that have captivated generations, fostering a deep appreciation for the enduring legacy of this remarkable civilization.

Explanation of the religious beliefs and cosmology of ancient Egypt

To understand the religious beliefs of ancient Egypt, it is essential to explore their cosmological framework, which shaped their perception of the universe and the divine. Ancient Egyptians conceived of the cosmos as an intricately ordered and interconnected system, governed by the principles of harmony and balance. At the core of their religious worldview was the concept of Ma'at, a multifaceted term encompassing notions of truth, justice, cosmic order, and harmony. Ma'at was not merely an abstract concept but a force that permeated every aspect of existence, from the movements of celestial bodies to the interactions between individuals in society.

Polytheism and the Divine Pantheon:

Ancient Egyptian religion was characterized by a rich and complex pantheon of gods and goddesses. Polytheism was the dominant religious framework, and the ancient Egyptians believed in the existence of multiple deities, each with their own distinctive attributes, roles, and mythological narratives. The divine pantheon comprised gods and goddesses associated with natural phenomena, celestial bodies, abstract concepts, and specific domains such as fertility, war, wisdom, and craftsmanship.

For example, Ra, the sun god, was considered the supreme deity, embodying the life-giving force of the sun. Osiris, the god of the afterlife and resurrection, symbolized the cycle of life, death, and rebirth. Isis, the goddess of magic and fertility, represented the nurturing and protective aspects of femininity. These deities, among many others, played pivotal roles in the religious and mythological narratives of ancient Egypt.

Creation Myths and the Origins of the Universe:

Ancient Egyptian cosmology encompassed various creation myths that sought to explain the origins of the universe and the divine order. One prominent myth involved the god Atum, who emerged from the primordial waters of Nun and brought forth creation through his creative powers. Atum was believed to have engendered the first divine couple, Shu (the god of air) and Tefnut (the goddess of moisture), who in turn gave rise to the world and the subsequent generations of deities.

Other creation myths centered around the god Ptah, who was revered as the divine craftsman responsible for shaping the world and all living beings. Ptah's creative act was envisioned as a result of his thoughts and words, symbolizing the power of divine utterance and the primacy of language in the act of creation.

The Duat: Underworld and the Journey of the Soul:

In ancient Egyptian belief, the afterlife held great significance, and the journey of the soul in the realm of the Duat played a central role in religious rituals and funerary practices. The Duat was conceived as an intricate underworld, through which the deceased would travel after death, encountering various challenges and tests. The ultimate goal of this journey was to reach the Hall of Ma'at, where the heart of the deceased would be weighed against the Feather of Ma'at, symbolizing the individual's adherence to moral and ethical principles.

To ensure a successful journey, ancient Egyptians engaged in complex funerary rituals, including mummification, the preservation of the body, and the provision of grave goods. They believed that these preparations would enable the deceased to maintain their physical form and continue their existence in the afterlife, where they could enjoy the blessings and rewards associated with a life well-lived.

Cult Practices and Rituals:

Ancient Egyptian religious practices were diverse and multifaceted, encompassing both temple rituals performed by priests and personal devotions carried out by individuals in their homes. Temples served as sacred spaces where the divine and human realms intersected, and rituals were conducted to maintain the cosmic order and honor the gods.

Examples of temple rituals included offerings of food, beverages, and incense, as well as the performance of complex liturgical ceremonies involving processions, music, and dance. Personal devotions involved the creation of household shrines, where individuals would make offerings and recite prayers to their chosen deities, seeking protection, guidance, and blessings in their daily lives.

Symbolism and Sacred Iconography:

Symbolism played a significant role in ancient Egyptian religious beliefs and practices. The use of intricate iconography and symbolism in temple reliefs, tomb decorations, and sacred objects served to convey religious concepts, evoke the presence of deities, and facilitate communication between the human and divine realms. For instance, the ankh, a symbol resembling a cross with a loop at the top, represented the concept of life and was often depicted in the hands of gods and goddesses. The scarab beetle symbolized rebirth and was associated with the sun god, Khepri.

Nature and Animal Worship:

Ancient Egyptians held a profound reverence for nature and believed that natural phenomena, animals, and plants were imbued with divine qualities. They worshipped a variety of animal deities, considering them as sacred manifestations of divine power. For instance, the cow-goddess Hathor was associated with fertility and nourishment, while the falcon-headed god Horus symbolized protection and royal authority.

Additionally, animals such as cats, crocodiles, and ibises were mummified and buried in special catacombs as offerings to the gods. These animal cults reflected the ancient Egyptians' deep connection with the natural world and their desire to honor and interact with the divine through the veneration of animal representations.

Conclusion:

The religious beliefs and cosmology of ancient Egypt were deeply ingrained in every aspect of their society and provided a comprehensive framework for understanding the universe, human existence, and the divine. Through the concepts of Ma'at, the polytheistic pantheon, creation myths, funerary practices, and symbolic representations, the ancient Egyptians sought to establish harmony with the cosmic order and ensure their spiritual well-being.

By studying the religious beliefs and cosmology of ancient Egypt, students can gain valuable insights into the profound complexities of this civilization and develop a deeper appreciation for the role of religion in shaping human societies throughout history. Through critical analysis of primary sources, engagement with thought-provoking questions, and exploration of practical exercises, students can further their understanding of ancient Egyptian religious practices and cultivate a broader perspective on the diversity of human spiritual expressions.

Examination of the importance of religion in ancient Egyptian society

Religion held a paramount position in ancient Egyptian society, permeating every aspect of life and shaping the cultural, social, and political landscape. The religious beliefs and practices of the ancient Egyptians played a fundamental role in maintaining social order, providing a sense of identity and purpose, and establishing a connection between the divine and the human realms. This section aims to explore the multifaceted importance of religion in ancient Egyptian society, drawing upon examples from various fields of study, including Witchcraft, Divination, Herbalism, Shamanism, Ecospirituality, and Magic in Ancient Egypt.

Social Cohesion and Cultural Identity:

Religion served as a unifying force in ancient Egyptian society, fostering a sense of communal identity and shared values. The belief in a pantheon of gods and goddesses, rituals, and religious festivals provided a common framework for individuals to come together, reinforcing social bonds and establishing a collective consciousness. For example, annual festivals held in honor of specific deities brought communities together, creating opportunities for social interaction, trade, and the expression of shared cultural traditions.

Religious rituals also played a crucial role in promoting social cohesion. Temples served as central gathering places where individuals from all walks of life, including priests, nobles, and commoners, could participate in ceremonies and engage in acts of worship. These communal rituals reinforced social hierarchies, with the king acting as the primary intermediary between the divine and the people.

Moral and Ethical Framework:

Ancient Egyptian religion provided a moral and ethical framework that guided individual behavior and interactions within society. The concept of Ma'at, representing truth, justice, and cosmic order, underpinned the moral principles of ancient Egyptian society. Ma'at served as a guiding principle for personal conduct, emphasizing virtues such as honesty, fairness, and compassion.

The teachings and myths associated with deities also conveyed moral lessons and ethical values. For example, the story of Osiris, who was unjustly killed by his brother Seth but ultimately resurrected and became the ruler of the afterlife, highlighted the importance of righteousness and the ultimate triumph of justice over chaos. These moral teachings fostered a sense of accountability and responsibility among individuals, promoting social harmony and stability.

Political Legitimacy and the Divine Kingship:

Religion played a crucial role in establishing and maintaining political legitimacy in ancient Egypt. The concept of divine kingship, wherein the pharaoh was believed to be a living embodiment of a god on Earth, provided the foundation for the ruler's authority and power. The pharaoh's close association with deities and their participation in religious rituals demonstrated their divine mandate to govern and ensure the welfare of the people.

The religious rituals performed by the pharaoh, such as the Sed festival or the Heb-Sed, were essential for renewing the ruler's divine powers and reaffirming their legitimacy. These ceremonies were public displays of the pharaoh's connection to the gods and their role as a mediator between the divine and human realms. By participating in these rituals, the pharaoh reinforced their position as the central figure in the religious and political life of ancient Egypt.

Personal Devotion and Individual Spirituality:

While religion played a significant role in the communal and political spheres, it also provided individuals with a framework for personal devotion and individual spirituality. Ancient Egyptians believed in a personal relationship with the gods and sought their guidance and protection through prayers, offerings, and rituals.

Individuals engaged in personal devotions at home, creating household shrines dedicated to specific deities or ancestral spirits. These intimate spaces allowed individuals to connect with the divine on a personal level, seeking solace, blessings, and guidance in their daily lives. Magical practices, such as spells and amulets, were also utilized to harness supernatural forces and protect against malevolent entities.

Interaction with the Supernatural and the Quest for Knowledge:

Ancient Egyptian religion provided a means for individuals to engage with the supernatural and explore the mysteries of the universe. Practices such as divination, witchcraft, and magical rituals were employed to gain insight into the future, seek healing, or manipulate natural forces. Divination techniques, such as interpreting dreams, reading omens, or consulting oracles, allowed individuals to tap into the divine realm and gain guidance for decision-making or understanding of future events.

Furthermore, the ancient Egyptians' pursuit of knowledge extended to the study of the cosmos, mathematics, medicine, and natural phenomena. Astronomy played a vital role in religious observations, with the movements of celestial bodies informing the timing of religious festivals and rituals. The study of medicine and herbalism was closely intertwined with religious beliefs, as healing practices were often associated with specific deities and magical rituals.

Conclusion:

In ancient Egyptian society, religion occupied a central and indispensable role. It provided a framework for social cohesion, shaping cultural identity, and reinforcing moral and ethical values. Religion also served as a means of political legitimacy, establishing the divine kingship and ensuring the pharaoh's authority. At an individual level, religion offered personal devotion, spiritual connection, and avenues for engaging with the supernatural.

The importance of religion in ancient Egypt is evident through its influence on various aspects of society, including art, architecture, governance, and personal beliefs. By examining the significance of religion in ancient Egyptian society, students can gain a deeper understanding of the complexities of this civilization and recognize the profound impact of religious beliefs on human cultures throughout history.

Class Exercises :

Analyze a religious festival from ancient Egypt and discuss its social and cultural significance.

Compare and contrast the moral principles of Ma'at with ethical frameworks in other ancient civilizations.

Investigate the role of divine kingship in ancient Egyptian politics and compare it to other systems of governance in the ancient world.

Reflect on personal religious practices today and draw parallels to the individual spirituality of ancient Egyptians.

Examine the role of divination and magic in ancient Egyptian society and discuss its implications for understanding human desires for knowledge and control over the supernatural.

Analysis of the role of gods, goddesses, and divine entities in ancient Egyptian mythology and religious practices

The ancient Egyptian pantheon comprised a vast array of gods, goddesses, and divine entities, each possessing unique attributes, powers, and responsibilities. These deities played a pivotal role in ancient Egyptian mythology and religious practices, serving as intermediaries between the mortal realm and the divine. This section aims to provide a comprehensive analysis of the role of gods, goddesses, and divine entities in ancient Egyptian religion, drawing upon examples from various fields of study, including Witchcraft, Divination, Herbalism, Shamanism, Ecospirituality, and Magic in Ancient Egypt.

Intermediaries and Protectors:

The gods and goddesses of ancient Egypt were considered intermediaries between humans and the divine. They acted as benevolent forces, providing protection, guidance, and blessings to individuals and communities. Each deity had a specific domain or area of influence, ranging from fertility and agriculture to warfare and wisdom.

For example, the goddess Isis, revered as the mother goddess, was associated with fertility, healing, and magic. She was believed to assist women in childbirth, offer protection to the vulnerable, and possess knowledge of powerful spells and enchantments. Through rituals and prayers dedicated to Isis, individuals sought her favor and intervention in matters related to fertility, health, and protection.

Similarly, the god Thoth, known as the god of wisdom, writing, and magic, was regarded as the patron of scribes and scholars. Thoth was believed to have invented hieroglyphic writing, serving as the divine scribe and mediator between the gods and humans. Individuals seeking knowledge, guidance, or assistance in matters of learning and communication would invoke Thoth through prayers, rituals, and the offering of incense and writing implements.

Cosmic Order and Balance:

Ancient Egyptian mythology emphasized the notion of cosmic order and balance, known as Ma'at. Ma'at represented the harmonious functioning of the universe, characterized by principles such as truth, justice, and balance. The gods and goddesses played essential roles in upholding Ma'at and maintaining cosmic equilibrium.

For instance, the god Horus, the divine falcon, was associated with kingship, the sun, and the protection of Ma'at. As the son of Osiris and Isis, Horus symbolized the rightful succession and continuity of kingship. In the mythological narrative, Horus engaged in a battle with his uncle, Seth, to avenge the murder of his father, Osiris, and restore order to the kingdom. This mythic struggle between Horus and Seth symbolized the eternal struggle between order and chaos, emphasizing the gods' role in maintaining Ma'at.

Exploring the Rituals, Beliefs, and Syncretism of Ancient Egyptian Religion

Cults and Religious Rituals:

The worship of specific gods and goddesses in ancient Egypt gave rise to cults and religious rituals dedicated to their veneration. Temples served as the focal points for religious activities, where priests and devotees would conduct rituals, offer sacrifices, and perform ceremonies to honor the gods.

One prominent example is the cult of Amun-Ra, a combination of the god Amun and the sun god Ra. Amun-Ra was regarded as the king of the gods, embodying the creative and life-giving power of the sun. The Karnak Temple in Thebes was dedicated to Amun-Ra and served as a significant religious center. The grand processions, festivals, and offerings held at Karnak Temple were intended to secure Amun-Ra's favor and ensure the prosperity and well-being of Egypt.

Personal Devotion and Popular Deities:

While the worship of gods and goddesses occurred on a grand scale within temples, personal devotion to specific deities was also widespread among the ancient Egyptian populace. Individuals would develop personal relationships with certain gods or goddesses, seeking their assistance and guidance in various aspects of life.

For example, the goddess Bastet, associated with protection, fertility, and the home, was highly popular among individuals seeking safety, prosperity, and familial blessings. Devotees would create statues, amulets, and personal shrines dedicated to Bastet, performing daily rituals and offering food, incense, and prayers.

Dissenting Views and Interpretations:

It is important to note that interpretations of ancient Egyptian mythology and religious practices may vary, and dissenting views exist within the scholarly community. Some scholars argue that the ancient Egyptian pantheon should be viewed more as a fluid and evolving system rather than a fixed and rigid hierarchy of gods and goddesses. They suggest that the role and prominence of certain deities might have shifted over time due to political, social, and cultural changes.

Furthermore, the influence of syncretism—the merging of deities and religious beliefs—within ancient Egyptian religion challenges a strict categorization of gods and goddesses. The fusion of Egyptian and foreign deities, such as the combination of Amun and Ra into Amun-Ra, demonstrates the adaptability and flexibility of ancient Egyptian religious beliefs.

Conclusion:

The gods, goddesses, and divine entities of ancient Egypt held multifaceted roles in religious practices and mythology. They acted as intermediaries, protectors, and embodiments of cosmic order. Their worship was carried out through elaborate rituals and ceremonies within temples, while personal devotion to specific deities provided a more intimate connection between individuals and the divine.

However, it is essential to approach the study of ancient Egyptian religion with an open mind, acknowledging the possibility of differing interpretations and dissenting views. Such diversity of thought fosters critical thinking and encourages students to engage in discussions surrounding the complexities and nuances of ancient Egyptian mythology and religious practices.

Class Exercises:

Select a specific god or goddess from ancient Egyptian mythology and analyze their attributes, responsibilities, and depictions in art. Discuss their significance in ancient Egyptian society.

Compare and contrast the roles and characteristics of gods and goddesses in ancient Egyptian religion with those in another ancient civilization, such as Greek or Mesopotamian mythology.

Investigate the influence of syncretism in ancient Egyptian religion, providing examples of gods or goddesses that were merged or associated with foreign deities.

Analyze the significance of temple rituals and religious ceremonies in ancient Egyptian society, exploring their social, political, and cultural implications.

Discuss dissenting views and interpretations regarding the nature and hierarchy of gods and goddesses in ancient Egyptian religion, considering the arguments put forth by different scholars.

Discussion of the influence of religious beliefs on daily life, rituals, and social structures

The religious beliefs of ancient Egypt permeated every aspect of daily life, shaping rituals, social structures, and individual behaviors. This section aims to provide a detailed analysis of the profound influence of religious beliefs on various aspects of ancient Egyptian society, including daily practices, religious rituals, and the organization of social structures. Drawing upon examples from fields such as Witchcraft, Divination, Herbalism, Shamanism, Ecospirituality, and Magic in Ancient Egypt, we will explore how religious beliefs influenced and shaped the lives of ancient Egyptians.

Daily Life and Piety:

Religious beliefs played a central role in the daily lives of ancient Egyptians, influencing their behavior, values, and social interactions. The concept of ma'at, the harmonious functioning of the universe based on truth, justice, and balance, provided a moral framework that guided individual actions. Ancient Egyptians believed that by adhering to ma'at in their daily lives, they maintained cosmic harmony and ensured their own well-being.

For example, the practice of ethical conduct, including honesty, respect, and fairness, was deeply ingrained in ancient Egyptian society. Individuals believed that by upholding these virtues, they were contributing to the maintenance of ma'at. The negative confessions recorded in the Book of the Dead exemplify this ethical focus, where individuals would declare their innocence by proclaiming their adherence to ma'at and the avoidance of negative actions.

Rituals and Offerings:

Religious rituals and offerings were an integral part of daily life in ancient Egypt. These rituals aimed to maintain a harmonious relationship with the gods, seeking their favor and protection. Individuals would participate in various rituals, both within temple settings and in their own households.

For instance, the ritual of offering food and drink to the gods, known as "ritual meals," was a common practice. Egyptians believed that the deities required sustenance and nourishment, just like humans. They would prepare and present offerings of bread, beer, meat, fruits, and vegetables, believing that the essence of the offerings would be consumed by the gods, while the physical food was consumed by the worshippers.

Festivals and Celebrations:

Festivals held in honor of specific gods and goddesses were significant events in ancient Egyptian society. These celebrations brought communities together, fostering a sense of unity and reinforcing religious beliefs. Festivals often involved elaborate processions, music, dance, and communal feasting.

An example is the festival of Opet, dedicated to the rejuvenation of the god Amun. The festival involved a grand procession where the statues of Amun, his consort Mut, and their son Khonsu were carried from the Karnak Temple to the Luxor Temple. The procession, accompanied by priests, musicians, and dancers, symbolized the renewal of the divine energy and the reaffirmation of the gods' presence in the mortal realm.

Social Structures and Priesthood:

Religious beliefs also influenced the organization of social structures in ancient Egypt. The priesthood held a prominent position in society, serving as intermediaries between the gods and the people. The priests were responsible for performing rituals, maintaining temples, and overseeing the religious practices of the community.

The priesthood was structured hierarchically, with high-ranking priests associated with major temples and specific deities. They held considerable influence and power, both religious and political. For example, the High Priest of Amun in Thebes, who served as the chief priest of Amun-Ra, wielded significant authority and had close ties to the pharaoh.

Burial Practices and Afterlife Beliefs:

Religious beliefs significantly influenced burial practices and the concept of the afterlife in ancient Egypt. Egyptians believed in the continuation of life after death and the importance of preparing for the journey to the afterlife. They believed that the deceased would enter the realm of the gods, where they would be judged and undergo a process of purification.

To ensure a successful transition to the afterlife, individuals engaged in elaborate burial rituals and preparations. These included mummification, the preservation of the body, and the provision of grave goods, such as food, clothing, and personal belongings. The Book of the Dead, a collection of spells and rituals, was also placed in the tomb to guide and assist the deceased in the afterlife.

Counterarguments and Dissenting Views:

While the influence of religious beliefs on daily life, rituals, and social structures in ancient Egypt is widely acknowledged, it is important to consider dissenting views and alternative interpretations. Some scholars argue that the influence of religion may have been exaggerated in previous scholarship, suggesting that economic and political factors played equally significant roles in shaping ancient Egyptian society.

For example, they propose that the construction of monumental temples and the organization of festivals were not solely driven by religious motivations but were also influenced by political ambitions and the desire to consolidate power. Additionally, they argue that social structures and priesthoods might have been more fluid and flexible, with individuals assuming multiple roles and responsibilities within the religious hierarchy.

Conclusion:

Religious beliefs had a profound and pervasive influence on daily life, rituals, and social structures in ancient Egypt. They shaped ethical behavior, guided individual actions, and provided a framework for social cohesion. Rituals, festivals, and offerings were an integral part of ancient Egyptian society, fostering a sense of communal identity and reinforcing religious beliefs. The organization of social structures, particularly the role of the priesthood, was deeply intertwined with religious practices. Moreover, religious beliefs influenced burial practices and the concept of the afterlife, emphasizing the significance of preparing for the journey beyond death.

By critically analyzing the influence of religious beliefs on various aspects of ancient Egyptian society, students can develop a comprehensive understanding of the complexities and nuances of ancient Egyptian culture.

Class Exercises:

Research and analyze the ethical principles embodied in ancient Egyptian religious beliefs, comparing them with ethical systems in other ancient civilizations.

Investigate the economic and political factors that may have influenced the construction of temples and the organization of festivals in ancient Egypt, presenting arguments for both religious and non-religious motivations.

Chapter 2: Importance of Prayers, Hymns, Chants, and Spells in Ancient Egyptian Religious Practices

Exploration of the various forms of communication with the divine in ancient Egyptian religion

Prayers, hymns, chants, and spells held significant importance in the religious practices of ancient Egypt. These ritualistic forms of communication with the divine were central to the expression of devotion, the seeking of divine favor, and the maintenance of cosmic harmony. In this chapter, we will delve into the profound significance of prayers, hymns, chants, and spells in ancient Egyptian religion, examining their roles, functions, and underlying beliefs. Drawing upon examples from diverse fields such as Witchcraft, Divination, Herbalism, Shamanism, Ecospirituality, and Magic in Ancient Egypt, we will explore the various aspects of these practices and their implications for understanding the religious worldview of the ancient Egyptians.

The Power of Communication with the Divine:

Prayers, as a form of direct communication with the gods and goddesses, served as a vital link between the mortal realm and the divine realm. Ancient Egyptians believed that through prayers, they could establish a connection with the deities, express their devotion, and seek their guidance, protection, and blessings. Prayers were offered both in formal temple settings and in personal daily interactions.

For example, individuals might recite prayers to Ra, the sun god, at sunrise as an expression of gratitude and to invoke his benevolent presence throughout the day. In times of difficulty or illness, people would offer prayers to Sekhmet, the goddess of healing, beseeching her intervention for restoration and well-being. These prayers were composed with careful consideration of the appropriate language, tone, and formulaic expressions to convey respect and humility towards the gods.

Hymns and Chants in Worship:

Hymns and chants played a crucial role in religious rituals and temple ceremonies in ancient Egypt. They were performed by priests and worshippers to honor and celebrate the gods, to express gratitude, and to invoke divine presence. These melodic and rhythmic compositions served as a means to create a sacred atmosphere and to connect with the divine through the power of music and sound.

An example of the significance of hymns is the "Great Hymn to the Aten," composed during the reign of Pharaoh Akhenaten. This hymn praised the sun disk, Aten, as the supreme deity, highlighting its life-giving and sustaining qualities. The hymn not only expressed devotion but also reflected the religious reforms of Akhenaten, who sought to emphasize the worship of a single deity.

Spells and Incantations:

Spells and incantations held a central position in ancient Egyptian magical practices. These ritual formulas, often written in hieroglyphs or hieratic script, were believed to possess inherent power and could influence the supernatural forces. Spells were employed for various purposes, including protection, healing, love, and divination.

For instance, the "Book of the Dead" contains numerous spells and incantations intended to guide and assist the deceased in their journey through the afterlife. These spells were believed to enable the individual to navigate the dangers and challenges of the underworld, ensuring a successful transformation into a divine being.

The Role of Ritual Experts:

The performance of prayers, hymns, chants, and spells was primarily entrusted to ritual experts, including priests, magicians, and healers. These individuals possessed specialized knowledge, training, and understanding of the appropriate rituals and invocations to communicate effectively with the gods and manipulate the supernatural forces.

Ritual experts were responsible for preserving the sacred texts, maintaining temple rituals, and conducting magical ceremonies. They were highly respected in society for their ability to bridge the mortal and divine realms, and their services were sought after for various religious and magical purposes.

Counterarguments and Dissenting Views:

While the importance of prayers, hymns, chants, and spells in ancient Egyptian religious practices is widely accepted, some scholars argue that these rituals may have also served social, psychological, and therapeutic functions. They propose that the repetitive nature of prayers, chants, and hymns could induce a trance-like state or altered consciousness, facilitating psychological healing and personal transformation.

Moreover, these scholars suggest that the recitation of spells and incantations in magical rituals may have had a placebo effect, providing individuals with a sense of control and empowerment in challenging situations. They argue that the power of these rituals lies not only in their perceived supernatural efficacy but also in their psychological impact on the practitioners.

Conclusion:

Prayers, hymns, chants, and spells were integral components of ancient Egyptian religious practices, providing means of communication with the divine, fostering devotion, and seeking divine intervention. They held significant importance in both personal and communal worship, shaping the religious experiences of individuals and the collective identity of the ancient Egyptian society.

By studying the various forms of ritualistic communication with the divine, students can gain insights into the religious worldview of ancient Egypt and explore the interplay between the mortal and divine realms. To engage students in critical thinking and discussion, the following exercises are suggested:

Analyze and compare different prayers, hymns, and spells from ancient Egyptian religious texts, discussing their themes, stylistic features, and purposes.

Investigate the role of music and sound in ancient Egyptian religious rituals, exploring the connection between sound and the divine realm in other ancient cultures.

Examine the psychological and therapeutic aspects of repetitive rituals such as prayers and chants, drawing upon examples from other religious and spiritual practices.

Research the training and responsibilities of ritual experts in ancient Egypt, comparing them with similar roles in other ancient civilizations.

Discuss dissenting views on the efficacy of prayers, hymns, chants, and spells, considering the potential psychological and social functions of these rituals.

Examination of the roles and functions of prayers, hymns, chants, and spells within the religious context

Prayers, hymns, chants, and spells played diverse roles and functions within the religious context of ancient Egypt. These ritualistic practices were not only expressions of devotion and reverence but also served specific purposes and had tangible effects on the individual and the community. In this section, we will examine the roles and functions of these religious practices in ancient Egyptian society.

Communication with the Divine:

Prayers, as a form of direct communication with the gods and goddesses, were crucial for establishing a connection between humans and the divine realm. Through prayers, individuals expressed their gratitude, sought guidance and protection, and petitioned for divine intervention in various aspects of life. Prayers were considered a means of establishing a personal relationship with the gods, and they formed the basis for individual and communal worship.

Hymns and chants also played a role in communicating with the divine. These melodic and rhythmic compositions were performed during religious rituals and temple ceremonies to honor and celebrate the gods. Hymns expressed the greatness and qualities of specific deities, while chants created a sacred atmosphere and helped worshippers connect with the divine through music and sound.

Preservation of Ma'at:

Ma'at, the fundamental concept of cosmic order and harmony, was at the core of ancient Egyptian religious beliefs. Prayers, hymns, chants, and spells were essential in upholding and restoring Ma'at. By appealing to the gods through prayers, individuals sought to maintain balance in the world and ensure the continued functioning of the universe. Spells and incantations were employed to ward off chaos and protect against malevolent forces, thus safeguarding Ma'at.

Personal and Collective Well-being:

Religious practices, including prayers, hymns, chants, and spells, were closely linked to personal and collective well-being. Prayers and hymns were offered for the prosperity, health, and protection of individuals, families, and the entire community. They were believed to invoke divine blessings and ensure a harmonious and prosperous life.

Spells and incantations were used for various purposes, including healing, protection against illness and misfortune, love and fertility, and divination. These rituals aimed to address specific needs and concerns, providing individuals with a sense of control over their lives and offering comfort and reassurance in times of difficulty.

Ritualistic and Symbolic Functions:

Prayers, hymns, chants, and spells served important ritualistic and symbolic functions in ancient Egyptian religious practices. They formed an integral part of temple rituals and festivals, contributing to the ceremonial atmosphere and invoking the presence of the gods. These rituals often involved a combination of spoken or sung words, gestures, and offerings, creating a multisensory experience that engaged worshippers on multiple levels.

Moreover, the recitation of prayers, hymns, chants, and spells represented the spoken or written word as a potent vehicle of divine power. The correct utterance and recitation of these texts were believed to activate the inherent magical properties within the words, thus enabling individuals to manipulate supernatural forces and achieve desired outcomes.

In summary, prayers, hymns, chants, and spells played diverse roles and functions within the religious context of ancient Egypt. They facilitated communication with the gods, upheld cosmic order, contributed to personal and collective well-being, and served ritualistic and symbolic purposes. These practices were an integral part of ancient Egyptian religious life, shaping the beliefs, experiences, and interactions of individuals and communities with the divine.

Analysis of the ways in which these practices were believed to establish a connection between humans and the divine realm

The ancient Egyptians believed that prayers, hymns, chants, and spells served as powerful means to establish a connection between humans and the divine realm. These practices were believed to bridge the gap between mortal existence and the divine world, facilitating communication and interaction with the gods and goddesses. In this analysis, we will explore the ways in which these practices were perceived to establish a connection between humans and the divine realm in ancient Egyptian religious beliefs.

Invocation of Deity Presence:

Prayers, hymns, chants, and spells were seen as means to invoke the presence of the gods and goddesses. Through the recitation of specific words, sounds, and rituals, individuals sought to attract and engage the attention of the divine beings. It was believed that the correct recitation and performance of these practices would bring the gods and goddesses into the immediate presence of the worshippers. This connection was vital for communication and the exchange of offerings, devotion, and supplication.

Communication and Dialogue:

These religious practices were considered a direct form of communication and dialogue with the gods. Prayers allowed individuals to express their thoughts, desires, and concerns to the divine beings. By addressing the gods and goddesses directly, worshippers believed they could establish a personal relationship and receive guidance, protection, and blessings. Through prayers, individuals sought to articulate their needs and aspirations, seeking assistance and intervention from the divine realm.

Elevation of Consciousness:

Hymns, chants, and repetitive recitations were believed to elevate the consciousness of the worshippers. These practices aimed to create a sacred atmosphere, inducing a state of heightened awareness and spiritual receptivity. Through the melodic and rhythmic nature of hymns and chants, individuals were encouraged to transcend mundane existence and connect with the divine realm. The repetition of sacred words and phrases in spells and incantations also served to focus the mind and attune it to the divine frequencies, allowing for a deeper connection to be established.

Alignment with Divine Will:

Engaging in these religious practices was seen as a way to align oneself with the divine will and seek harmony with the cosmic order. By offering prayers, hymns, and rituals, individuals acknowledged their dependence on the gods and affirmed their commitment to upholding Ma'at, the fundamental principle of balance and order. It was believed that by actively participating in these practices, individuals could attune themselves to the divine plan and seek to live in accordance with the gods' intentions.

Activation of Magical Power:

Spells and incantations were considered to possess inherent magical power. These texts contained sacred words and formulas believed to have been bestowed upon humanity by the gods themselves. By correctly reciting and performing these spells, individuals sought to harness and activate this magical power. It was believed that the gods had empowered these words with divine energy and that their utterance could manipulate supernatural forces and bring about desired outcomes.

In summary, prayers, hymns, chants, and spells were perceived as powerful tools for establishing a connection between humans and the divine realm in ancient Egyptian religious beliefs. Through these practices, worshippers sought to invoke the presence of the gods, engage in direct communication, elevate their consciousness, align themselves with the divine will, and activate the inherent magical power within sacred words. These beliefs and practices formed the foundation of the ancient Egyptians' spiritual connection with the gods, shaping their religious experiences and interactions with the divine.

Discussion of the significance of rituals and incantations in expressing devotion, seeking divine assistance, and promoting harmony with the natural world

Rituals and incantations played a significant role in ancient Egyptian religious practices, serving as powerful means for expressing devotion, seeking divine assistance, and promoting harmony with the natural world. These ceremonial actions and sacred words were believed to have profound effects on the worshippers and their relationship with the gods, as well as their connection to the natural order. In this discussion, we will explore the significance of rituals and incantations in the context of expressing devotion, seeking divine assistance, and promoting harmony with the natural world.

Expressing Devotion:

Rituals and incantations provided a tangible way for individuals to express their devotion and reverence to the gods and goddesses. By meticulously following prescribed rituals and performing specific actions, worshippers demonstrated their commitment and dedication to the divine beings. These practices were not merely symbolic gestures but were believed to have real effects in the spiritual realm. The careful execution of rituals and the recitation of sacred incantations conveyed a deep sense of respect and devotion, reinforcing the bond between humans and the gods.

Seeking Divine Assistance:

Rituals and incantations were employed as a means to seek divine assistance and intervention in various aspects of life. Whether individuals were facing personal challenges, health issues, or seeking guidance, these practices provided a channel to communicate their needs to the gods and goddesses. By performing rituals and reciting specific incantations, individuals believed they could gain the attention and favor of the divine beings, who possessed the power to alleviate their troubles and grant blessings. The act of engaging in these practices was an active demonstration of faith and trust in the gods' ability to assist and protect.

Promoting Harmony with the Natural World:

Ancient Egyptian religious beliefs were deeply intertwined with the natural world, and rituals and incantations were employed to promote harmony and balance within this realm. Through agricultural rites, individuals sought to ensure the fertility of the land and a bountiful harvest. Rituals performed during celestial events, such as the annual flooding of the Nile or the rising of Sirius, were believed to facilitate the cyclical processes of nature. By participating in these rituals and uttering incantations, individuals aimed to maintain a harmonious relationship with the natural forces and invoke the blessings of the gods for the well-being of the community.

Connecting with Cosmic Forces:

Rituals and incantations were seen as a means to connect with cosmic forces and tap into the deeper mysteries of the universe. These practices were designed to align individuals with the cycles of creation and the cosmic order. By engaging in the precise movements, gestures, and recitations prescribed by the rituals, worshippers sought to attune themselves to the natural rhythms and energies that permeated the cosmos. The power of the incantations was believed to resonate with the divine frequencies, enabling individuals to access higher realms of consciousness and spiritual enlightenment.

Preserving Tradition and Cultural Identity:

Rituals and incantations were crucial for the preservation of ancient Egyptian tradition and cultural identity. These practices were passed down through generations, ensuring the continuity of religious beliefs and customs. By participating in rituals and learning the sacred incantations, individuals actively contributed to the perpetuation of their cultural heritage. The performance of rituals and the recitation of incantations served as a unifying force within the community, reinforcing a shared sense of identity and belonging.

In conclusion, rituals and incantations held great significance in ancient Egyptian religious practices. They provided a tangible means for expressing devotion, seeking divine assistance, promoting harmony with the natural world, connecting with cosmic forces, and preserving cultural identity. These practices were deeply ingrained in the daily lives of the ancient Egyptians and were seen as vital conduits for establishing a profound relationship with the gods and aligning oneself with the cosmic order.

Chapter 3: Purpose and Scope of the Book

In this chapter, we will delve into the purpose and scope of this book, which aims to provide a comprehensive exploration of the multifaceted aspects of ancient Egyptian religious practices. By examining the rich tapestry of rituals, beliefs, and spiritual traditions, we seek to offer students a deeper understanding of the religious landscape of ancient Egypt. This chapter serves as a roadmap, outlining the objectives and focal points that will be covered throughout the book.

The Purpose of the Book:

The primary purpose of this book is to present a thorough and in-depth analysis of ancient Egyptian religion, catering specifically to students seeking a bachelor's degree. By exploring the diverse religious practices of this ancient civilization, we aim to foster a comprehensive understanding of the complexities and nuances of Egyptian spirituality. Our goal is to provide a scholarly resource that engages students in critical thinking and encourages meaningful discussions surrounding the religious traditions of ancient Egypt.

Scope and Coverage:

The scope of this book encompasses a wide range of topics related to ancient Egyptian religion. We will examine not only the religious beliefs and cosmology of the ancient Egyptians but also the roles and functions of various religious practices, including prayers, hymns, chants, spells, rituals, and incantations. Furthermore, we will explore the influence of religious beliefs on daily life, social structures, and the natural world.

To facilitate a comprehensive understanding, we will draw upon examples and comparisons from various fields, including Witchcraft, Divination, Herbalism, Shamanism, Ecospirituality, and even Magic in Ancient Egypt. By incorporating these diverse perspectives, we aim to present a holistic view of ancient Egyptian religion and its connections to broader spiritual and cultural contexts.

Objectives and Learning Outcomes:

Throughout this book, we have outlined specific objectives and learning outcomes to guide students in their exploration of ancient Egyptian religion. By engaging with the content presented in each chapter, students will:

a) Gain a thorough understanding of the religious beliefs and cosmology of ancient Egypt, as well as their significance within the broader cultural and historical context.

b) Analyze the role of prayers, hymns, chants, spells, rituals, and incantations in ancient Egyptian religious practices, and comprehend their functions and purposes.

c) Evaluate the influence of religious beliefs on daily life, rituals, and social structures, as well as the interconnectedness of religion with other aspects of ancient Egyptian society.

d) Develop critical thinking skills by examining counterarguments and dissenting opinions surrounding ancient Egyptian religion, allowing for a balanced and objective perspective.

e) Apply the knowledge gained from the book to real-world scenarios and engage in problem-solving exercises that encourage deeper analysis and critical reflection.

Conclusion:

In conclusion, this chapter has introduced the purpose and scope of this book, which aims to provide students with a comprehensive understanding of ancient Egyptian religion. Through a detailed exploration of various topics, including religious beliefs, rituals, prayers, and their cultural significance, students will develop a well-rounded appreciation for the complexities of ancient Egyptian spirituality. By engaging with the material presented in this book, students will enhance their critical thinking skills, broaden their knowledge base, and gain a deeper appreciation for the religious practices of one of the world's most fascinating civilizations.

Examples, Problems, and Exercises:

Analyze a specific ancient Egyptian hymn and discuss its themes, poetic elements, and its reflection of the religious beliefs and values of the time.

Compare and contrast the use of spells in ancient Egyptian religion with their use in modern Witchcraft traditions, highlighting similarities and differences.

Discuss the significance of religious rituals in promoting social cohesion and reinforcing power structures within ancient Egyptian society.

Explore the role of divination practices in ancient Egyptian religious contexts and their impact on decision-making processes.

Examine the ecological and environmental aspects of ancient Egyptian religious practices, such as the worship of nature deities and rituals honoring the natural world.

Explanation of the objectives and goals of the book

The objectives and goals of this book are multi-faceted, aiming to provide students seeking a comprehensive understanding of ancient Egyptian religion with a detailed analysis of its various aspects. By delving into the religious beliefs, practices, and cultural significance of this ancient civilization, we seek to achieve the following objectives:

Knowledge Acquisition: The primary objective of this book is to facilitate the acquisition of knowledge regarding ancient Egyptian religion. Through a systematic exploration of various topics, students will gain an in-depth understanding of the religious beliefs, cosmology, rituals, and deities of ancient Egypt. The book will draw upon a wide range of primary sources, scholarly research, and comparative examples from related fields to present a comprehensive and well-rounded examination of the subject matter.

Critical Analysis: Another key objective is to foster critical thinking skills. Students will be encouraged to engage in critical analysis and evaluation of the information presented in the book. They will be challenged to question assumptions, evaluate evidence, and consider alternative viewpoints. By examining different perspectives, students will develop the ability to think critically, assess arguments, and form well-reasoned opinions. This skill is crucial for academic success and intellectual growth.

Contextualization: A fundamental goal of this book is to provide students with a broader contextual understanding of ancient Egyptian religion. In addition to exploring the religious beliefs and practices themselves, the book will examine the socio-cultural, historical, and political factors that influenced them. By contextualizing ancient Egyptian religion within its specific time period and geographical location, students will gain insights into the interconnectedness of religion with various aspects of society. This contextual understanding will enhance their appreciation and comprehension of the subject matter.

Cultural Appreciation: This book aims to foster an appreciation for the cultural and religious diversity of ancient Egypt. By examining the rituals, prayers, hymns, chants, and spells of this civilization, students will gain an understanding of their significance within the cultural framework of ancient Egyptian society. The book will explore the ways in which religious practices intersected with other aspects of daily life, such as Witchcraft, Divination, Herbalism, Shamanism, Ecospirituality, and Magic, to provide a comprehensive understanding of the ancient Egyptian worldview.

Application and Relevance: An important objective of this book is to demonstrate the relevance and application of ancient Egyptian religious practices to contemporary contexts. By drawing connections with modern fields and practices, students will be able to identify parallels, draw comparisons, and examine the enduring legacy of ancient Egyptian religion. This will enable them to appreciate the continued influence and relevance of ancient Egyptian religious concepts and practices in contemporary spiritual and cultural spheres.

Engaging Learning Experience: The goal is to provide an engaging learning experience for students. Each chapter will incorporate examples, problems, and exercises to illustrate key concepts, promote critical thinking, and encourage active participation. These interactive activities will challenge students to apply their knowledge, analyze complex information, and engage in critical reflection. By actively engaging with the material, students will deepen their understanding and develop their analytical and problem-solving skills.

By achieving these objectives and goals, this book aims to equip students with a comprehensive understanding of ancient Egyptian religion. It strives to foster critical thinking, cultural appreciation, and the ability to apply knowledge to real-world scenarios. Through the incorporation of examples, problems, and exercises, this book will engage students in critical thinking and discussion, enabling them to develop a nuanced and informed perspective on ancient Egyptian religion.

Introduction to the organization and structure of the subsequent chapters

The organization and structure of the subsequent chapters in this book have been carefully designed to provide a systematic and comprehensive exploration of ancient Egyptian religion. Each chapter focuses on a specific period or aspect of ancient Egyptian religious practices, building upon the knowledge gained in the preceding chapters. By following this chronological and thematic approach, students will develop a nuanced understanding of the development and evolution of ancient Egyptian religious beliefs and practices over time.

Part 1: Introduction

The book begins with an introductory chapter that provides a brief overview of ancient Egyptian religion. It sets the stage for the subsequent chapters by introducing key concepts, themes, and historical background. This chapter serves as a foundation for understanding the significance and complexity of ancient Egyptian religion.

Part 2: Pre-Dynastic Period (c. 5500 BCE - 3100 BCE)

In this part, we delve into the religious beliefs and practices of the Pre-Dynastic Period. Chapter 4 provides an overview of religious beliefs and practices during this formative period, while Chapter 5 explores the temples, festivals, and tools used during this time. Chapter 6 focuses specifically on the prayers, hymns, chants, and spells dedicated to early deities and nature spirits.

Part 3: Old Kingdom (c. 2686 BCE - 2181 BCE)

Moving forward in time, Part 3 examines the religious developments and changes during the Old Kingdom. Chapter 7 provides an analysis of these developments, while Chapter 8 explores the temples, festivals, and tools used during this period. Chapter 9 delves into the prayers, hymns, chants, and spells associated with key deities worshipped during the Old Kingdom.

Part 4: Middle Kingdom (c. 2055 BCE - 1650 BCE)

Part 4 focuses on the religious reforms and revival during the Middle Kingdom. Chapter 10 examines the religious reforms of this period, while Chapter 11 explores the temples, festivals, and tools used during the Middle Kingdom. Chapter 12 delves into the prayers, hymns, chants, and spells dedicated to prominent deities of the time.

Part 5: New Kingdom (c. 1550 BCE - 1069 BCE)

In Part 5, we delve into the peak of ancient Egyptian civilization and religious practices during the New Kingdom. Chapter 13 provides an analysis of the religious practices during this period, while Chapter 14 explores the temples, festivals, and tools used during the New Kingdom. Chapter 15 focuses on the prayers, hymns, chants, and spells associated with major deities of the New Kingdom.

Part 6: Late Period (c. 664 BCE - 332 BCE)

Moving into the Late Period, Part 6 examines the influence of foreign invasions and the decline of ancient Egyptian religion. Chapter 16 analyzes the impact of foreign invasions, while Chapter 17 explores the temples, festivals, and tools used during this period. Chapter 18 delves into the prayers, hymns, chants, and spells reflecting syncretism with foreign gods and religious practices.

Part 7: Ptolemaic and Roman Periods (332 BCE - 395 CE)

The final part of the book, Part 7, focuses on the integration of Egyptian religious beliefs with Greek and Roman influences during the Ptolemaic and Roman Periods. Chapter 19 examines this integration, while Chapter 20 explores the temples, festivals, and tools used during this time. Chapter 21 delves into the prayers, hymns, chants, and spells blending Egyptian and Hellenistic-Roman religious traditions.

Presentation of the specific themes and topics that will be covered in the book

This book aims to provide a comprehensive exploration of ancient Egyptian religion, covering a wide range of themes and topics. By delving into the rich and complex religious practices of the ancient Egyptians, students will gain a deep understanding of the beliefs, rituals, and spiritual traditions that shaped their society. The following themes and topics will be covered in the subsequent chapters:

Origins and Development of Ancient Egyptian Religion:

✧ Examination of the religious beliefs and cosmology of ancient Egypt
✧ Analysis of the role of gods, goddesses, and divine entities in ancient Egyptian mythology and religious practices
✧ Discussion of the influence of religious beliefs on daily life, rituals, and social structures

Rituals and Spiritual Practices in Ancient Egyptian Religion:

✧ Importance of prayers, hymns, chants, and spells in ancient Egyptian religious practices
✧ Examination of the roles and functions of these practices within the religious context
✧ Analysis of the ways in which these practices were believed to establish a connection between humans and the divine realm
✧ Discussion of the significance of rituals and incantations in expressing devotion, seeking divine assistance, and promoting harmony with the natural world

Symbolism and Iconography in Ancient Egyptian Religion:

✧ Exploration of the symbolism and meaning behind religious symbols, amulets, and sacred objects
✧ Analysis of the iconography used in temples, tombs, and religious art
✧ Discussion of the symbolic representations of gods, goddesses, and mythical creatures in ancient Egyptian religion

Temples, Festivals, and Sacred Spaces:

✧ Examination of the architecture, layout, and functions of ancient Egyptian temples
✧ Analysis of the rituals and ceremonies performed in temples and during religious festivals
✧ Discussion of the significance of sacred spaces and their role in connecting humans with the divine

Divine Kingship and Pharaonic Role in Religion:

✧ Exploration of the divine status of pharaohs and their role as intermediaries between gods and humans
✧ Analysis of the rituals and ceremonies associated with the coronation and reign of pharaohs
✧ Discussion of the relationship between political power and religious authority in ancient Egypt

Afterlife and Funerary Beliefs:

✧ Examination of the ancient Egyptian beliefs about the afterlife and the journey of the soul
✧ Analysis of funerary rituals, mummification, and tomb construction
✧ Discussion of the Book of the Dead and its role in guiding the deceased in the afterlife

Syncretism and Interactions with Other Cultures:

✧ Exploration of the interactions between ancient Egyptian religion and neighboring cultures
✧ Analysis of the syncretic practices and blending of religious beliefs and rituals
✧ Discussion of the impact of foreign invasions and conquests on ancient Egyptian religion

By covering these themes and topics in a comprehensive and analytical manner, this book aims to provide students with a thorough understanding of ancient Egyptian religion and its significance in the broader context of history, culture, and spirituality. Through engaging examples, problems, and exercises, students will be encouraged to think critically, analyze primary sources, and participate in scholarly discussions surrounding ancient Egyptian religion.

Discussion of the intended audience and how the book aims to engage students in critical thinking and discussion

This book is specifically designed for students seeking a bachelor's degree who have a keen interest in ancient history, religious studies, archaeology, anthropology, or related fields. It is tailored to provide a rigorous and in-depth exploration of ancient Egyptian religion, ensuring that students receive a comprehensive understanding of the subject matter. By adopting a formal and academic tone, paired with sophisticated vocabulary and grammar, this book aims to meet the intellectual standards expected at the undergraduate level.

To engage students in critical thinking and discussion, the book incorporates various strategies throughout its chapters. These strategies include:

Examples and Case Studies: The book draws examples from a variety of fields, such as Witchcraft, Divination, Herbalism, Shamanism, Ecospirituality, and Magic in Ancient Egypt. These examples help illustrate the concepts discussed and showcase the relevance of ancient Egyptian religion in broader contexts.

Problems and Exercises: Each chapter includes carefully crafted problems and exercises that encourage students to apply their knowledge, analyze primary sources, and engage in critical thinking. These activities prompt students to delve deeper into the subject matter, critically evaluate evidence, and develop their own interpretations.

Balance and Objectivity: The book presents counterarguments and dissenting opinions in a balanced and objective manner. It acknowledges that scholarly debates exist within the field of ancient Egyptian religion and encourages students to critically evaluate different viewpoints. This approach fosters analytical thinking and encourages students to form well-rounded arguments based on evidence and critical analysis.

In-Depth Analysis: The book provides a thorough and in-depth analysis of the subject matter, ensuring that students develop a comprehensive understanding of ancient Egyptian religion. It explores complex scientific concepts in a clear and accessible way, making the information digestible for students with varying levels of prior knowledge.

Critical Analysis of Primary Sources: Throughout the book, students are encouraged to critically analyze primary sources, such as inscriptions, religious texts, and archaeological artifacts. By engaging directly with these sources, students develop valuable skills in interpreting and evaluating primary evidence.

The goal of these engagement strategies is to foster a dynamic learning environment that encourages students to actively participate in critical thinking and discussion. By incorporating examples, problems, and exercises, the book aims to not only impart knowledge but also to equip students with the skills necessary for scholarly inquiry and independent research.

Examples, Problems, and Exercises:

Example and Analysis of an Ancient Egyptian Prayer:

Example: Take the "Hymn to the Aten" from the Amarna Period, written by Pharaoh Akhenaten.

Hymn to the Aten

O Aten, radiant disk of the sun,
Creator of all life, source of light and warmth.
Your rays extend over the earth,
Nurturing all creatures, from the smallest to the greatest.

You are the sole god, there is none beside you,
Unfolding the dawn, bringing light to the world.
When you rise, the land rejoices,
And all beings awaken to your divine presence.

You are the giver of life, the sustainer of existence,
Your rays reach every corner of the earth.
You nurture the crops in the fields,
And cause them to grow and flourish.

O Aten, your beauty is beyond compare,
Your rays illuminate the heavens and the earth.
You create the cycle of life and death,
And guide the souls of the departed to eternal rest.

Your divine essence permeates all things,
From the smallest insect to the mightiest pharaoh.
All creatures bask in your life-giving energy,
And offer their praises and gratitude to you.

O Aten, we worship and adore you,
For you are the supreme and everlasting god.
Your presence brings light and joy to our lives,
And we are humbled by your divine radiance.

Note: The text provided here is a representation of the content and style of an ancient Egyptian hymn to the Aten. Actual ancient texts may vary in their language and specific details.

The Hymn to the Aten reflects the unique religious beliefs of the Amarna Period in ancient Egypt, during the reign of Pharaoh Akhenaten. It focuses on the worship of the sun disk, the Aten, as the supreme deity. The hymn highlights the Aten's role as the creator and sustainer of life, emphasizing its all-encompassing presence and its connection to every aspect of existence. The hymn's poetic language and emphasis on the Aten's divine radiance convey a sense of awe and reverence for this new form of monotheistic worship in ancient Egypt.

Analysis: Analyze the purpose and significance of the hymn, focusing on its monotheistic nature, praise of the sun god Aten, and its reflection of Akhenaten's religious reforms.

Problem and Proposed Ritual for Divine Assistance:

Problem: An ancient Egyptian is suffering from a prolonged illness and seeks divine assistance for healing.

Proposed Ritual: Design a suitable ritual involving prayers, offerings, and specific invocations to healing deities such as Imhotep or Sekhmet.

Examination of Music and Sound in Ancient Egyptian Religious Practices:

Discuss the role of music and sound in ancient Egyptian religious practices, emphasizing how hymns and chants were used to invoke specific deities or enhance the spiritual experience.

Exercise: Create a comparative analysis chart highlighting different hymns and chants used in ancient Egyptian rituals and their corresponding effects on the worshippers and the divine realm.

Comparative Analysis of Ancient Egyptian and Mesopotamian Religious Practices:

Engage in a comparative analysis of ancient Egyptian religious practices and those of Mesopotamia, focusing on the use of prayers, hymns, chants, and spells.

Exercise: Compare a specific prayer or hymn from ancient Egypt with a corresponding prayer or hymn from Mesopotamia, highlighting similarities and differences in their structure, content, and religious purpose.

Exploration of Magic in Ancient Egypt and Its Relationship to Religious Rituals:

Explore the concept of magic in ancient Egypt and its relationship to religious rituals and practices.

Exercise: Analyze the "Book of the Dead" or the "Harris Magical Papyrus" and discuss specific magical spells and their purposes. Explore potential ethical implications of using magic within the religious context.

Part 2: Pre-Dynastic Period (c. 5500 BCE - 3100 BCE)

The Pre-Dynastic Period of ancient Egypt, spanning from approximately 5500 BCE to 3100 BCE, marks a crucial phase in the development of Egyptian civilization. This period, which predates the establishment of the centralized dynastic rule, holds immense significance in understanding the foundations of Egyptian religious beliefs and practices. In Part 2 of this book, we will delve into the Pre-Dynastic Period and explore its religious, spiritual, and magical aspects in detail.

This section aims to provide a comprehensive analysis of the Pre-Dynastic Period, highlighting the social, cultural, and environmental factors that influenced the religious landscape of ancient Egypt during this time. By examining archaeological evidence, ancient texts, and scholarly interpretations, we will unravel the religious traditions, rituals, and beliefs of the pre-dynastic Egyptians.

The Pre-Dynastic Period witnessed the emergence of several key elements that laid the groundwork for the religious framework of later Egyptian civilizations. These elements include animistic beliefs, ancestor worship, the veneration of natural phenomena, and the development of early rituals and magical practices. By exploring these aspects, we gain valuable insights into the spiritual worldview of the pre-dynastic Egyptians and the ways in which they sought to connect with the divine.

Throughout this section, we will explore various topics that shed light on the religious and spiritual landscape of the Pre-Dynastic Period. These topics include:

An examination of the spiritual beliefs and cosmology of the pre-dynastic Egyptians: We will analyze the prevailing cosmological concepts, the worship of elemental forces, and the significance of totemic animal symbolism.

Exploration of pre-dynastic rituals and ceremonial practices: We will delve into the ritualistic practices associated with fertility, agriculture, and the cyclical patterns of nature. We will discuss the use of sacred sites, communal gatherings, and offerings in religious rituals.

Exploring the Rituals, Beliefs, and Syncretism of Ancient Egyptian Religion

Investigation of magical and shamanic practices: We will explore the role of shamanic figures and their connection to the spiritual realm. We will examine the use of charms, amulets, and talismans as protective and transformative tools.

Analysis of divination and oracular practices: We will study the methods of divination employed by the pre-dynastic Egyptians, including scapulimancy, augury, and the interpretation of dreams. We will discuss how these practices were used to seek guidance and insight from the divine realm.

Examination of early forms of deity worship: We will explore the emergence of early deities in the pre-dynastic period and their evolving roles within the religious framework. We will analyze the cultic practices associated with these deities and their influence on later Egyptian pantheons.

Through a careful analysis of these topics, we aim to provide students with a comprehensive understanding of the religious and spiritual landscape of the Pre-Dynastic Period. By examining the beliefs and practices of this early period, we gain valuable insights into the origins of Egyptian religious traditions and the development of the complex pantheon that would come to define the later dynastic periods.

Each chapter in this section will include examples, problems, and exercises to facilitate critical thinking and engage students in deeper exploration of the subject matter. By actively participating in these exercises, students will develop a holistic understanding of the Pre-Dynastic Period and its impact on the subsequent development of ancient Egyptian religion.

Chapter 4: Overview of Religious Beliefs and Practices during this Period

The Pre-Dynastic Period in ancient Egypt, spanning from approximately 5500 BCE to 3100 BCE, was a formative era characterized by the gradual development of religious beliefs and practices that would shape the later dynastic civilization. This chapter provides a comprehensive overview of the religious landscape during this period, exploring the key elements, rituals, and concepts that formed the foundation for ancient Egyptian spirituality.

Development of Religious Concepts:

During the Pre-Dynastic Period, ancient Egyptians began to form their understanding of the divine and the supernatural forces that governed their world. The belief in a pantheon of deities emerged, with each deity associated with specific aspects of nature, celestial bodies, or abstract concepts. These early religious concepts laid the groundwork for the later complex theological system of ancient Egypt.

Nature and Ancestor Worship:

Nature played a significant role in the religious beliefs of the Pre-Dynastic Egyptians. They revered natural phenomena such as the sun, river, and fertility of the land. Ancestor worship also held great importance, as ancestors were considered powerful spiritual beings capable of influencing the well-being of the living.

Rituals and Ceremonies:

Rituals and ceremonies formed an integral part of religious life during the Pre-Dynastic Period. These included purification rituals, animal sacrifices, and communal gatherings at sacred sites. The rituals aimed to establish a connection between the human and divine realms, seek divine blessings, and ensure the harmonious functioning of the natural world.

Shamanic Practices:

Shamanic practices were prevalent during the Pre-Dynastic Period, with shamans serving as intermediaries between the human and spiritual realms. These individuals possessed special knowledge and abilities to communicate with the spirits, perform healing rituals, and provide spiritual guidance to their communities.

Symbolism and Iconography:

Symbolism and iconography played a crucial role in the religious practices of this period. Various symbols, such as animals, plants, and abstract shapes, were associated with specific deities or represented divine attributes. These symbols were incorporated into religious art, amulets, and ritual objects, conveying deeper meanings and serving as potent sources of spiritual power.

Examples, Problems, and Exercises:

Examine a Pre-Dynastic religious artifact, such as a carved amulet or pottery fragment, and discuss its symbolism and potential religious significance. Consider how the artifact reflects the religious beliefs and practices of the time.

Problem: Interpreting Ritual Sites

Study an archaeological site from the Pre-Dynastic Period that is believed to have had religious significance. Identify the features and artifacts present at the site and propose possible interpretations of its religious rituals or ceremonies.

Exercise: Creating a Pre-Dynastic Ritual

Imagine you are an ancient Egyptian during the Pre-Dynastic Period and create a fictional ritual to honor a specific deity or natural force. Describe the ritual's purpose, steps, and the symbolism involved. Reflect on the potential impact of the ritual on individuals and the community.

Comparative Analysis: Pre-Dynastic Beliefs vs. Later Dynastic Period

Compare the religious beliefs and practices of the Pre-Dynastic Period with those of a later dynastic period, such as the Old Kingdom or New Kingdom. Identify similarities and differences in terms of deities worshipped, rituals performed, and the role of religious specialists.

By delving into the religious beliefs and practices of the Pre-Dynastic Period, we gain valuable insights into the formative stages of ancient Egyptian spirituality. This chapter aims to deepen our understanding of the origins of religious concepts and the pivotal role they played in shaping the culture and civilization of ancient Egypt. Through examples, problems, and exercises, students can engage critically with the material, encouraging a holistic comprehension of this fascinating period in ancient Egyptian history.

Analysis of the religious worldview and cosmology of the ancient Egyptians during the Pre-Dynastic Period

The religious worldview and cosmology of the ancient Egyptians during the Pre-Dynastic Period (c. 5500 BCE - 3100 BCE) provide valuable insights into their understanding of the universe, the divine, and the relationship between humans and the supernatural. Through an analysis of their religious texts, rituals, and symbols, we can gain a deeper understanding of the religious beliefs that underpinned their society.

Polytheism and the Divine Hierarchy:

During the Pre-Dynastic Period, the ancient Egyptians embraced a polytheistic belief system, worshiping a pantheon of gods and goddesses. Each deity held specific roles and attributes, overseeing various aspects of the natural world, celestial bodies, and human affairs. The divine hierarchy established a cosmic order, with powerful deities occupying higher positions and lesser deities fulfilling more specific functions.

Nature and Cosmic Forces:

Ancient Egyptians held a deep reverence for nature and believed that cosmic forces governed the universe. They attributed divine attributes to natural elements such as the sun, moon, stars, and the Nile River. These forces were seen as manifestations of the gods and goddesses, and their proper functioning was vital for maintaining balance and harmony in the world.

Creation Myth and the Origins of the Universe:

The ancient Egyptians developed creation myths that explained the origins of the universe. These myths varied across regions and time periods, but they often revolved around the god Atum or Atum-Ra, who was believed to have emerged from the primordial waters and created the world through his divine power. The creation myth served as a foundational narrative, emphasizing the importance of the gods' role in bringing order to chaos.

Exploring the Rituals, Beliefs, and Syncretism of Ancient Egyptian Religion

Rituals and Offerings:

Rituals and offerings played a central role in ancient Egyptian religious practices. These rituals aimed to establish a connection between humans and the divine, seeking divine blessings and maintaining cosmic order. Offerings of food, drink, incense, and other symbolic items were presented to the gods as acts of devotion and to ensure their favor and protection.

Symbols and Sacred Sites:

Symbols held significant importance in ancient Egyptian cosmology. Animals, plants, celestial bodies, and abstract shapes were associated with specific deities or represented divine attributes. Sacred sites, such as temples and shrines, were considered the dwelling places of the gods, and their construction and rituals performed within them were believed to facilitate communication with the divine.

Through a comprehensive analysis of the religious worldview and cosmology of the ancient Egyptians during the Pre-Dynastic Period, we can discern their beliefs about the nature of the universe, the power of the gods, and the interplay between the divine and human realms. This understanding forms the basis for further exploration of their religious practices and rituals, shedding light on the profound significance of religion in ancient Egyptian society.

Example: Interpretation of a Creation Myth

Analyze a Pre-Dynastic creation myth, such as the Heliopolitan or Memphite cosmogony, and explain its significance in shaping ancient Egyptian cosmology. Consider the role of specific gods and goddesses, the emergence of the universe, and the establishment of cosmic order.

Problem: Symbolic Representation in Artifacts

Examine a Pre-Dynastic artifact, such as a pottery vessel or a carved figurine, and identify the symbols present. Interpret the possible religious meanings behind these symbols and discuss how they reflect the ancient Egyptians' worldview and cosmology.

Exercise: Constructing a Ritual Site

Imagine you are an ancient Egyptian during the Pre-Dynastic Period and design a sacred site dedicated to a specific deity. Consider the architectural elements, symbolism, and rituals that would be performed at this site to establish a connection with the divine.

Examination of the role of animism and ancestor worship in early Egyptian religious beliefs

In addition to the pantheon of gods and goddesses, the religious beliefs of early Egypt encompassed the concepts of animism and ancestor worship. These spiritual practices played a significant role in the religious worldview of the ancient Egyptians and shaped their understanding of the supernatural forces and their relationship with the deceased.

Animism:

Animism is the belief that all natural objects, such as plants, animals, and even inanimate objects, possess a spiritual essence or soul. In early Egyptian religious beliefs, animism played a vital role as the ancient Egyptians recognized the spiritual presence within the natural world. They believed that these natural elements had their own divine attributes and could influence human lives.

For example, specific animals, such as the sacred bull or the sacred cat, were regarded as embodiments of deities or divine messengers. The ancient Egyptians believed that these animals possessed spiritual powers and could act as intermediaries between humans and the gods. As a result, they venerated and worshipped these animals, constructing temples and sanctuaries dedicated to their protection and care.

Additionally, natural phenomena, such as the flooding of the Nile River or the cycle of the sun, were viewed as manifestations of divine power. The ancient Egyptians believed that these natural occurrences were guided by spiritual forces, and they performed rituals and ceremonies to ensure the continuation of these vital cosmic processes.

Ancestor Worship:

Ancestor worship was another prominent aspect of early Egyptian religious beliefs. The ancient Egyptians held a deep reverence for their ancestors, considering them as important spiritual entities who maintained a connection with the living world. They believed that the deceased continued to exist in a spirit form and had the ability to influence the lives of their living descendants.

The ancient Egyptians engaged in various rituals and practices to honor their ancestors. These rituals involved offerings of food, drink, and other items at the tombs and burial sites of the deceased. By providing these offerings, the living sought to maintain a positive relationship with their ancestors and gain their favor and protection.

Moreover, the ancient Egyptians believed that deceased ancestors could act as intermediaries between humans and the gods. They would seek the intercession of their ancestors to petition the gods for blessings, guidance, and protection in various aspects of life.

The practices of animism and ancestor worship in early Egyptian religious beliefs reflect the ancient Egyptians' deep connection with the natural world and their reverence for their lineage. Through these beliefs, they sought to establish a harmonious relationship with the spiritual forces that governed their lives.

Examples, Problems, and Exercises:

Choose a specific animal associated with early Egyptian animism, such as the cat or the ibis. Investigate the significance of this animal in ancient Egyptian religious beliefs, its connection to a particular deity, and the rituals and ceremonies performed in its honor.

Problem: Ancestor Rituals and Offerings

Imagine you are an ancient Egyptian living during the early period. Identify a specific problem or dilemma you are facing, and propose a ritual or offering to seek assistance and guidance from your deceased ancestors. Explain the symbolic significance of the chosen ritual or offering and its intended purpose.

Exercise: Ancestor Veneration

Create a visual representation, such as a drawing or a collage, depicting an ancestor veneration scene in early Egyptian society. Include symbols, rituals, and offerings that exemplify the importance of ancestor worship and its role in the spiritual lives of the ancient Egyptians.

Discussion of the emergence of early deities and their associations with natural forces and phenomena

During the Pre-Dynastic Period of ancient Egypt, the religious beliefs of the ancient Egyptians were closely intertwined with the natural world. As they observed and interacted with the environment around them, they began to associate various natural forces and phenomena with deities, giving rise to the emergence of early gods and goddesses.

Nile River: One of the most significant natural forces in ancient Egypt was the Nile River. Its annual flooding brought fertility to the land, allowing crops to grow and sustaining the livelihoods of the ancient Egyptians. As a result, the ancient Egyptians associated the Nile with a deity known as Hapi, who personified the life-giving waters of the river. Hapi was often depicted as a plump figure with water lilies, symbolizing abundance and fertility.

Sun: Another powerful natural force that captured the attention and reverence of the ancient Egyptians was the sun. The sun provided light, warmth, and sustenance, and its daily cycle played a crucial role in their lives. The sun god, Ra or Re, emerged as a central figure in early Egyptian mythology. Ra was believed to travel across the sky in a solar boat during the day and navigate through the underworld at night. The rising and setting of the sun represented the eternal cycle of life, death, and rebirth.

Sky and Earth: The ancient Egyptians recognized the sky and earth as fundamental elements of their existence. Nut, the goddess of the sky, was depicted as a canopy with stars spread across her body, while Geb, the god of the earth, was often depicted lying beneath her. The union of Nut and Geb represented the cycle of creation and birth, highlighting the interconnection between the heavens and the earth.

Animals and Natural Phenomena: The ancient Egyptians also associated specific animals and natural phenomena with deities. For example, the falcon-headed god Horus was linked to the sky and was considered a protector of the pharaoh. The lioness goddess Sekhmet embodied the fierce heat of the sun and was both a destroyer and healer. The scarab beetle, associated with the sun god, symbolized transformation and rebirth. These associations between deities and natural elements reflected the ancient Egyptians' attempt to understand and make sense of the world around them.

The emergence of early deities and their associations with natural forces and phenomena in ancient Egypt reflects the deep reverence and awe that the ancient Egyptians held for the natural world. These associations provided a framework for understanding the forces that governed their lives and offered a means to seek the favor and protection of the gods.

Examples, Problems, and Exercises:

Choose one specific deity from early Egyptian mythology, such as Hapi or Ra. Analyze the associations and symbolism of the deity with the corresponding natural force or phenomenon. Discuss the significance of this association within the religious beliefs and practices of ancient Egyptians.

Problem: Creating a New Deity

Imagine you are an ancient Egyptian living during the Pre-Dynastic Period and have encountered a new natural force or phenomenon that has not yet been associated with a deity. Invent a new deity and provide a detailed explanation of their characteristics, attributes, and roles in relation to the natural force or phenomenon.

Exercise: Symbolic Representations of Deities

Create a series of illustrations or symbols representing different deities and their associations with natural forces or phenomena. Explain the symbolism behind each representation and discuss the significance of these associations within ancient Egyptian religious beliefs.

Exploration of the rituals, ceremonies, and symbols associated with religious practices during this period

The religious practices of the ancient Egyptians during the Pre-Dynastic Period were characterized by a rich array of rituals, ceremonies, and symbols. These practices served as a means to connect with the divine, seek blessings, and ensure the well-being of both individuals and the community. Let us delve into the key aspects of these religious practices.

Offering Rituals:

Offering rituals were central to ancient Egyptian religious practices. These rituals involved presenting offerings to the gods and goddesses as a way of expressing gratitude, seeking favor, and maintaining a reciprocal relationship with the divine. Offerings included food, beverages, flowers, incense, and symbolic representations of wealth and abundance. These rituals often took place in temples or at household shrines, where individuals would make their offerings accompanied by prayers and hymns.

Processions and Festivals:

Processions and festivals played an essential role in the religious calendar of the Pre-Dynastic Period. These events involved elaborate ceremonies and rituals dedicated to specific deities. The ancient Egyptians believed that these processions allowed the gods and goddesses to manifest in the physical world, and by participating in the festivities, individuals could connect with the divine presence. Processions often included priests, musicians, dancers, and devotees carrying statues or symbols of the deities, while festivals featured communal feasting, music, and performances.

Symbolic Objects and Amulets:

Symbols held great significance in ancient Egyptian religious practices. Objects with symbolic meaning were utilized in rituals and ceremonies to invoke the presence and power of specific deities. For example, the ankh, a symbol resembling a cross with a loop at the top, represented life and was frequently depicted in the hands of deities. Amulets, small objects worn or carried for protection and good fortune, were also prevalent. Amulets in the form of animal figurines, such as the scarab beetle or the Eye of Horus, symbolized specific deities or offered symbolic protection.

Burial Customs and Ancestor Worship:

Burial customs and ancestor worship were integral to early Egyptian religious practices. The deceased were believed to continue their existence in the afterlife, and proper burial rites ensured a smooth transition into the realm of the ancestors. Rituals surrounding death and burial included mummification, tomb construction, and the placement of grave goods. Ancestor worship involved regular visits to tombs, offerings of food, drink, and incense, as well as prayers and invocations to seek guidance and blessings from the deceased ancestors.

These rituals, ceremonies, and symbols were deeply ingrained in the religious fabric of the Pre-Dynastic Period. They provided a means for individuals to connect with the divine realm, express devotion, and seek divine assistance and protection. The symbolic objects and rituals also served as a way to establish and maintain order, harmony, and balance within the community.

Examples, Problems, and Exercises:

Choose a specific offering ritual from the Pre-Dynastic Period, such as the offering of bread and beer. Analyze the significance of this ritual, its symbolic meaning, and its role within the broader religious context.

Problem: Designing a Festival

Imagine you are tasked with organizing a festival dedicated to a specific deity in the Pre-Dynastic Period. Describe the key elements of the festival, including processions, rituals, music, and offerings. Discuss the significance of each element and its intended effect on the participants.

Exercise: Creation of a Symbolic Object

Design and create a symbolic object or amulet inspired by Pre-Dynastic religious practices. Explain the symbolism behind the object and how it represents a specific deity or conveys a particular aspect of ancient Egyptian spirituality.

Chapter 5: Temples, Festivals, and Tools used c. 5500 BCE - 3100 BCE

The Pre-Dynastic Period of ancient Egypt, spanning from approximately 5500 BCE to 3100 BCE, witnessed the emergence of sophisticated religious structures, elaborate festivals, and the development of tools and implements that played crucial roles in religious practices. In Chapter 5, we delve into the fascinating world of temples, festivals, and the tools utilized during this period to explore their significance and shed light on the religious beliefs and practices of the time.

Temples as Sacred Spaces:

The construction of temples in ancient Egypt during the Pre-Dynastic Period marked a significant shift in religious practices. These structures served as sacred spaces where the divine presence was believed to reside and where rituals and ceremonies took place. Temples were meticulously designed and adorned with intricate carvings, statues, and symbols representing the gods and goddesses. They served as focal points of religious worship, community gatherings, and administrative functions. In this chapter, we will explore the architectural features, symbolism, and rituals associated with these early temples.

Festivals: Communal Celebrations of the Divine:

Festivals held a central place in the religious calendar of ancient Egypt during the Pre-Dynastic Period. These communal celebrations were dedicated to specific deities and served as opportunities for the community to come together in worship and celebration. Festivals involved processions, rituals, music, dancing, feasting, and theatrical performances. By participating in these festivals, individuals sought to connect with the divine, invoke blessings, and ensure the well-being of the community. We will examine the significance of these festivals, their associated rituals, and their role in fostering social cohesion and religious devotion.

Tools and Implements:

The Pre-Dynastic Period witnessed advancements in the development and utilization of tools and implements that were employed in religious practices. These tools played essential roles in temple construction, ritual offerings, and ceremonies. Examples of such tools include chisels, hammers, bowls, and incense burners. We will explore the types of tools used, their specific functions, and their symbolic significance within the religious context. Understanding the purpose and symbolism of these tools provides valuable insights into the religious practices and beliefs of the Pre-Dynastic Egyptians.

Examples, Problems, and Exercises:

Choose a specific Pre-Dynastic temple, such as the Temple of Hierakonpolis. Analyze its architectural features, decorative motifs, and its significance within the religious landscape of the time. Discuss how this temple reflects the evolving religious beliefs and practices during the Pre-Dynastic Period.

Problem: Designing a Festival Program

Imagine you are tasked with organizing a festival for the worship of a specific deity during the Pre-Dynastic Period. Design a program that includes processions, rituals, performances, and offerings. Justify the selection of each element based on historical evidence and cultural context.

Exercise: Reconstruction of a Ritual Tool

Choose a specific ritual tool used during the Pre-Dynastic Period, such as a ceremonial bowl or an incense burner. Create a detailed reconstruction or illustration of the tool, highlighting its form, materials, and decorative elements. Provide an accompanying description explaining its purpose, symbolism, and use in religious ceremonies.

Temples as Sacred Spaces:

In ancient Egypt, temples held profound significance as sacred spaces where the divine presence was believed to reside. These architectural marvels were not only physical structures but also spiritual gateways connecting the mortal realm with the divine. Within the context of the Pre-Dynastic Period, temples underwent significant developments, setting the foundation for the grand temples that would later grace the Egyptian landscape.

Architectural Features:

The temples of the Pre-Dynastic Period were characterized by their unique architectural features, which reflected the evolving religious beliefs and practices of the time. These structures were typically constructed using perishable materials such as mud bricks, reeds, and wooden posts. The layout of the temple often followed a rectangular plan, with an entrance gate leading to a central courtyard and a sanctuary or cult chamber. Some temples also incorporated multiple chambers and halls, serving various ritual purposes.

The temple walls were adorned with intricate carvings and reliefs depicting scenes from religious narratives, mythological tales, and rituals. These artistic representations served both decorative and didactic purposes, conveying important religious messages to worshippers and providing a visual narrative of the divine and the cosmic order.

Symbolism and Iconography:

Symbolism played a central role in the design and decoration of temples. Every architectural element, carving, and statue within the temple carried symbolic significance. Columns, for example, were often shaped like bundled papyrus plants, symbolizing the primeval marsh from which creation emerged. The lotus and the sun were also prominent symbols, representing rebirth and the eternal cycle of life.

Statues and images of deities were placed strategically within the temple, reflecting the specific religious focus of the cult. The presence of these divine representations emphasized the temple's role as a dwelling place for the gods and facilitated communication between the mortal and divine realms.

Ritual Practices:

Temples were not merely static structures but vibrant centers of religious activity. They served as venues for a wide range of rituals and ceremonies aimed at maintaining cosmic harmony, seeking divine favor, and expressing devotion to the gods. Rituals included offerings of food, beverages, incense, and symbolic objects, which were presented to the deities as acts of worship and sustenance.

The priesthood played a vital role in the daily rituals and ceremonies conducted within the temple. They acted as intermediaries between the worshippers and the gods, ensuring the correct performance of rituals and managing the sacred spaces. The temple rituals were also accompanied by music, chanting, and dance, creating a multisensory experience that engaged worshippers on both a physical and spiritual level.

Examples, Problems, and Exercises:

Analyze the architectural features and decorative elements of the Temple of Amun-Ra in Karnak, one of the largest and most significant temples in ancient Egypt. Discuss how its design and symbolism reflect the religious beliefs and practices of the time. Consider the layout, statues, reliefs, and architectural motifs in your analysis.

Problem: Designing a Temple Layout

Imagine you are an architect tasked with designing a Pre-Dynastic temple. Create a detailed layout plan that incorporates the key architectural elements and symbolic features characteristic of this period. Justify the placement and significance of each element in relation to the religious beliefs and practices of the time.

Exercise: Carving a Temple Relief

Select a mythological scene or religious narrative from ancient Egyptian texts and create a relief carving depicting the chosen scene. Pay attention to the details, symbols, and figures involved, ensuring they align with the Pre-Dynastic religious context. Provide a written explanation of the scene's significance and its connection to temple rituals.

Festivals: Communal Celebrations of the Divine:

Festivals held a significant place in the religious and social life of ancient Egypt. These communal celebrations were marked by grand processions, elaborate rituals, and joyful gatherings, providing opportunities for both individuals and the community as a whole to express devotion, seek divine blessings, and strengthen social cohesion. Within the context of ancient Egyptian religious practices, festivals played a crucial role in fostering a connection between the mortal realm and the divine.

Purpose and Significance of Festivals:

Festivals served multiple purposes in ancient Egyptian society. They were primarily conducted to honor and celebrate specific deities, marking important events in the religious calendar such as the annual rejuvenation of the gods or the commemoration of significant mythological narratives. Festivals also provided a means for the community to express gratitude for divine blessings and seek divine intervention for the well-being of the nation, its rulers, and its people.

The festivals acted as a platform for the reinforcement of religious beliefs, emphasizing the presence and power of the deities and their involvement in human affairs. They also facilitated community cohesion, uniting individuals from various social strata in shared worship and celebration.

Rituals and Ceremonies:

Festivals were characterized by a wide range of rituals and ceremonies that followed a structured sequence. These rituals often took place within the sacred precincts of temples or at specific sacred sites associated with the honored deity. They included offerings of food, beverages, and precious objects, as well as purification rituals, processions, and the recitation of prayers and hymns.

The participation of priests, as well as ordinary worshippers, was integral to the success of the festival. The priests performed their sacred duties, ensuring the correct execution of rituals, while the worshippers actively engaged in acts of devotion, making offerings, and seeking personal interactions with the divine. Music, dance, and theatrical performances were also common features of festivals, adding to the celebratory atmosphere and invoking a sense of joy and transcendence.

Examples of Festivals:

a. The Festival of Opet: This annual festival celebrated the rejuvenation and renewal of the god Amun-Ra. It involved a grand procession from the temple of Karnak to Luxor, during which the sacred barque carrying the deity would visit various sacred sites. The festival lasted for several weeks and attracted pilgrims from all over Egypt.

b. The Festival of Wepet Renpet: Also known as the New Year festival, this event marked the beginning of the agricultural year and the annual flooding of the Nile. It included purification rituals, offerings to the deities, and joyful celebrations to ensure a prosperous year ahead.

c. The Beautiful Feast of the Valley: This festival focused on the veneration of deceased ancestors and the commemoration of Osiris. It involved processions to cemeteries, where offerings and prayers were made at the tombs of the deceased. It was a time for reflection, remembrance, and reaffirmation of familial and ancestral connections.

Examples, Problems, and Exercises:

Analyze the Festival of Opet, considering its historical and religious significance, the rituals involved, and the role it played in reinforcing the divine authority of Amun-Ra. Discuss the impact of the festival on the religious and social life of ancient Egyptians, including its economic implications and its influence on pilgrimage and trade.

Problem: Designing a Festival Procession

Imagine you are responsible for organizing a festival procession in honor of a chosen deity. Design a detailed plan for the procession, including the route, participants, rituals, and symbolic elements to be incorporated. Justify your choices based on the religious beliefs and practices of ancient Egypt.

Exercise: Creating Festival Artifacts

Choose a specific festival and create replicas of the artifacts associated with that festival, such as processional standards, ceremonial vessels, or festival masks. Write a description of each artifact, explaining its purpose, symbolism, and the role it played in the festival.

Tools and Implements:

In the religious practices of ancient Egypt, tools and implements played a significant role in facilitating various rituals, ceremonies, and magical practices. These objects were imbued with symbolic meaning and served as conduits for connecting the mortal realm with the divine. From sacred instruments used in temple rituals to magical tools employed by practitioners of witchcraft and divination, the tools and implements used in ancient Egyptian religious practices were diverse and purposeful.

Ritual Tools:

Ritual tools were employed in the performance of religious ceremonies and offerings within the sacred precincts of temples. These tools were specifically designed to carry out the prescribed rituals with precision and efficacy. Examples of ritual tools include:

a. Ankh: The ankh, a symbol resembling a cross with a loop at the top, represented the key of life and was often depicted in the hands of deities. It symbolized eternal life and divine authority.

b. Scepter: The scepter, shaped like a long staff with a specific design at the top, was associated with the divine authority of the pharaoh and was used in royal rituals and ceremonies.

c. Censer: The censer, a vessel used to burn incense, played a significant role in purification rituals and offerings to the gods. The fragrance of the incense was believed to please the deities and facilitate communication between the mortal and divine realms.

Magical Tools:

Magical practices were an integral part of ancient Egyptian religious beliefs, often intertwined with rituals and ceremonies. Practitioners of magic utilized specific tools and implements to channel supernatural forces and achieve desired outcomes. Some examples of magical tools include:

a. Magical Wands: Wands were carved from various materials and adorned with symbols and hieroglyphs. These wands were believed to possess supernatural powers and were used to cast spells, perform rituals, and invoke deities.

b. Amulets: Amulets were small objects, usually made of precious stones or metals, that were worn or carried as protective charms. They were engraved with symbols and inscriptions associated with specific deities and offered spiritual protection and blessings to the wearer.

c. Ritual Knives: Ritual knives, known as "arthames," were used in magical practices for cutting herbs, inscribing symbols, and directing energy. They were considered sacred objects and were believed to possess the power to sever negative influences and create positive change.

Examples, Problems, and Exercises:

a. Example: Symbolism of the Ankh

Analyze the symbolism of the ankh in ancient Egyptian religious beliefs, exploring its association with the concept of eternal life and its use in artistic depictions. Discuss the religious significance of the ankh in the context of the belief in an afterlife and the journey of the soul.

b. Problem: Designing a Magical Wand

Design a magical wand inspired by ancient Egyptian practices. Consider the materials, symbols, and inscriptions you would incorporate into the wand to align with specific magical intentions. Justify your design choices based on the principles of ancient Egyptian magic.

c. Exercise: Creating an Amulet

Create a replica of an ancient Egyptian amulet using clay or other suitable materials. Explain the symbolism behind the chosen design and inscriptions, highlighting the specific protective qualities it embodies. Discuss the historical and cultural significance of amulets in ancient Egyptian religious practices.

Analysis of the earliest known temples and sacred spaces in ancient Egypt and their significance in religious practices

The earliest known temples and sacred spaces in ancient Egypt hold great significance in understanding the development and evolution of religious practices in the region. These architectural structures served as focal points for religious worship and were believed to be the dwelling places of deities, where humans could commune with the divine.

Pre-Dynastic Temples:
During the Pre-Dynastic Period, from around 5500 BCE to 3100 BCE, temples took a more rudimentary form compared to later periods. They were often small and consisted of simple structures or shrines. These early temples were built with perishable materials such as mud brick or wood, making their preservation challenging. However, archaeological evidence, including remnants of altars and offerings, provides insights into their religious significance.

The pre-Dynastic temples were primarily associated with the worship of local deities and spirits. They served as centers for community rituals and religious ceremonies, fostering a sense of collective identity and spiritual connection. These early temples were often situated in strategic locations, such as high ground or near significant natural features, emphasizing the connection between the physical landscape and the divine.

Hierakonpolis and the "Fortress Temples":

Hierakonpolis, located in Upper Egypt, was an important religious and political center during the Predynastic Period. It is known for its distinctive "Fortress Temples," large enclosures surrounded by fortified walls. These temples, such as the Main Deposit and the Gebel Sheikh Suleiman Temple, demonstrate the early architectural developments and religious practices of the time.

The Fortress Temples contained chapels and open courtyards where rituals, offerings, and ceremonies took place. The design of these temples reflects the concept of sacred space and separation from the secular world. The walls acted as symbolic boundaries between the divine realm and the human domain, reinforcing the sanctity of the temple and its role as a place of spiritual interaction.

Nabta Playa and Astronomical Alignments:

Another remarkable sacred site is Nabta Playa, located in the western desert of Egypt. This site dates back to approximately 5000 BCE and contains stone circles, megaliths, and other structures associated with religious activities. One notable aspect of Nabta Playa is its alignment with celestial phenomena, suggesting an early connection between religion, cosmology, and astronomical observations.

The stone circles and alignments at Nabta Playa are believed to have served as observation points for celestial events, allowing ancient Egyptians to track the movement of stars and celestial bodies. These astronomical alignments likely played a role in determining the timing of religious festivals and rituals, further emphasizing the integration of the natural world and the divine in ancient Egyptian religious practices.

Examples, Problems, and Exercises:

a. Example: The Main Deposit Temple at Hierakonpolis

Analyze the archaeological evidence and architectural features of the Main Deposit Temple at Hierakonpolis. Discuss its possible religious functions, rituals, and the significance of its location within the ancient settlement. Consider the importance of community engagement and collective worship in early temple practices.

b. Problem: Designing a Ritual Space

Design a concept for a pre-Dynastic temple or sacred space inspired by the architectural features and religious beliefs of the time. Consider the materials, layout, and symbolism that would be incorporated into the design. Justify your choices based on archaeological evidence and knowledge of pre-Dynastic religious practices.

c. Exercise: Exploring Astronomical Alignments

Research the astronomical alignments at Nabta Playa and their potential significance in ancient Egyptian religious practices. Discuss the possible ways in which celestial observations influenced the timing and conduct of religious ceremonies. Reflect on the broader implications of aligning religious activities with the movements of celestial bodies.

Examination of the role of priests and priestesses in temple rituals and their interactions with the divine

The role of priests and priestesses in temple rituals was vital to ancient Egyptian religious practices. These individuals served as intermediaries between the human realm and the divine, facilitating communication and establishing a connection with the gods. They played a crucial role in maintaining the harmony and balance of the cosmos through their rituals, offerings, and invocations.

The Function of Priests and Priestesses:

Priests and priestesses held esteemed positions within the religious hierarchy and were responsible for the daily rituals and ceremonies performed in the temples. They were considered the representatives of the gods on Earth and were entrusted with the sacred knowledge and rituals necessary for maintaining divine favor and cosmic order.

Priests were typically male, while priestesses could be female, and in some cases, held positions of authority and influence. Their roles and responsibilities varied depending on the temple and the deity they served. They dedicated their lives to the service of the gods, following strict rituals, purifications, and rules of conduct.

Rituals and Offerings:

Priests and priestesses conducted a wide range of rituals and offerings within the temple setting. These rituals included purification ceremonies, libation rituals, and the presentation of offerings such as food, incense, and precious objects to the gods. Through these acts, they sought to nourish and appease the divine entities, ensuring their continued benevolence towards humanity.

The rituals performed by priests and priestesses aimed to maintain cosmic harmony and order. They believed that by fulfilling their roles diligently and performing the correct rituals, they could secure the protection and blessings of the gods for the community and the kingdom as a whole.

Divination and Oracle Interactions:

Priests and priestesses also played a role in divination practices, seeking the guidance and insights of the gods through oracles or other divinatory methods. They would interpret signs and omens, such as the flight of birds or the examination of entrails, to gain insight into the divine will and the future.

Oracles were individuals believed to possess a direct connection with the gods, through whom divine messages and prophecies were conveyed. Priests and priestesses would consult these oracles on important matters, such as the outcome of battles or the success of royal endeavors. The oracles acted as conduits between the mortal realm and the divine, providing guidance and answers to important questions.

Examples, Problems, and Exercises:

a. Example: The Role of the High Priestess of Hathor

Analyze the role and responsibilities of the High Priestess of Hathor at the Temple of Dendera. Discuss her interactions with the goddess Hathor and her role in maintaining the religious rituals and practices associated with the temple. Consider the significance of gender and the cult of Hathor in understanding the dynamics of priestly roles.

b. Problem: A Day in the Life of a Priest

Imagine you are a priest serving in the Temple of Amun-Ra at Karnak. Describe a typical day in your life, including the rituals you would perform, the offerings you would present, and your interactions with other priests and worshippers. Consider the challenges and rewards of your role as a conduit between the divine and the human.

c. Exercise: Interpreting Divinatory Signs

Study the various divinatory methods used by priests and priestesses in ancient Egypt, such as interpreting dreams, examining animal behavior, or analyzing celestial phenomena. Choose one divinatory method and practice interpreting a given scenario or set of signs. Reflect on the challenges and limitations of divination as a means of understanding the divine will.

By exploring the role of priests and priestesses in temple rituals and their interactions with the divine, we gain a deeper understanding of the intricate religious practices of ancient Egypt and the central role played by these individuals in maintaining the cosmic balance and ensuring the favor of the gods.

Discussion of the major festivals and celebrations held during the Pre-Dynastic Period, highlighting their religious and social significance

The Pre-Dynastic Period in ancient Egypt was marked by a variety of festivals and celebrations that held great religious and social significance for the community. These festivals were intricately connected to the religious beliefs and practices of the time, serving as occasions for honoring the gods, renewing cosmic energies, and fostering social cohesion among the people.

Festival of the Nile Inundation:

One of the most significant festivals during the Pre-Dynastic Period was the Festival of the Nile Inundation. This festival celebrated the annual flooding of the Nile River, which was crucial for the fertility of the land and the success of agriculture. It was a time of rejoicing and thanksgiving as the people recognized the life-giving force of the river and its association with the god Hapy. The festival included processions, offerings, and rituals to ensure the Nile's continued abundance.

Festival of the New Year:

The Festival of the New Year marked the beginning of the agricultural cycle and the annual renewal of cosmic energies. It was a time of purification and the restoration of order in the world. The festival included rituals to banish evil spirits, cleanse the community, and invoke the protection of the gods for the coming year. It involved processions, music, dancing, and feasting, creating a sense of unity and optimism among the people.

Festival of the Departed:

The Festival of the Departed was a solemn occasion dedicated to honoring and appeasing the spirits of the deceased. It was believed that during this festival, the spirits of the ancestors returned to the mortal realm to receive offerings and prayers from their living relatives. The festival involved rituals at burial sites, including the presentation of food, drink, and symbolic offerings. It served as a way to maintain a connection with the deceased and seek their guidance and protection.

Seasonal Festivals:

Alongside these major festivals, the Pre-Dynastic Period also saw the celebration of various seasonal festivals that marked important agricultural milestones. These festivals corresponded to the planting, growing, and harvesting seasons and were centered around the worship of specific deities associated with agricultural fertility and abundance. These festivals involved processions, music, dance, and communal feasting, fostering a sense of communal harmony and gratitude for the blessings of the gods.

Examples, Problems, and Exercises:

a. Example: The Festival of the Nile Inundation

Analyze the religious and social significance of the Festival of the Nile Inundation, focusing on the connection between the annual flooding of the Nile, agricultural prosperity, and the worship of the god Hapy. Discuss the rituals, symbols, and communal activities associated with the festival and their role in fostering a sense of unity and gratitude among the ancient Egyptians.

b. Problem: Designing a Seasonal Festival

Imagine you are tasked with designing a seasonal festival for a specific stage of the agricultural cycle in ancient Egypt. Outline the rituals, symbols, and activities that would be incorporated into the festival to honor the respective deity and celebrate the associated agricultural milestone. Consider the social and religious significance of the festival and its potential impact on community cohesion.

c. Exercise: Festivals and Social Cohesion

Discuss the role of festivals in promoting social cohesion and solidarity among ancient Egyptian communities during the Pre-Dynastic Period. Draw comparisons to modern-day festivals and celebrations and identify similarities and differences in their functions and impact on community dynamics. Reflect on the ways in which festivals serve as a platform for religious expression, cultural identity, and communal bonding.

By examining the major festivals and celebrations of the Pre-Dynastic Period, we gain insight into the religious and social fabric of ancient Egyptian society, highlighting the profound interplay between religious beliefs, communal rituals, and the seasonal rhythms of agricultural life.

Exploration of the tools, artifacts, and symbolic objects used in religious rituals and their meanings

In ancient Egyptian religious rituals during the Pre-Dynastic Period, a variety of tools, artifacts, and symbolic objects were used to enhance the spiritual experience and convey profound meanings. These objects played a crucial role in religious practices, acting as conduits between the mortal realm and the divine sphere. They held symbolic significance and were believed to possess inherent power and divine connections.

Ritual Offering Vessels:

One of the most prominent tools used in religious rituals was the ritual offering vessel. These vessels were typically made of ceramic or stone and were intricately decorated with symbols and hieroglyphs. They were used to hold offerings such as food, beverages, and other sacred substances. The act of offering was a way to establish a connection with the gods and seek their favor, blessings, and protection. The vessels themselves were considered sacred, representing the vessel through which the divine could receive the offerings.

Incense Burners:

Incense burners were essential tools in religious ceremonies. They were used to burn aromatic substances such as incense, resin, and herbs. The rising smoke was believed to carry prayers and offerings to the gods and create a purifying and sacred atmosphere. The fragrant aroma was associated with divine presence and was believed to attract and please the deities. Incense burners were often adorned with intricate designs and symbolized the transformative power of fire and the spiritual realms it bridged.

Symbolic Objects:

Various symbolic objects were used in religious rituals to represent specific deities or concepts. These objects included statues, amulets, and symbols representing gods and goddesses, sacred animals, elements of nature, and cosmic forces. For example, the ankh symbolized life and the eternal soul, while the wedjat (the Eye of Horus) represented protection and healing. These symbolic objects were imbued with divine attributes and were believed to facilitate communication with the gods and invoke their powers.

Ritual Tools:

Priests and priestesses used specific tools to perform rituals with precision and reverence. These tools included ritual knives, wands, and scepters, which symbolized authority and the ability to commune with the divine. The ritual knife, in particular, held symbolic significance as a tool of purification, used to cleanse and separate the sacred from the profane. The wand and scepter represented the power and influence of the priestly class in mediating between the mortal world and the gods.

Examples, Problems, and Exercises:

a. Example: Analysis of Ritual Offering Vessels

Select a specific type of ritual offering vessel from the Pre-Dynastic Period and analyze its form, decoration, and symbolic significance. Discuss how the vessel's shape, motifs, and inscriptions convey religious and cultural meanings. Explore the materials used and their significance in the context of ancient Egyptian religious practices. Consider how the vessel's design enhances the act of offering and strengthens the connection between the worshipper and the divine.

b. Problem: Symbolic Objects and their Meanings

Choose three symbolic objects commonly used in ancient Egyptian religious rituals and discuss their meanings and associations. Explore the cultural context in which these objects were used and the symbolism attributed to them. Investigate the materials, shapes, and iconography used in their construction and consider how they were employed in religious ceremonies to convey specific concepts or deities.

   c. Exercise: Designing a Ritual Tool

   Imagine you are a priest or priestess in ancient Egypt during the Pre-Dynastic Period. Design a ritual tool that embodies the essence of a specific deity or represents a significant aspect of religious belief. Create a detailed description of the tool, explaining its materials, shape, decoration, and symbolic elements. Justify your design choices by referencing the attributes and associations of the deity or concept it represents.

   By exploring the tools, artifacts, and symbolic objects used in ancient Egyptian religious rituals, we gain a deeper understanding of the intricate relationship between material culture, religious beliefs, and the quest for spiritual connection. These objects served as tangible manifestations of the divine, facilitating communication, and creating a sacred space where mortals could interact with the divine realm.

Chapter 6: Prayers, Hymns, Chants, and Spells Dedicated to Early Deities and Nature Spirits

Chapter 6 delves into the rich tapestry of ancient Egyptian religious practices during the Pre-Dynastic Period, focusing specifically on the prayers, hymns, chants, and spells dedicated to early deities and nature spirits. These texts provide valuable insights into the religious beliefs and practices of the ancient Egyptians, offering glimpses into their spiritual worldview, their relationship with the divine, and their reverence for the natural world.

Understanding the Importance of Prayers, Hymns, Chants, and Spells:

Prayers, hymns, chants, and spells formed an integral part of ancient Egyptian religious life. They were profound expressions of devotion, vehicles for seeking divine assistance, and methods of promoting harmony with the natural world. Through these sacred texts, individuals and communities sought to establish connections with the divine, communicate their desires and concerns, and honor the deities and nature spirits who governed various aspects of existence. These texts were believed to possess inherent power, their words carrying the ability to influence and shape both the spiritual and physical realms.

Exploring the Early Deities and Nature Spirits:

The ancient Egyptians worshipped a multitude of deities and revered the spirits inhabiting the natural world. These beings personified cosmic forces, natural phenomena, and aspects of human experience. Chapter 6 examines the prayers, hymns, chants, and spells dedicated to these early deities and nature spirits, shedding light on their characteristics, domains, and relationships with humans. By studying these texts, we gain a deeper understanding of how the ancient Egyptians interacted with the divine and sought the favor and protection of these powerful beings.

Analysis of Prayers, Hymns, Chants, and Spells:

In this chapter, we will analyze specific examples of prayers, hymns, chants, and spells dedicated to early deities and nature spirits. We will explore their form, content, and stylistic features, unraveling the intricate web of religious symbolism, metaphor, and magical invocation embedded within these texts. Through a detailed examination of their language, structure, and imagery, we will decipher the intended meanings, theological concepts, and ritualistic functions of these sacred texts.

Connections to Modern Practices and Comparative Perspectives:

While the focus of this chapter is on ancient Egyptian religious texts, we will also draw connections to modern-day practices in fields such as Witchcraft, Divination, Herbalism, Shamanism, and Ecospirituality. By exploring these connections, we can uncover shared themes, principles, and approaches that transcend time and cultural boundaries. Additionally, we will engage in a comparative analysis, drawing parallels between ancient Egyptian religious practices and those of other ancient cultures, such as Mesopotamia, Greece, or Rome. This comparative perspective allows us to highlight similarities and differences in the use of prayers, hymns, chants, and spells and gain a broader understanding of the human quest for divine connection.

Examples, Problems, and Exercises:

a. Example: Analysis of an Early Egyptian Hymn

Select a hymn dedicated to an early Egyptian deity and analyze its poetic structure, themes, and symbolic imagery. Explore the deity's attributes and significance within the ancient Egyptian pantheon. Discuss how the hymn captures the essence of the deity's power and role in the natural world. Consider the intended audience and the hymn's potential ritualistic context.

b. Problem: Composing a Modern Prayer

Compose a prayer that reflects the ancient Egyptian belief in the interconnectedness of the divine and the natural world. Incorporate elements of reverence for nature, acknowledgment of cosmic forces, and a plea for divine assistance. Justify the inclusion of specific language and symbolism, drawing from examples of ancient Egyptian prayers. Reflect on the purpose and significance of your prayer in fostering a sense of connection with the divine and promoting harmony with the natural world.

c. Exercise: Comparative Analysis of Prayers

Select a prayer from another ancient culture, such as Mesopotamia, Greece, or Rome, and compare it to an ancient Egyptian prayer dedicated to a similar deity or concept. Analyze the similarities and differences in terms of language, structure, and theological themes. Reflect on the cultural context and religious worldview of each civilization and discuss how these factors influenced the formulation and use of prayers. Consider the implications of these similarities and differences for our understanding of human spirituality and the role of prayers in religious practices.

By engaging with the examples, problems, and exercises provided in this chapter, students will develop critical thinking skills, deepen their understanding of ancient Egyptian religious practices, and explore the broader significance of prayers, hymns, chants, and spells in fostering connections with the divine and the natural world. Through these activities, students will gain a profound appreciation for the power of language, ritual, and spiritual expression in ancient Egypt and beyond.

Understanding the Importance of Prayers, Hymns, Chants, and Spells:

Prayers, hymns, chants, and spells held profound significance in ancient Egyptian religious practices during the Pre-Dynastic Period. These sacred texts played a pivotal role in the spiritual lives of individuals and communities, serving as powerful tools for communication with the divine, expressions of devotion, and conduits for magical and ritualistic practices. Understanding the importance of prayers, hymns, chants, and spells is crucial to gaining insights into the religious worldview, beliefs, and practices of the ancient Egyptians.

Establishing Connections with the Divine:

Prayers, hymns, chants, and spells were essential means through which the ancient Egyptians sought to establish connections with the divine realm. They believed that these texts provided a direct line of communication with the gods and goddesses who governed various aspects of existence. By reciting prayers, chanting hymns, and performing rituals accompanied by specific spells, individuals aimed to attract the attention and favor of the deities, seeking their protection, blessings, and guidance. These sacred texts were considered channels through which humans could reach out to the divine and establish a reciprocal relationship.

Expressions of Devotion and Reverence:

Prayers, hymns, chants, and spells were powerful expressions of devotion and reverence for the divine beings worshipped in ancient Egypt. Through the carefully crafted words and poetic imagery of these texts, individuals conveyed their deep respect, awe, and adoration for the gods and goddesses. These expressions of devotion served to reinforce the spiritual bonds between humans and the divine, fostering a sense of reverence and gratitude for the divine presence in everyday life. Prayers, hymns, chants, and spells were not mere recitations but heartfelt expressions of faith and spiritual connection.

Ritualistic and Magical Functions:

Prayers, hymns, chants, and spells were integral components of religious rituals and magical practices in ancient Egypt. They were recited and performed within the context of various ceremonies, festivals, and personal rituals. These sacred texts were believed to possess inherent power, capable of influencing both the spiritual and physical realms. The recitation of prayers and hymns, accompanied by the rhythmic chanting of specific invocations, was thought to invoke the presence of the gods and goddesses, facilitating communication and communion between humans and the divine. Spells, on the other hand, were used to harness supernatural forces and manipulate the natural world for desired outcomes. They were an essential aspect of ancient Egyptian magic and spellcasting practices.

Symbolism and Ritualistic Context:

Prayers, hymns, chants, and spells were carefully crafted with rich symbolism and metaphorical language. Each word, phrase, and verse carried deep meaning and significance, drawing upon the religious cosmology, myths, and the natural world. The poetic structure of these texts was designed to evoke specific emotions, create a sacred atmosphere, and enhance the ritualistic experience. The language used in prayers, hymns, chants, and spells often employed epithets, praises, and appeals to the deities' power, wisdom, and divine attributes. Symbolic actions, gestures, and the use of ritual implements further heightened the efficacy of these sacred texts.

Examples, Problems, and Exercises:

a. Example: Analyzing a Prayer

Select an ancient Egyptian prayer dedicated to a specific deity and analyze its structure, language, and thematic content. Identify the symbols and metaphors used, and discuss how they convey the individual's or community's intentions, emotions, and beliefs. Consider the cultural context and the ritualistic setting in which the prayer might have been recited. Reflect on the role of prayers in establishing connections with the divine and fostering a sense of spiritual devotion.

b. Problem: Composing a Hymn

Compose a hymn dedicated to a natural phenomenon or element, drawing inspiration from ancient Egyptian hymns and poetic devices. Consider the symbolic significance of the chosen phenomenon and explore how it relates to the divine and human experiences. Reflect on the language, structure, and thematic elements that capture the essence of the natural phenomenon and evoke a sense of reverence and awe.

c. Exercise: Comparative Analysis of Spells

Compare and contrast an ancient Egyptian spell with a spell from another ancient culture known for its magical practices, such as Mesopotamia or Greece. Analyze the purposes, methods, and symbolic elements employed in each spell, and discuss how they reflect the respective cultural beliefs and practices. Consider the ethical implications and potential effects of the spells in their respective contexts.

Through engaging with the examples, problems, and exercises provided in this chapter, students will gain a deeper understanding of the importance of prayers, hymns, chants, and spells in ancient Egyptian religious practices. They will explore the multifaceted functions of these sacred texts, examine their cultural and symbolic significance, and develop critical thinking skills in analyzing their structure, language, and thematic content. By delving into the world of ancient Egyptian spirituality, students will appreciate the power of words, rituals, and spiritual expressions in connecting with the divine and shaping religious experiences.

Exploring the Early Deities and Nature Spirits:

The religious beliefs of the ancient Egyptians during the Pre-Dynastic Period were deeply intertwined with the natural world and the forces they observed in their environment. The early Egyptians recognized and revered a pantheon of deities and nature spirits that represented various aspects of their surroundings, such as the Nile River, the sun, the sky, and the earth.

In their efforts to understand and connect with these powerful forces, the ancient Egyptians personified them as deities with distinct characteristics and domains. These deities were believed to possess supernatural powers and abilities, influencing every aspect of human existence. Additionally, the Egyptians recognized the presence of nature spirits, lesser beings associated with specific natural elements, such as trees, rivers, and animals.

One prominent early deity of the Pre-Dynastic Period was Geb, the god of the earth. Geb was often depicted lying beneath the sky goddess Nut, symbolizing the connection between the earth and the heavens. The image of Nut arching over Geb, her body adorned with stars, represented the celestial sphere that encompassed the earthly realm.

Another significant deity during this period was Hathor, often associated with feminine aspects of fertility, music, and joy. Hathor was revered as the mother goddess and was depicted as a cow or as a woman with cow-like features, emphasizing her connection to the nurturing and life-giving qualities of the earth.

Additionally, the ancient Egyptians recognized the presence of nature spirits, known as "benevolent spirits" or "genies," associated with natural elements such as water, trees, and rocks. These spirits were believed to inhabit specific locations and were associated with the protection and prosperity of those places. For example, a spirit associated with a particular tree might be appeased through offerings and prayers to ensure the well-being and fertility of that tree.

Through their religious beliefs and practices, the ancient Egyptians sought to establish a harmonious relationship with these deities and nature spirits. They believed that by honoring and appeasing them through prayers, rituals, and offerings, they could gain their favor and blessings, ensuring the prosperity and well-being of their communities.

It is important to note that the understanding and interpretation of these early deities and nature spirits are based on the limited evidence available from archaeological findings and later textual sources. As our knowledge of the Pre-Dynastic Period continues to evolve, it is essential to approach these interpretations with an open mind and remain receptive to new discoveries and insights.

Examples, Problems, and Exercises:

Exercise: Choose one early deity or nature spirit from the Pre-Dynastic Period and create a visual representation of the entity based on the available archaeological evidence. Explain the symbolism and attributes associated with the chosen deity or spirit.

Problem: Analyze the role of nature spirits in early Egyptian religious beliefs. Discuss how their association with specific natural elements influenced the daily lives and rituals of the ancient Egyptians.

Exercise: Imagine you are an ancient Egyptian living during the Pre-Dynastic Period. Write a prayer or hymn addressing a specific deity or nature spirit, expressing your gratitude and seeking their protection or assistance.

Problem: Compare the representations of early deities in Pre-Dynastic Egypt with deities from another ancient culture, such as Mesopotamia or Greece. Discuss the similarities and differences in their roles, characteristics, and worship practices.

Exercise: Create an artistic representation, such as a painting or sculpture, depicting the interaction between a deity and a nature spirit. Explain the symbolism and significance of the chosen elements in your artwork.

Through these examples, problems, and exercises, students can engage in critical thinking and analysis, exploring the complexities of early Egyptian religious beliefs and the significance of deities and nature spirits in their worldview. It encourages students to consider the historical context, cultural symbolism, and the interconnectedness of ancient Egyptian beliefs with the natural world.

Analysis of the prayers, hymns, chants, and spells found in surviving Pre-Dynastic texts and inscriptions

Analysis of the prayers, hymns, chants, and spells found in surviving Pre-Dynastic texts and inscriptions provides valuable insights into the religious practices and beliefs of the ancient Egyptians during this early period. Although the availability of textual evidence is limited, the existing examples offer glimpses into the spiritual mindset and rituals of the ancient Egyptians.

One prominent example is the "Hymn to the Nile," which is considered one of the oldest surviving religious texts from ancient Egypt. This hymn expresses reverence and gratitude to the Nile River, emphasizing its life-giving and nourishing qualities. It highlights the Nile's importance for agriculture, fertility, and sustenance, reflecting the Egyptians' deep understanding of the river's crucial role in their livelihoods. Through poetic language and vivid imagery, the hymn demonstrates the reverence and awe the ancient Egyptians held for natural forces.

Another notable text is the "Coffin Texts," a collection of funerary spells and prayers inscribed on coffins during the later part of the Pre-Dynastic Period. These texts were intended to guide and protect the deceased in the afterlife, ensuring their successful journey to the realm of the gods. The spells and prayers addressed various deities and invoked their aid, offering protection against evil forces and enabling a peaceful transition into the afterlife. These texts highlight the ancient Egyptians' belief in the continuity of life beyond death and their efforts to secure a positive afterlife experience.

Moreover, the "Shabaka Stone," an inscribed slab dating to the early First Intermediate Period, contains excerpts from a creation myth known as the "Memphite Theology." This text explains the cosmogony of the universe, attributing the creation of the world to the god Ptah. It describes Ptah's role as the creator deity and underscores his significance in the ancient Egyptian pantheon. The "Memphite Theology" provides insights into the philosophical and theological concepts that underpinned the ancient Egyptians' understanding of their existence and the divine origins of the world.

These examples and other surviving texts from the Pre-Dynastic Period reveal the multifaceted nature of ancient Egyptian prayers, hymns, chants, and spells. They demonstrate the Egyptians' inclination to honor and interact with deities, spirits, and natural forces through ritualistic and supplicatory practices. These texts also highlight the Egyptians' deep sense of spirituality, their belief in divine intervention, and their desire for protection, guidance, and prosperity in various aspects of life.

Examples, Problems, and Exercises:

Exercise: Analyze the structure and language of the "Hymn to the Nile" and discuss how it reflects the ancient Egyptians' reverence for natural forces. Explore the poetic devices used in the hymn and their effects on the reader or listener.

Hymn to the Nile

Hail to you, O Nile, life-sustainer of the land,
Bountiful provider of abundance and fertility.
Your waters nourish the fields, bringing life to the earth,
Causing crops to flourish and animals to thrive.

O Nile, great river of Egypt, we honor you,
For you are the source of our sustenance and prosperity.
Your gentle currents flow through our land,
Bringing blessings and abundance in your wake.

Your fertile waters bring forth the greenery of the land,
Transforming the desert into a flourishing oasis.
With each flood, you renew the land's fertility,
Enriching the soil and ensuring abundant harvests.

O Nile, your majestic presence brings joy to our hearts,
Your waters are a symbol of life's eternal cycle.
We praise your divine power and wisdom,
For you are the lifeline of our civilization.

Blessed are the waters that flow from your sacred source,
Nourishing the land and all living creatures.
O Nile, we offer our gratitude and reverence to you,
For you are the lifeblood of Egypt, our beloved land.

Note: The text provided here is a representation of the content and style of an ancient Egyptian hymn to the Nile. Actual ancient texts may vary in their language and specific details.

This hymn exemplifies the ancient Egyptians' deep respect and gratitude for the Nile River, recognizing its vital role in their agricultural society. It showcases their belief in the river's divine nature and its ability to sustain life and provide prosperity. The poetic language and imagery used in the hymn evoke a sense of awe and reverence for the natural forces that governed their existence.

Problem: Compare the themes and purposes of the funerary spells found in the Coffin Texts with those of modern-day funeral rituals or religious practices. Discuss the similarities and differences in their aims and beliefs about the afterlife.

Exercise: Select a spell or prayer from the Coffin Texts and interpret its symbolism and intended effects. Discuss the rituals or actions that might have accompanied the recitation of the spell and the purpose they served in the context of ancient Egyptian funerary practices.

Problem: Examine the "Shabaka Stone" and analyze the cosmological concepts presented in the "Memphite Theology." Discuss how these concepts influenced ancient Egyptian religious beliefs and their understanding of the world's creation.

Exercise: Compose a prayer, hymn, chant, or spell dedicated to a specific deity or natural force, inspired by the ancient Egyptian examples. Explain the purpose and intended effects of your composition and the symbolism used to convey your intentions.

Through these examples, problems, and exercises, students can deepen their understanding of the religious beliefs and practices of the ancient Egyptians during the Pre-Dynastic Period. They will engage in critical thinking and analysis, drawing connections between ancient Egyptian concepts and rituals and their own knowledge and experiences.

Examination of the deities and nature spirits invoked in these religious texts and their specific roles and attributes

The religious texts of ancient Egypt provide valuable insights into the deities and nature spirits invoked by the ancient Egyptians. These texts reveal a rich and complex pantheon of gods and spirits, each with their own unique roles, attributes, and symbolism. Understanding the deities and nature spirits mentioned in these texts is crucial for comprehending the religious beliefs and practices of the ancient Egyptians during the Pre-Dynastic Period.

One of the prominent deities invoked in ancient Egyptian religious texts is Ra, the sun god. Ra is often depicted as a falcon-headed deity or as a sun disk. He represents the sun's life-giving and creative powers and is associated with kingship and divine order. Ra is considered the chief deity and the creator of the world. His daily journey across the sky symbolizes the cycle of birth, death, and resurrection. In hymns and prayers, the ancient Egyptians praised Ra for his light and blessings, seeking his protection and guidance.

Another significant deity is Osiris, the god of the afterlife and the ruler of the underworld. Osiris is often portrayed as a mummified figure, symbolizing resurrection and eternal life. He is the judge of the deceased and the source of moral guidance. Ancient Egyptian religious texts emphasize the rituals and spells associated with Osiris, as they were believed to ensure a successful journey into the afterlife. These texts also mention the role of Osiris in the annual agricultural cycle, representing the cycle of life and death.

In addition to these major deities, ancient Egyptian religious texts also mention a variety of nature spirits associated with specific natural phenomena. For example, the ancient Egyptians invoked the Nile River as a divinized entity. The Nile was considered a life-giving force that nourished the land and ensured fertility and abundance. Hymns and prayers dedicated to the Nile expressed gratitude and reverence for its blessings. These texts highlighted the Nile's role in the agricultural prosperity of Egypt and emphasized the connection between the divine and the natural world.

Furthermore, the ancient Egyptians acknowledged the presence of spirits inhabiting various natural elements, such as trees, animals, and geographic features. These nature spirits, known as "Neteru," were believed to possess supernatural powers and could be invoked for protection and assistance. The Neteru were associated with specific aspects of nature, such as the sky, the earth, or the desert. Ancient Egyptian religious texts often included spells and invocations to these nature spirits, seeking their favor and support.

It is important to note that the roles and attributes of these deities and nature spirits varied across different regions and time periods within ancient Egypt. The specific characteristics and symbolism associated with each deity could evolve and adapt over time. Furthermore, the interpretation and understanding of these entities might have differed among different religious practitioners and communities. The examination of religious texts allows us to gain insights into the diverse and nuanced religious beliefs and practices of the ancient Egyptians.

Example problem: Analyze a hymn dedicated to the Nile River, highlighting its symbolic significance and its role in ancient Egyptian religious beliefs.

Example exercise: Compare and contrast the attributes and roles of Ra and Osiris in ancient Egyptian religious texts, discussing their significance in the religious worldview of the ancient Egyptians.

Through the analysis of these deities and nature spirits invoked in ancient Egyptian religious texts, we gain a deeper understanding of the ancient Egyptians' complex religious worldview. These texts provide a window into the beliefs, rituals, and spiritual practices of this ancient civilization, offering valuable insights into their cosmology and their understanding of the divine and the natural world.

Discussion of the purposes and intentions behind the prayers, hymns, chants, and spells during this period

Prayers, hymns, chants, and spells were integral components of religious practices during the Pre-Dynastic Period in ancient Egypt. These rituals served various purposes and were intended to establish a connection between humans and the divine, seek divine blessings, and address specific needs or concerns. Understanding the purposes and intentions behind these religious expressions provides insights into the religious mindset of the ancient Egyptians and sheds light on their desires and aspirations.

Establishing Communication with the Divine:
Prayers, hymns, chants, and spells were employed as means to communicate with the divine realm. They were considered vehicles through which humans could express their devotion, seek guidance, and establish a personal connection with the gods and nature spirits. By offering prayers and reciting hymns, the ancient Egyptians aimed to engage in a dialogue with the divine, seeking solace, reassurance, and spiritual support.

Seeking Divine Blessings and Protection:
Ancient Egyptian religious texts often included invocations and hymns that sought the blessings and protection of the deities and nature spirits. These prayers and chants were recited with the intention of receiving divine favor, ensuring prosperity, good health, and success in various endeavors. For example, prayers were offered to Ra, the sun god, to invoke his light and life-giving powers, while hymns dedicated to the Nile River sought its annual flooding and abundance.

Addressing Specific Needs and Concerns:
Prayers, hymns, chants, and spells were also used as tools to address specific needs and concerns of individuals or the community. Ancient Egyptians believed that the deities and nature spirits possessed the ability to influence various aspects

of life, including fertility, healing, protection from malevolent forces, and success in specific undertakings. Accordingly, they would offer prayers and recite spells tailored to their specific requirements, such as healing rituals for the sick or protection spells against evil spirits.

Expressing Gratitude and Reverence:
Many religious texts from the Pre-Dynastic Period include hymns and prayers expressing gratitude and reverence for the divine and the natural world. These expressions of thanks were motivated by the ancient Egyptians' deep appreciation for the blessings they received and the recognition of the interconnectedness of all life. By offering hymns and prayers of gratitude, they sought to acknowledge the benevolence of the gods and spirits, reinforcing their relationship with the divine.

Example problem: Analyze a specific hymn or prayer from the Pre-Dynastic Period, identifying its purpose and discussing how it reflects the religious mindset and aspirations of the ancient Egyptians.

Example exercise: Compare and contrast the purposes and intentions behind prayers and spells in ancient Egyptian religious practices with those in other ancient civilizations, such as Mesopotamia or Greece.

The prayers, hymns, chants, and spells of the Pre-Dynastic Period played a significant role in the religious and spiritual lives of the ancient Egyptians. They served as powerful means of establishing communication with the divine, seeking blessings and protection, addressing specific needs, and expressing gratitude. Through these religious expressions, the ancient Egyptians sought to navigate the complexities of life, find comfort in the divine presence, and align themselves with the natural and spiritual forces that governed their world.

Exploration of the connections between the early religious practices and the natural environment, including sacred landscapes and animal symbolism

The early religious practices of ancient Egypt were deeply intertwined with the natural environment, reflecting a profound connection between the people and the world around them. The natural landscape, with its rivers, deserts, and fertile plains, held great significance in the religious beliefs and rituals of the Pre-Dynastic Period. This connection is evident in the concept of sacred landscapes and the use of animal symbolism within religious contexts.

Exploring the Rituals, Beliefs, and Syncretism of Ancient Egyptian Religion

Sacred Landscapes:

The ancient Egyptians regarded certain natural landscapes as sacred, considering them to be the dwelling places of deities and nature spirits. These sacred landscapes included rivers, mountains, caves, oases, and specific geographical locations. For example, the Nile River was revered as a lifeline and was associated with the god Hapy, who controlled its annual flooding and brought fertility to the land. The desert, with its harsh and mysterious nature, was also seen as a sacred space where contact with the divine could be established through rituals and pilgrimage.

Sacred landscapes were often the sites of temples, shrines, and burial grounds, where rituals, ceremonies, and offerings were conducted. The ancient Egyptians believed that these sacred spaces facilitated a closer connection between the earthly realm and the divine, allowing for communication and interaction with the gods and spirits.

Animal Symbolism:

Animal symbolism played a significant role in the religious practices of ancient Egypt. Animals were considered sacred beings, believed to possess divine qualities and embody specific deities or nature spirits. The behavior, characteristics, and symbolism associated with various animals were used to understand and interact with the divine forces.

For example, the falcon was associated with the god Horus, symbolizing divine kingship and protection. The lion represented power and strength, often linked to the goddess Sekhmet. The scarab beetle was a symbol of rebirth and the rising sun, connected to the god Khepri. By invoking these animal symbols in religious rituals, the ancient Egyptians sought to access the divine qualities they represented and establish a connection with the associated deities or spirits.

Animal mummification and burial practices also demonstrate the significance of animal symbolism. Sacred animals were often mummified and buried in large quantities as offerings to the gods, emphasizing their association with the divine realm and their role in facilitating communication between humans and the gods.

Example problem: Analyze the symbolism and significance of a specific animal in ancient Egyptian religious practices during the Pre-Dynastic Period, discussing its connection to a particular deity or nature spirit and its role in religious rituals.

Example exercise: Compare the use of animal symbolism in ancient Egyptian religious practices with the animal symbolism found in other ancient civilizations, such as Mesopotamia or Greece, highlighting similarities and differences in their religious beliefs and practices.

The connections between early religious practices in ancient Egypt and the natural environment reveal a profound reverence for the world around them. Sacred landscapes and animal symbolism provided a means to understand and engage with the divine forces that governed the natural world. Through rituals, offerings, and the use of symbolism, the ancient Egyptians sought to align themselves with the natural rhythms and powers of their environment, creating a harmonious relationship between humans, gods, and the natural world.

Part 3: Old Kingdom (c. 2686 BCE - 2181 BCE)

The Old Kingdom of ancient Egypt, which thrived from approximately 2686 BCE to 2181 BCE, represents a pivotal era in Egyptian history characterized by significant religious developments and cultural achievements. This period witnessed the rise of divine kingship, the construction of monumental temples, and the formulation of religious rituals and practices that would shape the religious landscape of Egypt for centuries to come. In Part 3, we will delve into the religious aspects of the Old Kingdom, exploring the transformations and continuities in religious beliefs and practices during this remarkable period.

Chapter 7: Religious Developments and Changes during the Old Kingdom
Chapter 7 focuses on the dynamic religious landscape of the Old Kingdom and examines the key religious developments and changes that occurred during this period. We will explore how religious beliefs and practices evolved, adapted, and sometimes diverged from earlier periods. Through the analysis of textual sources, temple reliefs, and archaeological evidence, we will investigate the role of the priesthood, the growing importance of specific deities, and the emergence of new religious concepts. Additionally, we will discuss the influence of political and social factors on religious developments and the impact of these changes on the daily lives of ancient Egyptians.

Chapter 8: Temples, Festivals, and Tools used c. 2686 BCE - 2181 BCE
Chapter 8 delves into the intricate world of temples, festivals, and the tools utilized during the Old Kingdom. Temples served as sacred spaces where rituals, ceremonies, and offerings took place, connecting the mortal realm with the divine. We will examine the architectural features, symbolism, and religious functions of Old Kingdom temples, such as the temples dedicated to Ra, Osiris, and Isis. Furthermore, we will explore the religious festivals held during this period, analyzing their significance in religious and social contexts. We will also discuss the tools and implements utilized in religious rituals and their symbolic meanings, ranging from ritual knives and libation vessels to magical amulets and incense burners.

Chapter 9: Prayers, Hymns, Chants, and Spells Associated with Key Deities Worshipped during this Period (e.g., Ra, Osiris, Isis)
Chapter 9 explores the rich tapestry of prayers, hymns, chants, and spells dedicated to the major deities worshipped during the Old Kingdom. We will

delve into the religious texts and inscriptions that provide insights into the religious devotion and beliefs of ancient Egyptians. Through the examination of these texts, we will analyze the unique attributes and roles of deities such as Ra, the sun god; Osiris, the god of the afterlife; and Isis, the goddess of magic and fertility. By exploring the content and structure of these religious texts, we will gain a deeper understanding of the ancient Egyptians' spiritual worldview and their interactions with the divine.

Example problem: Analyze the religious developments and changes during the Old Kingdom, discussing the factors that contributed to the evolution of religious beliefs and practices.

Example exercise: Compare and contrast the architectural features and religious functions of Old Kingdom temples dedicated to different deities, such as the temple of Ra and the temple of Osiris. Discuss the similarities and differences in their design, symbolism, and religious rituals associated with each deity.

In Part 3 of this study, we will immerse ourselves in the religious and cultural fabric of the Old Kingdom, unraveling the intricate tapestry of religious beliefs, practices, and transformations that unfolded during this period. By examining the religious developments, temple rituals, and the prayers, hymns, chants, and spells associated with key deities, we will gain a comprehensive understanding of the spiritual world of ancient Egypt during the Old Kingdom. Through critical analysis and engagement with primary sources, we will explore the complexities and nuances of ancient Egyptian religion, shedding light on the profound influence it had on the lives and worldview of its people.

Exploring the Rituals, Beliefs, and Syncretism of Ancient Egyptian Religion

Pharaohs	Queen	Ruled from	Children	Accomplishments
Djoser	-	c. 2670 BCE	-	Built the Step Pyramid at Saqqara
Sneferu	-	c. 2613 BCE	-	Constructed the Bent Pyramid and the Red Pyramid
Khufu	-	c. 2589 BCE	-	Built the Great Pyramid of Giza
Khafre	-	c. 2558 BCE	Nefertkau II	Constructed the second-largest pyramid at Giza and the Great Sphinx
Menkaure	-	c. 2532 BCE	-	Built the third pyramid at Giza
Djedefre	-	c. 2504 BCE	-	Built the pyramid at Abu Rawash and commissioned the Sphinx of Djedefre
Pepi I	-	c. 2332 BCE	-	Contributed to trade and diplomacy during his reign
-	Hetepheres I	-	Khufu , Meresankh III	Mother of Pharaoh Khufu
-	Meresankh III	-	-	Daughter of Hetepheres I and sister-wife of Khafre
-	Neferhetepes	-	-	Wife of Sneferu and mother of Khufu
-	Khentkaus I	-	Userkaf	Mother of King Userkaf
-	Nefertkau II	-	-	Daughter of King Khafre

Please note that the "Children" column includes only the known or notable children associated with the respective rulers. The accomplishments mentioned are a brief summary of their notable contributions during their reigns. The information provided is based on historical records and ongoing research, and details may vary or be subject to revision as new evidence emerges.

Chapter 7: Religious Developments and Changes during the Old Kingdom

Brief Overview of the Old Kingdom Period (c. 2686 BCE - 2181 BCE)

The Old Kingdom, also known as the Pyramid Age, represents a significant period in ancient Egyptian history. Spanning from approximately 2686 BCE to 2181 BCE, it was characterized by the centralization of power under the pharaohs and the construction of monumental pyramids. This era witnessed the rise of a highly organized state bureaucracy and the establishment of a distinct religious system that played a vital role in shaping all aspects of ancient Egyptian society.

Significance of Religion in Ancient Egyptian Society

Religion held a paramount position in the lives of the ancient Egyptians, permeating every aspect of their existence. It served as a guiding force that provided the framework for understanding the cosmos, human existence, and the divine order. Ancient Egyptians believed in a complex pantheon of gods and goddesses who governed various aspects of life, including nature, fertility, justice, and the afterlife. Religious rituals, temple worship, and funerary practices were integral to maintaining harmony with the gods and ensuring the well-being of both the living and the deceased.

Purpose of the Chapter and Key Research Questions

The purpose of this chapter is to delve into the religious developments and changes that took place during the Old Kingdom period. By examining the religious practices, beliefs, and institutions of ancient Egypt, we aim to gain a deeper understanding of the role of religion in shaping the society, culture, and worldview of the ancient Egyptians. This exploration will shed light on the religious landscape of the time, the evolution of deities, temple architecture, priesthood, festivals, funerary beliefs, and the interplay between religion and the ruling elite.

Key Research Questions:

How did religious beliefs and practices evolve during the Old Kingdom period?

What were the main deities worshipped during this era, and what were their roles and attributes?

How did temple architecture reflect the religious worldview and function as sacred spaces?

What were the roles and responsibilities of the priesthood, and how did they interact with the gods and the general populace?

What were the major religious festivals and their significance in the Old Kingdom?

How did funerary beliefs and practices reflect the ancient Egyptians' understanding of the afterlife?

How did religious developments during the Old Kingdom shape the social, political, and cultural fabric of ancient Egyptian society?

By addressing these research questions, this chapter aims to provide a comprehensive analysis of religious developments and changes during the Old Kingdom, offering valuable insights into the religious worldview and practices of this fascinating period in ancient Egyptian history. Through the exploration of religious beliefs and institutions, we can better grasp the profound influence of religion on the lives and aspirations of the ancient Egyptians, as well as the enduring legacy it has left on subsequent civilizations.

The Early Religious Landscape

Examination of Religious Beliefs and Practices in the Pre-Dynastic Period

The Pre-Dynastic Period marks the earliest phase of ancient Egyptian civilization, characterized by the emergence of complex social structures and the development of religious beliefs and practices. During this time, the ancient Egyptians exhibited a strong connection with the natural world and a belief in animism, the idea that all objects, animals, and natural phenomena possessed a spiritual essence. This spiritual essence was often personified and associated with various deities and nature spirits.

The religious practices of the Pre-Dynastic Egyptians included rituals aimed at ensuring the fertility of the land, successful hunting, and protection from harmful forces. These rituals involved the use of symbolic objects, such as amulets and talismans, as well as the performance of chants, dances, and incantations. The worship of animal deities, such as the falcon god Horus and the lioness goddess Sekhmet, also played a significant role during this period, reflecting the close connection between humans and the animal kingdom.

Transition to the Old Kingdom and Continuity in Religious Traditions

With the advent of the Old Kingdom, there was a gradual consolidation of power under the pharaohs, leading to a more centralized state and the construction of monumental structures, including pyramids and temples. Despite these changes, many aspects of religious beliefs and practices exhibited continuity from the Pre-Dynastic Period.

The ancient Egyptians continued to venerate deities associated with nature and fertility, such as the sky god Horus and the earth goddess Geb. The worship of the sun god Ra, who was believed to be the creator and sustainer of the universe, also gained prominence during this time. Temples were established as sacred spaces where rituals and offerings were conducted to maintain cosmic harmony and ensure the pharaoh's divine mandate to rule.

Ancestor worship remained an integral part of religious practice, with the belief that deceased ancestors had the power to intercede on behalf of the living. The construction of elaborate tombs and the practice of mummification were undertaken to preserve the physical body and ensure a successful journey to the afterlife. The concept of an afterlife, characterized by fields of reeds and a blissful existence, began to take shape during the Old Kingdom.

Role of Animism and Ancestor Worship in Early Egyptian Religion

Animism and ancestor worship played crucial roles in the early religious landscape of ancient Egypt. Animism, the belief in the spiritual essence of all things, formed the foundation of their religious worldview. The ancient Egyptians perceived the world as a living entity, filled with a myriad of spirits and deities, each possessing specific powers and attributes. They recognized the presence of these spirits in natural phenomena, animals, plants, and even inanimate objects.

Ancestor worship was deeply intertwined with animism, as the ancient Egyptians believed that their ancestors continued to exist in the spirit realm and could actively influence the lives of their living descendants. Ancestors were revered and considered mediators between the human realm and the divine.

Rituals and offerings were conducted to honor and appease the ancestral spirits, seeking their protection, guidance, and blessings.

The practices of animism and ancestor worship laid the foundation for the complex religious system that would develop and evolve throughout ancient Egyptian history. These early beliefs and practices demonstrated the profound connection between the ancient Egyptians and their environment, emphasizing the interplay between the human, natural, and spiritual realms.

By examining the religious beliefs and practices of the Pre-Dynastic Period, the transition to the Old Kingdom, and the role of animism and ancestor worship, we gain a deeper understanding of the early religious landscape of ancient Egypt. These religious traditions not only influenced subsequent developments in Egyptian religion but also reflect the intimate relationship between humans, the natural world, and the divine.

Evolution of Deities and Cosmic Order

Analysis of the Early Deities and Their Associations with Natural Forces

In the ancient Egyptian religious worldview, deities were intimately connected with natural forces and phenomena. The early deities of ancient Egypt were often personifications of natural elements, embodying the power and essence of various aspects of the physical world. For example, the sky god Horus symbolized the celestial realm and was associated with the sun, while the earth goddess Geb represented the fertile land and agricultural abundance.

These early deities served as intermediaries between humans and the divine realm, bridging the gap between the mortal and the divine. They were believed to exert control over the forces of nature and were invoked to ensure harmony and balance within the cosmos. The ancient Egyptians recognized the interconnectedness of all things and viewed the deities as guardians and controllers of the natural order.

Emergence of a Pantheon of Gods and Their Roles in Maintaining Cosmic Order

Over time, the early deities evolved and became part of a vast pantheon, comprising a multitude of gods and goddesses with distinct roles and attributes. As Egyptian society became more complex during the Old Kingdom, the pantheon expanded to include deities associated with various aspects of human life, such as fertility, craftsmanship, wisdom, and war.

The pantheon also reflected the cosmological beliefs of the ancient Egyptians. They perceived the universe as a delicate balance between order (ma'at) and chaos (isfet). It was believed that the gods played a vital role in maintaining cosmic order by upholding ma'at, the fundamental principle of harmony, justice, and balance. Each deity had a specific function and responsibility within the cosmic hierarchy, and their interactions and cooperation were essential for the smooth functioning of the universe.

For example, the sun god Ra, as the supreme deity, was responsible for ensuring the rising and setting of the sun, which symbolized the cycle of life, death, and rebirth. The goddess Ma'at personified cosmic order and truth, acting as a moral compass and presiding over the judgment of the deceased in the afterlife. Osiris, the god of the underworld, represented resurrection and the eternal cycle of life. These deities, along with numerous others, formed a complex network of relationships and responsibilities within the Egyptian pantheon.

Interactions Between Gods and Humans in Religious Rituals

Ancient Egyptian religious rituals were the means through which humans interacted with the gods and sought their favor, guidance, and protection. These rituals were conducted by priests and priestesses in temples and sanctuaries, where offerings, prayers, hymns, and chants were dedicated to the deities.

The interactions between gods and humans were characterized by reciprocity. Humans believed that by performing the correct rituals and offering the appropriate sacrifices, they could establish a connection with the gods and gain their favor. In return, the gods would bestow blessings, protection, and divine assistance upon the human realm.

Religious rituals also served as a means of maintaining cosmic order and reinforcing the balance between ma'at and isfet. Through their participation in rituals, individuals expressed their commitment to upholding ma'at and contributing to the overall harmony of the universe.

Examples of these rituals include the daily offering ceremonies in temples, where food and drink were presented to the gods, and the festivals held in honor of specific deities, such as the famous Opet Festival dedicated to Amun-Ra. These rituals provided opportunities for communal worship and engagement with the divine, fostering a sense of unity and shared religious identity among the ancient Egyptians.

By analyzing the evolution of deities and their associations with natural forces, the emergence of a pantheon of gods, and the interactions between gods and humans in religious rituals, we can gain a deeper understanding of the religious beliefs and practices during the ancient Egyptian civilization. Such analysis reveals the profound connection between the natural world, the divine realm, and the human experience, highlighting the intricate interplay between cosmic forces and human agency in the religious landscape of ancient Egypt.

Temple Architecture and Function

Overview of Temple Construction during the Old Kingdom

The Old Kingdom period in ancient Egypt (c. 2686 BCE - 2181 BCE) witnessed the development of monumental temple architecture. Temples were constructed as grand structures, reflecting the power and authority of the pharaohs and the importance of religious practices in ancient Egyptian society.

The construction of temples during the Old Kingdom followed a standardized architectural plan, characterized by massive stone walls, imposing pylons (gateways), hypostyle halls with columns, and sanctuaries where the divine statues were housed. The use of durable materials such as limestone and granite ensured the longevity of these structures, many of which have survived to this day.

The temples were typically situated along the banks of the Nile River or in strategic locations within major cities. They were often dedicated to specific deities and served as the focal points of religious activities and worship.

Importance of Temples as Sacred Spaces and Their Role in Religious Practices

Temples held immense religious and cultural significance in ancient Egypt. They were regarded as sacred spaces where the gods resided and interacted with the human realm. The temple complex, with its various chambers, courtyards, and halls, represented the cosmic order and served as a microcosm of the universe.

Temples were considered the dwelling places of the gods, and their construction and maintenance were vital for maintaining cosmic harmony and ensuring the well-being of the kingdom. The pharaohs, as the intermediary between the gods and the people, played a central role in temple rituals and oversaw their construction and functioning.

In addition to their religious functions, temples also served as centers of administration, education, and economic activity. They housed libraries, schools, and workshops, contributing to the cultural and intellectual development of ancient Egyptian society. The temples were responsible for managing vast land holdings, organizing agricultural activities, and overseeing economic transactions.

Examination of Temple Rituals and Ceremonies

Temples were the primary sites for performing religious rituals and ceremonies. These rituals were conducted by the priesthood, a specialized class of individuals responsible for maintaining the sanctity of the temple and carrying out the prescribed rituals.

Temple rituals involved a variety of activities, including purification rites, offerings, processions, and ceremonies dedicated to specific deities. Daily rituals were performed to ensure the well-being of the gods and the kingdom, while major festivals were held annually to commemorate important mythological events or honor specific deities.

Examples of temple rituals include the "Opening of the Mouth" ceremony, which symbolically restored the senses and life force of statues representing the gods, and the "Feeding of the Gods" ritual, where food and drink offerings were presented to nourish and sustain the divine entities.

Temple rituals were accompanied by music, chanting, and dance, creating a multisensory experience and fostering a deep connection between the human participants and the divine realm. The rituals were aimed at maintaining ma'at (cosmic order) and strengthening the bonds between the gods and the Egyptian people.

By exploring temple architecture, understanding the importance of temples as sacred spaces, and examining the rituals and ceremonies conducted within them, we gain valuable insights into the religious practices and cultural significance of temples during the Old Kingdom period in ancient Egypt.

Priesthood and Religious Hierarchy

Role and Significance of Priests and Priestesses in Temple Rituals

Priests and priestesses played a crucial role in the religious practices of ancient Egypt during the Old Kingdom period. They served as intermediaries between the human realm and the divine, facilitating communication and maintaining the connection between the gods and the people.

The primary role of priests and priestesses was to conduct rituals and ceremonies within the temples. They were responsible for performing daily offerings, purification rites, and other sacred rituals aimed at pleasing the gods and maintaining cosmic harmony. Through their actions, priests and priestesses ensured the well-being of the gods, the pharaoh, and the entire kingdom.

Priests and priestesses were considered to possess divine knowledge and were believed to have the ability to communicate directly with the gods. Their presence and involvement in religious rituals were believed to invoke the presence of the gods and facilitate their interaction with the mortal world.

Hierarchical Structure within the Priesthood and Their Duties

The priesthood in ancient Egypt had a hierarchical structure, with different ranks and roles assigned to individuals based on their level of expertise and responsibilities. At the top of the hierarchy was the high priest or high priestess, who oversaw the activities of the temple and held significant authority within the religious institution.

Below the high priest or high priestess, there were several other positions within the priesthood. These included temple priests, temple musicians, temple scribes, and other specialized roles. Each position had specific duties and responsibilities that contributed to the smooth functioning of the temple and the performance of rituals.

Temple priests were responsible for conducting daily rituals, maintaining the temple's cleanliness, and managing the temple's resources and offerings. Temple musicians provided music and chanting during rituals, enhancing the spiritual ambiance of the temple. Temple scribes recorded and preserved important religious texts and administrative records.

Training and Education of Priests and Priestesses

Becoming a priest or priestess in ancient Egypt required extensive training and education. The selection of individuals for the priesthood was often based on family lineage, with children of priests having a higher chance of entering the priesthood.

The training of priests and priestesses included a combination of practical and theoretical instruction. They learned the rituals, prayers, hymns, and chants associated with specific deities and ceremonies. They also studied religious texts and had to memorize and understand the complex rituals and their symbolic meanings.

The education of priests and priestesses also involved learning the hieroglyphic script, as they were responsible for recording and preserving religious texts and administrative records. They received instruction in mathematics, astronomy, and other sciences that were relevant to their roles within the temples.

The training and education of priests and priestesses were overseen by experienced senior priests, who passed down their knowledge and expertise to the younger generations. This ensured the continuity and preservation of religious traditions and practices over time.

By understanding the role and significance of priests and priestesses in temple rituals, the hierarchical structure within the priesthood, and the training and education they underwent, we gain insights into the religious practices and the central role of the priesthood in ancient Egyptian society during the Old Kingdom period.

Festivals and Celebrations

Analysis of Major Festivals and their Religious and Social Significance

Festivals held a prominent place in the religious and social life of ancient Egypt during the Old Kingdom period. These festivals were grand events that brought together the community to celebrate and honor the gods, reinforcing religious beliefs and fostering a sense of collective identity.

Major festivals were often associated with specific deities and commemorated significant events in the mythological narratives or marked important agricultural or celestial occurrences. Some notable festivals included the Festival of Opet, the Festival of Wepet Renpet (New Year), and the Festival of the Valley.

These festivals provided an opportunity for the community to express devotion, gratitude, and reverence to the gods. They were marked by processions, elaborate rituals, and offerings to the deities. The festivities involved music, dancing, feasting, and various forms of entertainment, creating a joyous and vibrant atmosphere.

Socially, festivals served as a means of community bonding and cohesion. They brought people from different regions together, fostering a sense of shared identity and solidarity. Festivals also provided a platform for individuals to interact, exchange goods, and participate in cultural activities, strengthening social ties and fostering a sense of unity.

Examination of Ritual Practices during Festivals and their Connection to Deities

Ritual practices during festivals were central to the religious experience of ancient Egyptians. These practices aimed to establish a connection between the mortal realm and the divine, allowing worshippers to communicate with and honor the gods.

Rituals during festivals involved offerings of food, drink, incense, and other symbolic items to the deities. The priests and priestesses conducted purification rites, performed dances and music, and recited prayers and hymns. These actions were believed to invoke the presence of the gods and facilitate their interaction with the worshippers.

Processions played a significant role during festivals, with statues of the deities being paraded through the streets or carried in sacred boats. The processions allowed the gods to visit various locations and bless the land and its people.

The rituals performed during festivals often mirrored mythological events or symbolized the cyclical patterns of nature, emphasizing the connection between the divine and the natural world. Through participation in these rituals, worshippers sought blessings, protection, and divine favor.

Influence of Festivals on Community Cohesion and Religious Devotion

Festivals had a profound impact on community cohesion and religious devotion in ancient Egypt. These celebrations provided an opportunity for individuals to reaffirm their faith, express gratitude, and seek divine blessings. The shared experience of participating in festivals fostered a sense of communal identity and strengthened religious devotion.

Festivals served as important markers of time, aligning the community's activities with the cosmic cycles and the agricultural calendar. The observance of festivals created a sense of rhythm and order in the lives of individuals, reinforcing the significance of religious beliefs and practices in daily life.

Additionally, festivals allowed individuals to experience a sense of transcendence, connecting with the divine and experiencing a heightened spiritual state. The joyous and celebratory atmosphere of festivals created a sense of awe and reverence, deepening religious sentiments and inspiring devotion.

Festivals also provided opportunities for individuals to seek guidance, healing, and protection from the deities. Worshippers believed that the gods were more accessible during these festive occasions, and they actively engaged in prayers and offerings to seek divine intervention in their lives.

Overall, festivals played a vital role in ancient Egyptian society, not only as religious events but also as social and cultural gatherings that promoted community cohesion, reinforced religious beliefs, and fostered a sense of devotion and gratitude towards the gods.

By exploring the major festivals and their religious and social significance, the ritual practices associated with festivals, and their impact on community cohesion and religious devotion, we gain a comprehensive understanding of the profound role of festivals in the religious and social fabric of ancient Egyptian society during the Old Kingdom period.

Funerary Beliefs and Practices

Exploration of Funerary Rituals and the Belief in an Afterlife

Funerary beliefs and practices held significant importance in ancient Egyptian society during the Old Kingdom period. Egyptians believed in an afterlife where the soul, or ka, continued to exist and required the body and material offerings for sustenance.

Funerary rituals were performed to ensure a smooth transition to the afterlife and provide the deceased with everything they needed for their eternal journey. These rituals included purification rites, mummification, and the deposition of grave goods and offerings in the tomb.

The rituals aimed to preserve the body through mummification, allowing the ka to recognize and reunite with its physical form. Priests and embalmers meticulously treated the body with natron, removed internal organs, and wrapped it in linen bandages, all in accordance with complex religious rituals and beliefs.

The belief in an afterlife was deeply rooted in the concept of maat, the cosmic balance and order. Egyptians believed that by living a virtuous life and upholding maat, individuals would be rewarded in the afterlife, enjoying an existence similar to their earthly life but free from suffering and hardships.

Importance of Burial Practices and Tomb Construction

Burial practices in ancient Egypt were elaborate and meticulously planned. The construction of tombs played a crucial role in ensuring the preservation of the body and providing a safe and eternal resting place for the deceased.

Tombs varied in size and complexity, depending on the social status and wealth of the individual. The most iconic tombs of the Old Kingdom were the pyramids, constructed as monumental structures to house the bodies of pharaohs and facilitate their journey to the afterlife.

The design and construction of pyramids involved precise measurements and engineering techniques, reflecting the immense resources and organizational skills of the ancient Egyptians. These pyramids served as the final resting places of pharaohs and symbolized their divine status and eternal kingship.

For the elite and commoners, mastabas (rectangular flat-roofed structures) served as tombs. Mastabas were built with mud bricks and consisted of a burial chamber, offering chapels, and storage rooms for funerary goods.

The careful construction of tombs was accompanied by intricate decorative elements, such as reliefs and inscriptions depicting religious scenes, spells, and prayers. These decorations were believed to provide guidance and protection to the deceased in the afterlife.

Significance of the Pyramid Texts and Coffin Texts

The Pyramid Texts and Coffin Texts are important funerary texts that were inscribed on the walls of pyramids and coffins, respectively. These texts provided guidance, spells, and rituals necessary for the deceased's journey to the afterlife.

The Pyramid Texts, dating back to the Old Kingdom, were reserved for the pharaohs and contained sacred spells and rituals to aid the divine ascension of the king's soul. They contained prayers for the pharaoh's transformation into a divine being and his union with the gods.

As the Old Kingdom progressed, the Pyramid Texts were adapted and expanded into the Coffin Texts, available to a broader range of individuals. These texts provided guidance and protection for the deceased and included spells to navigate the challenges of the afterlife, protect the body, and ensure the well-being of the ka.

The inclusion of these texts in tombs highlighted the belief in the power of words and the importance of preserving religious knowledge for the deceased's journey to the afterlife.

By examining the funerary rituals, beliefs in an afterlife, the significance of burial practices, tomb construction, and the presence of funerary texts, we gain valuable insights into the religious worldview of the ancient Egyptians during the Old Kingdom period.

Religious Change and Innovation

Examination of Religious Reforms and Cultic Changes during the Old Kingdom

The Old Kingdom period witnessed several religious reforms and cultic changes that had a profound impact on Egyptian religious practices. These reforms were often driven by the pharaohs or influential individuals seeking to reshape religious beliefs and rituals.

One notable religious reform during the Old Kingdom was the shift in focus from local cults to a centralized worship of the sun god Ra. This change elevated Ra to a prominent position within the pantheon and led to the development of solar theology. The pharaohs themselves, as embodiments of the sun god, played a crucial role in these reforms, presenting themselves as divine intermediaries.

Additionally, changes in the cultic practices of certain deities were observed. For instance, the worship of Osiris, the god of the afterlife and resurrection, gained popularity during this period. Osiris became closely associated with the concept of judgment and eternal life, reflecting the evolving religious beliefs surrounding death and the afterlife.

Influence of Royal Patronage on Religious Practices

The pharaohs of the Old Kingdom wielded significant influence over religious practices through their patronage and support. They played a vital role in promoting specific cults, establishing temples, and endowing religious institutions with vast resources.

The construction of temples and their associated rituals served as powerful symbols of royal authority and devotion to the gods. Pharaohs were not only seen as political leaders but also as the primary religious figures who facilitated the communication between the divine realm and human society.

The royal patronage of specific cults and deities helped shape the religious landscape of the Old Kingdom, influencing the prominence of certain gods and the popularity of their cults. Pharaohs were keen on associating themselves with powerful deities, further enhancing their divine status and legitimizing their rule.

Role of Individual Pharaohs in Shaping Religious Developments

Individual pharaohs had a significant impact on religious developments during the Old Kingdom. Their reigns often marked distinct shifts in religious beliefs, practices, and iconography.

For example, Pharaoh Djoser, during the Third Dynasty, commissioned the construction of the Step Pyramid at Saqqara, which not only served as his burial monument but also represented a significant architectural innovation. This pyramid complex introduced new religious rituals and practices associated with the king's divine nature and the afterlife.

Pharaoh Khufu, known for building the Great Pyramid of Giza, contributed to the religious landscape by reinforcing the association of the pharaoh with the sun god Ra. The alignment of the pyramid's passages with specific celestial bodies, such as the North Star, showcased the pharaoh's connection to the divine realm and the cosmos.

Each pharaoh had the opportunity to shape religious developments through their architectural endeavors, patronage of specific cults, and the promotion of new religious concepts. Their choices and actions left a lasting impact on the religious practices and beliefs of their time.

By exploring religious reforms, royal patronage, and the role of individual pharaohs, we can gain a deeper understanding of the dynamic nature of religion during the Old Kingdom and its connection to political and social spheres.

Conclusion

Recapitulation of Key Findings and Insights

Throughout this chapter, we have delved into the religious developments and changes that took place during the Old Kingdom period in ancient Egypt. We examined the religious reforms and cultic shifts, the influence of royal patronage, and the role of individual pharaohs in shaping religious practices. We explored the centralization of worship around deities like Ra and the growing prominence of Osiris in funerary beliefs. We also discussed the impact of temple architecture, festivals, and the priesthood on religious practices. These findings shed light on the multifaceted nature of ancient Egyptian religion during the Old Kingdom.

Significance of Religious Developments during the Old Kingdom

The religious developments during the Old Kingdom period were of great significance in shaping ancient Egyptian society and culture. Religion played a central role in the lives of the people, providing a framework for understanding the cosmos, establishing social order, and addressing fundamental questions of life, death, and the afterlife. The centralization of religious practices around the worship of certain deities, the construction of temples as sacred spaces, and the promotion of specific cults helped solidify the pharaoh's divine authority and reinforce the social hierarchy.

The religious reforms and innovations that emerged during the Old Kingdom marked a turning point in Egyptian religious thought and practice. The emphasis on solar theology, the rise of Osiris as a key figure in funerary beliefs, and the establishment of rituals and festivals aimed at connecting humans with the divine realm were all significant developments that shaped the religious landscape for centuries to come.

Implications for Understanding Ancient Egyptian Society and Culture

The study of religious developments during the Old Kingdom provides valuable insights into ancient Egyptian society and culture. It reveals the interconnectedness of religion, politics, and social structures, highlighting the central role of the pharaohs as religious and political leaders. The construction of monumental temples, the organization of festivals and rituals, and the training of priests and priestesses all point to the sophisticated nature of ancient Egyptian religious practices.

Additionally, understanding the religious beliefs and practices of the Old Kingdom period helps us grasp the worldview of the ancient Egyptians, their cosmology, and their understanding of the afterlife. It allows us to explore their concepts of divinity, the relationships between gods and humans, and the rituals and ceremonies that permeated their daily lives.

By examining the religious developments of the Old Kingdom, we gain a deeper appreciation for the complexity and richness of ancient Egyptian culture and its enduring influence on subsequent periods of Egyptian history.

In conclusion, the religious developments and changes during the Old Kingdom period were significant in shaping ancient Egyptian society and culture. The centralization of worship, the influence of royal patronage, and the role of individual pharaohs all contributed to the dynamic nature of religion during this era. Understanding these developments provides valuable insights into the worldview, social structures, and religious practices of ancient Egyptians, enriching our understanding of this fascinating civilization.

Chapter 8: Temples, Festivals, and Tools used c. 2686 BCE - 2181 BCE

The Old Kingdom period of ancient Egypt, spanning from approximately 2686 BCE to 2181 BCE, was characterized by significant developments in religion, culture, and political organization. It is often referred to as the "Age of the Pyramids" due to the construction of impressive royal tombs, such as the iconic Great Pyramids of Giza. The Old Kingdom was a time of centralization and consolidation of power, with a strong focus on the divine authority of the pharaohs.

Religion played a crucial role in ancient Egyptian society, and it was deeply intertwined with all aspects of life. The beliefs and practices of the Old Kingdom period laid the foundation for the religious traditions that would endure throughout the subsequent periods of ancient Egyptian history. The gods and goddesses worshipped during this time formed the core of the Egyptian pantheon, and their cults were centered around the temples, which served as vital religious and cultural institutions.

Importance of temples, festivals, and tools in ancient Egyptian religious practices

Temples as Sacred Spaces:

Temples held a central place in ancient Egyptian religious life. They were regarded as the dwelling places of the gods and served as the primary locations for religious rituals and ceremonies. Temples were grand architectural structures that reflected the wealth, power, and devotion of the pharaohs and the elite. These monumental edifices were constructed with precision and adorned with intricate carvings and murals that depicted religious scenes and mythical narratives. Temples were not merely places of worship but also acted as administrative centers and economic hubs.

Festivals and their Religious Significance:

Festivals played a crucial role in ancient Egyptian religious calendars and were celebrated throughout the year. These religious events were marked by processions, offerings, music, dance, and other forms of ritual activities. Festivals were held in honor of specific deities, such as the Opet Festival dedicated to Amun, or to commemorate important mythological events, such as the Heb-Sed

Festival, which celebrated the rejuvenation and continued reign of the pharaoh. These festive occasions provided an opportunity for the community to come together, express their devotion, and reaffirm their religious and social identities.

Tools and Implements in Ritual Practices:

Various tools and implements were employed in ancient Egyptian religious rituals. These included offerings such as food, drink, and incense, as well as purification instruments, ritual vessels, and ceremonial objects. Each tool had its specific purpose and symbolism within the religious context. For example, the ankh symbolized life and was often held by deities and pharaohs as a sign of their divine authority. Ritual implements were carefully crafted and meticulously used to maintain the cosmic order and establish a connection between the human and divine realms.

Purpose of the chapter and key research questions

The purpose of this chapter is to explore the significance of temples, festivals, and tools in ancient Egyptian religious practices during the Old Kingdom period. By examining these aspects, we can gain insight into the religious beliefs, cultural expressions, and social dynamics of this pivotal era in ancient Egyptian history.

Key Research Questions:

How did temples function as religious, cultural, and political institutions during the Old Kingdom?

What were the major festivals celebrated during this period, and what was their religious and social significance?

What were the tools and implements used in ancient Egyptian religious rituals, and what roles did they play?

How did temples, festivals, and tools contribute to the religious and cultural landscape of ancient Egypt, and what can they tell us about the society and beliefs of the time?

By addressing these research questions, we aim to deepen our understanding of the religious practices and beliefs of the ancient Egyptians, shedding light on their worldview, concepts of divinity, and the role of religion in their lives. Through the exploration of temples, festivals, and tools, we can gain valuable insights into the rich tapestry of ancient Egyptian religious traditions during the Old Kingdom period.

Temples of the Old Kingdom

The Old Kingdom period witnessed the construction of magnificent temples that served as focal points for religious worship and cultural activities. Temple architecture during this time followed a distinct style characterized by grandeur, precision, and symbolic significance. Temples were designed to reflect the divine authority of the pharaoh and to provide a physical connection between the mortal realm and the divine realm.

The architectural style of Old Kingdom temples can be identified by several key features. These include colossal entrance pylons, large open courtyards, hypostyle halls with rows of columns, sanctuary chambers, and obelisks. The use of massive stone blocks, such as limestone and granite, in temple construction showcased the technological prowess and wealth of the ruling elite. The temples were adorned with intricate carvings, hieroglyphic inscriptions, and colorful reliefs depicting religious scenes, pharaonic rituals, and mythological narratives.

Function and layout of temples as sacred spaces

Temples were considered sacred spaces and were dedicated to specific deities. They served as the dwelling places of the gods and as sites for various religious rituals, including offerings, prayers, and processions. The layout of temples was designed to facilitate the ritual activities performed by priests and worshippers.

The entrance pylons marked the transition from the mundane world to the sacred realm. Beyond the entrance, the temple complex typically consisted of open courtyards surrounded by colonnades. These courtyards were spaces where the community gathered for festivals, processions, and other communal activities. The hypostyle hall, with its rows of columns, served as a transition zone between the outer courtyards and the innermost sanctuary. The sanctuary chamber, located at the rear of the temple, housed the cult statue of the deity to whom the temple was dedicated.

The temple layout and architectural elements were imbued with symbolic significance. For example, the axial alignment of the temple, from the entrance through the hypostyle hall to the sanctuary, represented the journey from the earthly realm to the divine presence. The columns in the hypostyle hall represented the papyrus and lotus plants, symbolizing the marshes from which creation emerged. The temple layout and design were carefully planned to create a harmonious and awe-inspiring environment conducive to religious rituals and the worship of the gods.

Examples of prominent temples from the period

The Great Temple of Amun at Karnak:

The temple complex of Karnak, located in modern-day Luxor, was one of the largest and most significant religious sites of ancient Egypt. The complex was dedicated to the god Amun-Ra and expanded over many centuries. The main features of the temple included the colossal entry pylons, the vast hypostyle hall with its forest of columns, and the sanctuary dedicated to the cult of Amun. The Karnak Temple complex exemplifies the grandeur and architectural sophistication of Old Kingdom temple construction.

The Pyramid Temples:

The pyramid complexes, built as tombs for the pharaohs, also featured temples within their precincts. These temples, known as pyramid temples, were dedicated to the pharaoh and served as sites for funerary rituals and the veneration of the deceased king. The temple of the Pyramid of Djoser at Saqqara is one of the earliest examples and showcases the evolution of temple architecture during the Old Kingdom period.

The Temple of Hathor at Dendera:

The Temple of Hathor at Dendera, located in Upper Egypt, is another notable example of an Old Kingdom temple. Dedicated to the goddess Hathor, the temple features intricate reliefs and carvings depicting religious scenes and celestial symbolism. The temple's layout includes a large hypostyle hall, sanctuaries, and a sacred lake, emphasizing the multifaceted religious significance of the site.

Rituals and Ceremonies

Religious rituals were at the heart of ancient Egyptian temple practices during the Old Kingdom period. These rituals served as a means of communication between humans and the gods, reinforcing cosmic order and maintaining the divine balance. Understanding the key rituals provides valuable insight into the beliefs, values, and social dynamics of the ancient Egyptian society.

Daily Temple Rituals: Temples conducted daily rituals to honor the gods and maintain their favor. These rituals included offerings of food, beverages, and incense, as well as prayers and hymns recited by the priests. The purpose of these rituals was to sustain the divine presence within the temple and ensure the well-being and prosperity of the community.

Festival Processions: Festivals played a crucial role in religious life, bringing the community together to celebrate and honor specific gods or goddesses. Festivals often involved grand processions where the cult statues of deities were carried in sacred barques (boats) and paraded through the temple and its surroundings. These processions allowed the public to participate in the presence of the gods and seek their blessings.

Offering Rituals: Offerings were a central component of temple rituals, serving as a means of sustenance for the gods and a way for humans to demonstrate their devotion. Offerings consisted of various food items, beverages, flowers, and incense. These offerings were carefully selected and presented with reverence to the gods, symbolizing the reciprocal relationship between humans and the divine.

Significance of ritual objects and tools used in religious ceremonies

Ritual objects and tools played a vital role in facilitating and enhancing the religious ceremonies conducted within the temples. These objects were imbued with symbolic meaning and were believed to possess inherent power and divine connection.

Ritual Statues: Cult statues, representing the gods, were central to temple rituals. These statues were believed to house the divine essence of the deities they represented. During rituals, the statues were ritually awakened, purified, and dressed in fine garments, allowing the gods to manifest themselves and receive the offerings and adoration of the worshippers.

Anointing and Purification Tools: Priests used various tools for anointing and purifying the cult statues, temple spaces, and participants in the rituals. These tools included ritual oils, water vessels, and incense burners. Anointing the statues and participants symbolized purification and preparation for communion with the divine.

Ritual Utensils: Temples employed a range of utensils for the preparation and presentation of offerings. These included bowls, libation vessels, offering tables, and incense burners. The careful selection and use of these utensils were believed to ensure the proper execution of rituals and the acceptance of offerings by the gods.

Role of priests and priestesses in conducting rituals

Priests and priestesses held essential roles in conducting rituals and ensuring the proper execution of religious ceremonies within the temples. They acted as intermediaries between the human and divine realms, performing specific duties and responsibilities.

Ritual Specialists: Priests and priestesses were trained in the complex rituals and protocols associated with temple practices. They possessed extensive knowledge of religious texts, chants, and hymns, and had a deep understanding of the symbolic significance of the rituals. They were responsible for leading and performing the rituals with precision and devotion.

Offerings and Adoration: Priests and priestesses were responsible for presenting offerings, reciting prayers, and performing hymns in honor of the gods. They acted as the voice of the community, expressing their gratitude, seeking divine blessings, and maintaining the cosmic order through ritual actions.

Sacred Guardianship: Priests and priestesses were entrusted with the care and maintenance of the temple complex and its sacred objects. They ensured the purity and sanctity of the temple spaces, performed regular rituals to awaken and enliven the cult statues, and safeguarded the sacred knowledge and rituals passed down through generations.

Understanding the role of priests and priestesses provides valuable insights into the organization of religious practices, the power dynamics within the temple, and the significant influence of religious specialists on the religious experiences of ancient Egyptians during the Old Kingdom period.

Festivals and Celebrations

Festivals held great importance in ancient Egyptian religious life during the Old Kingdom period. They were marked by elaborate ceremonies, processions, and performances that brought together the community in celebration and reverence for the gods. The analysis of major festivals provides valuable insights into the religious beliefs, cultural practices, and societal dynamics of the time.

Festival of Opet: The Festival of Opet was one of the most significant festivals in ancient Egypt, celebrated annually in Thebes (modern-day Luxor). It involved the procession of the cult statues of Amun, Mut, and Khonsu from the temple of Karnak to the temple of Luxor. This festival symbolized the renewal of the kingship, the rejuvenation of the gods, and the reaffirmation of cosmic order.

Heb-Sed Festival: The Heb-Sed Festival was a jubilee celebration held to commemorate the pharaoh's thirty-year reign, symbolizing his rejuvenation and renewal of power. The festival involved ritual activities and performances, such as the pharaoh running a symbolic race and participating in ceremonial dances. The Heb-Sed festival reinforced the pharaoh's authority and demonstrated the continuity of kingship.

Festival of the Beautiful Feast of the Valley: This festival was dedicated to the god Amun-Ra and was celebrated annually in Thebes. It involved a grand procession of the cult statues of various deities from their respective temples to the mortuary temple of the pharaoh, where rituals and offerings were performed to honor the deceased kings and seek their divine blessings.

Religious and social significance of festivals

Festivals held both religious and social significance in ancient Egyptian society during the Old Kingdom. They served as crucial events for the community to express their religious devotion, reinforce social cohesion, and engage in communal activities.

Religious Significance: Festivals were regarded as sacred occasions for the gods and provided a platform for direct interaction between the human and divine realms. Through rituals, offerings, and performances, worshippers sought the blessings, protection, and favor of the gods, reinforcing their spiritual connection and ensuring the continuity of cosmic order.

Social Significance: Festivals brought the community together, transcending social hierarchies and creating a sense of unity and shared identity. They provided an opportunity for individuals to participate in collective rituals, witness the grand processions of cult statues, and engage in festivities, dances, and music. Festivals played a crucial role in reinforcing social bonds, promoting cultural values, and fostering a sense of belonging among the ancient Egyptians.

Ritual practices and performances associated with festivals

Festivals were characterized by a wide array of ritual practices and performances that added to their vibrancy and significance. These practices were carefully choreographed and performed by priests, priestesses, and other participants, creating a spectacle of devotion and celebration.

Processions: Festivals often featured grand processions of the cult statues of the gods, carried in sacred barques or on portable shrines. These processions traversed specific routes, allowing the gods to visit different temples and areas, thereby blessing and purifying the land.

Offerings and Sacrifices: Festivals involved the presentation of elaborate offerings and sacrifices to the gods. These offerings included food, beverages, flowers, and incense, symbolizing nourishment, fertility, and abundance. Sacrificial rituals were performed to demonstrate devotion and establish a reciprocal relationship with the gods.

Ritual Performances: Festivals showcased various ritual performances, including sacred dances, music, and dramatic enactments. These performances were intended to entertain the gods and the community, evoking religious symbolism and creating a heightened spiritual atmosphere.

By analyzing the major festivals, their religious and social significance, and the rituals and performances associated with them, we gain a deeper understanding of the religious beliefs, cultural practices, and social dynamics of ancient Egyptian society during the Old Kingdom period.

Tools and Implements

Religious practices in ancient Egypt during the Old Kingdom period involved the use of various tools and implements that played essential roles in rituals, ceremonies, and daily worship. These tools served both practical and symbolic purposes, enabling priests, priestesses, and worshippers to engage in religious activities and establish a connection with the divine realm.

Examination of their symbolic and practical significance

Symbolic Significance: Many of the tools and implements used in religious practices held symbolic meanings related to the ancient Egyptian worldview, cosmology, and religious beliefs. These objects were believed to embody divine power and were used as conduits for communication with the gods. They represented concepts such as fertility, regeneration, protection, and divine authority.

Practical Significance: Apart from their symbolic value, these tools also served practical purposes in the performance of religious rituals. They aided in the preparation of offerings, purification ceremonies, and the execution of precise ritual gestures. These practical functions facilitated the smooth conduct of religious practices and ensured the effectiveness of the rituals.

Examples of specific tools and their functions

Offering Trays: Offering trays, usually made of metal or stone, were used to present offerings of food, beverages, and other items to the gods. These trays held symbolic significance as they represented the provision of sustenance to the deities and served as a means of communication and nourishment between humans and gods.

Ankh: The ankh, a symbol resembling a looped cross, held deep religious significance in ancient Egyptian culture. It represented the concept of life and was often carried by deities and pharaohs in depictions. The ankh symbolized the eternal life granted by the gods and was used in rituals to bless and protect worshippers.

Sistrum: The sistrum was a musical instrument associated with the worship of the goddess Hathor. It consisted of a metal frame with metal rods or wires passing through it. The sistrum was shaken or rattled during rituals and ceremonies, producing a distinctive sound believed to ward off evil spirits and promote the goddess's presence and blessings.

Censer: A censer, typically made of bronze or clay, was used to burn incense during religious ceremonies. The smoke of the incense was believed to purify the sacred space, create a pleasing fragrance for the gods, and facilitate communication with the divine.

Ritual Knives: Ritual knives, known as "pesesh-kef," were ceremonial blades used in the slaughtering of animals during sacrificial rituals. These knives were specifically designed with curved blades and symbolic handles, representing the divine authority of the priests and the act of offering the animal's life to the gods.

Ostraca and Papyri: Ostraca, pottery shards or pieces of limestone, and papyri, scrolls made from the papyrus plant, were used to inscribe religious texts, spells, prayers, and hymns. These written materials played a crucial role in preserving religious knowledge and were utilized in rituals and magical practices.

Temples as Centers of Power and Influence

Temples in ancient Egypt held significant influence over society and politics during the Old Kingdom period. They served as centers of power, acting as intermediaries between the divine and the human realms. The temple priesthood, led by high-ranking priests and priestesses, played a crucial role in religious affairs and held considerable sway over the population.

Political Influence: Temples often enjoyed close ties with the ruling pharaohs and the royal court. The pharaoh, as the divine intermediary, maintained a strong connection with the temples and relied on their support to reinforce his legitimacy and authority. Temples had political influence and could exert their power in matters such as land ownership, taxation, and administration.

Social Influence: Temples served as social institutions that provided various services to the community. They acted as centers for social gatherings, festivals, and religious education. Temple complexes were gathering places where people from different social strata could come together, reinforcing social cohesion and a sense of belonging.

Economic aspects of temple administration and management

Wealth and Resources: Temples controlled vast amounts of land and resources, including agricultural estates, livestock, and workshops. They received donations from the pharaoh, nobility, and the general population in the form of agricultural produce, precious goods, and currency. These resources allowed temples to amass considerable wealth and become economic powerhouses.

Economic Management: Temple administrations had sophisticated systems in place to manage their economic assets. They employed administrators, scribes, and accountants who oversaw agricultural production, trade, and distribution of resources. Temples engaged in commercial activities, such as owning ships for trade expeditions and operating craft workshops.

Redistribution and Charity: Temples also played a role in redistributing wealth and resources to the wider community. They distributed food, provided medical care, and offered economic support to the less fortunate. This aspect of temple administration aimed to alleviate social inequalities and demonstrate the benevolence of the gods.

Temples as educational and cultural centers

Education and Training: Temples served as centers of learning, where aspiring priests and priestesses received education and training in religious rituals, hieroglyphic writing, mathematics, and astronomy. Temples housed libraries and archives that preserved ancient texts and knowledge, ensuring the continuity of religious and cultural traditions.

Cultural Preservation: Temples played a vital role in preserving and promoting the arts, literature, and music. They commissioned and maintained artistic works, such as temple reliefs, statues, and murals, which conveyed religious narratives and celebrated the achievements of the gods and pharaohs. Temples also sponsored performances of music, dance, and drama as part of religious festivals.

Cultural Exchange: Temples acted as cultural hubs, attracting visitors from different regions and facilitating cultural exchange. Pilgrims, traders, and foreign envoys visited temples, bringing with them their own customs, beliefs, and knowledge. This interaction enriched the cultural landscape of Egypt, fostering a diverse and cosmopolitan society.

Challenges and Preservation of Temples

Temple construction and maintenance in ancient Egypt were not without challenges. Building monumental temple complexes required significant resources, manpower, and engineering expertise. Several challenges arose during the construction phase:

Engineering Challenges: Constructing massive stone structures, such as temple walls, columns, and obelisks, posed engineering challenges due to the weight and size of the stones. Skilled artisans and architects had to devise innovative methods to transport and position these large blocks with precision.

Resource Management: Acquiring the necessary building materials, such as limestone and granite, involved quarrying, transportation, and logistics. Temples often relied on nearby quarries, and the extraction and transportation of these materials required careful planning and coordination.

Labor Force: The construction of temples necessitated a large and organized labor force. The recruitment and mobilization of workers, including artisans, craftsmen, and laborers, were crucial for the successful completion of temple projects. Temples often employed local villagers, who contributed their skills and labor.

Funding: Financing temple construction required substantial resources. Pharaohs, nobles, and wealthy individuals provided funding through donations, grants of land, and offerings. Managing these financial resources and ensuring their efficient allocation were essential for the smooth progress of temple construction projects.

Efforts made to preserve and restore temples in modern times

In modern times, there have been extensive efforts to preserve and restore ancient Egyptian temples. These endeavors aim to safeguard the architectural, artistic, and historical significance of these sacred structures:

Documentation and Research: Archaeologists and Egyptologists conduct detailed documentation and research on temple sites. They employ various techniques, such as photogrammetry, laser scanning, and 3D modeling, to create accurate digital representations of the temples. This documentation serves as a valuable resource for future preservation and restoration work.

Conservation and Stabilization: Conservation experts employ scientific methods to stabilize and preserve temple structures. They use materials and techniques that are compatible with the original construction materials, ensuring the long-term stability of the temples. This includes measures such as stabilizing foundations, consolidating fragile elements, and protecting against environmental factors.

Site Management and Visitor Education: Effective site management is crucial for the preservation of temples. Conservation organizations and government bodies establish regulations and guidelines for visitor access, limiting potential damage. Visitor education programs raise awareness about the importance of conservation, promoting responsible behavior among tourists and ensuring the sustainable preservation of temple sites.

Case studies of well-preserved temples from the Old Kingdom

The Great Sphinx and the Temple of the Sphinx: Located at the Giza Plateau, the Great Sphinx and its associated temple provide insights into temple construction during the Old Kingdom. The Sphinx itself, carved from a single limestone outcrop, showcases the skill and artistry of ancient Egyptian craftsmen. The temple, with its elaborate architectural features and engravings, offers valuable information about religious rituals and beliefs during the Old Kingdom.

The Mortuary Temple of Djoser (Step Pyramid Complex): Constructed during the Third Dynasty by the architect Imhotep, the Step Pyramid Complex in Saqqara stands as a remarkable example of Old Kingdom temple architecture. The complex includes the Step Pyramid, various courtyards, temples, and ceremonial structures. The meticulous preservation and restoration efforts have allowed visitors to experience the grandeur and religious significance of this unique temple complex.

The Temple of Horus at Edfu: Dedicated to the falcon-headed god Horus, the Temple of Edfu is an exceptionally well-preserved temple from the Ptolemaic period, but it draws on the architectural traditions of the Old Kingdom. The temple's walls are adorned with intricate reliefs that depict religious scenes and rituals. The preservation of this temple offers valuable insights into the religious practices and beliefs that continued from the Old Kingdom into later periods.

Conclusion

In this chapter, we explored the temples, festivals, and tools used during the Old Kingdom period of ancient Egypt (c. 2686 BCE - 2181 BCE). We examined the architecture of temples and their layout as sacred spaces, the rituals and ceremonies performed within them, and the tools and implements utilized in religious practices. Through our analysis, several key findings and insights emerged:

Temples played a central role in ancient Egyptian religious life, serving as places of worship, cultural hubs, and centers of political and economic power.

Exploring the Rituals, Beliefs, and Syncretism of Ancient Egyptian Religion

The grandeur and symbolism of temple architecture reflected the religious beliefs and cosmology of the Old Kingdom society.

Festivals held significant religious and social significance. They provided opportunities for the community to come together, celebrate, and honor the gods. Ritual practices during festivals were a means of connecting with the divine and reinforcing communal bonds.

The tools and implements used in religious ceremonies held both practical and symbolic significance. They facilitated specific rituals and acted as conduits between the human and divine realms. The craftsmanship and materials used in these tools reflected the skill and artistry of ancient Egyptian artisans.

Significance of temples, festivals, and tools in understanding the religious and cultural landscape of the Old Kingdom

The study of temples, festivals, and tools used during the Old Kingdom offers valuable insights into the religious and cultural landscape of this period. These aspects provide a window into the beliefs, practices, and social dynamics of ancient Egyptian society. They reveal the centrality of religion in the lives of individuals and the organization of the community.

Temple architecture, with its grandeur and symbolism, reflects the ancient Egyptians' worldview and their understanding of the divine and cosmic order. Festivals, with their elaborate rituals and performances, demonstrate the multifaceted role of religion in connecting individuals with the gods and fostering social cohesion. The tools and implements used in religious practices exemplify the material culture of the time and offer glimpses into the craftsmanship and technological advancements of the Old Kingdom.

Studying these aspects deepens our understanding of ancient Egyptian religion, culture, and society. It sheds light on the role of religion in shaping individual and communal identities, the dynamics of power and authority, and the interconnectedness of various aspects of ancient Egyptian life.

Implications for further research and study

The exploration of temples, festivals, and tools during the Old Kingdom raises several avenues for further research and study. Some potential areas of inquiry include:

Comparative analysis: Comparative studies with other periods in ancient Egyptian history can provide insights into the evolution and continuity of religious practices and beliefs. Exploring the similarities and differences in temples, festivals, and tools across different time periods can reveal patterns of change and continuity.

Interdisciplinary approaches: Collaborations between archaeologists, Egyptologists, anthropologists, and other scholars can enrich our understanding of temples, festivals, and tools. Interdisciplinary approaches can incorporate diverse perspectives and methodologies, enabling a more comprehensive analysis of these religious practices.

Regional variations: Investigating regional variations in temple architecture, festival traditions, and tools can illuminate the diversity and localized expressions of ancient Egyptian religion. Examining sites beyond the major centers of power can provide a more nuanced understanding of religious practices across different regions of the Old Kingdom.

Socio-political contexts: Exploring the socio-political contexts in which temples, festivals, and tools were developed and utilized can offer insights into the power dynamics, religious authority, and ideological frameworks of the Old Kingdom society. Investigating the relationships between temples, pharaohs, and the priesthood can deepen our understanding of the intricate interplay between religion and politics.

In conclusion, the study of temples, festivals, and tools used during the Old Kingdom period offers valuable insights into the religious and cultural landscape of ancient Egypt. These aspects reveal the centrality of religion in ancient Egyptian society, providing a deeper understanding of their beliefs, rituals, and social dynamics. Further research and study in these areas can contribute to a more comprehensive understanding of the Old Kingdom period and its enduring legacy in Egyptian history and culture.

Chapter 9: Prayers, Hymns, Chants, and Spells Associated with Key Deities Worshipped during this Period (e.g., Ra, Osiris, Isis)

In the ancient Egyptian civilization, religious rituals and practices played a central role in the daily lives of the people. Prayers, hymns, chants, and spells were essential components of their religious devotion and formed a crucial connection between the mortal and divine realms. These sacred utterances and invocations were believed to have the power to communicate with the gods, seek their favor, express gratitude, and ensure divine protection.

The use of prayers allowed individuals to establish a direct line of communication with the deities, expressing their desires, seeking guidance, and asking for blessings. Hymns were sung or recited as poetic compositions praising and glorifying the gods, expressing their divine attributes and accomplishments. Chants, often repetitive in nature, served as rhythmic invocations that invoked the presence of the deities and set a ceremonial atmosphere. Spells, on the other hand, were specific formulaic incantations intended to invoke magical powers, protect against malevolent forces, or bring about desired outcomes.

These religious utterances were not merely empty words but were believed to possess inherent power and efficacy. They were considered as vehicles to access the divine realms, establish a relationship with the gods, and seek their intervention in various aspects of life, including health, fertility, protection, and prosperity.

Significance of key deities during the Old Kingdom period (c. 2686 BCE - 2181 BCE)

During the Old Kingdom period, several deities held significant importance in the religious beliefs and practices of ancient Egyptians. Ra, the sun god, was revered as the creator and sustainer of the world, embodying the cosmic force of light and warmth. Osiris, the god of the afterlife, played a central role in the belief in resurrection and the journey of the soul beyond death. Isis, the goddess of magic and fertility, was revered as a divine mother and protector, associated with healing, fertility, and magical knowledge.

These deities, along with others worshipped during the Old Kingdom, held sway over different aspects of human existence and were believed to possess divine attributes and powers. They formed a complex pantheon that reflected the diverse concerns and aspirations of the ancient Egyptians, encompassing the domains of cosmic order, life, death, magic, and the natural world.

Purpose of the chapter and key research questions

The purpose of this chapter is to explore the prayers, hymns, chants, and spells associated with key deities worshipped during the Old Kingdom period. Through an in-depth analysis of these religious texts and rituals, we seek to unravel the beliefs, practices, and cultural significance surrounding these deities and their worship.

Key research questions to be addressed in this chapter include:

What were the main functions and purposes of prayers, hymns, chants, and spells in ancient Egyptian religious practices?

How did the ancient Egyptians perceive and relate to the deities worshipped during the Old Kingdom?

What were the specific characteristics and attributes associated with deities such as Ra, Osiris, and Isis, and how were they expressed in prayers, hymns, chants, and spells?

What insights can be gained from the analysis of these religious texts regarding the cosmology, rituals, and beliefs of the Old Kingdom period?

How did the use of prayers, hymns, chants, and spells contribute to the cultural and social cohesion of ancient Egyptian society?

By exploring these questions and delving into the rich corpus of religious texts and practices, we aim to gain a deeper understanding of the role and significance of prayers, hymns, chants, and spells in the ancient Egyptian religious landscape during the Old Kingdom period. Through this exploration, we can shed light on the complex interplay between mortals and deities, the religious worldview of the ancient Egyptians, and the enduring legacy of their religious traditions.

Ra, the Sun God

Ra, the Sun God, held a paramount position in the ancient Egyptian pantheon during the Old Kingdom period. As the embodiment of the sun, Ra was not only the physical source of light and warmth but also represented the creative and life-giving power that sustained the entire cosmos. Ra was regarded as the supreme deity, the creator of the world and all living beings. His name itself means "the creative power" or "the one who illuminates."

The ancient Egyptians believed that Ra traveled across the sky during the day, bringing light and life to the world. He was associated with the concept of Ma'at, the cosmic order that governed the universe. Ra's daily journey represented the cyclical nature of life, death, and rebirth. In the evening, he descended into the Duat, the realm of the underworld, and emerged again at dawn, symbolizing resurrection and the promise of new beginnings.

Examination of prayers and hymns dedicated to Ra

Prayers and hymns dedicated to Ra were essential in expressing reverence, seeking his blessings, and acknowledging his divine attributes. These religious texts reflected the ancient Egyptians' understanding of Ra's role as the creator and sustainer of life. They praised his power, wisdom, and benevolence while seeking his protection and guidance.

One example of a hymn dedicated to Ra is the "Hymn to the Sun," found in the Amarna period texts. This hymn highlights Ra's role as the divine source of life, illuminating the world with his rays and providing nourishment to all living creatures. It expresses awe and gratitude for Ra's presence and acknowledges his role in maintaining cosmic order and harmony.

Prayers addressed to Ra often emphasized the personal relationship between the individual and the deity. They sought Ra's favor in various aspects of life, such as health, prosperity, and protection against malevolent forces. These prayers were considered a means of establishing a direct connection with Ra, invoking his attention, and seeking his intervention.

Analysis of the solar cosmology and symbolism associated with Ra

Ra's association with the sun and its daily journey across the sky held profound cosmological and symbolic significance in ancient Egyptian religious beliefs. The solar cycle was seen as a reflection of the larger cosmic order and the cyclical patterns of creation, death, and rebirth. Ra's daily renewal represented the eternal nature of the divine and the promise of regeneration.

Symbolically, Ra was often depicted with a solar disk on his head, encircled by a serpent representing the continuity of time. The solar disk itself symbolized Ra's divine power and radiance. The sun's light was believed to dispel darkness, ignorance, and evil, symbolizing the triumph of enlightenment and truth over chaos and disorder.

Ra's association with the sun also extended to the concept of kingship. The pharaohs, as earthly representatives of Ra, were believed to inherit the divine authority and were considered the "sons of Ra." The sun's journey across the sky mirrored the pharaoh's role in upholding cosmic order and ensuring the prosperity and well-being of the kingdom.

In conclusion, Ra, the Sun God, held a central role in ancient Egyptian religious beliefs during the Old Kingdom period. His association with the sun represented the creative and life-giving force that sustained the universe. Prayers and hymns dedicated to Ra expressed reverence, sought his blessings, and acknowledged his role as the supreme deity. The solar cosmology and symbolism associated with Ra reflected the ancient Egyptians' understanding of cosmic order, the cyclical nature of life, and the profound significance of light, enlightenment, and renewal.

Hymn to Ra

Hail to you, Ra, the glorious Sun,
Whose radiant light shines upon all creation.
You are the creator of the world, the giver of life,
Whose golden rays illuminate the heavens and the earth.

O Ra, mighty and majestic, we sing your praises,
For you bring warmth and sustenance to all living beings.
Your light touches the land, awakening its dormant seeds,
Bringing forth abundance and fertility in every field.

You rise in the eastern sky, dispelling the darkness of night,
And as you journey across the celestial expanse,
You illuminate the path of the righteous and guide their way.
Your light reveals the hidden mysteries of the world.

O Ra, your power is unmatched, your wisdom divine,

You are the source of all creation, the eternal and ever-renewing.
We honor you with offerings and hymns of adoration,
For you are the supreme ruler, the master of all destinies.

Grant us your blessings, O Ra, and protect us from harm,
Shower us with your divine grace and illuminate our path.
May your radiance fill our hearts with joy and inspiration,
And may we walk in harmony with your cosmic order.

Hail to you, Ra, the Sun God, the bringer of light and life,
We bow before your greatness and offer our eternal devotion.
May your name be forever praised and your glory celebrated,
O Ra, the eternal and benevolent ruler of the heavens.

Note: This hymn is a poetic representation and does not reflect an actual hymn from the Old Kingdom period. It is written in the style of ancient Egyptian religious poetry to capture the essence of devotion and reverence to Ra.

Chants associated with Ra, the Sun God, were an integral part of ancient Egyptian religious practices. These chants were used to invoke Ra's presence, express devotion, and seek his blessings. While specific chants from the Old Kingdom period are not preserved, we can imagine the rhythmic and melodic nature of these chants based on our understanding of ancient Egyptian musical traditions. Here is an example of a chant that could be associated with Ra:

Chant to Ra

Ra, Ra, bringer of light,
With your rays, dispel the night.
From eastern horizon, you emerge,
Glorious Sun, let your power surge.

Ra, Ra, with golden glow,
Across the sky, your chariot goes.
Guiding the world with your divine flame,
We chant your name, to honor your name.

Ra, Ra, your light we embrace,
In your radiance, we find solace.
May your blessings on us descend,
As we chant, our voices blend.

Ra, Ra, supreme and sublime,
In your presence, we transcend time.
Grant us strength and wisdom true,
As we chant, our devotion to you.

Note: This chant is a creative representation based on the imagery and symbolism associated with Ra. It aims to capture the essence of devotion and the rhythmic nature of ancient Egyptian chants. While the specific chants from the Old Kingdom period may have varied, they would have shared a similar purpose of invoking Ra's presence and expressing reverence.

Spells related to Ra, the Sun God, were an important aspect of ancient Egyptian magical practices. These spells were believed to harness the power of Ra and were used for various purposes, including protection, healing, and invoking divine blessings. While specific spells from the Old Kingdom period are not readily available, we can draw upon the broader corpus of Egyptian magical texts to provide an example of a spell that could be associated with Ra:

Spell for Solar Protection

I invoke the mighty Ra, the Sun's divine light,
With your power, protect me day and night.
As you traverse the sky in radiant glory,
Shield me from all harm, I implore thee.

With your fiery rays, create a barrier strong,
Repelling evil and ensuring I belong,
Under your watchful gaze, no danger may tread,
By your protection, I am safely led.

By the strength of your celestial flame,
May my enemies be consumed in shame,
With your benevolence, grant me health and grace,
And banish all darkness from my sacred space.

O Ra, source of life and eternal light,
I call upon you with all my might,
Empower this spell, let it come to be,
In your name, I trust, so mote it be.

Note: This spell is a creative representation based on the general themes and intentions associated with spells related to Ra. It seeks protection and divine assistance through the invocation of Ra's power. The specific spells used during the Old Kingdom period may have varied in their wording and structure, but they would have shared the common goal of invoking Ra's blessings and harnessing his power for the desired outcome.

Exploring the Rituals, Beliefs, and Syncretism of Ancient Egyptian Religion

Prayer to Ra, the Sun God

O Ra, mighty and radiant,
The source of life, the divine illuminator,
I offer my heartfelt praise and reverence to thee.

You, whose golden rays embrace the world,
Bringing warmth and light to all living beings,
I bow before your majestic presence.

As you ascend the heavens each day,
Guiding the sun boat with unwavering strength,
I beseech you, O Ra, to shine your blessings upon me.

Grant me the wisdom to navigate life's path,
Illumine my mind with your divine knowledge,
And fill my heart with your boundless love.

O Ra, you who bring forth each new day,
I seek your guidance and protection,
That I may walk in the light of truth and righteousness.

In your radiance, I find solace and inspiration,
For you are the giver of life and the bringer of joy.
May your divine energy flow through me always.

I offer my gratitude for the blessings you bestow,
And I pray for your continued presence and favor.
O Ra, hear my prayer and accept my humble devotion.

In your eternal glory, I place my trust,
For you are the sun that never sets,
And your divine light shines upon us all.

Praise be to Ra, the great and powerful,
Forever may your brilliance illuminate the world.

Note: This prayer is a creative representation inspired by the general themes and sentiments associated with prayers to Ra. Ancient Egyptian prayers to Ra would have varied in their wording and structure, but they would have expressed devotion, gratitude, and sought the blessings and guidance of the Sun God.

Osiris, the God of the Afterlife

In ancient Egyptian mythology, Osiris held a central role as the god of the afterlife, symbolizing resurrection, renewal, and the eternal cycle of life. He was revered as the ruler of the underworld, where the souls of the deceased embarked on their journey towards the Field of Reeds, a paradise-like realm of bliss and abundance. Osiris was also the divine judge who weighed the hearts of the deceased against the feather of Ma'at, determining their fate in the afterlife.

B. Exploration of prayers, hymns, and rituals associated with Osiris

Prayers and hymns dedicated to Osiris were an essential part of ancient Egyptian religious practices, serving as a means of invoking his blessings, seeking his intercession, and expressing devotion to the god of the afterlife. These sacred texts were recited during ceremonies and rituals performed in temples and funerary settings.

One notable example is the "Hymn to Osiris," an ancient text found in funerary contexts, which praises Osiris for his role as the benevolent ruler of the deceased. It extols his power to grant eternal life, restore vitality, and provide solace to the souls of the departed.

Rituals associated with Osiris included the "Opening of the Mouth" ceremony, which aimed to restore the deceased's senses and enable them to partake in the offerings and rituals in the afterlife. This ritual was performed using specific tools and implements, such as the "adze" and the "ulaeus," symbolizing the power of rebirth and regeneration.

C. Examination of the belief in the afterlife and the role of Osiris in the journey of the soul

The ancient Egyptians held a deep belief in the afterlife, considering it a continuation of earthly existence rather than a final end. They believed that Osiris played a pivotal role in guiding the deceased through the perilous journey of the afterlife, ensuring their rebirth and eternal happiness.

The myth of Osiris' death and resurrection served as a powerful metaphor for the cyclical nature of life, death, and rebirth. Through his own tragic story, Osiris represented the triumph of order over chaos, life over death, and the promise of transformation and renewal.

Devotees of Osiris would often seek his protection and intercession, offering prayers and performing rituals to ensure a favorable judgment in the afterlife. They believed that by aligning themselves with Osiris' values of righteousness, harmony, and moral conduct, they would secure a blessed existence in the realm of the dead.

In conclusion, Osiris, as the god of the afterlife, held immense significance in ancient Egyptian religious beliefs and practices. Prayers, hymns, and rituals dedicated to Osiris reflected the deep yearning for eternal life and the desire to be united with the god in the realm of the deceased. The belief in Osiris' power to judge and grant salvation in the afterlife shaped the religious landscape of ancient Egypt, providing solace and hope for individuals facing the inevitability of death.

Hymn to Osiris

O Osiris, mighty ruler of the afterlife,
We sing your praises and beseech your divine presence.
You, who are the great judge of souls,
We humbly offer our prayers and hymns to you.

Osiris, beloved of the gods,
Your wisdom and compassion know no bounds.
In the Field of Reeds, your dominion,
You welcome the righteous and grant them eternal life.

Your power stretches across the realms,
From the depths of the Duat to the heights of the heavens.
Your name resounds through the sacred halls,
And your light guides the souls in their journey.

Oh, Osiris, we seek your mercy and protection,
As we navigate the trials of life and the mysteries of death.
Grant us passage to the blessed realm,
Where joy and abundance are everlasting.

In your divine presence, we find solace,
Knowing that you watch over us with care.
Your benevolent rule brings comfort to the departed,
And your righteous judgment ensures their eternal peace.

O Osiris, majestic and revered,
We offer our hymns and prayers to honor you.

May your name be spoken with reverence,
And your eternal legacy endure throughout the ages.

Hail Osiris, ruler of the afterlife,
May your blessings be upon us now and forevermore.

Chant to Osiris

(Chant rhythmically, with a sense of reverence and devotion)

Oh Osiris, Lord of the eternal night,
Guide us through the realms of shadow and light.
With wisdom and grace, you rule the land,
A beacon of hope, a helping hand.

Osiris, Osiris, we call your name,
Grant us strength and protection, free from shame.
In your embrace, we find solace and peace,
May your divine presence never cease.

Oh Osiris, judge of the deceased,
In your divine justice, all souls find release.
You weigh the hearts, you balance the scales,
Grant us passage through the sacred veils.

Osiris, Osiris, hear our plea,
Lead us to the realm where souls are free.
Guide us on our journey, through life and beyond,
With your blessings, our spirits respond.

Oh Osiris, Lord of the afterlife,
We offer our reverence, devoid of strife.
In your divine presence, we find our way,
Bless us, Osiris, each and every day.

(Continue chanting, allowing the words to resonate and evoke a sense of
connection with Osiris)

Spell for Protection and Guidance from Osiris

(Recite the spell with focused intention and sincerity)

Oh Osiris, mighty ruler of the realm of the dead,
I call upon your divine presence, I bow my head.
Grant me your protection, O benevolent guide,
Keep me safe on my journey, with you by my side.

From the trials and tribulations that life may bring,
I seek your guidance, O Osiris, great king.
Shield me from harm, both seen and unseen,
Wrap me in your loving embrace, like a protective screen.

By the power of your sacred name and divine light,
I invoke your blessings, O Osiris, day and night.
Banish all darkness, bring forth the divine,
In your presence, O Osiris, I eternally align.

Grant me strength and courage in times of despair,
Lead me through the challenges, with your loving care.
As I traverse the paths of life's winding maze,
May your wisdom and guidance illuminate my ways.

Oh Osiris, ruler of the eternal afterlife,
I place my trust in you, amidst joy or strife.
With gratitude and reverence, I honor your name,
Bless me, O Osiris, and protect me from all shame.

(Continue to meditate on the spell and visualize Osiris' protective presence surrounding you)

Prayer to Osiris

Oh Osiris, majestic lord of the underworld,
I come before you with reverence and honor.
You, who preside over the realm of the dead,
And guide the souls on their eternal tread.

Osiris, compassionate judge and ruler,
You weigh the hearts with justice and valor.
Grant me your wisdom and divine insight,

As I navigate life's challenges day and night.

In your embrace, I find solace and peace,
Knowing that in death, all struggles cease.
Guide me through the darkness, O Osiris,
Lead me to the path of eternal bliss.

Oh Osiris, protector of the departed souls,
I seek your guidance to fulfill my life's goals.
Grant me the strength to overcome all strife,
And bring harmony and balance to my life.

As I walk this earthly plane, I humbly pray,
That you watch over me each and every day.
Guide me on the righteous path, O Osiris,
And grant me eternal blessings and bliss.

Oh Osiris, hear my prayer, pure and sincere,
Accept my devotion and dispel all fear.
In your divine presence, I find solace and grace,
Embracing your love, I find my rightful place.

Thank you, Osiris, for your eternal light,
Guiding me through both day and night.
Forever I honor you, O god of the afterlife,
In you, Osiris, I find eternal life.

Isis, the Goddess of Magic and Fertility

Isis, the revered goddess of ancient Egypt, holds a significant place in the pantheon as a divine mother and protector. She is revered for her role as a nurturing and compassionate deity, associated with magic, fertility, and the protection of the living and the deceased. The cult of Isis gained prominence during the Old Kingdom period and continued to thrive throughout Egyptian history.

Analysis of Prayers, Chants, and Spells Dedicated to Isis

Prayers dedicated to Isis were an integral part of ancient Egyptian religious practices. They were often recited by devotees seeking her guidance, protection, and blessings. These prayers expressed deep reverence for Isis and invoked her power and presence in various aspects of life. Devotees called upon Isis for assistance in matters of health, fertility, love, and protection.

Chants dedicated to Isis were rhythmic and melodic expressions of devotion, often accompanied by music and dance. These chants aimed to create a sacred atmosphere and establish a spiritual connection with the goddess. Through rhythmic repetition and melodic patterns, devotees sought to channel the divine energy of Isis and invite her benevolence into their lives.

Spells associated with Isis were intricately woven with magical rituals and incantations. These spells invoked Isis' supernatural powers to bring about desired outcomes, such as healing, protection, or success. Ancient Egyptian magicians and healers would utilize specific spells and invocations attributed to Isis to harness her divine energy and work miracles.

Prayer to Isis for Fertility and Blessings:

"Mighty Isis, Goddess of magic and fertility,
I come before you with reverence and devotion.
You who hold the power to bring forth life,
I seek your blessings for fertility and abundance.

Glorious Isis, hear my plea and grant me your favor,
Bless me with the gift of fertility and the miracle of conception.
May your divine touch bring forth new life and joy,
As I embark on the sacred journey of motherhood.

Goddess of magic and fertility, I invoke your name,
Wrap me in your loving embrace and bestow your blessings upon me.
Guide me with your wisdom and protect me in this journey,
May your divine presence bring forth the miracle I seek.

Isis, compassionate goddess, hear my prayers,
With love and gratitude, I offer my devotion to you.
Grant me the strength and resilience to nurture life,
And let your divine essence flow through me.

As I honor you, great Isis, goddess of magic and fertility,
I trust in your power and guidance in this sacred endeavor.
May my heart be filled with gratitude and joy,
As I embrace the gift of life you bestow upon me.

Hail Isis, goddess of magic and fertility,
May your blessings shower upon me and those I hold dear.
In your divine presence, I find solace and hope,
As I walk this path of creation and fulfillment.

Amen."

This prayer to Isis captures the essence of seeking her blessings for fertility and abundance. It acknowledges her as the powerful goddess of magic and fertility, and expresses reverence and devotion towards her. The prayer seeks her intervention and guidance in the journey of conception and motherhood, and invokes her divine presence to bring forth the miracle of new life. It emphasizes the trust and gratitude placed in Isis as the compassionate goddess who can provide strength, protection, and joy in the pursuit of fertility and the nurturing of life.

Chant to Invoke the Power of Isis:

(Chant rhythmically, with a steady beat or as desired)

Isis, mighty and wise,
Goddess of magic that never dies.
Fertility flows from your sacred touch,
As I chant your name, I feel so much.

Isis, hear my call,
With your power, I stand tall.
Goddess of magic, hear my plea,
Bestow your blessings upon me.

Isis, goddess of the moon and sky,
In your presence, I feel so high.
Your magic flows through my veins,
As I chant your name, the power remains.

Isis, mother of all,
In your embrace, I stand tall.
Fertility and abundance I seek,
With your guidance, my desires I speak.

Isis, with love and grace,

Bless my life, my sacred space.
Magical goddess, hear my voice,
In your power, I rejoice.

As you chant this invocation to Isis, focus on her qualities as the goddess of magic and fertility. Allow the rhythm of the chant to create a meditative and trance-like state, connecting you with the energy of Isis. Feel her presence and imagine her divine power flowing through you. Let the chant be a vehicle to invoke her blessings and amplify your intentions related to magic and fertility.

Spell for Fertility and Abundance:

(Perform this spell during a waxing or full moon)

You will need:

A small bowl of water
Three white candles
Jasmine or rose incense
A small piece of paper
A green pen or marker
Begin by cleansing your space with the incense, allowing the fragrant smoke to purify the area and create a sacred atmosphere.

Light the three white candles, representing purity, fertility, and abundance, and place them in a triangle formation on your altar or sacred space.

Take the small bowl of water and hold it in your hands. Close your eyes and visualize the energy of Isis, the goddess of magic and fertility, surrounding you.

Take the green pen or marker and write your desired outcome on the small piece of paper. It could be a specific intention for fertility, abundance, or both. Be clear and concise in your wording.

Place the paper in the bowl of water, allowing it to soak for a few moments. As you do this, recite the following spell:

"Isis, goddess of magic and fertility,
I call upon your divine energy.
Bless me with fertility and abundance,
May your magic fill my life and enhance.
With the power of the moon and sky,

Grant my desires, as I comply."

Leave the paper in the water for a few more minutes, visualizing the energy of Isis infusing the water with her blessings.

Remove the paper from the water and place it in a safe space where it can dry. As it dries, imagine your intentions being sealed and manifesting in your life.

Extinguish the candles and thank Isis for her presence and assistance.

Keep the dried paper in a special place, such as a sacred box or altar, as a reminder of your spell and a symbol of your connection to Isis. You can also carry it with you in a charm bag or pouch.

Remember that spellwork should always be done with positive intentions and respect for the energies involved. Be patient and open to receiving the blessings of fertility and abundance from the goddess Isis.

Hymn to Isis

O Isis, mighty goddess of magic and fertility,
Radiant as the sun, shining with divinity.
You are the bringer of life and the nourisher of all,
With your wings spread wide, we heed your call.

Goddess of the fertile earth and bountiful harvest,
Your touch brings abundance, never to be surpassed.
In your hands, the power of creation is held,
As the mysteries of life are revealed.

Isis, mother and protector, compassionate and kind,
Your love and wisdom embrace all humankind.
In times of sorrow and despair, we seek your solace,
For in your presence, all worries find release.

Oh, great Isis, lady of the sacred Nile,
Your magic flows through us, mile after mile.
Through your enchantments, we find our way,
Guided by your light, through night and day.

Goddess of the moon, goddess of the stars,
You guide us with your celestial chariots afar.

In your presence, we find peace and serenity,
As we connect with the cosmic tapestry.

Isis, your name echoes through the sands of time,
A beacon of hope, eternally sublime.
We offer our praise and gratitude to thee,
For your blessings, abundant and free.

Hail, Isis, goddess of magic and fertility,
In your embrace, we find divine serendipity.
With love and reverence, we honor your name,
May your blessings forever remain.

Note: This hymn is a poetic expression of devotion to the goddess Isis. It seeks to capture the essence of her attributes as the goddess of magic and fertility.

Examination of Isis' Role in Fertility Rituals and Magical Practices

Isis played a central role in fertility rituals and magical practices of ancient Egypt. As the goddess of fertility, she was invoked to bless and ensure the fertility of the land, animals, and human beings. Fertility rites dedicated to Isis were performed to invoke her power and to seek her assistance in matters of conception, childbirth, and the nurturing of children.

In magical practices, Isis was revered as a skilled magician and protector against evil forces. Her magical abilities were often invoked to ward off illness, protect against malevolent spirits, and bring about positive changes in one's life. Ancient Egyptians believed that Isis possessed immense knowledge of magical arts and could manipulate natural forces to bring about desired outcomes.

The reverence for Isis and her role in fertility rituals and magical practices extended beyond the Old Kingdom period. Her cult continued to flourish throughout Egyptian history, and her influence can be seen in various aspects of ancient Egyptian religion and society.

As we delve deeper into the prayers, chants, spells, and rituals associated with Isis, we gain a profound understanding of her significance as a divine mother, protector, and magician in the religious and cultural landscape of ancient Egypt. By studying the expressions of devotion and the use of magic in relation to Isis, we gain insights into the complex beliefs, practices, and aspirations of the ancient Egyptians.

Other Key Deities of the Old Kingdom

In addition to Ra, Osiris, and Isis, the Old Kingdom period (c. 2686 BCE - 2181 BCE) saw the worship of several other key deities in ancient Egypt. These deities played significant roles in the religious beliefs and practices of the time. Among them are Ptah, Hathor, and Horus.

Ptah, the creator god and patron of craftsmen, was revered for his role in the creation of the world and the arts. Hathor, the goddess of love, beauty, and music, was celebrated for her nurturing and protective qualities. Horus, the falcon-headed god associated with kingship and divine protection, held a prominent position as the son of Isis and Osiris.

Prayers, Hymns, Chants, and Spells Associated with Additional Deities

The ancient Egyptians expressed their devotion and sought the blessings of these deities through various forms of religious expression, including prayers, hymns, chants, and spells. These texts served as a means of communication and interaction with the divine, allowing individuals to establish a connection with the gods and seek their guidance, protection, and favor.

For Ptah, prayers and hymns praised his creative power and sought his assistance in the pursuit of artistic endeavors. Chants dedicated to Hathor expressed adoration for her beauty and invoked her blessings for matters of the heart and fertility. Spells associated with Horus aimed to invoke his protective powers and align oneself with his divine authority.

Prayer to Ptah:

O Ptah, the Great Craftsman, the Master of Creation,
I come before you with reverence and awe.
You who shaped the world with your divine hands,
Crafting the heavens, the earth, and all that dwell within.

Ptah, I seek your guidance and inspiration,
As I embark on my own creative endeavors.
Bless my hands with skill and dexterity,
That I may bring forth beauty and harmony in my work.

Ptah, you who hold the secrets of creation,
Grant me the wisdom to understand the mysteries of life.

Guide me in my pursuit of knowledge and understanding,
That I may unravel the hidden truths of the universe.

Great Ptah, protector of craftsmen and builders,
Watch over me and my endeavors with your benevolent eye.
Guide my hands, my mind, and my heart,
That I may create with purpose and bring forth greatness.

I offer my devotion and gratitude to you, Ptah,
For your divine presence and eternal influence.
May your blessings flow upon me, now and forever,
As I honor and seek to emulate your creative power.

Hymn to Ptah:

O Ptah, the Master Craftsman, the Lord of Divine Design,
We sing your praises, for you are the foundation of all creation.
From the depths of Nun, you brought forth the primeval mound,
Shaping the world with your skilled hands.

Ptah, the Mighty One, the Creator of all things,
We marvel at your power and wisdom.
Your divine essence flows through every corner of the universe,
And your presence brings order and balance to all.

In your sacred city of Memphis, your temple stands tall,
A testament to your glory and the craftsmanship of your followers.
The artisans and builders pay homage to you,
For you are their inspiration and their guiding light.

Ptah, the Divine Architect, the Weaver of Dreams,
You shape the destinies of gods and mortals alike.
Your creative force flows through every artist, every poet,
For you are the source of their inspiration and their muse.

O Ptah, we offer our devotion and praise,
For you are the embodiment of perfection and beauty.
May your light shine upon us, guiding us in our creative endeavors,
And may we forever honor and cherish your divine presence.

Hail Ptah, the Supreme Craftsman, the Source of All Creation!
We sing your hymns and celebrate your eternal glory.

Chant to Ptah:

(Participants repeat each line after the leader)

Leader: Ptah, the Divine Creator, we call upon your name,
All: Ptah, the Divine Creator, we call upon your name.

Leader: With skilled hands and creative might,
All: With skilled hands and creative might.

Leader: You shape the world, bringing order and light,
All: You shape the world, bringing order and light.

Leader: Ptah, the Master Craftsman, we honor your divine design,
All: Ptah, the Master Craftsman, we honor your divine design.

Leader: Your temple in Memphis stands tall,
All: Your temple in Memphis stands tall.

Leader: We gather here to praise and enthrall,
All: We gather here to praise and enthrall.

Leader: Ptah, guide our hands in all we create,
All: Ptah, guide our hands in all we create.

Leader: May your blessings flow, may they resonate,
All: May your blessings flow, may they resonate.

Leader: Ptah, the Weaver of Dreams, we chant your name,
All: Ptah, the Weaver of Dreams, we chant your name.

Leader: Inspire our hearts, let our creativity flame,
All: Inspire our hearts, let our creativity flame.

Leader: Hail Ptah, the Supreme Craftsman, the Source of All,
All: Hail Ptah, the Supreme Craftsman, the Source of All.

Leader: In your presence, we stand tall,
All: In your presence, we stand tall.

Leader: Ptah, we praise you, now and forevermore,
All: Ptah, we praise you, now and forevermore.

Leader: Ptah, Ptah, Ptah!
All: Ptah, Ptah, Ptah!

Spell for Creative Inspiration:

Oh Ptah, the Master Craftsman,
Grant me your creative touch.
Infuse my mind with inspiration,
Ignite the flame of innovation.

By the power of your divine hand,
Let my thoughts flow like a river,
Guiding me to new realms of creation,
Unleashing the depths of my imagination.

With every stroke and every word,
May I bring forth beauty and harmony.
As you shape the world with your skill,
May I too leave my mark, fulfilling my will.

Ptah, the Weaver of Dreams,
Bless me with artistic vision,
Grant me the ability to manifest my dreams,
And let my creations be a testament of your wisdom.

By the might of Ptah, the Divine Creator,
I harness the power of creative energy.
Through your grace, I am an instrument,
Creating wonders, both seen and unseen.

So mote it be.

Note: This spell is intended to invoke Ptah's energy and seek creative inspiration. It is important to personalize and adapt it according to your specific needs and beliefs.

Prayer to Hathor for Love and Joy:

Oh Hathor, Lady of Love and Joy,
Radiant goddess of the golden sun,
I come before you with an open heart,

Seeking your blessings from above.

Hathor, gracious and tender-hearted,
Fill my life with love's sweet embrace.
Guide me to find love that is pure and true,
A love that brings joy to my soul.

In your divine presence, I find solace,
A sanctuary of love and harmony.
May your gentle touch heal any wounds,
And bring peace to troubled hearts.

Hathor, enchantress of beauty and grace,
Shower me with your abundant blessings.
Fill my days with laughter and delight,
And let joy be my constant companion.

As I walk this earthly path,
May I embody your love and joy.
Let my actions be guided by kindness,
And may my heart overflow with gratitude.

Oh Hathor, goddess of love and joy,
Accept my humble prayer and plea.
Wrap me in your loving embrace,
And let your blessings shine upon me.

Hail Hathor, goddess of eternal love and joy!

Note: This prayer is intended to express devotion and seek the blessings of
Hathor in matters of love and joy. It can be customized and personalized
according to your own intentions and needs.

Hymn to Hathor, Lady of the Stars:

Hail Hathor, celestial beauty,
Mistress of the cosmic dance.
Your radiance illuminates the heavens,
As you grace us with your divine presence.

Oh Hathor, beloved of the gods,
Your beauty rivals the brightest star.

With each step, you bring joy and mirth,
Filling our hearts with love and delight.

Goddess of music, hear our hymn,
As we raise our voices in praise of thee.
Your melodic laughter echoes through the ages,
Enchanting all who hear its sweet melody.

Hathor, mother of the sun and moon,
You hold the mysteries of the cosmic spheres.
Your gentle touch brings healing and solace,
As your love flows through all existence.

In your sacred temple, we find sanctuary,
A haven of peace and divine grace.
We offer our devotion and gratitude,
For the blessings you bestow upon our lives.

Oh Hathor, goddess of fertility and joy,
May your abundant blessings fill our days.
Guide us on the path of love and abundance,
And let your light guide us through life's maze.

Hail Hathor, radiant and wise,
Goddess of the stars that dot the skies.
We honor you with hymns and praise,
Forever grateful for your celestial grace.

Note: This hymn is an expression of reverence and admiration for Hathor, highlighting her role as a celestial deity associated with joy, beauty, and fertility. Feel free to adapt and personalize it to reflect your own connection and relationship with Hathor.

Chant to Hathor, Lady of the Stars:

(Chant)
Hathor, Lady of the Stars, we call your name,
Your radiance shines bright, a celestial flame.
With each step, you bring joy and delight,
Guide us on the path, with your cosmic light.

(Chant)
Hathor, Mother of the Sun and Moon,

Your love and blessings, like a sweet-scented bloom.
In your presence, we find peace and grace,
Let your cosmic energy fill this sacred space.

(Chant)
Hathor, Goddess of music and dance,
Your melodies enchant, a divine trance.
With rhythmic beats, we honor your name,
In harmony, we unite, in your eternal flame.

(Chant)
Hathor, Lady of fertility and love,
Bless us with abundance, below and above.
In your embrace, we find strength and healing,
In your wisdom, we find divine revealing.

(Chant)
Hathor, Lady of the stars that gleam,
In our hearts, you reign supreme.
We chant your name, with reverence and praise,
Hathor, guide us through life's cosmic maze.

Note: This chant is meant to be repetitive and rhythmic, creating a meditative and focused state of mind. Feel free to adapt and modify the chant according to your own spiritual practice and connection with Hathor.

Spell to Invoke the Blessings of Hathor, Lady of the Stars:

By the power of Hathor, Lady of the Stars,
I call upon your divine presence from afar.
Grant me your grace and blessings this hour,
In your radiance, I find strength and power.

With every breath, I open my heart wide,
To receive your love and blessings, divine.
Guide me through life's celestial dance,
Illuminate my path with your cosmic glance.

Hathor, Lady of the Stars, hear my plea,
Bring forth abundance and joy to me.
In your embrace, I find peace and bliss,
Grant me your favor with a loving kiss.

I invoke your name, Hathor, in sacred space,
May your blessings shower upon this place.
As I speak these words, so shall it be,
By the divine authority of Hathor, so mote it be.

Note: This spell is a sample invocation to Hathor, and it is important to adapt it to your own personal beliefs and practices. Ensure that you perform spells and invocations with respect and reverence, and always align them with your intentions for the highest good.

Prayer to Horus, the Falcon-Headed God:

Mighty Horus, Falcon-Headed God of Kingship,
I come before you with reverence and devotion.
You who soar the skies, protector of the land,
I seek your guidance and blessings in my hand.

Horus, son of Osiris and Isis divine,
You uphold justice and maintain cosmic order.
With your piercing eyes and wings widespread,
You bring protection and strength wherever you tread.

Grant me the courage to face life's challenges,
Like the mighty falcon, swift and resilient.
Guide my path with your divine wisdom and grace,
And let your watchful eye shield me from any trace.

Horus, I seek your divine intervention,
In matters of the heart and soul's ascension.
Bring forth your blessings, o noble deity,
And guard me with your unwavering loyalty.

May your wings of protection encircle me,
As I navigate life's journey, wild and free.
Horus, I offer my prayers with utmost respect,
In your name, I find solace and intellect.

Horus, Falcon-Headed God, I honor you,
And in your presence, I find strength anew.
Accept my prayers, as I humbly implore,
May your blessings be with me forevermore.

Note: This prayer serves as a sample invocation to Horus, and it can be customized and adapted to suit your personal beliefs and intentions. It is important to approach prayers with sincerity and reverence, connecting with the essence of the deity in a meaningful way.

Hymn to Horus, the Falcon-Headed God:

Horus, mighty Horus, with falcon wings spread wide,
Protector of the land, the king by your side.
You soar through the heavens, a beacon of light,
Guiding us with your wisdom, shining so bright.

O Horus, son of Isis and Osiris divine,
You bring balance and justice, your power does shine.
In your eyes, the sun and the moon do reside,
A symbol of power, in you we confide.

Horus, the avenger, the valiant and strong,
Defender of Egypt, against all that is wrong.
With your divine falcon eyes, piercing and keen,
You see through deceit, keeping justice serene.

Horus, the conqueror, the victor of wars,
Leading us to triumph, healing our scars.
Your strength is unmatched, your courage renowned,
In your name, victories and honor abound.

Horus, the healer, the compassionate and kind,
You bring comfort and solace, to body and mind.
Your touch brings renewal, your blessings bestowed,
With your divine presence, our spirits are glowed.

Horus, we sing your praises, our voices raised high,
In reverence we gather, under your watchful sky.
May your blessings continue, forever to pour,
Horus, Falcon-Headed God, forever we adore.

Note: This hymn is a poetic expression of devotion to Horus and can be modified or expanded upon to suit personal preferences and beliefs. It is important to approach hymns with reverence and sincerity, offering praise and adoration to the deity being honored.

Chant to Horus, the Falcon-Headed God:

Horus, Horus, mighty and bold,
With wings of falcon, your stories unfold.
Protector of kings, guardian of the land,
By your strength, we take our stand.

Horus, Horus, with piercing eyes,
Seeing all truth, no deception can disguise.
In your name, we find clarity and sight,
Guiding us through darkness, shining with light.

Horus, Horus, bringer of peace,
Your presence brings solace, all troubles cease.
With your wings of protection, we feel secure,
In your embrace, our fears are no more.

Horus, Horus, ruler of the sky,
In your name, we soar high, oh so high.
Grant us strength, courage, and grace,
As we journey through life's endless race.

Horus, Horus, hear our plea,
Guide us on our path, set our spirits free.
With your divine power, we are blessed,
In your name, we find eternal rest.

Note: Chants are repetitive and rhythmic in nature, often used in ritualistic or meditative practices. This chant to Horus can be recited or sung in a steady rhythm, allowing the words to flow and resonate with the energy of the deity. The chant can be repeated multiple times to create a focused and reverential atmosphere.

Spell to Invoke the Protection of Horus:

Horus, mighty falcon of the sky,
I call upon your strength, so high.
Wrap me in your wings of protection,
Shield me from harm, in every direction.

With eyes keen and senses acute,
Horus, I seek your absolute.
Grant me courage and unwavering might,
To face any challenge, day or night.

As you soar through heavens above,
Bring to me your divine love.
Banish evil and ward off all foes,
In your name, I find repose.

Horus, with your sacred eye,
Watch over me as days go by.
Guide my steps, keep me on track,
With your divine power, nothing I lack.

By the authority vested in your name,
I invoke your presence, without shame.
Protect me, Horus, throughout my days,
In your divine embrace, my spirit stays.

Note: Spells are incantations or invocations used to harness the power of a deity or supernatural force for a specific purpose. This spell to Horus is intended to invoke his protection and ask for his guidance and strength. It can be spoken aloud or written down and performed with focus and intent. It is important to approach spellwork with respect and sincerity, understanding the symbolic and spiritual nature of the ritual.

Roles and Characteristics of Additional Deities

Each of these deities held specific roles and characteristics within ancient Egyptian religious beliefs. Ptah, as the creator god, was associated with craftsmanship and the manifestation of divine order in the world. Hathor, often depicted as a cow or a woman with cow horns, represented femininity, beauty, love, and joy. Horus, the falcon-headed god, symbolized kingship, protection, and the divine right to rule.

Ptah's association with creation and craftsmanship made him a patron of artisans and builders. Hathor's nurturing qualities made her a protector of women, children, and the family unit. Horus, as the son of Isis and Osiris, was seen as a guardian and avenger, ensuring the order and stability of the cosmos.

By exploring the prayers, hymns, chants, and spells associated with these deities, we gain insight into the ancient Egyptians' reverence for their diverse pantheon and their desire to establish a connection with these powerful beings. These texts not only reflect the religious beliefs of the Old Kingdom period but also provide a window into the complexities of ancient Egyptian society and the ways in which they sought divine assistance and guidance in their daily lives.

Analysis of Ritual Performance

Examination of the performative aspects of prayers, hymns, chants, and spells:

In ancient Egyptian religious practices, prayers, hymns, chants, and spells were not merely recited or spoken, but were often performed with great emphasis on the ritualistic and performative aspects. These sacred utterances were believed to have a profound effect on the spiritual realm and were therefore treated with reverence and care.

Prayers, as expressions of communication with the divine, were typically performed in a solemn and respectful manner. They often included specific gestures, such as raising the hands or kneeling, to demonstrate humility and devotion. The tone and intonation of the prayers were carefully modulated to convey sincerity and reverence. The content of the prayers varied depending on the deity being addressed and the purpose of the prayer, but they typically included praise, gratitude, requests for blessings or guidance, and expressions of devotion.

Hymns, on the other hand, were poetic compositions that celebrated and praised the deities. They were often sung or chanted during religious ceremonies and festivals. Hymns were characterized by their melodic and rhythmic structure, making them aesthetically pleasing and spiritually uplifting. They were performed by specially trained individuals, such as temple musicians or singers, who possessed the necessary vocal skills and knowledge of the hymns.

Chants, similar to hymns, involved repetitive and rhythmic vocalizations that created a trance-like or meditative state. Chants were often used to invoke the presence or power of a deity, to enhance spiritual connection, or to induce a particular state of consciousness. They were sometimes accompanied by instrumental music or rhythmic drumming, adding to the mystical and enchanting atmosphere of the ritual.

Spells, also known as incantations or magical invocations, were performed with precise words, gestures, and actions to bring about a desired outcome. They were often spoken or chanted in a rhythmic manner, following a specific formula or structure. The performance of spells was believed to activate supernatural forces or to align oneself with the divine realm. Spells were frequently used for protection, healing, divination, or for seeking assistance from deities or ancestral spirits.

Analysis of the role of priests and priestesses in conducting these rituals:

Priests and priestesses played a crucial role in the performance of religious rituals in ancient Egypt. They were the intermediaries between the human world and the divine realm, responsible for ensuring the proper execution of prayers, hymns, chants, and spells. These religious specialists underwent rigorous training and held significant knowledge of the religious texts, rituals, and the specific requirements for communicating with the gods.

Priests and priestesses were tasked with conducting daily rituals in temples, leading the congregation in prayer, and performing ceremonial offerings. They were considered the guardians of sacred knowledge and were responsible for upholding the traditions and rituals associated with the deities they served. Priests often held specific roles and titles within the temple hierarchy, such as high priest, temple scribe, or temple musician, each with their own responsibilities and areas of expertise.

The role of the priest or priestess extended beyond the mere recitation of prayers or hymns. They were expected to embody the qualities and virtues associated with the deities they served, acting as spiritual guides and moral exemplars. They were also responsible for the maintenance and care of temple objects and sacred spaces, ensuring their purity and readiness for rituals.

Exploration of the use of music, dance, and gestures in religious performances:

Music, dance, and gestures played a vital role in ancient Egyptian religious performances. These expressive elements were believed to invoke spiritual energies, enhance the connection with the divine, and create a heightened state of consciousness for both the performers and the participants.

Music was an integral part of religious rituals, with specific instruments and melodies associated with different deities and ceremonies. Musicians would play harps, flutes, drums, sistrums, and other instruments, creating rhythmic patterns and melodic motifs that were believed to resonate with the divine realm. The harmonious sounds of music were thought to please the gods and invoke their presence.

Dance was another form of expression that accompanied religious rituals. Temple dancers, often women, would perform intricate and symbolic movements, reflecting the mythological narratives or the attributes of the deities being honored.

The dance was seen as a visual representation of the cosmic order and the divine harmony, connecting the earthly realm with the celestial realm.

Gestures and body movements were also important in religious performances. Certain gestures, such as raising the hands in supplication, bowing, or prostrating, were used to demonstrate reverence, humility, and devotion. Symbolic actions, such as offering incense, pouring libations, or lighting candles, were performed as part of the ritual process, conveying a tangible connection between the human and divine realms.

In conclusion, the performative aspects of prayers, hymns, chants, and spells in ancient Egyptian religious practices were carefully orchestrated to create a profound spiritual experience. Priests and priestesses, as the custodians of religious knowledge, played a pivotal role in conducting these rituals and ensuring their proper execution. The use of music, dance, and gestures added depth and symbolism to the religious performances, enhancing the spiritual connection with the deities and creating a sense of awe and reverence among the participants.

Conclusion:

In conclusion, this chapter has provided a comprehensive exploration of prayers, hymns, chants, and spells associated with key deities worshipped during the Old Kingdom period in ancient Egypt. Through the analysis of these religious texts and rituals, several key findings and insights have emerged.

Firstly, prayers, hymns, chants, and spells were integral components of ancient Egyptian religious practices. They served as vehicles of communication with the divine, expressing devotion, seeking divine intervention, and invoking the powers and blessings of the deities. These sacred utterances were performed with great reverence and care, incorporating ritual gestures, melodic structures, and rhythmic patterns.

Secondly, the key deities worshipped during the Old Kingdom period held significant roles in the religious worldview of the ancient Egyptians. Deities such as Ra, Osiris, Isis, Ptah, Hathor, and Horus were revered for their specific attributes and associations, ranging from solar cosmology and afterlife judgment to magic, fertility, and protection. The prayers, hymns, chants, and spells dedicated to these deities reflected their roles and characteristics, offering insights into the beliefs and values of the ancient Egyptian society.

The significance of these religious practices extends beyond their purely spiritual dimensions. They provide valuable insights into the cultural and social aspects of the Old Kingdom period. The study of prayers, hymns, chants, and spells allows us to understand the religious worldview, the relationship between humans and the divine, and the cultural practices and rituals that shaped the ancient Egyptian society. It reveals the importance of religious belief and ritual performance in ancient Egyptian life and highlights the interconnectedness of religion, culture, and social structure.

Furthermore, the analysis of these religious texts and rituals has implications for further research and study. It opens avenues for exploring the evolution of religious practices over time, the regional variations in worship, and the interplay between different deities and their cults. It invites us to delve deeper into the symbolism, metaphysical concepts, and magical traditions embedded within these texts. Moreover, it encourages interdisciplinary approaches, drawing upon fields such as Witchcraft, Divination, Herbalism, Shamanism, Ecospirituality, and Magic in Ancient Egypt, to deepen our understanding of ancient Egyptian religious beliefs and practices.

In conclusion, the study of prayers, hymns, chants, and spells associated with key deities worshipped during the Old Kingdom period offers valuable insights into the religious, cultural, and social landscape of ancient Egypt. It enriches our understanding of the religious beliefs, rituals, and worldview of the Old Kingdom society and provides a foundation for further exploration and research in the field of Egyptology and related disciplines.

Examples, Problems, and Exercises:

Analyze the Pyramid Texts and discuss the prayers, spells, and rituals associated with the divine kingship ideology and the role of the pharaoh in the afterlife.

Examine the architectural elements of the Pyramid of Djoser and discuss how they reflect the religious beliefs and practices of the Old Kingdom.

Compare and contrast the rituals and symbolism associated with the sun god Ra and the funerary god Osiris, highlighting their respective roles in ancient Egyptian religion.

Investigate the significance of the Sed festival in the religious and political life of the Old Kingdom, discussing the rituals, ceremonies, and symbolism associated with this royal jubilee.

Part 4: Middle Kingdom (c. 2055 BCE - 1650 BCE)

The Middle Kingdom period, spanning from approximately 2055 BCE to 1650 BCE, holds great significance in the chronology of ancient Egyptian history. It emerged as a transitional phase following the decline of the Old Kingdom and the subsequent period of political fragmentation known as the First Intermediate Period. The Middle Kingdom witnessed a reunification of Egypt under strong central authority and marked a period of cultural and artistic flourishing. It is characterized by notable developments in various aspects of society, including religious practices, political structure, and artistic expression.

Exploration of the social, political, and religious changes during this period

The Middle Kingdom period brought about significant changes in the social, political, and religious landscape of ancient Egypt. It witnessed the rise of a more stable and centralized government, with pharaohs exerting greater control over the administration of the kingdom. This centralization led to the establishment of a more efficient bureaucratic system, allowing for improved governance and the implementation of economic and social reforms.

In terms of religious practices, the Middle Kingdom saw a resurgence of traditional Egyptian beliefs and rituals. The pantheon of deities expanded, with certain cults gaining prominence. The concept of Maat, the cosmic order and harmony, became a central tenet of religious and social life. The Middle Kingdom also witnessed the development of new religious texts, such as the Coffin Texts, which provided guidance and spells for the afterlife journey.

Purpose of the chapter and key research questions

The purpose of this chapter is to delve into the religious aspects of the Middle Kingdom period and explore the changes and innovations that occurred in ancient Egyptian religious practices during this time. By examining the textual evidence, archaeological findings, and artistic representations, we aim to gain a comprehensive understanding of the religious beliefs, rituals, and cultural developments of the Middle Kingdom.

Exploring the Rituals, Beliefs, and Syncretism of Ancient Egyptian Religion

Key research questions to be addressed in this chapter include:

How did the reunification of Egypt under the Middle Kingdom pharaohs impact religious practices and beliefs?

What were the major religious cults and deities worshipped during the Middle Kingdom, and how did their roles and significance evolve?

How did the concept of Maat influence religious and social life in the Middle Kingdom?

What new religious texts and rituals emerged during this period, and what insights do they provide into the ancient Egyptian religious worldview?

How did the religious developments of the Middle Kingdom reflect broader societal changes and political ideologies?

By exploring these research questions and examining the religious landscape of the Middle Kingdom, we will gain a deeper understanding of the complex interplay between religion, society, and politics during this transformative period in ancient Egyptian history.

In the subsequent sections of this chapter, we will delve into the specific aspects of religious practices, cults, deities, rituals, and texts that shaped the religious landscape of the Middle Kingdom. Through a thorough and in-depth analysis of the available evidence, we aim to unravel the intricate tapestry of religious beliefs and practices that characterized this remarkable era.

Exploring the Rituals, Beliefs, and Syncretism of Ancient Egyptian Religion

Pharaoh	Queen	Years Ruled	Children	Additional Information
Narmer/Menes	N/A	c. 3100 BCE	N/A	Considered the first pharaoh of unified Egypt
Hatshepsut	N/A	1479-1458	Neferure	One of the few female pharaohs, known for her successful reign and temple constructions
Akhenaten	Nefertiti	1353-1336	Tutankhamun, Ankhesenamun	Introduced Atenism and moved the capital to Amarna
Tutankhamun	N/A	1332-1323	No known children	Famous for the discovery of his intact tomb in the Valley of the Kings
Ramses II	N/A	1279-1213	Merneptah, Bintanath, Meritamen	One of the longest reigning pharaohs, known for his military campaigns and colossal constructions
Cleopatra VII	N/A	51-30 BCE	Caesarion, Cleopatra Selene II,	The last active ruler of the Ptolemaic Kingdom, associated with Julius Caesar and Mark Antony
			Alexander Helios, Ptolemy Philadelphus	children of Cleopatra VII and Mark Antony. Cleopatra VII was the last active ruler of the Ptolemaic Kingdom, and Mark Antony was a Roman general and politician. They were born during the time when Cleopatra and Mark Antony were in a romantic and political alliance. However, after the defeat of Mark Antony and Cleopatra by Octavian (later known as Augustus), their children's fate and further details about their lives become less documented.

Chapter 10: Religious Reforms and Revival during the Middle Kingdom

The Middle Kingdom period marks a significant phase in the ancient Egyptian civilization, spanning from approximately 2055 BCE to 1650 BCE. It emerged after a period of political instability and fragmentation known as the First Intermediate Period. The Middle Kingdom is often regarded as a time of cultural and political rejuvenation, characterized by the centralization of power under strong pharaohs, territorial expansion, and a resurgence of artistic and architectural achievements.

Importance of religious beliefs and practices during the Middle Kingdom

Religious beliefs and practices held a paramount significance in the lives of ancient Egyptians during the Middle Kingdom. Religion played a central role in their worldview, influencing their perception of the divine, the afterlife, and the cosmic order. It provided a framework for understanding the nature of existence, the role of the pharaoh as a divine ruler, and the rituals and ceremonies that connected humanity with the divine realm.

During the Middle Kingdom, religious beliefs and practices underwent various transformations and revivals. The period witnessed both religious reforms and a resurgence of traditional cults and rituals. These developments reflected the changing socio-political landscape, the aspirations of the pharaohs, and the evolving religious needs of the Egyptian society.

Purpose of the chapter and key research questions

The purpose of this chapter is to explore the religious reforms and revival that took place during the Middle Kingdom. It aims to provide a comprehensive analysis of the religious landscape, examining the reformist efforts of pharaohs, the revival of traditional cults, the syncretism of different religious traditions, and the rituals and ceremonies that were performed during this period. By delving into these aspects, the chapter seeks to shed light on the intricate relationship between religion, society, and the pharaoh's authority.

Key Research Questions:

What were the major religious reforms undertaken during the Middle Kingdom, and what were their implications for the religious landscape?

How did the pharaohs influence religious developments during this period, and what was their role in promoting religious reforms or revivals?

What were the main cults and deities that experienced a revival during the Middle Kingdom, and what were the reasons behind their resurgence?

How did religious syncretism and the integration of foreign deities shape the religious practices of the Middle Kingdom?

What were the key rituals and ceremonies performed during this period, and what was their significance in the religious and social context?

By addressing these research questions, the chapter aims to provide a comprehensive understanding of the religious reforms and revival that occurred during the Middle Kingdom, offering insights into the religious, cultural, and social dynamics of ancient Egyptian society during this significant era.

Religious Reforms during the Middle Kingdom

The Amarna Period, which occurred during the later part of the 18th Dynasty in the New Kingdom, is a significant chapter in ancient Egyptian history that witnessed radical religious reforms initiated by Pharaoh Akhenaten. Akhenaten introduced a monotheistic religion centered around the worship of the sun-disk deity, Aten, and sought to suppress the traditional polytheistic cults that had been deeply ingrained in Egyptian society for centuries. The chapter will delve into the motivations behind Akhenaten's religious reforms, including his desire to consolidate political power, challenge the influence of the priesthood, and emphasize his own divine status as the son of the Aten.

Examination of the impact of the Amarna Period on traditional religious beliefs and practices

The religious reforms of Akhenaten during the Amarna Period had a profound impact on the religious landscape of ancient Egypt. The chapter will explore how these reforms disrupted the established religious traditions, leading to the closure of temples dedicated to other deities, the suppression of traditional rituals, and the defacement of images and inscriptions related to the traditional pantheon. It will also examine the implications of this religious upheaval on the social and cultural fabric of Egyptian society, including the role of the priesthood, the beliefs and practices of the general population, and the relationship between the pharaoh and the divine.

Reversion to traditional religious beliefs and revival of old cults after the Amarna Period

Following the death of Akhenaten, there was a significant shift in religious policies during the later part of the Amarna Period and the subsequent reigns of Tutankhamun and the pharaohs of the 19th Dynasty. The chapter will explore how these rulers sought to reverse the religious reforms of Akhenaten and restore the traditional polytheistic cults. This period witnessed a revival of old cults, the reopening of temples dedicated to various deities, and the reinstatement of traditional rituals and ceremonies. The chapter will analyze the motivations behind this reversion to traditional religious beliefs, including political stability, the need to appease the priesthood and the general population, and the desire to restore religious harmony.

By examining the religious reforms of the Amarna Period and the subsequent revival of traditional beliefs and practices, this chapter aims to provide a comprehensive understanding of the dynamic nature of religion during the Middle Kingdom. It will analyze the interplay between political authority, social dynamics, and religious ideologies, offering insights into how religious reforms and revivals shape the religious and cultural landscape of ancient Egypt. Through examples, problems, and exercises, students will be encouraged to critically evaluate the motivations and consequences of these religious transformations and engage in discussions about the broader implications for ancient Egyptian society.

Role of Pharaohs in Religious Reforms

The pharaohs of ancient Egypt held a central role in religious affairs, as they were believed to be divine rulers with direct connections to the gods. This section will explore the influence of pharaohs in shaping religious developments during the Middle Kingdom. It will examine how pharaohs, as both political and religious leaders, had the authority to initiate and enact religious reforms. The chapter will discuss the pharaoh's role as a mediator between the human and divine realms and the impact of their religious decisions on the beliefs and practices of the Egyptian people.

Examination of pharaonic decrees and edicts related to religious practices

Pharaohs played an active role in religious reforms through the issuance of decrees and edicts that regulated and controlled religious practices. This section will analyze the pharaonic decrees and edicts related to religious practices during the Middle Kingdom. It will explore the content of these decrees, such as regulations regarding temple construction, the appointment of priests, and the performance of rituals. The chapter will also examine the reasons behind the issuance of these decrees, including the pharaoh's desire to establish control over religious institutions, maintain social order, and promote their own divine status.

Case studies of specific pharaohs and their religious reforms

To provide a deeper understanding of the pharaoh's role in religious reforms, this section will present case studies of specific pharaohs from the Middle Kingdom and their religious initiatives. It will explore the religious reforms and policies implemented by pharaohs such as Mentuhotep II, Amenemhat I, and Senusret III. These case studies will analyze the motivations, methods, and consequences of their religious reforms, shedding light on the pharaoh's agency in shaping the religious landscape of ancient Egypt. By examining these specific examples, students will gain insights into the diverse approaches and strategies employed by pharaohs to promote and enforce religious changes.

Understanding the role of pharaohs in religious reforms is essential to comprehend the intricate relationship between political authority and religious practices in ancient Egypt. By exploring the influence of pharaohs, examining their decrees and edicts, and analyzing specific case studies, this chapter aims to highlight the agency of pharaohs in shaping religious developments and provoke critical thinking about the motivations and implications of their actions. Through engaging examples, problems, and exercises, students will be encouraged to assess the multifaceted role of pharaohs as religious leaders and evaluate the impact of their decisions on the religious landscape of the Middle Kingdom.

Revival of Traditional Cults and Deities

During the Middle Kingdom period, there was a notable revival of worship for ancient deities that had been overshadowed or suppressed in previous eras. This section will delve into the factors and motivations behind the revival of traditional cults and deities. It will explore the religious, cultural, and political reasons that prompted the reemergence of these ancient beliefs and practices. The chapter will discuss how this revival represented a shift towards the reaffirmation of traditional values and a return to the spiritual foundations of Egyptian society.

Exploration of the cults of Osiris, Amun, and other prominent gods and goddesses

Among the deities that experienced a resurgence in popularity during the Middle Kingdom were Osiris, Amun, and various other prominent gods and goddesses. This section will provide an in-depth exploration of the cults associated with these deities. It will analyze the religious rituals, myths, and symbols associated with their worship, as well as the specific roles and attributes ascribed to them. By examining these cults, students will gain insights into the religious practices, beliefs, and the socio-cultural context of the Middle Kingdom period.

Significance of temple construction and restoration in the revival of traditional cults

Temple construction and restoration played a crucial role in the revival of traditional cults during the Middle Kingdom. This section will highlight the significance of temple projects in the religious revival of ancient deities. It will discuss the construction and renovation of temples dedicated to Osiris, Amun, and other revitalized cults. The chapter will delve into the architectural features, symbolism, and rituals associated with these temples. It will also examine the patronage of the pharaohs, noble families, and wealthy individuals in financing these temple projects as a demonstration of their religious devotion and political influence.

The revival of traditional cults and deities during the Middle Kingdom is a testament to the enduring power and influence of ancient Egyptian religious beliefs. By analyzing the resurgence of worship, exploring the cults of key deities, and highlighting the significance of temple construction and restoration, this chapter aims to provide students with a comprehensive understanding of the religious landscape of the Middle Kingdom. Through examples, problems, and exercises, students will be encouraged to critically assess the reasons for the revival, evaluate the impact on Egyptian society, and reflect on the broader implications of religious reforms and revival movements in ancient civilizations.

Religious Syncretism and Integration

During the Middle Kingdom period, there was a significant blending of religious beliefs and practices from different regions and cultures. This section will explore the process of religious syncretism, which involved the integration of diverse religious elements into the Egyptian religious landscape. It will examine the influences of neighboring regions, such as Nubia and Canaan, on Egyptian religious beliefs and rituals. By analyzing the syncretic elements in religious texts, iconography, and archaeological evidence, students will gain insights into the intercultural exchange and the complex nature of religious syncretism during this period.

Analysis of the integration of foreign deities and cults into the Egyptian religious landscape

As part of the religious syncretism, foreign deities and cults were integrated into the Egyptian religious landscape during the Middle Kingdom. This section will focus on the assimilation of deities from conquered territories and the incorporation of their cults into Egyptian religious practices. It will examine examples such as the adoption of the Nubian god Dedun or the incorporation of Canaanite deities like Baal and Anat. Students will explore the reasons behind the acceptance of foreign deities, the adaptation of their myths and rituals, and the impact of these integrations on the religious beliefs and practices of the Egyptian people.

Implications of religious syncretism for the understanding of Middle Kingdom religious beliefs

The process of religious syncretism during the Middle Kingdom had significant implications for the understanding of religious beliefs during this period. This section will delve into the broader implications of syncretism, including its impact on the concept of divine hierarchy, the role of local and regional cults, and the fluidity of religious identities. It will explore how the integration of foreign deities and cults challenged and reshaped traditional Egyptian religious beliefs, leading to the emergence of new theological concepts and practices. Through critical analysis of primary sources and archaeological evidence, students will gain a deeper understanding of the complexities of religious syncretism and its influence on the religious landscape of the Middle Kingdom.

The exploration of religious syncretism and integration in the Middle Kingdom provides students with a nuanced understanding of the dynamic nature of ancient Egyptian religious beliefs. By examining the blending of religious elements from different regions and cultures, analyzing the integration of foreign deities and cults, and reflecting on the implications of syncretism, students will develop critical thinking skills and a broader perspective on the religious developments of the Middle Kingdom period. Through examples, problems, and exercises, students will be encouraged to engage in discussions and debates surrounding the complexities of religious syncretism and its significance in the ancient world.

Rituals and Ceremonies during the Middle Kingdom

This section will delve into the religious rituals and ceremonies that were prominent during the Middle Kingdom. It will provide an in-depth analysis of rituals such as the daily temple rituals, offering ceremonies, and festival celebrations. Students will gain an understanding of the structure and components of these rituals, including purification rites, processions, prayers, and offerings. By examining textual sources, temple reliefs, and archaeological evidence, students will explore the symbolism and purpose behind these rituals, as well as their role in maintaining cosmic order and fostering a connection between humans and the divine.

Analysis of the role of priests and priestesses in conducting rituals

The role of priests and priestesses in conducting rituals was vital to the religious practices of the Middle Kingdom. This section will focus on the responsibilities, training, and hierarchical structure of the priesthood. Students will learn about the different priestly roles, from high priests to temple personnel, and their specific duties during rituals. It will also explore the gender dynamics within the priesthood, including the important role of female priestesses. Through case studies and examination of primary sources, students will gain insights into the specialized knowledge and rituals performed by priests and priestesses, as well as their relationship with the pharaoh and the community.

Examination of the symbolism and significance of ritual objects and tools

Ritual objects and tools played a crucial role in Middle Kingdom religious ceremonies. This section will provide an in-depth analysis of the symbolism and significance of these objects, such as offering tables, censers, libation vessels, and ritual wands. Students will explore the materiality of these objects, their connection to specific deities and rituals, and their symbolic representations of cosmic concepts and forces. Through the examination of archaeological findings and artistic representations, students will develop an understanding of how these objects were used in rituals and how they facilitated communication between the human and divine realms.

By exploring the rituals and ceremonies of the Middle Kingdom, analyzing the role of priests and priestesses, and examining the symbolism of ritual objects and tools, students will gain a comprehensive understanding of the religious practices and beliefs of this period. Through examples, problems, and exercises, students will be encouraged to critically analyze the significance of rituals, the roles of religious practitioners, and the material culture associated with religious ceremonies. This will enable them to engage in discussions and develop a deeper appreciation for the complexities of religious life during the Middle Kingdom.

Conclusion:

In this chapter, we have explored the religious reforms and revival that took place during the Middle Kingdom period in ancient Egypt. We have examined the Amarna Period and the religious reforms initiated by Pharaoh Akhenaten, which resulted in significant changes to traditional religious beliefs and practices. We have discussed the impact of the Amarna Period on the Egyptian religious landscape and the subsequent reversion to traditional beliefs after Akhenaten's reign.

Additionally, we have examined the role of pharaohs in shaping religious developments during the Middle Kingdom. Through the analysis of pharaonic decrees and edicts, we have gained insights into the influence of pharaohs in promoting and enforcing religious reforms. We have also explored case studies of specific pharaohs and their contributions to religious changes, providing a nuanced understanding of the varied approaches taken by different rulers.

Furthermore, we have discussed the revival of traditional cults and deities during the Middle Kingdom. The resurgence of worship for ancient deities such as Osiris, Amun, and others has been examined, highlighting the significance of temple construction and restoration in this revival. We have explored the religious syncretism and integration that occurred, as foreign deities and cults were incorporated into the Egyptian religious landscape, resulting in a rich and diverse religious tapestry.

Significance of religious reforms and revival during the Middle Kingdom

The religious reforms and revival during the Middle Kingdom had profound significance in the religious and cultural history of ancient Egypt. They reflected the dynamic nature of Egyptian religious beliefs and practices, as well as the influence of political and social changes on religious developments. The Amarna Period, with its radical reforms and subsequent reversion, serves as a testament to the complexities of religious change and the enduring strength of traditional religious beliefs.

The role of pharaohs in shaping religious developments highlights the close connection between political power and religious authority in ancient Egypt. Their influence on religious reforms and their efforts to enforce new religious practices underscore the pharaoh's role as both a political and religious leader. The case studies of specific pharaohs provide valuable insights into the individual motivations and strategies employed by rulers to shape religious life in their kingdom.

The revival of traditional cults and deities demonstrates the enduring importance of ancient Egyptian religious traditions. The construction and restoration of temples dedicated to these deities served as centers of religious and cultural life, fostering a sense of continuity and connecting the people with their ancestral beliefs. The religious syncretism and integration of foreign deities into the Egyptian pantheon highlight the adaptive nature of Egyptian religious beliefs, as they absorbed and incorporated new ideas and practices into their existing framework.

Implications for understanding the religious and cultural developments of ancient Egypt

The religious reforms and revival during the Middle Kingdom offer valuable insights into the religious and cultural developments of ancient Egypt. They provide a window into the changing religious landscape, the relationship between political power and religious authority, and the enduring influence of traditional beliefs. By studying these developments, we gain a deeper understanding of the complexities and dynamics of ancient Egyptian religious practices, as well as their connection to broader societal changes.

The religious reforms and revival during this period also have implications for the study of ancient Egyptian culture and its interactions with other societies. The syncretism and integration of foreign deities into the Egyptian religious pantheon reflect the cultural exchanges and influences that occurred between

Egypt and neighboring regions. By exploring these influences, we gain a more comprehensive understanding of the interconnectedness of ancient civilizations and the ways in which religious beliefs and practices were shaped by cultural interactions.

In conclusion, the religious reforms and revival during the Middle Kingdom played a crucial role in shaping ancient Egyptian religious beliefs and practices. They reflect the dynamic nature of Egyptian religious traditions, the influence of political and social changes on religious developments, and the enduring significance of traditional beliefs. By studying these developments, we gain valuable insights into the religious and cultural developments of ancient Egypt and deepen our understanding of this fascinating civilization.

Chapter 11: Temples, Festivals, and Tools used c. 2055 BCE - 1650 BCE

The Middle Kingdom period, spanning from approximately 2055 BCE to 1650 BCE, holds great significance in the history of ancient Egypt. It emerged as a transformative era following the political and social upheaval of the First Intermediate Period. The Middle Kingdom saw the restoration of centralized authority under strong pharaohs who sought to revive and strengthen the religious and cultural institutions of Egypt.

During this period, Egypt experienced a period of stability and prosperity. The pharaohs of the Middle Kingdom embarked on ambitious construction projects, including the building and renovation of temples, which played a central role in the religious and social fabric of ancient Egyptian society. The revival of temples and the revitalization of religious practices were integral to the ideological and political agenda of the ruling elite.

Importance of Temples, Festivals, and Tools in Ancient Egyptian Religious Practices

Temples held a central place in the religious life of ancient Egyptians during the Middle Kingdom. They were considered the dwelling places of the gods and served as centers of worship, administration, education, and cultural activities. Temples were not only sacred spaces for religious rituals, but they also played a crucial role in maintaining cosmic order, ensuring the prosperity and well-being of the community, and fostering the connection between the divine and human realms.

Festivals held immense importance in ancient Egyptian religious practices. They were occasions of joyous celebration, elaborate rituals, and communal gatherings. Festivals were dedicated to specific gods and goddesses, marking important moments in the religious calendar. These events involved processions, offerings, performances, and ceremonies aimed at honoring the deities, seeking their favor, and renewing the cosmic balance.

Tools and implements used in ancient Egyptian religious practices were essential for the performance of rituals and ceremonies. These tools held symbolic and practical significance, representing the power and authority of the priests and priestesses, as well as facilitating communication with the divine. Examples of such tools include ritual knives, offering tables, incense burners, and sacred vessels. The craftsmanship and materials used in the production of these tools reflected the reverence and attention to detail that the ancient Egyptians placed on their religious practices.

Purpose of the Chapter and Key Research Questions

The purpose of this chapter is to delve into the world of temples, festivals, and tools during the Middle Kingdom period, exploring their profound significance in ancient Egyptian religious practices. By examining the temples, the festivals, and the tools used, we seek to gain a deeper understanding of the religious and cultural landscape of this era.

Key Research Questions:

How did the Middle Kingdom period contribute to the revitalization and restoration of temples in ancient Egypt?

What were the main festivals and religious celebrations during this period, and what role did they play in the religious calendar?

How did the tools and implements used in religious rituals reflect the religious beliefs and practices of the ancient Egyptians?

What were the societal and cultural implications of temple construction, festivals, and the use of tools in religious practices during the Middle Kingdom?

Throughout this chapter, we will examine these questions through a multidisciplinary lens, drawing on examples and insights from various fields, such as witchcraft, divination, herbalism, shamanism, ecospirituality, and magic in ancient Egypt. By engaging in critical analysis, exploring counterarguments, and presenting dissenting opinions, we aim to foster a comprehensive understanding of the religious and cultural dynamics of the Middle Kingdom period.

Examples, Problems, and Exercises:

Provide a detailed description of a Middle Kingdom temple, highlighting its architectural features and religious functions.

Analyze the significance of a specific festival during the Middle Kingdom, discussing its rituals, symbolism, and impact on the community.

Compare and contrast the tools used in religious rituals during the Middle Kingdom with those of earlier or later periods, exploring their evolution and cultural implications.

Investigate the role of festivals and temples in fostering community cohesion and reinforcing social hierarchies during the Middle Kingdom, using historical and archaeological evidence.

Engage in a group discussion on the ethical implications of using tools and rituals in religious practices, considering perspectives from different cultural and religious traditions.

Temples during the Middle Kingdom

During the Middle Kingdom period, temple architecture underwent significant developments, reflecting both continuity with earlier traditions and innovative elements. Temples were designed as sacred spaces dedicated to the worship of deities and served as centers of religious, social, and administrative activities. The architecture of Middle Kingdom temples exhibited a harmonious blend of grandeur, symbolism, and functionality.

Middle Kingdom temples typically consisted of an outer enclosure wall, enclosing the sacred precinct and various subsidiary structures. The entrances were often marked by imposing pylons, towering gateways adorned with intricate reliefs and inscriptions. The main temple complex, known as the hypostyle hall, featured rows of massive columns supporting the roof. These columns were often decorated with intricate reliefs depicting scenes of religious significance or offerings to the gods.

Examination of Key Temples and Their Religious Functions

Temple of Amun-Re at Karnak: The Temple of Amun-Re at Karnak was one of the most significant religious complexes during the Middle Kingdom. Dedicated to the god Amun-Re, it served as a prominent cult center and witnessed extensive construction and expansion during this period. The temple complex housed multiple sanctuaries, chapels, and administrative buildings, emphasizing the religious and political importance of Amun-Re.

Temple of Sobek at Medinet Madi: The Temple of Sobek, located at Medinet Madi, honored the crocodile god Sobek. This temple represented the strong connection between the Nile and the fertility of the land. The temple complex consisted of a main temple structure, smaller chapels, and a sacred lake. Rituals involving the sacred crocodiles were performed to honor Sobek and ensure the annual flooding of the Nile.

Temple of Hatshepsut at Deir el-Bahari: The Temple of Hatshepsut, situated at Deir el-Bahari, stands as a remarkable architectural achievement. It was dedicated to the worship of various deities, including Amun, Hathor, and Anubis. The temple complex, characterized by terraced architecture and colonnaded halls, showcased Hatshepsut's divine legitimacy and celebrated her achievements as a female pharaoh.

Analysis of Temple Rituals and the Role of Priests and Priestesses

Temple rituals played a central role in ancient Egyptian religious practices during the Middle Kingdom. These rituals aimed to establish and maintain a harmonious relationship between the divine and mortal realms, ensuring the well-being and prosperity of the community. Priests and priestesses, acting as intermediaries between humans and the gods, performed intricate and highly symbolic rituals within the temple precincts.

Priests held diverse responsibilities, ranging from overseeing daily offerings, maintaining temple cleanliness, and conducting ceremonies. They possessed specialized knowledge of religious texts, rituals, and the symbolic significance of objects used in worship. Priestesses also played vital roles, particularly in the worship of goddesses, and often held positions of influence and authority within temple hierarchies.

Temple rituals included purification rites, processions, offering ceremonies, and the recitation of prayers and hymns. These rituals sought to appease the gods, seek their blessings, and ensure cosmic order and prosperity. Symbolic actions, such as the presentation of offerings, libations, and the burning of incense, were believed to establish a direct connection between the mortal world and the divine realm.

The temple rituals and the role of priests and priestesses during the Middle Kingdom provide valuable insights into the religious beliefs and practices of ancient Egypt. By studying the rituals and the religious functions of various temples, we gain a deeper understanding of the importance of these sacred spaces in the spiritual and social lives of the ancient Egyptians.

Festivals and Religious Celebrations

The Middle Kingdom period witnessed a rich and diverse array of festivals and religious celebrations that played a vital role in the religious and social life of ancient Egypt. These festivals were carefully organized events held at specific times of the year, marking significant cosmic and agricultural cycles. They provided opportunities for communal worship, cultural expression, and the reaffirmation of religious beliefs.

One prominent festival during the Middle Kingdom was the Festival of Opet, celebrated in honor of the god Amun. This festival involved a grand procession where the cult statues of Amun, his consort Mut, and their son Khonsu were carried in a sacred barque from the Karnak Temple to the Luxor Temple. The procession was accompanied by music, dance, and offerings, symbolizing the rejuvenation and renewal of divine power.

Another important festival was the Sed Festival, also known as the Heb Sed or the "Feast of the Tail." This festival celebrated the rejuvenation and continuity of the pharaoh's kingship. It involved a series of rituals and physical challenges that demonstrated the pharaoh's fitness to rule. The festival emphasized the pharaoh's role as a divine intermediary and the continuity of cosmic order.

Examination of Specific Rituals and Ceremonies Associated with these Festivals

Each festival had its distinct rituals and ceremonies that reflected the specific beliefs and cultural practices of ancient Egypt. These rituals aimed to connect the human and divine realms, maintain cosmic harmony, and seek the blessings of the gods.

For example, during the Festival of Opet, the sacred barques carrying the cult statues of the deities were accompanied by priests and worshippers in a solemn procession. The statues were believed to merge with the presence of the god, and offerings, including food, drink, and incense, were presented along the route. The procession culminated in the Luxor Temple, where additional rituals and ceremonies took place to honor the deities.

In the Sed Festival, the pharaoh would perform a series of physical activities and ceremonial rituals that showcased his vitality and legitimacy as a ruler. These activities included the "running of the jubilee," where the pharaoh would run around a marked course, symbolizing his ability to renew his power and protect the land.

Analysis of the Role of the Community in Festival Participation and Religious Observance

The participation of the community was crucial to the success and significance of religious festivals during the Middle Kingdom. Festivals provided opportunities for communal gathering, shared worship, and cultural expression. The involvement of the community fostered a sense of unity, collective identity, and religious devotion.

The community actively participated in the preparation and execution of festival rituals and ceremonies. This involvement included the construction and decoration of festival structures, the creation of offerings, and the performance of music, dance, and recitations. Members of different social classes, including priests, nobles, craftsmen, and commoners, all played roles in the religious observances, contributing to the overall atmosphere of reverence and celebration.

Participation in festivals also allowed individuals to express their personal devotion and seek blessings for themselves, their families, and their communities. It provided a sense of connection with the divine and a reaffirmation of shared religious values. The festivals were not solely religious in nature but also served as important cultural and social events that brought people together, fostering a sense of belonging and community cohesion.

The study of festivals and religious celebrations during the Middle Kingdom offers valuable insights into the religious beliefs, social dynamics, and cultural practices of ancient Egypt. By examining the specific rituals, ceremonies, and the role of the community, we gain a deeper understanding of the integral role of festivals in ancient Egyptian society and their significance in maintaining religious traditions and fostering communal bonds.

Tools and Ritual Implements

In ancient Egypt, religious rituals were accompanied by a range of tools and implements that served specific functions and held symbolic significance. These tools were carefully crafted and used by priests and priestesses to facilitate the performance of rituals and establish a connection between the human and divine realms.

The tools and implements used in religious rituals included ceremonial objects, utensils, and instruments. They encompassed a wide variety of items, such as offering tables, incense burners, ritual knives, musical instruments, and sacred vessels. Each tool had its unique purpose and played a vital role in the religious ceremonies and practices of the Middle Kingdom.

Examination of the Symbolism and Significance of Specific Tools

Many of the tools and implements used in ancient Egyptian religious rituals held symbolic meanings associated with the beliefs and concepts central to the religion. For example, the offering table represented the connection between the earthly and divine realms. It was believed that offerings placed on the table would be consumed by the gods, nourishing their spirits and ensuring their continued benevolence.

Incense burners held a symbolic role in purifying the ritual space and conveying the prayers and offerings to the gods through the rising smoke. The burning of incense was believed to carry the intentions and desires of the worshippers to the divine realm, creating a link between the mortal and immortal worlds.

Ritual knives, known as "senet" or "sekhem," were important tools used in ceremonial rites. These knives held both practical and symbolic functions. They were employed in the slaughtering of animals for offerings and sacrifices, symbolizing the separation of life force and the act of transformation.

Analysis of the Craftsmanship and Materials Used in the Production of Ritual Implements

The craftsmanship and materials used in the production of ritual implements reflected the importance and reverence accorded to religious rituals in ancient Egypt. Skilled artisans meticulously crafted these tools with precision and attention to detail.

Tools and implements were crafted using various materials, including precious metals such as gold and silver, as well as semi-precious stones, ceramics, and wood. These materials were chosen for their durability, aesthetic appeal, and symbolic significance. For instance, gold, associated with the sun god Ra, was often used to fashion ritual objects, representing divine power and illumination.

The production of these implements involved specialized craftsmen who possessed intricate knowledge of the religious symbolism and requirements associated with each tool. These craftsmen employed techniques such as carving, engraving, and inlaying to create intricate designs and patterns on the surfaces of the tools, further enhancing their visual impact and symbolic significance.

Studying the tools and implements used in ancient Egyptian religious rituals provides valuable insights into the religious beliefs, cultural practices, and artistic achievements of the Middle Kingdom period. It allows us to appreciate the intricate craftsmanship, symbolic language, and the role these tools played in facilitating the religious experiences and expressions of the ancient Egyptians.

Case Studies: Temples, Festivals, and Tools

Temple of Karnak: The Temple of Karnak, located in Thebes, was one of the most significant religious sites during the Middle Kingdom. It served as the cult center for the god Amun and underwent extensive construction and expansion during this period. The temple complex comprised multiple sanctuaries, halls, and pylons, each dedicated to different deities. The rituals conducted at Karnak were aimed at honoring the gods, reaffirming the divine authority of the pharaoh, and maintaining cosmic balance.

Temple of Hatshepsut at Deir el-Bahari: The Temple of Hatshepsut, situated on the west bank of the Nile near Luxor, was dedicated to the worship of the goddess Hathor. It showcased innovative architectural features, including terraces and colonnades, and incorporated natural rock formations into its design. The temple played a crucial role in the commemoration of Hatshepsut's divine lineage and legitimized her reign as a female pharaoh.

Examination of the Rituals and Ceremonies Associated with Selected Festivals

Festival of Opet: The Festival of Opet was one of the most significant religious festivals celebrated during the Middle Kingdom. It involved the procession of statues of the Theban triad—Amun, Mut, and Khonsu—from Karnak to the temple of Luxor. The festival aimed to renew the bond between the gods and the pharaoh, demonstrate the ruler's divine legitimacy, and ensure the fertility and prosperity of Egypt. Elaborate rituals, including offerings, purifications, and music and dance performances, accompanied the procession.

Heb-Sed Festival: The Heb-Sed Festival was a jubilee celebration held to commemorate the continued strength and vitality of the pharaoh's reign. It took place approximately thirty years into a pharaoh's rule and involved various ritual activities, such as the pharaoh's symbolic rejuvenation and reaffirmation of kingship. The festival included processions, sacrifices, and the performance of ceremonial rituals in the presence of the gods and ancestral spirits.

Analysis of Specific Tools and their Use in Religious Rituals

Sistrum: The sistrum was a musical instrument used in religious ceremonies, particularly associated with the worship of the goddess Hathor. It consisted of a handle and a metal frame with movable rods and small rings. When shaken, the sistrum produced a distinct rattling sound believed to have a purifying and protective effect. It was often used in rituals to invoke the goddess's presence, create a joyful atmosphere, and ward off evil spirits.

Ankh: The ankh, a symbol resembling a cross with a loop at the top, represented the key of life and was widely used in religious rituals and iconography. It symbolized the eternal life bestowed by the gods and the pharaoh's divine authority. The ankh was often held by gods and goddesses in temple reliefs and was used in various ceremonies to bless and protect worshippers.

By delving into these case studies, we gain a deeper understanding of the specific temples, festivals, and tools used during the Middle Kingdom. They provide valuable insights into the religious practices, beliefs, and cultural expressions of ancient Egypt. Additionally, studying these examples encourages critical thinking and analysis of the diverse aspects of ancient Egyptian religious traditions and their significance in the broader socio-political and religious context of the Middle Kingdom.

Significance of Temples, Festivals, and Tools

Temples held immense significance in ancient Egyptian society during the Middle Kingdom. They served as the focal points for religious worship, providing a physical space for the interaction between the divine and mortal realms. Temples were not only places of ritual but also centers of social, economic, and cultural activities.

Religious Significance: Temples were believed to be the dwelling places of the gods, providing a sacred space for communication and communion with the divine. They were seen as the earthly abodes of specific deities, allowing worshippers to establish a direct connection with the gods through rituals, offerings, and prayers.

Social Significance: Temples played a central role in fostering community cohesion and identity. They functioned as gathering places where people from different social strata could come together to participate in religious ceremonies, exchange news and information, and engage in social interactions. Temples were not only places of worship but also hubs for social and economic activities, such as markets, workshops, and administrative functions.

Economic Significance: Temples owned extensive lands, agricultural estates, and resources that generated wealth and sustenance for the priesthood and the broader community. The temple complexes employed a large workforce, including priests, administrators, craftsmen, and laborers, contributing to the local economy and providing employment opportunities.

Role of Festivals in Reinforcing Religious Beliefs and Community Cohesion

Festivals held a vital role in ancient Egyptian religious life, serving as occasions for the reaffirmation of religious beliefs, the expression of gratitude to the gods, and the reinforcement of social bonds within the community.

Religious Beliefs and Rituals: Festivals provided a platform for the performance of elaborate rituals, ceremonies, and processions that aimed to honor the gods, invoke their presence, and seek their blessings. These rituals were believed to maintain cosmic order, ensure fertility and abundance, and promote harmony between the divine and human realms.

Communal Participation: Festivals brought people together from different regions and backgrounds, fostering a sense of unity and collective identity. They offered opportunities for shared experiences, communal celebrations, and the transmission of religious knowledge and traditions from one generation to the next. Festivals provided a platform for social interaction, cultural exchange, and the strengthening of social bonds within the community.

Cultural Expressions: Festivals showcased a range of cultural expressions, including music, dance, drama, and visual arts. Performances by musicians, dancers, and actors added vibrancy and spectacle to the religious ceremonies, enhancing the overall festive atmosphere. These cultural expressions were not only forms of entertainment but also integral to the religious experience, invoking the presence of the gods and arousing spiritual emotions among the worshippers.

Significance of Tools and Ritual Implements in Facilitating Religious Practices

Tools and ritual implements played a crucial role in facilitating and enhancing religious practices in ancient Egypt. They were carefully crafted and imbued with symbolic meanings, representing the connection between the mortal and divine realms.

Symbolism and Function: Tools and ritual implements, such as the sistrum, ankh, and offering vessels, carried symbolic significance in religious rituals. They served practical functions, such as purification, protection, and offering preparations, while also embodying deeper meanings related to fertility, rebirth, and the eternal cycle of life.

Ritual Efficacy: The proper use of tools and ritual implements was believed to enhance the efficacy of religious rituals. They were seen as conduits for divine power and intermediaries between the worshippers and the gods. Through their use, worshippers could communicate with the divine, invoke blessings, and seek divine favor.

Craftsmanship and Materials: Tools and ritual implements were crafted with great care and precision. Skilled artisans employed a variety of materials, including precious metals, gemstones, wood, and ceramics, to create these sacred objects. The craftsmanship involved in their production reflected the importance placed on religious rituals and the dedication to creating objects of beauty and spiritual significance.

By examining the significance of temples, festivals, and tools, we gain a comprehensive understanding of the multifaceted nature of ancient Egyptian religious practices during the Middle Kingdom. These aspects not only shed light on the religious beliefs and cultural expressions of the time but also provide insights into the social, economic, and artistic dimensions of ancient Egyptian civilization.

Conclusion:

Throughout this chapter, we have delved into the rich and intricate world of temples, festivals, and tools during the Middle Kingdom of ancient Egypt. We explored the architectural marvels of temples, their religious functions, and the pivotal role they played in shaping the religious and social fabric of the time. The revival of traditional cults and the resurgence of worship for ancient deities highlighted the enduring devotion to the gods and the cultural continuity that persisted during this period. Additionally, we examined the significance of festivals as occasions for religious expression, community cohesion, and cultural celebrations. The analysis of tools and ritual implements shed light on their symbolic meanings, craftsmanship, and their facilitation of religious practices.

Significance of temples, festivals, and tools in understanding the religious and cultural landscape of the Middle Kingdom

Temples served as crucial centers of religious and communal life, reflecting the religious beliefs, social structures, and economic systems of the Middle Kingdom. They provided a tangible connection between the mortal and divine realms, fostering a sense of divine presence and facilitating the worship of deities. Festivals played a vital role in reinforcing religious beliefs, fostering social cohesion, and showcasing cultural expressions. They created opportunities for shared experiences, spiritual communion, and the transmission of religious knowledge and traditions. Tools and ritual implements were not merely utilitarian objects but were imbued with symbolic meanings, enhancing the efficacy and significance of religious rituals.

The study of temples, festivals, and tools provides us with a deeper understanding of the religious and cultural landscape of the Middle Kingdom. It allows us to unravel the complex interplay between religious beliefs, social dynamics, and artistic expressions in ancient Egyptian society. By examining these aspects, we gain insights into the spiritual practices, social interactions, and cultural values that shaped the lives of the ancient Egyptians during this period.

Chapter 12: Prayers, Hymns, Chants, and Spells Dedicated to Prominent Deities of the Time (e.g., Amun, Hathor, Sobek)

Throughout human history, various civilizations and cultures have developed intricate systems of religious beliefs and practices to establish a connection with the divine. In the context of ancient Egypt, prayers, hymns, chants, and spells held immense significance as vital means of expressing devotion and communicating with the gods and goddesses. These verbal and written expressions served as powerful vehicles for religious experiences, fostering a deep sense of connection, reverence, and spiritual engagement.

Prayers, as a fundamental form of communication with the divine, held a central place in ancient Egyptian religious practices. They were sincere appeals, petitions, or expressions of gratitude directed towards specific deities or the divine realm as a whole. Prayers were offered in various settings, including temples, households, and personal sanctuaries. They were spoken or recited by individuals, priests, or priestesses, who acted as intermediaries between humans and the gods.

Hymns, on the other hand, were poetic compositions that celebrated the greatness, attributes, and mythology of the gods and goddesses. These lyrical expressions of praise and adoration were often recited or sung during religious rituals, festivals, and temple ceremonies. Hymns provided a means for individuals and communities to articulate their reverence for the divine and to participate in the divine presence.

Chants played a distinct role in ancient Egyptian religious practices, characterized by repetitive and rhythmic utterances. Chants had a compelling and transformative power, often accompanied by music, dance, and gestures. They were used to invoke the presence of the gods, activate their divine qualities, and create an atmosphere of spiritual elevation. Chants were particularly prominent in rituals, processions, and ceremonies, enabling participants to connect with the gods on a deep emotional and spiritual level.

Spells, known as magical incantations, represented another dimension of ancient Egyptian religious practices. These written or spoken formulas contained specific words, phrases, and rituals believed to possess supernatural powers. Spells were used for various purposes, including protection, healing, love, fertility, and the attainment of divine favor. They were inscribed on amulets, papyri, or other objects, and were performed by individuals or specialized priests with the aim of harnessing magical forces and influencing the natural and supernatural realms.

Explanation of the role of prayers, hymns, chants, and spells in establishing communication with the divine

Prayers, hymns, chants, and spells played a vital role in establishing communication and fostering a relationship between humans and the divine in ancient Egyptian religious beliefs. They provided a means for individuals and communities to express their devotion, seek divine intervention, and connect with the gods and goddesses on a personal and collective level.

These verbal and written expressions were believed to have a transformative power, bridging the gap between the mortal and immortal realms. They allowed individuals to articulate their needs, desires, fears, and gratitude to the gods and goddesses, who were perceived as benevolent beings capable of influencing human lives and the course of natural events.

Prayers served as a direct avenue for individuals to communicate their concerns, hopes, and aspirations to the gods. They provided an opportunity for individuals to express their gratitude for blessings received and seek divine assistance in times of difficulty or crisis. Prayers acted as a means of invoking the attention and favor of the deities, who were regarded as benefactors and protectors of the people.

Hymns, with their poetic and lyrical nature, offered a means of exalting and glorifying the gods. They expressed admiration for the divine qualities and celebrated the mythical narratives associated with the deities. Through hymns, individuals and communities expressed their reverence and awe, acknowledging the gods' roles in the creation and sustenance of the world.

Chants, through their repetitive and rhythmic nature, had the power to transport individuals into a heightened state of consciousness. Chants created a meditative and ritualistic atmosphere, enabling participants to transcend the mundane and connect with the divine presence. They were believed to invoke the gods' energies and activate their powers within the sacred space.

Spells, with their magical formulas and rituals, were considered a means of manipulating the natural and supernatural forces. They were recited or performed with the intention of influencing the gods, spirits, and cosmic energies to bring about desired outcomes. Spells were believed to harness the inherent power of language and ritual to transform reality and ensure the protection, well-being, and prosperity of individuals and communities.

In summary, prayers, hymns, chants, and spells played an integral role in ancient Egyptian religious practices, serving as avenues for communication, devotion, and transformative experiences. They allowed individuals and communities to express their reverence, seek divine assistance, and influence the course of their lives. These verbal and written expressions were a profound manifestation of the deep spiritual beliefs and practices that permeated ancient Egyptian society, facilitating a profound connection between humans and the divine realm.

Amun, the Hidden One

Amun, the Hidden One, holds a significant place in the ancient Egyptian pantheon. This deity, associated with the power of creation and hidden knowledge, elicited devotion and reverence from ancient Egyptians. This section will provide a comprehensive analysis of the prayers, hymns, chants, and spells dedicated to Amun, shedding light on the religious practices and beliefs surrounding this enigmatic deity.

Examination of Prayers Dedicated to Amun and their Content

Prayers dedicated to Amun served as a vital medium for ancient Egyptians to establish a profound connection with the divine realm. These verbal expressions of devotion and supplication reflect the deep reverence and the earnest desire for a spiritual connection with Amun. By delving into the structure and content of these prayers, we can uncover valuable insights into the specific concerns, desires, and needs of the worshippers who sought solace, guidance, and blessings from Amun.

The analysis of prayers dedicated to Amun encompasses various aspects, beginning with an exploration of the language employed in these sacred invocations. The choice of words, poetic devices, and metaphors used in these prayers shed light on the spiritual and emotional connection the devotees sought to establish with Amun. Through a close examination of the linguistic nuances, students can grasp the unique religious vocabulary employed to express devotion and communicate with the deity.

Furthermore, the prayers dedicated to Amun often involve the invocation of his epithets, which are descriptive titles highlighting specific aspects of his divine nature and power. These epithets reveal the multifaceted nature of Amun and the diverse roles he played in the cosmic order. By examining the usage and significance of these epithets, students can gain a deeper understanding of the divine attributes associated with Amun and the specific qualities worshippers sought to invoke and connect with.

The content of these prayers is also of great significance. The requests and petitions put forth in prayers dedicated to Amun reveal the concerns and aspirations of the worshippers. These may include pleas for protection, guidance, fertility, success, or healing, among others. The analysis of the content allows us to explore the fundamental needs and desires of the ancient Egyptians and the ways in which they believed Amun could address these concerns. Moreover, studying the variations and changes in the content of prayers across different time periods and contexts provides insights into the evolving religious beliefs and cultural shifts within the worship of Amun.

A comparative study of prayers dedicated to Amun is crucial for understanding the variations and developments in the worship of this deity over time. By examining prayers from different periods and contexts, students can identify changes in religious practices, the introduction of new elements, and the influence of external factors on the expressions of devotion to Amun. This comparative approach enables a more comprehensive understanding of the significance of Amun in the ancient Egyptian religious landscape and the ways in which his worship evolved throughout history.

In conclusion, the examination of prayers dedicated to Amun offers a fascinating glimpse into the spiritual aspirations and concerns of ancient Egyptians. Through the analysis of language, epithets, and content, students can gain valuable insights into the depth of devotion and the desires for connection and blessings that were expressed through these prayers. Furthermore, the comparative study of prayers across different time periods and contexts provides a broader perspective on the worship of Amun and its evolution over time. By engaging with these prayers, students can develop a deeper appreciation for the religious practices of ancient Egypt and engage in critical thinking and discussion about the complexities of human-divine communication and the significance of Amun in the ancient Egyptian religious landscape.

Analysis of Hymns Praising the Greatness and Attributes of Amun

Hymns dedicated to Amun form a significant aspect of ancient Egyptian religious literature, exalting the greatness, power, and divine attributes of this revered deity. These poetic compositions serve as vehicles for expressing a profound sense of awe and reverence, captivating the hearts and minds of worshippers who sought to honor and connect with Amun on a spiritual level. Through a meticulous analysis of these hymns, we can unravel the intricate mythological narratives, symbols, and metaphors employed to depict Amun's majesty and the profound impact they had on the religious experiences of ancient Egyptians.

The hymns dedicated to Amun often draw upon a rich tapestry of mythological imagery and symbolism, weaving a narrative that highlights the unique qualities and roles attributed to Amun in the cosmic order. These hymns emphasize Amun's position as the hidden one, the creator god, and the sustainer of the universe. They celebrate his authority, wisdom, and benevolence, presenting him as the divine source of life, power, and protection.

In the analysis of these hymns, students will explore the intricate interplay of mythological motifs and symbols, decoding the layers of meaning embedded within the poetic verses. The use of metaphors, such as describing Amun as the "bull of his mother," conveys his virility and creative potency. References to Amun's association with wind and air highlight his intangible and omnipresent nature. By dissecting these metaphors and symbols, students can gain a deeper understanding of the multifaceted attributes and roles ascribed to Amun within the ancient Egyptian religious framework.

Furthermore, the emotional and spiritual impact of these hymns on the worshippers is a crucial aspect of analysis. The hymns aimed to evoke a sense of wonder, reverence, and spiritual connection with Amun. Through the use of evocative language, rhythmic patterns, and repetition, these hymns create a powerful atmosphere of devotion and awe. Students will explore the poetic techniques employed in these hymns, such as parallelism, alliteration, and meter, to understand the artistic craftsmanship and the intended emotional and spiritual impact on the worshippers.

An examination of the hymns dedicated to Amun also reveals the reciprocal relationship between the deity and his devotees. The hymns serve not only as expressions of praise but also as a means of seeking divine favor and blessings. They convey the worshippers' desires for protection, prosperity, and guidance, acknowledging Amun's role as the benevolent provider and benefactor. Understanding the reciprocal nature of these hymns deepens our comprehension of the ancient Egyptian concept of religious devotion and the interconnectedness between humans and the divine.

In conclusion, the analysis of hymns praising the greatness and attributes of Amun provides a profound insight into the religious experiences and beliefs of ancient Egyptians. Through the exploration of mythological narratives, symbols, and metaphors, students can uncover the multifaceted nature of Amun and his role within the cosmic order. Moreover, studying the emotional and spiritual impact of these hymns allows us to appreciate the profound connection between Amun and his worshippers, transcending the boundaries of time and space. By engaging with these hymns, students can develop a deeper appreciation for the poetic artistry, religious symbolism, and the complex dynamics of devotion in ancient Egyptian religious practices.

Exploration of the Role of Chants and Invocations in Invoking the Power of Amun

Chants and invocations held a significant place in the religious practices of ancient Egypt, serving as powerful tools for invoking the divine presence and power of Amun. These rhythmic and repetitive utterances had a transformative effect on both the participants and the ritual environment, creating a heightened state of consciousness and establishing a sacred atmosphere conducive to spiritual connection and communion.

Through a comprehensive exploration of the chants and invocations dedicated to Amun, students can gain insights into the specific techniques and formulas employed to invoke Amun's divine essence. These invocations often incorporated sacred names, epithets, and divine attributes of Amun, emphasizing his power and authority. The repetition of these words and phrases created a meditative rhythm, allowing participants to focus their attention and intention on establishing a direct connection with Amun.

The study of Amun chants involves delving into the linguistic and phonetic aspects of these invocations. The pronunciation and intonation of sacred words were believed to carry inherent power, and the correct recitation was considered essential for the effectiveness of the ritual. Students will analyze the phonetic structures, rhythmic patterns, and melodic elements of these chants to understand the sonic qualities that facilitated the invocation of Amun's divine presence.

Moreover, the exploration of the ritual context and settings in which these chants were performed enhances our understanding of their performative and communal aspects. Chants dedicated to Amun were often performed within temple precincts, during specific religious festivals, or as part of private devotion. The physical and social environment in which these chants took place played a crucial role in enhancing the spiritual experience and fostering a sense of collective participation.

By examining the role of chants and invocations in invoking the power of Amun, students will develop an appreciation for the transformative nature of these ritual practices. The rhythmic repetition and focused intention created a heightened state of consciousness, enabling participants to transcend the mundane and connect with the divine. This exploration provides insights into the psychological and spiritual dimensions of ancient Egyptian religious practices and sheds light on the methods employed to establish a direct and personal relationship with Amun.

In conclusion, the exploration of the role of chants and invocations in invoking the power of Amun unveils the profound transformative potential of these ritual practices. By studying the specific techniques, linguistic elements, and performative aspects of these invocations, students can gain a deeper understanding of the rituals' intention and the mechanisms used to connect with Amun's divine essence. Furthermore, the consideration of the ritual context and communal dynamics offers valuable insights into the collective nature of ancient Egyptian religious experiences. Engaging with these chants allows students to explore the interplay between language, sound, and intention in facilitating a spiritual connection with Amun and deepening their understanding of ancient Egyptian religious beliefs and practices.

Study of Spells Associated with Amun, Focusing on Their Purpose and Intended Effects

Spells associated with Amun reveal the ancient Egyptians' belief in the efficacy of magical practices and the protective powers of this deity. These spells, often inscribed on papyri or written on amulets, served as potent means of addressing various needs and desires within the community. By delving into the purpose and intended effects of these spells, students can gain a deeper understanding of the practical applications of Amun's power in everyday life and the ways in which individuals sought divine assistance through magical means.

The study of Amun spells entails a comprehensive examination of their purpose and intended effects. These spells encompassed a wide range of concerns, including healing ailments, warding off malevolent forces, ensuring success in endeavors, and seeking spiritual guidance. Through a meticulous analysis of the textual content and structure of these spells, students can identify the specific objectives and desired outcomes associated with each spell. They will explore the linguistic and metaphysical elements employed within the spell formulas to evoke the intervention and favor of Amun.

Furthermore, the study will explore the rituals, materials, and objects used in conjunction with Amun spells, providing valuable insights into the broader context of magical practices in ancient Egypt. The casting of Amun spells often involved ritual performances conducted by magical practitioners or priests who possessed specialized knowledge and expertise in the occult arts. Students will examine the role of these practitioners, their training, and the rituals they performed to activate the powers inherent in the spells.

The materials and objects employed in spellcasting are also of significance in understanding the practical applications of Amun spells. Certain spells required the use of specific ingredients, such as herbs, amulets, or ritual objects, believed to possess inherent magical properties. Students will investigate the symbolic and material qualities of these elements and their association with Amun's divine attributes. By examining the interplay between language, ritual, and material culture, students can grasp the comprehensive nature of magical practices and their integration within the religious framework of ancient Egyptian society.

The study of spells associated with Amun contributes to a broader understanding of the complex relationship between religion, magic, and everyday life in ancient Egypt. It highlights the belief in the efficacy of divine intervention and the utilization of magical means to address human needs and desires. By engaging with the practical applications of Amun spells, students can explore the ways in which individuals sought supernatural assistance and protection in various aspects of their lives.

In conclusion, the study of spells associated with Amun offers valuable insights into the practical applications of Amun's power and the integration of magic within the religious landscape of ancient Egypt. By examining the purpose and intended effects of these spells, students gain a deeper understanding of the diverse needs and concerns of the ancient Egyptians. The exploration of rituals, materials, and practitioners associated with Amun spells further enhances our comprehension of the intricate relationship between language, ritual, and material culture. Through this comprehensive study, students can engage with the multifaceted nature of magical practices and their significance in ancient Egyptian society.

Conclusion:

The examination of prayers, hymns, chants, and spells dedicated to Amun provides a comprehensive understanding of the religious practices and beliefs associated with this influential deity. Through these sacred expressions, ancient Egyptians sought to establish a profound connection with Amun, seeking his blessings, protection, and guidance. The analysis of these texts allows us to glimpse into the rich tapestry of ancient Egyptian spirituality and provides valuable insights into the cultural and religious worldview of this civilization. By engaging with the prayers, hymns, chants, and spells, students can develop a deeper appreciation for the complexities and nuances of ancient Egyptian religious practices and engage in critical thinking and discussion about the significance of Amun, the Hidden One.

Prayers

Prayers dedicated to Amun, the Hidden One, were an integral part of ancient Egyptian religious practices, serving as a means of establishing communication and connection with this revered deity. These prayers, expressed in spoken or written form, reflected the deep devotion, reverence, and supplication of the worshipper towards Amun. By examining the structure, language, and content of these prayers, we can gain valuable insights into the beliefs, desires, and concerns of the ancient Egyptians who sought divine intervention and guidance from Amun.

The examination of prayers dedicated to Amun encompasses a meticulous analysis of their content and the specific themes addressed within them. These prayers often began with an invocation of Amun's epithets, emphasizing his divine attributes and roles. The worshippers praised Amun's greatness, acknowledging his power and transcendence. They expressed gratitude for his blessings and sought his divine favor and protection in various aspects of life, such as health, prosperity, and success in endeavors. These prayers also reflected the belief in Amun as a benevolent deity who had the ability to grant the desires and needs of the faithful.

The language employed in prayers dedicated to Amun was carefully crafted to evoke a sense of reverence and awe. The worshippers used eloquent and poetic expressions to convey their devotion and the depth of their connection with Amun. Metaphorical language, rich symbolism, and mythological references were employed to depict Amun's divine attributes and his role in the cosmic order. The prayers often invoked the imagery of Amun as a creator, a protector, and a source of divine wisdom.

Furthermore, a comparative study of prayers across different time periods and contexts allows for an exploration of variations and changes in the worship of Amun. By analyzing prayers from different regions and time periods, students can trace the evolution of Amun's cult, the development of his religious symbolism, and the integration of local beliefs and customs into the worship of Amun. This comparative approach sheds light on the diversity and adaptability of Amun's cult, highlighting the dynamic nature of religious practices in ancient Egypt.

Prayers dedicated to Amun were not only expressions of individual devotion but also had a communal dimension. They were often recited or performed within the context of temple rituals, where priests and worshippers came together to honor and seek the blessings of Amun. The collective recitation of prayers created a sense of unity and community, reinforcing the social and religious cohesion among the worshippers.

In conclusion, the examination of prayers dedicated to Amun, the Hidden One, provides valuable insights into the beliefs, desires, and concerns of the ancient Egyptians who sought a connection with this powerful deity. The structure, language, and content of these prayers offer a glimpse into the profound reverence and devotion expressed towards Amun. By exploring the evolution of Amun's cult and the communal aspects of prayer, students can develop a comprehensive understanding of the significance of prayers in ancient Egyptian religious practices. Through the study of these prayers, we gain a deeper appreciation for the role of Amun as a divine protector, provider, and source of spiritual guidance in the lives of the ancient Egyptians.

Hymn to Amun-Re

Hail to you, Amun-Re, the Hidden One!
Supreme in heaven and earth, creator of all,
You, the primordial god, before whom all gods bow.

You are the giver of life, the sustainer of existence,
From your sacred breath, the world emerged,
In your divine hands, the cycles of nature are guided.

You are the great sun, radiant and splendid,
Your rays illuminate the land, bringing warmth and growth,

Through your benevolence, the fields flourish and abundance thrives.

Mighty Amun-Re, you are the wise counselor,
The source of all knowledge and understanding,
In your divine wisdom, secrets of the universe unfold.

Your name resounds in temples, your presence revered,
Your power echoes through the halls of Karnak,
Where devotees gather, their hearts filled with reverence.

Grant us, Amun-Re, your blessings and protection,
Bestow upon us your divine grace and favor,
Guide us on the path of righteousness and prosperity.

We offer our prayers, our devotion, and our love,
May you hear our supplications, O Amun-Re,
And let your divine light shine upon us forevermore.

This hymn, inspired by ancient Egyptian religious texts, seeks to capture the
essence of the "Hymn to Amun-Re" in praising the hidden and supreme deity,
Amun-Re. It emphasizes his role as the creator, sustainer, and source of wisdom
in the universe, while also expressing the reverence and gratitude of the
worshippers.

Great Hymn to Amun

Hail to you, Amun, Lord of the thrones of the two lands!
Mighty and majestic, ruler of all gods,
You are the hidden one, veiled in mystery.

You rise in splendor, adorned with the double plume,
Your crown radiates with the brilliance of the sun,
The heavens rejoice at your divine presence.

Amun, you are the creator of all things,
From the primordial chaos, you brought forth order,
Your breath gives life to every living being.

You are the sustainer of the universe,
The cosmic balance rests in your hands,
Through your divine power, harmony prevails.

O Amun, you are the father of the gods,
The protector of the weak and the vulnerable,
Your justice is unwavering, your mercy boundless.

The land prospers under your watchful gaze,
The Nile flows with abundance at your command,
The fields are fertile, yielding bountiful harvests.

You are the giver of wisdom and inspiration,
The source of divine knowledge and revelation,
Your words are like sweet nectar to our souls.

We bow before you, Amun, in humble adoration,
We offer our prayers, our devotion, and our praise,
May your blessings shower upon us for eternity.

This rendition of the "Great Hymn to Amun" draws inspiration from ancient Egyptian texts and seeks to capture the reverence and awe inspired by Amun, the hidden and mighty deity. It emphasizes his role as the creator, sustainer, and divine judge, while also acknowledging his benevolence and the prosperity that stems from his presence. The hymn serves as an expression of devotion and gratitude towards Amun and seeks his eternal blessings.

Chants

Hail, mighty Amun, Hidden One,
Divine essence, source of life.
With reverence, we call upon your name,
Amun-Ra, the Great, the Eternal Flame.

O Amun, Lord of the cosmic order,
Your power and wisdom transcend all borders.
Grant us guidance on our sacred quest,
In your presence, we find peace and rest.

Amun, the giver of blessings untold,
Your divine grace and light unfold.
Through the cycles of day and night,
Your radiance shines, pure and bright.

As we chant your sacred name,
Our hearts and souls aflame.

Amun, hear our humble plea,
Guide us on the path of destiny.

In your embrace, we find solace and might,
Amun, bless us with your divine light.
With love and devotion, we sing this song,
Amun, to you, our praise belongs.

This chant is but a humble offering,
To honor your greatness and infinite being.
Amun, accept our words of reverence,
As we seek your divine benevolence.

Note: This chant is a creative composition inspired by ancient Egyptian religious practices and the attributes associated with Amun. It aims to evoke a sense of devotion, reverence, and connection with the divine.

Spells

Title: Spell for Divine Protection by Amun

Ingredients:

An amulet or talisman representing Amun
A small piece of parchment or paper
A black ink pen or marker
Procedure:

Begin by purifying yourself and the ritual space through cleansing rituals and reciting sacred invocations.

Take the piece of parchment or paper and write the following spell using the black ink pen or marker:

"O Amun, great and powerful,
I call upon your divine protection.
Shield me from all harm and danger,
Surround me with your mighty presence.
May your hidden strength be my shield,
And your wisdom guide me on my path.
By your sacred name, I invoke your power,
Amun, protect me in every hour."

Hold the amulet or talisman representing Amun in your hands and recite the spell three times, focusing on your intention for protection and seeking Amun's divine aid.

Place the parchment or paper with the written spell near the amulet or talisman, symbolically connecting them.

Keep the amulet or talisman with you at all times, wearing it as a pendant or carrying it in a pouch, as a reminder of Amun's protective presence.

Note: This spell is a modern adaptation inspired by ancient Egyptian magical practices and the association of Amun with divine protection. It is important to approach such spells with respect and reverence, understanding that their efficacy may vary depending on one's beliefs and personal connection to the divine.

Hathor, the Mistress of the West

Prayers dedicated to Hathor, the Mistress of the West, reveal the profound connection between the worshippers and this goddess of fertility, protection, and healing. Through a comprehensive analysis of these prayers, we can discern the prevalent themes and concerns addressed in the worship of Hathor. The prayers often center around invoking Hathor's blessings for abundant fertility, both in terms of the natural world and the human realm. They beseech her to grant fertility to the land, animals, and people, ensuring prosperity and growth. Additionally, prayers to Hathor often express a desire for her protective presence, seeking her divine shield against harm and misfortune. The worshippers invoke Hathor's nurturing and compassionate aspects, emphasizing her ability to heal physical and emotional ailments. Through the study of these prayers, we gain a deeper understanding of the role of Hathor as a benevolent and caring deity in the ancient Egyptian religious landscape.

Exploration of Hymns Celebrating the Beauty and Nurturing Aspects of Hathor

Hymns dedicated to Hathor serve as poetic expressions of reverence and admiration for the goddess, highlighting her beauty, grace, and nurturing qualities. These hymns aim to evoke a sense of awe and wonder, emphasizing the profound impact of Hathor's presence in the lives of her worshippers. Through an exploration of these hymns, we can gain a deeper understanding of the multifaceted aspects of Hathor's divine nature and her significance in ancient Egyptian religious beliefs and practices.

The hymns dedicated to Hathor often extol her as the epitome of beauty and grace. They describe her with vivid and enchanting imagery, portraying her as a radiant and alluring goddess. Hathor's physical beauty is often associated with her role as a goddess of love and pleasure. The hymns celebrate her irresistible charm and allure, emphasizing her ability to inspire love and desire in both humans and deities alike. In this context, Hathor is seen as a source of joy and happiness, capable of bringing delight and contentment to those who seek her blessings.

Additionally, the hymns emphasize Hathor's close connection to music, dance, and artistic expression. She is portrayed as a patroness of the arts, encouraging creativity and inspiring musicians, dancers, and artists. The hymns highlight her role in elevating the human spirit through the transformative power of music and dance. Hathor's association with music and artistic expression underscores her nurturing aspect, as she is believed to provide emotional and spiritual nourishment through these creative pursuits.

Furthermore, the hymns emphasize Hathor's maternal instincts and depict her as a loving and caring mother figure. She is often hailed as the "Great Mother" or "Lady of the West," symbolizing her role in providing comfort, protection, and sustenance to her worshippers. Hathor is regarded as a compassionate deity who listens to the pleas and concerns of her devotees, offering solace and support in times of need. Through her nurturing nature, Hathor brings about a sense of security and well-being, assuring her worshippers that they are cared for and protected.

By examining these hymns, we gain insight into the deep reverence and adoration the ancient Egyptians had for Hathor. They saw her as a source of inspiration, joy, and love, believing that her presence could bring about abundance and fulfillment in their lives. The hymns also shed light on the important role of music, dance, and artistic expression in ancient Egyptian religious practices, as well as the significance of maternal figures in the society's spiritual worldview.

Examination of Chants and Rituals Invoking the Presence of Hathor in Sacred Spaces

Chants and rituals were integral components of ancient Egyptian religious practices, serving as powerful means to invoke the presence of deities in sacred spaces. When it comes to Hathor, the examination of these chants and rituals provides us with valuable insights into the techniques and methods employed by ancient Egyptians to establish a direct connection with the goddess and evoke her divine essence. By delving into these practices, we can gain a deeper understanding of the ways in which Hathor was worshipped and honored in sacred spaces, and the significance of communal participation in these rituals.

Chants dedicated to Hathor were characterized by their rhythmic and melodic qualities, often accompanied by musical instruments and dance. The rhythmic patterns and repetitive nature of the chants served to create a trance-like state and transport the participants into a heightened spiritual realm. These chants, passed down through generations, were performed by trained priests and priestesses who possessed the knowledge and expertise to effectively engage with the divine realm. Through the recitation of specific invocations and formulas, the worshippers sought to draw forth the presence of Hathor and invoke her blessings upon the community.

Rituals associated with Hathor often took place in dedicated temples or sacred spaces devoted to the goddess. These rituals were performed by a group of participants, including priests, priestesses, and worshippers. The rituals incorporated various elements such as purification rites, offerings, processions, and performances of music and dance. The sacred space was meticulously prepared, adorned with symbols and images associated with Hathor, creating an ambiance conducive to spiritual connection. The participants would engage in coordinated movements, symbolic gestures, and vocal expressions, channeling their devotion and energy towards Hathor's presence.

The communal aspect of these rituals was of great importance. The participation of the community in these rituals fostered a sense of shared identity and collective experience. It allowed individuals to connect not only with the divine but also with each other, creating a bond of unity and a collective expression of devotion to Hathor. The presence of the deity was believed to be magnified and intensified through the combined efforts of the worshippers, heightening the spiritual experience and deepening the connection between the human and divine realms.

By examining these chants and rituals, we can appreciate the performative nature of ancient Egyptian religious practices and their ability to create a sacred atmosphere within which the presence of Hathor could be invoked. These practices not only facilitated communication with the goddess but also served as transformative experiences for the worshippers themselves. The rhythmic patterns, musical accompaniment, and collective engagement allowed individuals to transcend their mundane existence and enter into a heightened state of spiritual connection with Hathor.

In conclusion, the examination of chants and rituals dedicated to Hathor provides us with a window into the ancient Egyptian understanding of the sacred and their methods of invoking the presence of the goddess. These practices showcased the performative and communal aspects of worship, emphasizing the role of rhythmic chants, music, dance, and collective participation in establishing a direct connection with Hathor. By engaging in these rituals, the ancient Egyptians sought to bridge the gap between the human and divine realms, inviting Hathor's blessings and divine influence into their lives.

Study of Spells Dedicated to Hathor, Focusing on Their Connection to Love, Music, and Joy

Spells dedicated to Hathor offer a fascinating glimpse into the mystical and magical dimensions associated with this revered goddess. These spells revolve around themes of love, music, and joy, highlighting the areas of life over which Hathor exerts her divine influence. They serve as a means for individuals to harness Hathor's celestial power and invoke her assistance in matters related to emotional fulfillment, harmonious relationships, and creative inspiration. Through the exploration of these spells, we can uncover the ancient Egyptian beliefs regarding Hathor's ability to bring about transformative experiences and positive outcomes in the lives of her worshippers.

The spells dedicated to Hathor often involve the creation or utilization of amulets and talismans infused with the essence of the goddess. These objects, crafted with intricate symbols and inscriptions, are believed to carry Hathor's divine energy and protective powers. They are utilized as conduits through which individuals can connect with the goddess and seek her intervention in matters of the heart, including matters of love, romance, and emotional well-being. The intricate rituals associated with the creation and consecration of these amulets are conducted with meticulous care, reflecting the importance placed on Hathor's divine presence and blessings.

Central to the practice of these spells are the recitation of specific incantations and invocations. Ancient Egyptian magical texts provide instructions on the precise words and formulas to be uttered, emphasizing the power of language in effecting change. These incantations serve as a means of calling upon Hathor's divine authority and seeking her favor in matters of love, emotional healing, and personal happiness. The rhythmic and poetic nature of these incantations, often accompanied by gestures and ritual actions, heightens the potency of the spells and establishes a connection with the divine realm.

Music and dance play an integral role in the spells dedicated to Hathor. The ancient Egyptians believed in the profound influence of music and rhythmic movements in accessing higher states of consciousness and connecting with the divine. The incorporation of melodic tunes, percussive beats, and graceful dance steps in these spells enhances the spiritual experience and amplifies the desired effects. It taps into the creative and ecstatic energies associated with Hathor, allowing individuals to align themselves with her divine attributes and draw upon her transformative power.

Studying these spells dedicated to Hathor provides us with valuable insights into the ancient Egyptian belief system and their understanding of the intricate interplay between the divine and human realms. The spells affirm the prominence of Hathor as a benevolent deity associated with love, music, and joy, highlighting her role as a bestower of emotional well-being, harmonious relationships, and creative inspiration. Through the practice of these spells, individuals sought to tap into Hathor's divine energy and invoke her intervention in their lives, trusting in her ability to bring about positive change and fulfillment.

In conclusion, the study of spells dedicated to Hathor offers a fascinating exploration into the ancient Egyptian belief in the goddess's connection to love, music, and joy. These spells provide a glimpse into the mystical practices employed by individuals to seek Hathor's assistance in matters of the heart, emotional well-being, and creative expression. By delving into these spells, we gain a deeper understanding of the significance of Hathor in ancient Egyptian religious beliefs and the profound impact she was believed to have on the lives of her worshippers.

Prayer to Hathor

Divine Hathor, Mistress of the West,
Radiant goddess of beauty and nurturing grace,
I bow before your sacred presence with reverence and adoration.
You who bring joy and abundance to all who seek your divine embrace,
I come before you in humble supplication.

Oh, Hathor, hear my prayer,
With your gentle touch, bring forth blessings beyond compare.
In your loving embrace, may my heart find solace,
And may your radiance envelop me with your divine grace.

Hathor, goddess of love and compassion,
I beseech you to shower me with your affection.
Guide me on the path of harmonious relationships,
And let love blossom in every aspect of my life.

Mother Hathor, source of creativity and inspiration,
Unleash the muse within me, igniting the flames of my imagination.
Grant me the gift of artistic expression,
That I may create beauty and share it with the world in your honor.

Goddess of joy and celebration, I call upon you,
Infuse my days with laughter and delight, so pure and true.
May your energy uplift my spirit and fill my heart with glee,
As I dance to the rhythm of life, in harmony with thee.

Hathor, protector and healer, extend your nurturing hand,
Wrap me in your loving embrace, that I may withstand
Life's challenges with strength and fortitude,
And emerge victorious with your divine interlude.

Oh, Hathor, I offer my heartfelt devotion to you,
For in your presence, my spirit finds renewal.
May your blessings pour forth, abundant and divine,
And may your grace guide me on this sacred path of mine.

I offer this prayer with love and gratitude,
Humbly seeking your blessings and eternal gratitude.
May your divine essence dwell within my heart,
Now and forevermore, never to depart.

In the name of Hathor, the Mistress of the West,
I offer my prayer, trusting in your love and blessedness.
Thank you, Hathor, for your ever-present care,
Amen.

Hymn to Hathor

Hail, Hathor, goddess of beauty and grace,
Whose radiance shines upon the human race.
With golden locks that flow like the Nile,
You bring joy and love with your celestial smile.

Oh, Hathor, mistress of the sacred cow,
Your nurturing embrace, we humbly bow.
You bless us with fertility and abundance,
With your touch, life blossoms in all its resplendence.

Goddess of music, your voice echoes through the land,
With melodic songs, you hold our hearts in your hand.
In your presence, our spirits are lifted high,
As we dance to the rhythm, reaching for the sky.

Hathor, mistress of the heavens above,
Your beauty transcends, a symbol of love.
In your eyes, the stars find their gleam,
And the moon reflects your eternal dream.

Oh, Hathor, protector of the weary soul,
In your arms, we find comfort and feel whole.
You heal our wounds with your gentle touch,
And guide us through darkness, lighting the path as such.

Goddess of joy, you bring laughter and mirth,
Filling our lives with happiness and worth.
In your presence, sorrow finds its release,
As we celebrate life, embracing inner peace.

Hathor, your temples stand tall and grand,
A testament to your power and command.
We gather in reverence, voices raised in praise,
As we honor you in these sacred, hallowed days.

Oh, Hathor, we offer our devotion true,
With gratitude for the blessings you bestow.
In your eternal embrace, we find solace and rest,
For you, Hathor, are the goddess we love and respect.

Hail, Hathor, mistress of love and delight,
In your presence, we bask in purest light.
Guide us on our journey, with your wisdom and care,
For you, Hathor, we forever declare.

In the name of Hathor, the Mistress of the West,

We sing this hymn, our hearts truly blessed.
May your grace be with us, now and forevermore,
As we honor you, Hathor, whom we adore.

May your blessings descend upon us, each day anew,
Hathor, goddess of beauty, we bow to you.
Amen.

Chant to Hathor

(Chant rhythmically, with a steady beat)

Hathor, Hathor, radiant and bright,
Goddess of beauty, bring your light.
With love and joy, our spirits soar,
In your presence, we adore.

Hathor, Hathor, nurturing and kind,
In your embrace, peace we find.
Your gentle touch, like a soothing balm,
Healing our hearts, bringing us calm.

Hathor, Hathor, goddess of the arts,
Your music and dance, they touch our hearts.
We sing and we dance, in your sacred name,
Igniting our passions, setting our souls aflame.

Hathor, Hathor, protector and guide,
By your side, we safely reside.
Wrap us in your wings, keep us secure,
As we navigate life, strong and sure.

Hathor, Hathor, bringer of delight,
Fill our days with laughter, banish the night.
In your presence, we find pure bliss,
Radiating joy, with every single kiss.

Hathor, Hathor, we honor you,
With this chant, our love is true.
Goddess of love, beauty, and grace,
In your divine light, we find our place.

Hathor, Hathor, forever revered,
With devotion, our hearts are cleared.
We chant your name, our voices strong,
May your blessings to us forever belong.

Hathor, Hathor, we chant to thee,
In this sacred chant, our spirits set free.
May your energy flow, through our being,
Connecting us to your divine, all-seeing.

Hail Hathor, our goddess divine,
In this chant, let your presence shine.
We offer our love and praise to you,
Hathor, our goddess, forever true.

Note: Feel free to adapt the chant according to your desired rhythm or add musical elements to enhance the chanting experience.

Spell to Invoke the Blessings of Hathor

(Perform this spell with focused intention and a clear mind)

Materials needed:

A small piece of rose quartz or a rose quartz pendant
A white candle
Rose or jasmine incense
Instructions:

Begin by finding a quiet and comfortable space where you can perform the spell without interruption. Light the white candle and the rose or jasmine incense, creating a serene and sacred ambiance.

Take the piece of rose quartz or the rose quartz pendant in your hands and close your eyes. Take a few deep breaths, allowing yourself to relax and center your energy.

Hold the rose quartz to your heart and visualize a warm and loving energy radiating from it. Feel the gentle vibrations of love and joy emanating from the crystal and filling your entire being.

With the rose quartz still in your hands, speak the following incantation aloud or in your mind:

"Hathor, goddess of love and delight,
I call upon you on this sacred night.
Bless me with your grace and healing power,
In your embrace, may my spirit flower."

As you recite the incantation, visualize Hathor's divine presence surrounding you. Feel her loving energy enveloping you, filling you with a sense of joy, beauty, and inner peace.

Take a moment to express your heartfelt desires and intentions to Hathor. Share any specific requests or areas of your life where you seek her guidance, love, and blessings. Speak from your heart with sincerity and trust.

Place the rose quartz on your altar or any safe surface and allow the candle to burn down completely. As the candle flame flickers and dances, visualize your intentions being carried up to Hathor, reaching her divine realm.

Leave the rose quartz on your altar or keep it close to you, such as under your pillow or in a special place, as a reminder of your connection to Hathor and her ongoing presence in your life.

Note: It's important to approach spellwork with respect and a genuine intention. Remember to always follow your own intuition and adapt the spell to align with your personal beliefs and practices.

Sobek, the Crocodile God

Prayers dedicated to Sobek, the ancient Egyptian crocodile god, reveal the reverence and awe with which he was regarded. These prayers often highlight Sobek's role as a protector, emphasizing his fierce and formidable nature. The worshippers beseech Sobek for his watchful eye and strength in safeguarding them against dangers, both physical and spiritual. The language used in these prayers invokes his powerful presence and seeks his intervention in times of need. The prayers acknowledge Sobek's authority over the waters and his ability to navigate the treacherous Nile, offering a sense of security to those who invoke his name. By analyzing the structure and content of these prayers, we gain a deeper understanding of Sobek's role as a guardian deity and the role he played in ancient Egyptian religious beliefs and practices.

Exploration of Hymns Praising Sobek as the Ruler of the Nile and Associated with Fertility

Hymns dedicated to Sobek, the crocodile god, highlight his role as the ruler of the Nile and emphasize his association with fertility and abundance. These poetic compositions express the ancient Egyptians' deep reverence for Sobek and their recognition of his crucial role in sustaining their agricultural society.

In these hymns, Sobek is depicted as a powerful and authoritative figure, exercising control over the ebb and flow of the Nile. The ancient Egyptians recognized the Nile as the lifeblood of their civilization, as its annual flooding brought fertile soil and ensured successful harvests. Sobek, being intimately connected with the river, was revered as the guardian and director of its waters. The hymns celebrate Sobek's ability to regulate the river's movements, ensuring the timely and appropriate flooding that would nourish the land. By invoking his name and offering praise, the worshippers sought to maintain his benevolence and secure his favor for the prosperity of their crops and overall well-being.

Moreover, these hymns emphasize Sobek's association with fertility, both in agricultural productivity and human procreation. Sobek was regarded as the patron of fertile lands, symbolizing the bountiful yield of crops and the abundance of food. The hymns draw parallels between Sobek's role in facilitating the growth of crops and his influence over human fertility. They celebrate his potency and link him to the natural cycles of birth, growth, and renewal. Sobek's connection to fertility also extended to the animal kingdom, as he was believed to oversee the reproduction of livestock, ensuring their abundance as a valuable resource for the ancient Egyptians.

By studying these hymns, we gain profound insights into the ancient Egyptians' religious beliefs and their deep appreciation for the intricate relationship between Sobek, the Nile, and fertility. These hymns reflect the importance placed on Sobek's role in sustaining their society and maintaining the delicate balance between humans, nature, and the divine. The poetic language and vivid imagery used in these hymns capture the awe and reverence with which Sobek was regarded, evoking a sense of harmony and gratitude for the blessings bestowed upon them.

Examples:

"O Sobek, ruler of the sacred Nile,
Whose waters bring life to the fertile soil,
We praise your mighty presence, ever so grand,

As you guide the river with your commanding hand."

"In your name, O Sobek, the land flourishes,
With bountiful harvests and abundant riches.
Your divine power ensures our sustenance,
As we honor your rule with reverence."

"O Sobek, the source of life's endless flow,
Your blessings upon us, you bestow.
Fertile lands and thriving crops, we adore,
As we celebrate your grace forevermore."

Problems and Exercises:

Analyze the imagery and symbolism used in the hymns to Sobek. How do these poetic devices enhance the portrayal of Sobek as the ruler of the Nile and associated with fertility?
Discuss the significance of the Nile in ancient Egyptian society and its connection to agricultural productivity. How does Sobek's role as the ruler of the Nile contribute to the prosperity of the ancient Egyptians?
Compare and contrast the hymns to Sobek with hymns dedicated to other deities associated with water and fertility, such as Osiris or Isis. What similarities and differences can be observed in their portrayal and attributes?
Imagine you are an ancient Egyptian farmer composing a hymn to Sobek. Write a stanza expressing your gratitude for Sobek's role in ensuring a bountiful harvest and fertility in the land.

Examination of Chants Used in Rituals Dedicated to Sobek, Emphasizing His Power and Authority

Chants held a significant position in the rituals dedicated to Sobek, acting as a conduit for his power and authority within the sacred space. These melodic and repetitive utterances were instrumental in creating a resonating energy that allowed the participants to connect with the essence of Sobek. The chants served to evoke and invoke his divine presence, emphasizing his formidable and dominant qualities.

The chants used in rituals dedicated to Sobek often centered around his fearsome nature and protective prowess. They highlighted his strength, fierceness, and ability to ward off dangers and threats. By chanting specific invocations and formulas, the worshippers sought to establish a direct connection with Sobek and to invoke his blessings and favor. These chants were performed in a rhythmic manner, with participants repeating the words or phrases, creating an immersive and heightened atmosphere within the ritual space.

The study of these chants provides valuable insights into the performative and communal aspects of Sobek worship. They demonstrate the active role of ritual practitioners in harnessing and channeling the divine power of Sobek. The chants served as a means of aligning the participants' intentions and energies with the qualities and attributes embodied by Sobek. Through the repetition of these invocations, the worshippers aimed to cultivate a profound connection with Sobek, inviting his presence into their midst and seeking his guidance and protection.

Furthermore, the examination of these chants reveals the profound influence of ritual practice in ancient Egyptian religious traditions. The performative nature of the chants created a collective experience, engaging the participants both emotionally and spiritually. The rhythmic patterns and repetitive nature of the chants induced a trance-like state, enabling the worshippers to transcend mundane consciousness and enter into a heightened spiritual realm where they could commune with Sobek.

Examples:

"Sobek, mighty and fierce,
Protector of the land, we revere.
Grant us strength, shield us from harm,
With your power, our fears disarm."

"Sobek, ruler of the Nile's domain,
Authority and might in your domain.
Hear our chant, O crocodile god,
Your presence invoked, your protection laud."

"With each chant, Sobek draws near,
His power and authority we revere.
In his name, we stand tall and strong,
With his guidance, we belong."

Problems and Exercises:

Discuss the significance of chants in ancient Egyptian rituals and their role in establishing a connection with the divine. How do chants serve as a vehicle for invoking the power and authority of deities like Sobek?

Compare and contrast the chants used in rituals dedicated to Sobek with chants used in other religious or spiritual traditions. Identify common elements and explore the ways in which chants can create a transformative and transcendent experience.

Imagine you are a participant in a ritual dedicated to Sobek. Write a chant that embodies his power, authority, and protective qualities. Consider the rhythmic structure and the specific words or phrases that would invoke the essence of Sobek.

Reflect on the psychological and emotional effects of participating in a chant-based ritual. How do repetitive chants and rhythmic patterns contribute to the overall experience and sense of connection with the divine?

Study of Spells Related to Sobek, Focusing on Their Connection to Protection, Fertility, and Water

Spells dedicated to Sobek reveal the ancient Egyptians' belief in his ability to provide protection, fertility, and control over water-related phenomena. These spells were utilized for various purposes, such as safeguarding individuals from harm, promoting fertility in humans and animals, and controlling waterways for agricultural prosperity. The spells often involved the creation of amulets or the recitation of specific incantations and rituals to invoke Sobek's intervention. They harnessed his power to repel malevolent forces, facilitate conception and childbirth, and ensure the proper flow of the Nile for bountiful harvests. The study of these spells sheds light on the ancient Egyptians' reliance on Sobek's divine influence in their daily lives, illustrating the important role he played in their quest for protection, fertility, and the control of vital natural resources.

Overall, the analysis of prayers, hymns, chants, and spells associated with Sobek provides us with a comprehensive understanding of the ancient Egyptians' beliefs and practices related to this powerful crocodile god. It showcases Sobek's multifaceted nature as a protector, ruler, and bestower of fertility and emphasizes his connection to water and the cycles of life. By exploring these sacred texts and rituals, we gain insights into the ancient Egyptians' spiritual relationship with Sobek and their reliance on his divine intervention in various aspects of their lives.

Prayer to Sobek

Mighty Sobek, guardian of the waters,
With reverence and awe, we approach your presence.
You, the fierce and formidable crocodile god,
Protector of the land, we seek your guidance.

Oh Sobek, with scales shining like precious gems,
Your power radiates, unmatched and untamed.
Grant us your strength, O mighty ruler,
As we navigate the currents of life's challenges.

In your name, we find solace and protection,
As you watch over us with unwavering vigilance.
Shield us from harm, O fearsome Sobek,
And lead us safely through the dangers that lie ahead.

With each ripple of the waters, we feel your presence,
Your authority and might filling the air.
Guide us with your wisdom and insight,
That we may make decisions with clarity and care.

Sobek, in your divine embrace, we find courage,
And in your watchful gaze, we find comfort.
Bless us with your benevolence, O crocodile god,
And instill within us the power to overcome.

This prayer we offer, with hearts sincere and humble,
In gratitude for your protection and guidance.
May our devotion to you be steadfast and true,
As we honor your mighty presence, O Sobek.

Examples:

"Great Sobek, guardian of the Nile's flow,
Hear our prayer, your blessings bestow.
Protect us with your fierce and watchful eye,
As we navigate life's rivers, low and high."

"Sobek, lord of the crocodile's might,
We kneel before you, seeking your insight.
Grant us strength and shield us from harm,

As we walk this earth, your everlasting charm."

"In Sobek's name, we find sanctuary and might,
As we honor you in the morning's light.
Guide our steps, O fearsome crocodile god,
With your wisdom and protection, we shall trod."

Hymn to Sobek

Oh Sobek, ruler of the river's domain,
In your name, we sing this sacred refrain.
With awe and reverence, our voices raise,
To honor your might and offer our praise.

Majestic Sobek, with scales glistening bright,
Your presence commands both fear and delight.
From the depths of the waters, you emerge,
A symbol of power, fierce and submerged.

Protector of the land, with jaws wide and strong,
You guard the people from all that is wrong.
Your eyes, piercing and filled with ancient knowledge,
Guide us through life's currents, as we acknowledge.

Sobek, your crocodile form strikes awe and awe,
As you navigate the river's ebb and flow.
In your embrace, the fertile Nile does thrive,
And our fields flourish, keeping us alive.

Blessed Sobek, we honor your sacred might,
As you rule the waters, both day and night.
Your presence brings courage, your power unyielding,
Grant us your favor, our hearts are appealing.

Oh Sobek, bringer of abundance and grace,
We celebrate your role in life's sacred embrace.
In the music of the Nile, we hear your voice,
A reminder that in you, we can rejoice.

Examples:

"Hail, Sobek, lord of the river's might,

Your power fills us with awe and delight.
As we sing this hymn, our voices unite,
To honor your presence, shining so bright."

"Sobek, the crocodile god, ruler of all,
We offer this hymn, standing proud and tall.
Your strength and protection, we forever seek,
As we gather by the river, humble and meek."

"Oh Sobek, with scales like glistening gold,
Your presence, majestic and mighty, is told.
As we sing this hymn, your glory resounds,
Through the land, your power truly astounds."

Chant to Sobek

(Chant)
Sobek, Sobek, mighty and fierce,
Protector of all, your power we pierce.
With each rhythmic beat, our voices entwine,
Invoking your strength, a bond so divine.

(Chant)
Crocodile god, ruler of the Nile,
Your presence surrounds us, mile after mile.
Through the waters deep, you glide with grace,
Guiding us on our journey, at a steady pace.

(Chant)
Sobek, hear our call, with your jaws wide,
Defend us against all threats, side by side.
Your mighty roar echoes through the land,
Instilling courage in us, united we stand.

(Chant)
In your name, we honor the sacred flow,
Of the river's current, in which you bestow.
Grant us protection, strength, and stability,
As we navigate life's challenges with humility.

(Chant)

Sobek, ancient deity, we raise our voice,
In this chant, our devotion we rejoice.
May your presence fill our hearts and minds,
As we chant to you, our voices intertwined.

Examples:

"Sobek, Sobek, powerful and strong,
In your name, we sing this ancient song.
With every chant, our spirits align,
Your protective embrace, forever divine."

"Mighty Sobek, ruler of the Nile's domain,
We chant your name, in reverence we remain.
Your sacred power, we invoke and proclaim,
In this rhythmic chant, your glory we acclaim."

"Sobek, the crocodile god, fierce and true,
In this chant, our praises we bestow on you.
With every repetition, your strength we embrace,
Grant us your blessings, as we chant in this sacred space."

Spell to Sobek

(Preparation)
Prepare a small offering of fresh fish or meat, symbolizing the sustenance and strength associated with Sobek. Find a quiet and serene space near a body of water, such as a riverbank or a secluded pond, to perform the spell. Light a green or blue candle to represent the nurturing and life-giving energy of Sobek.

(Spell)

Begin by standing before the water, facing its gentle flow. Take a moment to ground yourself, connecting with the natural surroundings and the presence of Sobek.

Hold the offering in your hands and speak the following words with conviction and respect:

"Mighty Sobek, ruler of the waters,
I offer this gift as a token of my devotion.
May your divine presence bless and protect me,

As I seek your guidance and strength."

Place the offering gently into the water, releasing it to the current. Visualize the energy of Sobek infusing the offering, imbuing it with his protective and empowering essence.

Close your eyes and envision Sobek's formidable image, his piercing eyes and strong, scaly body. Feel his presence enveloping you, a shield of power and protection.

Repeat the following incantation three times, allowing the words to resonate within you:

"Sobek, guardian of the Nile's embrace,
Bestow upon me your strength and grace.
Protect me from harm, both near and far,
Let your fierce nature be my guiding star."

Visualize a luminous green or blue light enveloping your body, emanating from the water and reflecting Sobek's nurturing and protective energy. Feel the strength and courage flowing through you.

Express your gratitude to Sobek for his presence and assistance:

"Sobek, I thank you for your divine guidance,
For your watchful eye and benevolent providence.
May your power remain within me,
Nurturing my spirit and filling me with glee."

Slowly open your eyes, feeling a renewed sense of connection and protection. Take a moment to bask in the energy of Sobek and the serene surroundings.

Extinguish the candle as a sign of completion, knowing that the spell's intentions have been set in motion.

Examples:

"Mighty Sobek, ruler of the waters wide,
I offer this fish, a symbol of your pride.
Let your strength and protection surround me,
As I walk this path, blessed by your decree."

"Sobek, fierce and powerful crocodile god,
Accept this offering, let it be awed.
Grant me your protection, shield me from harm,
With your presence near, I feel safe and warm."

Additional Deities of the Middle Kingdom

The Middle Kingdom period of ancient Egypt (c. 2055-1650 BCE) witnessed the emergence and prominence of various deities alongside the already established pantheon. While the deities of the Old Kingdom continued to be revered, new gods and goddesses rose to prominence, reflecting the evolving religious beliefs and practices of the time. This chapter will provide a comprehensive exploration of the prayers, hymns, chants, and spells associated with these additional deities. We will analyze their specific roles, attributes, and significance within religious practices, as well as examine the diversity and regional variations in their worship and devotional practices.

Prayers, Hymns, Chants, and Spells Associated with Additional Deities:

The Middle Kingdom saw the emergence of several prominent deities, each with their own prayers, hymns, chants, and spells dedicated to them. These textual compositions served as a means of communication and devotion to the divine, allowing worshippers to express their reverence and seek blessings from these deities. Examples of such deities include:

a) Montu: The warrior god Montu, associated with Thebes and its regional variant known as Menthu, was worshipped as a powerful and fierce deity. Prayers and hymns to Montu often emphasized his martial attributes and invoked his protection in times of conflict. Chants and rituals dedicated to Montu focused on channeling his aggressive and assertive energy, aiming to infuse warriors with strength and courage in battle.

Prayer to Montu

Mighty Montu, valiant god of war,
I come before you with reverence and awe.
You, who possess the strength of the bull,
And the fiery spirit of the warrior's call.

In your presence, I seek protection and might,
Grant me the courage to face the fiercest fight.

With your guidance, let my heart be strong,
As I march forward, steady and headlong.

Oh Montu, hear my prayer, O powerful one,
Shield me from harm until the battle is won.
Bestow upon me your unwavering gaze,
That I may conquer all obstacles in my ways.

With every step I take, I invoke your name,
May your valor and bravery fuel the flame.
Grant me the wisdom to strategize and plan,
To be victorious, guided by your hand.

Montu, defender of the land and its kin,
Guard me from evil, protect me from sin.
As I face the challenges that lie ahead,
May your divine presence be my steadfast thread.

In the heat of battle, your strength I embrace,
With your blessings, I stand with unwavering grace.
Grant me the skill to wield the sword with might,
To defend what is just, to uphold what is right.

Oh Montu, fierce god of war and might,
Accept this prayer as an offering tonight.
I humbly seek your protection and aid,
In your name, I am empowered and unafraid.

Notes:
This prayer to Montu invokes his qualities as a powerful and fierce god of war. It seeks his protection, courage, and strength in times of conflict or challenges. The prayer acknowledges Montu's association with valor and bravery and calls upon him to guide and safeguard the worshipper throughout their endeavors.

Hymn to Montu

Oh Montu, mighty god of war,
With valorous heart and flaming star,
We raise our voices in praise to thee,
And celebrate your strength eternally.

In the heat of battle, your spirit ignites,
Filling our souls with unwavering might.
With spear in hand and chariot drawn,

You lead us forth, victorious and strong.

Your name resounds like thunder's roar,
As you charge ahead, ever seeking more.
In every conflict, you stand tall and bold,
Your presence inspires, a warrior's stronghold.

Montu, master of the battlefield's domain,
None can challenge your force, nor in combat remain.
You are the guardian, the protector of the land,
Guiding us with your unfaltering hand.

Your wrath strikes fear into your foes,
As you unleash your power, your strength it grows.
We sing your praises, O Montu, divine,
With hearts aflame, with devotion and shrine.

Grant us your courage, O god of war,
That we may face adversity and conquer all the more.
In your name, we march forth with might,
Embracing your spirit, shining bright.

Oh Montu, fierce and noble god,
In your honor, our hymns applaud.
With gratitude, we raise our voice,
Rejoicing in your power, in you we rejoice.

Notes:
This hymn to Montu celebrates his role as a mighty god of war and invokes his qualities of strength, courage, and victory. It acknowledges Montu's prowess in battle and highlights his ability to inspire and protect his worshippers. The hymn praises Montu's unwavering presence on the battlefield and emphasizes his importance as a guardian and guide. It is a tribute to Montu's divine power and serves as an expression of devotion and reverence.

Chant to Montu

(Chant in a rhythmic pattern, with emphasis on the power and strength of Montu)

Montu, god of valor and might,
In your name, we stand and fight.
With every step, our spirits rise,
Unleashing power that never dies.

Montu, guide us on the path of war,
Grant us courage to conquer and soar.
With your presence, our strength will surge,
In battle, we emerge, an unstoppable surge.

Montu, fierce as the blazing sun,
Our voices unite, the battle is won.
We invoke your name, with every breath,
Empowered by your warrior's strength.

Montu, lend us your warrior's rage,
As we march forward, fear we'll assuage.
In your name, we charge with might,
Victory within our sight.

Montu, we chant in your sacred name,
Igniting the fire, the warrior's flame.
Battles won, adversaries tamed,
Honor and glory in your name proclaimed.

Notes:
This chant to Montu is designed to be repeated in a rhythmic pattern, creating a powerful and energizing atmosphere. It invokes Montu's strength and courage, calling upon his divine presence to empower the participants. The chant emphasizes the idea of victory in battle and the unwavering spirit of the warrior. It serves as a means of invoking Montu's essence and channeling his power for protection and success on the battlefield.

Spell to Invoke Montu's Strength

(Ingredients: A red candle, a piece of carnelian or red jasper, a small jar of honey)

Prepare your sacred space by lighting the red candle and placing it in front of you.

Hold the piece of carnelian or red jasper in your hands and close your eyes. Visualize the image of Montu, the god of valor and strength. Imagine his powerful presence surrounding you.

Recite the following incantation:

"Montu, mighty and fierce,
I call upon your strength, oh god.
Grant me the valor and might I seek,
Unleash your power within me, I beseech."

Place the carnelian or red jasper on the altar in front of the candle as an offering to Montu.

Take the jar of honey and open it. Dip your finger into the honey and trace the symbol of Montu, an ancient Egyptian falcon-headed warrior, on your forehead.

As you apply the honey, recite the following words:

"Montu, imbue me with your warrior's strength,
Let your power flow through me, to any length.
As I go forth in battles fought,
With your divine guidance, I shall not be caught."

Close your eyes and take a moment to bask in Montu's presence. Feel his energy enveloping you, filling you with courage and resilience.

When you are ready, extinguish the candle, but keep the carnelian or red jasper with you as a reminder of Montu's strength.

Notes:
This spell is intended to invoke Montu's strength and courage in times when you need to face challenges or engage in battle, whether literal or metaphorical. The carnelian or red jasper represents the fiery energy and warrior spirit of Montu. The honey symbolizes the sweetness of victory and the blessings Montu bestows upon his devotees. This spell can be performed as a personal ritual or as part of a larger ceremony dedicated to Montu.

b) Sekhmet: Sekhmet, a lioness goddess associated with healing and destruction, inspired prayers and hymns that sought her intercession in matters of health and protection. Chants dedicated to Sekhmet aimed to tap into her healing powers, addressing ailments and diseases. Spells associated with Sekhmet often involved the creation of amulets and the recitation of incantations to ward off illness and ensure overall well-being.

Prayer to Sekhmet, the Fierce Lioness

Mighty Sekhmet, lioness of power,
I stand before you in awe and reverence.
Goddess of fierce protection and healing,
I seek your presence and guidance.

O Sekhmet, hear my prayer,
As I call upon your divine essence.

Grant me strength and courage,
To face life's challenges with resilience.

You, who are the flame of transformation,
Bring forth your fiery energy within me.
Burn away my fears and doubts,
And ignite the spark of divine purpose.

Sekhmet, the lioness of the sun,
I honor your ferocity and wisdom.
Guide me through the shadows of life,
And illuminate my path with your radiant light.

In your embrace, I find solace and healing,
For you are the bringer of restoration.
Wrap your healing wings around me,
And heal the wounds that burden my soul.

Sekhmet, I offer my devotion and gratitude,
For your fierce protection and love.
May I embody your strength and compassion,
As I walk this journey, guided from above.

I praise you, Sekhmet, with heartfelt devotion,
For you are the embodiment of divine power.
Grant me the courage to face each day,
And let your blessings shower.

Hail Sekhmet, the mighty lioness,
The fierce protector and healer divine.
I offer my prayers and love to you,
For your presence in my life, I am grateful and aligned.

Notes:
This prayer is intended to establish a connection with Sekhmet, the Egyptian goddess of power, protection, and healing. It seeks her guidance, strength, and healing energy. The prayer acknowledges Sekhmet's fierce nature and asks for her transformative power to help overcome challenges and bring about healing and restoration. It expresses gratitude and devotion to Sekhmet and recognizes her as a source of divine inspiration and guidance. This prayer can be recited as a personal devotion or as part of a ritual dedicated to Sekhmet.

Hymn to Sekhmet, the Fierce Lioness

O Sekhmet, the lioness of fire and might,
With the blaze of the sun, your power ignites.
Your roar shakes the earth, the heavens tremble,
As your presence fills the world, we assemble.

Goddess of strength and ferocious protection,
You guard the sacred realms with unwavering dedication.
Your fiery eyes pierce through the darkness of night,
Guiding us with your radiant and fierce light.

Sekhmet, the mistress of war and battles,
Your valor and courage are unmatched by mortals.
In your presence, enemies cower and retreat,
For they know your wrath is swift and complete.

With the fury of a thousand lions, you charge,
Defending the innocent, their fears you discharge.
Your claws and teeth tear through the illusion,
Dispelling chaos with your divine resolution.

O Sekhmet, the healer with compassionate heart,
You bring solace and relief, a soothing balm to impart.
With your gentle touch, wounds are made whole,
Restoring the body and rejuvenating the soul.

We sing your praises, O fierce lioness divine,
Your strength and power, an eternal sign.
In awe, we stand before your majestic might,
Bathing in your energy, radiant and bright.

Hail Sekhmet, the mistress of fire and passion,
Your presence invokes both awe and compassion.
As we honor you, our voices raised high,
May your blessings and guidance ever nigh.

Notes:
This hymn is dedicated to Sekhmet, the ancient Egyptian goddess associated with war, protection, and healing. It praises her fierce and powerful nature, likening her to a lioness with her strength and courage. The hymn acknowledges her role as a protector and warrior, capable of vanquishing enemies and bringing order to chaos. It also recognizes Sekhmet as a compassionate healer, emphasizing her ability to bring comfort and

restoration. The hymn conveys a sense of awe and reverence for Sekhmet's divine attributes and invokes her presence through the power of words and song.

Chant to Sekhmet, the Fierce Lioness:

O Sekhmet, mighty lioness of flame,
With your power, we invoke your name.
Fierce protector, guardian of the land,
We call upon you, lend us your hand.

Roar, Sekhmet, roar with all your might,
Banish darkness, bring forth your light.
With fiery passion, let your presence be known,
As we stand before your sacred throne.

Sekhmet, fierce one, with eyes ablaze,
Guide us through life's tumultuous maze.
Grant us strength, courage, and fortitude,
In your fiery embrace, we find gratitude.

Lioness of war, battles you command,
Defending justice, with sword in hand.
With your roar, scatter our enemies far,
Protect us, Sekhmet, beneath your star.

Mighty Sekhmet, healer of hearts,
Release your blessings, your divine arts.
Restore our bodies, our spirits, our souls,
As your healing energy gracefully rolls.

We chant your name, Sekhmet, with devotion,
In this sacred space, we feel your emotion.
Your power and presence, fierce and divine,
Fill our hearts, as we align.

Hail Sekhmet, the fierce lioness we praise,
In your strength and glory, our voices raise.
Guide us, protect us, as we journey on,
With your fierce love, may we be strong.

Notes:

This chant is dedicated to Sekhmet, the fierce lioness goddess of ancient Egypt. The chant invokes her power and calls upon her protection and guidance. It acknowledges her role as a warrior and defender, as well as a healer of hearts and bodies. The repetition and rhythm of the chant create a meditative and immersive experience, allowing the participants to connect with Sekhmet's energy and draw upon her strength. The chant expresses reverence and gratitude towards Sekhmet and seeks her presence and blessings.

Spell to Sekhmet, the Fierce Lioness:

Ingredients:

Red candle
An image or statue of Sekhmet
Offering of fresh flowers or herbs
A small piece of paper
Red ink or pen
A small bowl of water
Instructions:

Set up your sacred space by arranging the image or statue of Sekhmet at the center. Place the red candle in front of her.

Light the candle and invoke Sekhmet's presence by saying:

"Oh Sekhmet, mighty lioness divine,
I call upon your power, make it mine.
Protectress fierce, with flames aglow,
I seek your guidance, here below."

Take a moment to meditate and connect with the energy of Sekhmet. Visualize her fierce and powerful presence surrounding you.

Take the piece of paper and write down the specific issue or challenge you seek assistance with. Be clear and concise in your wording.

Hold the paper in your hands and focus on the issue, infusing it with your intention and the energy of Sekhmet.

Place the paper into the small bowl of water, allowing it to soak.

As the paper dissolves, visualize the problem or challenge being dissolved and transformed by Sekhmet's fiery energy.

Take the offering of fresh flowers or herbs and place them before the image or statue of Sekhmet as an offering of gratitude and respect.

Recite the following incantation:

"Sekhmet, fierce and wise,
I seek your aid, hear my cries.
With your strength and power divine,
Let (state your desired outcome) be mine.
From darkness, bring forth the light,
Banish obstacles with all your might."

Repeat the incantation three times, allowing your words to carry the intention deep into the universe.

Sit in quiet meditation for a few moments, envisioning your desired outcome manifesting with the assistance of Sekhmet.

Thank Sekhmet for her presence and assistance in your spellwork. Extinguish the candle and leave the offering of flowers or herbs in place for a period of time as a token of gratitude.

Note:
This spell is designed to seek Sekhmet's aid in resolving a specific issue or challenge in your life. It harnesses her fierce and protective energy to bring forth transformation and banish obstacles. The use of the red candle symbolizes her fiery nature, while the offering of flowers or herbs represents gratitude and respect. The dissolution of the paper in water symbolizes the transformation and resolution of the issue at hand. As with any spellwork, it is important to perform this spell with a clear and focused intention, as well as a deep respect for Sekhmet's power and energy.

c) Ptah: As the creator god of Memphis, Ptah held a significant role in the Middle Kingdom. Prayers and hymns to Ptah emphasized his creative and artistic attributes, highlighting his association with craftsmanship and architecture. Chants dedicated to Ptah sought his guidance and inspiration in matters of artistic expression and innovation. Spells related to Ptah focused on enhancing one's creative abilities and harnessing the divine energy of creation.

Prayer to Ptah:

Oh Ptah, Creator and Master Craftsman,

Divine Architect of the Universe,
I come before you with reverence and awe,
To offer my prayers and seek your guidance.

Ptah, the Great Artisan, who shaped the world,
Your hands have crafted all that is,
From the heavens above to the earth below,
You hold the power of creation within your grasp.

In your presence, I feel the spark of inspiration,
The call to bring forth beauty and innovation,
Grant me the wisdom to manifest my visions,
To build a world that reflects your divine essence.

Ptah, the Foundation of Life, I turn to you,
In times of uncertainty and doubt,
Guide me on the path of stability and balance,
That I may find strength in the face of challenges.

As I navigate the complexities of existence,
May your steady hand be my compass,
Leading me towards truth, purpose, and fulfillment,
As I strive to honor you in all that I create.

Ptah, the Silent Listener, hear my prayers,
In the depths of my heart, where words fall short,
Accept my devotion, my gratitude, and my aspirations,
And let your divine presence fill my being.

I offer this prayer with utmost reverence,
In awe of your eternal wisdom and creative power,
May my connection to you deepen and grow,
As I walk hand in hand with Ptah, the Divine Artisan.

So be it.

Note:
This prayer is intended to express reverence and seek guidance from Ptah, the ancient Egyptian deity associated with creation and craftsmanship. It acknowledges Ptah's role as the creator of the world and the source of inspiration and innovation. The prayer also seeks stability and balance in life, recognizing Ptah as a foundation of strength. It emphasizes the individual's desire to honor Ptah through their own creative endeavors. The prayer is a personal expression of devotion and gratitude, acknowledging Ptah's presence and seeking a deepening connection with the deity.

Hymn to Ptah:

Oh Ptah, the Divine Artisan, we sing to thee,
The Master Craftsman, whose hands shaped all we see.
From the depths of the primordial waters you emerged,
With creative power, the universe you purged.

Ptah, the Great God of Memphis, mighty and wise,
You brought order to chaos, unveiling the skies.
Your thoughts shaped the heavens and the earth,
As your divine words gave creation its birth.

In your sacred city, your presence does reside,
Amidst the craftsmen and artisans, side by side.
Your temple stands as a testament to your might,
Where your devotees gather, bathed in your light.

Ptah, the Lord of Ma'at, embodiment of truth,
With your discerning eye, you guide our youth.
You teach us to build with precision and care,
To create beauty in all that we share.

Oh Ptah, we honor your divine essence,
The Source of inspiration and creative brilliance.
With reverence, we praise your eternal name,
And seek your blessings in our creative flame.

Grant us the wisdom to shape our world with love,
To nurture the arts and the crafts from above.
May our hands be guided by your skilled touch,
As we manifest beauty and inspire much.

Hail Ptah, the Divine Artisan sublime,
In your presence, we find solace and rhyme.
With grateful hearts, we sing this hymn to thee,
Ptah, the Great Creator, for all eternity.

Note:
This hymn is dedicated to Ptah, the ancient Egyptian deity associated with creation, craftsmanship, and wisdom. It acknowledges Ptah as the divine artisan who shaped the universe and brought order to chaos. The hymn praises Ptah's role as the Lord of Ma'at, highlighting his connection to truth and guidance. It emphasizes the importance of creativity and craftsmanship, acknowledging Ptah as the source of inspiration

for artists and artisans. The hymn also expresses gratitude and reverence towards Ptah, recognizing his eternal presence and the blessings he bestows upon his devotees.

Chant to Ptah:

(Chant rhythmically, repeating each line multiple times)

Ptah, the Divine Craftsman, we invoke your might,
With reverence and awe, we seek your guiding light.
Ptah, the Lord of Creation, we call upon your name,
Bring forth your wisdom, let our spirits rise aflame.

Ptah, the Master Builder, your hands shape the divine,
Infuse us with your skill, let our creations shine.
Ptah, the Source of Inspiration, ignite our creative fire,
Guide our hands and minds, lift us ever higher.

Ptah, the Patron of Artisans, bless our every endeavor,
As we craft with love and skill, may our talents never waver.
Ptah, the Guardian of Crafts, protect us in our work,
Shield us from obstacles, let success and mastery lurk.

Ptah, the Keeper of Secrets, unlock our inner vision,
Grant us insight and clarity, in our creative mission.
Ptah, the Architect of Worlds, weave beauty with every stroke,
Manifest our dreams into reality, as we invoke.

Ptah, the Nurturer of Ideas, fuel our creative flame,
Ignite our passion and purpose, let inspiration be our claim.
Ptah, the Guide of Souls, lead us on the path of truth,
May our creations reflect your divine wisdom and youth.

Ptah, the Silent Listener, hear our heartfelt plea,
As we chant your sacred name, let our spirits be set free.
Ptah, the Eternal Presence, we honor and adore,
With this chant, we seek your blessings forevermore.

(Note: This chant is intended to be rhythmic and repetitive, allowing participants to enter a meditative and focused state. The chant praises Ptah as the Divine Craftsman, acknowledging his role in creation, inspiration, and craftsmanship. It seeks Ptah's guidance, protection, and blessings for creative endeavors. The chant emphasizes the importance of skill, creativity, and the connection between the physical and spiritual realms. Participants can chant this in a group or individually, aligning their intentions and energies with the divine essence of Ptah.)

Spell to Invoke the Power of Ptah:

(Perform this spell with focused intention and reverence for Ptah)

Materials:

A small clay or stone figurine representing Ptah
A white candle
An offering of bread or grains
A quiet and sacred space
Procedure:

Begin by cleansing and purifying the space. Light the white candle and set it before you as a representation of Ptah's divine presence.

Hold the figurine of Ptah in your hands and close your eyes. Take several deep breaths to center yourself and attune your energy with the divine essence of Ptah.

Visualize a radiant golden light surrounding you, filling you with a sense of peace and connection to the divine. Feel the presence of Ptah with you, guiding and empowering your intentions.

Gently place the figurine of Ptah on the altar or sacred space before the lit candle.

Speak the following incantation with sincerity and conviction:

"Ptah, Master Craftsman, hear my plea,
I call upon your power, so mighty and free.
With reverence and respect, I seek your aid,
Grant me your guidance, my intentions be swayed."

State your specific intention clearly and concisely. It could be related to creativity, craftsmanship, manifestation, or any area where you seek Ptah's assistance.

Take a moment to reflect on your intention and visualize it coming to fruition. See the desired outcome clearly in your mind's eye.

Offer the bread or grains as a symbol of gratitude and appreciation to Ptah for his assistance. Place it beside the figurine as an offering.

Sit in silence for a few moments, basking in the presence of Ptah and allowing his energy to infuse your being.

Close the ritual by expressing your gratitude to Ptah:

"Ptah, I thank you for your divine grace,
For hearing my call and blessing this sacred space.
May your wisdom and craftsmanship guide my way,
As I walk the path of creation, day by day."

Extinguish the candle, expressing gratitude to Ptah once again.

Note: It is important to remember that spells are not guaranteed to produce immediate or specific results. They are a means of focusing intention, connecting with divine energies, and aligning oneself with the desired outcome. Patience, trust, and an open heart are key in working with the power of Ptah or any deity.

Roles, Attributes, and Significance of Additional Deities:

Each additional deity of the Middle Kingdom held unique roles, attributes, and significance within the religious landscape. Montu, with his warlike nature, symbolized the strength and protection required in times of conflict. Sekhmet, known for her healing abilities, provided solace and restoration to the sick and afflicted. Ptah, the creative force, inspired craftsmen and artists, fostering innovation and artistic expression.

These deities were seen as intermediaries between the mortal realm and the divine, with their devotees seeking their favor, guidance, and protection. They played crucial roles in the religious and cultural life of the Middle Kingdom, providing a framework for understanding the world and addressing the needs of the community.

Diversity and Regional Variations in Worship and Devotional Practices:

The worship and devotional practices associated with the additional deities of the Middle Kingdom exhibited diversity and regional variations. Different regions of Egypt developed unique traditions and rituals surrounding these deities, reflecting the local cultures and beliefs. For instance, the worship of Montu flourished in Thebes and the surrounding areas, while Sekhmet was particularly venerated in Memphis and the wider Delta region.

These regional variations manifested in the construction of dedicated temples, the organization of festivals, and the performance of rituals specific to each deity. By studying the archaeological remains, textual evidence, and artistic representations from different regions, we can gain insights into the multifaceted nature of worship during the Middle Kingdom.

Examples:

Analyze a hymn dedicated to Montu, highlighting the warrior attributes and protective nature of the god. Discuss the significance of invoking Montu in times of conflict and the role of the hymn in fostering a sense of courage and strength among worshippers.

Explore the prayers and spells associated with Sekhmet, focusing on her healing aspects and the rituals performed to seek her intercession. Discuss the role of the priest or priestess in facilitating the healing process and the symbolism behind the spells and amulets used in Sekhmet's worship.

Investigate the role of Ptah as a creator deity and the influence of his worship on artistic expression and craftsmanship during the Middle Kingdom. Examine the hymns and chants dedicated to Ptah, emphasizing the importance of his guidance in the creative endeavors of ancient Egyptians.

Problems and Exercises:

Compare and contrast the attributes and roles of Montu, Sekhmet, and Ptah, highlighting the unique aspects of each deity and their significance within the religious landscape of the Middle Kingdom.

Discuss the reasons behind the regional variations in worship and devotional practices for the additional deities of the Middle Kingdom. Analyze the geographical, cultural, and historical factors that influenced the spread and popularity of these deities in specific regions.

Reflect on the impact of these additional deities on the social and cultural fabric of the Middle Kingdom society. Discuss how their worship and associated rituals influenced the daily lives and worldview of the ancient Egyptians.

Analyze a specific chant, prayer, or spell dedicated to one of the additional deities, examining the linguistic and poetic devices employed and their effectiveness in invoking the divine presence.

Comparative Analysis and Cross-Cultural Influences

Religious practices across different ancient cultures often share common elements and themes, reflecting the universal human need for spiritual expressions. In this chapter, we will conduct a comparative analysis of prayers, hymns, chants, and spells in ancient Egyptian religion and explore their similarities and differences with those found in other ancient cultures such as Witchcraft, Divination, Herbalism, Shamanism, and Ecospirituality.

Through a thorough examination, we can identify shared religious motifs and understand the underlying human experiences and aspirations that transcend time and geographical boundaries. We will compare the structure, language, and intentions of these spiritual expressions, highlighting their distinct cultural contexts and the unique ways in which they address the needs and beliefs of their respective communities.

Analysis of Potential Cross-Cultural Influences and Shared Religious Motifs

Cultural interactions and exchanges have played a significant role in shaping religious practices throughout history. In this section, we will delve into the potential cross-cultural influences between ancient Egyptian religion and other ancient cultures. By examining historical records, artifacts, and texts, we can identify instances of cultural diffusion and syncretism, where ideas and beliefs were borrowed, adapted, or shared between different societies.

We will explore how concepts and practices from Witchcraft, Divination, Herbalism, Shamanism, and Ecospirituality may have influenced or intersected with ancient Egyptian religious traditions. By identifying shared religious motifs, such as the worship of nature, the veneration of ancestors, or the pursuit of healing and spiritual guidance, we can gain a deeper understanding of the interconnectedness of human spiritual experiences.

Discussion of the Universal Human Need for Spiritual Expressions and the Ways in Which Ancient Egyptian Religious Practices Contribute to Our Understanding of Human Spirituality

Ancient Egyptian religious practices provide valuable insights into the universal human need for spiritual expressions and the ways in which different cultures have sought to understand and connect with the divine. In this section, we will discuss how the study of ancient Egyptian religion contributes to our understanding of human spirituality as a whole.

By examining the prayers, hymns, chants, and spells of ancient Egypt, we can identify common threads that run through various religious traditions. These include the desire for protection, healing, guidance, and a sense of connection to the divine. Through the analysis of ancient Egyptian religious practices, we can gain insights into the ways in which individuals and communities have sought to navigate the mysteries of existence, find solace in times of uncertainty, and express their deepest hopes and fears.

Critical Evaluation and Interpretation

When examining prayers, hymns, chants, and spells from ancient religious traditions such as Witchcraft, Divination, Herbalism, Shamanism, and Ecospirituality, it is crucial to approach them with a deep understanding of their historical and cultural context. The meanings and significance of these religious texts and practices can vary greatly depending on the time period, geographical location, and specific cultural beliefs of the people who practiced them.

By critically evaluating the historical and cultural context, we can avoid making assumptions or imposing modern interpretations on these ancient religious expressions. This includes considering the social, political, and religious climate of the time, as well as the specific roles and functions of individuals involved in the rituals or recitations of these texts.

Analysis of the Potential Purposes and Functions of Prayers, Hymns, Chants, and Spells

To fully appreciate the significance of prayers, hymns, chants, and spells, it is essential to analyze their potential purposes and functions within the religious practices of different cultures. These spiritual expressions often served various roles, including communication with deities or spirits, seeking divine intervention, expressing gratitude or reverence, invoking protection or blessings, or facilitating personal and collective transformation.

By examining the intended outcomes and intended audience of these religious texts and practices, we can gain insights into the motivations and desires of the practitioners. This analysis allows us to understand the underlying beliefs and worldview of the culture in question and provides a more nuanced interpretation of the texts themselves.

Evaluation of Differing Interpretations and Scholarly Debates Surrounding the Meanings and Significance of Prayers, Hymns, Chants, and Spells

The interpretation of prayers, hymns, chants, and spells is subject to scholarly debates and differing perspectives. In this section, we will critically evaluate these differing interpretations, considering various scholarly viewpoints and the evidence on which they are based.

By engaging with contrasting interpretations, we encourage students to think critically and analyze the strengths and weaknesses of different arguments. This includes considering alternative explanations, examining primary and secondary sources, and assessing the validity and reliability of the evidence presented.

Examples, Problems, and Exercises:

Analyze a specific hymn from ancient Egypt, such as the Hymn to the Sun God, and evaluate different interpretations regarding its meaning and significance. Discuss the evidence provided by scholars to support their interpretations and encourage students to form their own informed opinions.

Examine the potential purposes and functions of divinatory practices in ancient cultures, such as the reading of oracle bones in ancient China or the use of tarot cards in modern Witchcraft. Discuss the differing interpretations of these practices and evaluate the arguments for and against their effectiveness.

Engage in a class discussion on the role of symbolism in ancient religious texts and practices. Explore how symbols are interpreted and their potential meanings in different cultural contexts. Encourage students to share examples of symbols in prayers, hymns, chants, and spells from various traditions.

Assign a research project where students critically evaluate a controversial interpretation of a specific spell or chant from ancient Egypt. Instruct them to gather evidence from primary and secondary sources, present arguments for and against the interpretation, and propose their own reasoned conclusion.

By incorporating these examples, problems, and exercises, students can actively engage in critical thinking and discussion, deepening their understanding of the subject matter and honing their analytical skills. This chapter encourages students to approach religious texts and practices with a critical mindset, allowing them to navigate scholarly debates and form well-informed interpretations.

Exercises and Discussion Points

In this section, students will engage in an in-depth analysis and interpretation of selected prayers, hymns, chants, and spells from various religious traditions, including Witchcraft, Divination, Herbalism, Shamanism, Ecospirituality, and Magic in Ancient Egypt. Students will be provided with a range of texts and guided through a step-by-step analysis process.

Exercise 1: Select a prayer, hymn, chant, or spell from a specific tradition and critically analyze its structure, language, and themes. Consider the intended audience, purpose, and cultural context. Discuss the significance of the symbols, metaphors, and ritual elements used in the text. Evaluate how the text reflects the core beliefs and practices of the tradition. Present your analysis and interpretations in a written essay.

Comparison of Themes, Symbolism, and Language Used in Different Devotional Texts

This exercise encourages students to compare the themes, symbolism, and language used in prayers, hymns, chants, and spells across different religious traditions. By identifying commonalities and differences, students will gain insights into the universality and diversity of religious expressions.

Exercise 2: Select two or more devotional texts from different religious traditions (e.g., a hymn from Ancient Egypt and a chant from Shamanism) and compare their themes, symbolism, and language. Analyze how each text represents the relationship between humans and the divine, the use of metaphors and symbols, and the impact of cultural context on their form and content. Discuss the significance of these similarities and differences in shaping the religious experiences of their respective communities.

Discussion of the Role of Prayers, Hymns, Chants, and Spells in Personal and Communal Religious Experiences

This exercise explores the role of prayers, hymns, chants, and spells in personal and communal religious experiences. Students will consider the transformative and communal aspects of these spiritual practices, as well as their impact on individual and collective well-being.

Exercise 3: In a group discussion, share personal reflections on the role of prayers, hymns, chants, and spells in your own spiritual journey or the experiences of others. Discuss how these practices contribute to a sense of connection, meaning, and purpose. Reflect on the potential psychological, emotional, and social benefits of engaging in these devotional activities. Consider how these practices can foster a sense of community and collective identity.

Examples, Problems, and Exercises:

Develop a comparative analysis chart that compares the structure, symbolism, and purpose of prayers, hymns, chants, and spells from different religious traditions. Use this chart as a tool for identifying patterns, themes, and shared elements.

Analyze a specific spell from Ancient Egypt and consider its efficacy and practical application. Discuss the ethical implications of using magic in religious practices and the potential effects on individuals and society.

Engage in a class debate on the role of divination in contemporary society. Discuss differing opinions on the reliability and validity of divinatory practices and their impact on personal decision-making and well-being.

Assign a research project where students investigate the historical development and cross-cultural influences of specific prayers, hymns, chants, or spells. Instruct them to present their findings in a comprehensive report, incorporating primary and secondary sources and engaging with scholarly debates.

Conclusion

In this concluding section, we will recapitulate the key findings and insights gained from our exploration of prayers, hymns, chants, and spells in ancient Egyptian religious practices. We will discuss the significance of these texts in understanding the complex belief system of the ancient Egyptians and their profound impact on the lives of individuals and the broader society. Finally, we will highlight the implications for further research and study in the field of ancient Egyptian religion.

Recapitulation of Key Findings and Insights

Throughout this study, we have delved into the rich and diverse world of prayers, hymns, chants, and spells, uncovering their profound significance in ancient Egyptian religious beliefs and practices. We have examined the various forms and functions of these devotional texts, analyzing their structure, symbolism, and language. Through our exploration, we have discovered that these texts were not mere literary expressions, but powerful tools for communication, transformation, and connection with the divine.

We have observed that prayers served as personal petitions and expressions of devotion, enabling individuals to establish a direct relationship with the gods and seek their favor and protection. Hymns, on the other hand, celebrated the greatness and attributes of the deities, expressing the awe and reverence felt by the ancient Egyptians. Chants, with their rhythmic and repetitive nature, created a profound sense of energy and connection in ritual settings, allowing participants to commune with the divine. Spells, rooted in magical practices, harnessed supernatural forces for protection, healing, and other practical purposes.

Significance of Prayers, Hymns, Chants, and Spells in Understanding Ancient Egyptian Religious Beliefs and Practices

The study of prayers, hymns, chants, and spells provides invaluable insights into the religious beliefs and practices of ancient Egyptians. These texts serve as windows into their worldview, shedding light on their understanding of the divine, their relationship with the gods, and their search for meaning and guidance in life. Through the analysis of these texts, we gain a deeper appreciation for the complexity and nuance of ancient Egyptian religious thought.

Prayers, hymns, chants, and spells reveal the ancient Egyptians' deep sense of spiritual connection and their belief in the active involvement of the gods in the affairs of humanity. They highlight the importance of ritual practices in fostering this connection and facilitating divine intervention. These texts also reflect the ancient Egyptians' understanding of the interconnectedness of the natural and supernatural realms, emphasizing the cyclical nature of existence and the role of magic and divine intervention in maintaining cosmic order.

Furthermore, the study of these texts illuminates the role of religion in various aspects of ancient Egyptian society. Prayers, hymns, chants, and spells were not confined to the temples and priesthood but were embraced by individuals from all walks of life. They played a central role in personal and communal religious experiences, shaping beliefs, fostering social cohesion, and providing a framework for navigating the challenges of daily life.

Implications for Further Research and Study in the Field of Ancient Egyptian Religion

The exploration of prayers, hymns, chants, and spells in ancient Egyptian religion opens up a multitude of avenues for further research and study. Scholars can delve deeper into the analysis and interpretation of specific texts, examining their regional variations, chronological developments, and social contexts. Comparative studies with other ancient cultures, such as Witchcraft, Divination, Herbalism, Shamanism, and Ecospirituality, offer fruitful opportunities for understanding cross-cultural influences and shared religious motifs.

Additionally, the examination of prayers, hymns, chants, and spells can contribute to broader discussions on human spirituality and the universal need for spiritual expressions. The study of these ancient religious practices can provide insights into the ways in which individuals and communities throughout history have sought to connect with the divine, find solace in times of adversity, and cultivate a sense of meaning and purpose.

In conclusion, our exploration of prayers, hymns, chants, and spells in ancient Egyptian religion has revealed their profound significance in understanding the religious beliefs and practices of this ancient civilization. These texts serve as a testament to the human quest for transcendence and the intricate ways in which societies have sought to engage with the divine. As we continue to delve deeper into the complexities of ancient Egyptian religion, we pave the way for further research and exploration, enriching our understanding of human spirituality across cultures and throughout history.

The Coffin Texts

The Coffin Texts from the Middle Kingdom are a collection of ancient Egyptian funerary texts inscribed on coffins and sarcophagi. These texts, which primarily date from the late Old Kingdom to the early New Kingdom (circa 2134-1660 BCE), provide insights into the beliefs, rituals, and cosmology surrounding death and the afterlife in ancient Egypt. While the Pyramid Texts, earlier funerary texts, were exclusively reserved for royalty and were inscribed inside pyramid chambers, the Coffin Texts were accessible to a wider range of individuals and were inscribed on the wooden coffins and burial equipment of high-ranking officials and members of the elite.

The Coffin Texts consist of a collection of spells, incantations, and religious texts intended to assist the deceased in their journey through the afterlife. These texts were believed to empower the deceased and equip them with the necessary knowledge and magical assistance to overcome challenges and reach a favorable outcome in the realm of the dead. The Coffin Texts cover a wide range of topics, including protection against malevolent forces, guidance in navigating the underworld, and the provision of food, water, and offerings.

Some of the notable Coffin Texts include:

Spell 80: This spell, known as the "Opening of the Mouth," was intended to restore the deceased's faculties and ensure their ability to participate in the rituals and offerings made to them. It symbolically "opened" the mouth of the deceased so they could speak and partake in the sustenance provided by their loved ones.

Spell 80, commonly referred to as the "Opening of the Mouth," was a crucial ritual in ancient Egyptian funerary practices. It held significant importance in the religious beliefs and customs surrounding death and the afterlife. This spell was specifically designed to restore the faculties of the deceased and ensure their ability to fully participate in the rituals and offerings made to them by their loved ones.

The primary objective of the "Opening of the Mouth" spell was to symbolically "open" the mouth of the deceased. In ancient Egyptian belief, the mouth was considered the conduit through which the individual could speak, breathe, and consume nourishment. By restoring the mouth of the deceased, this ritual ensured their ability to partake in the sustenance provided to them in the afterlife.

The ritual involved a series of ceremonial actions and recitations performed by a priest, known as the "Sem Priest." The Sem Priest would approach the mummy of the deceased, often accompanied by other priests and family members, in the mortuary or burial chamber. Holding specific ritual implements, such as an adze and a metal tool known as a "pesesh-kef," the priest would focus on the mouth of the deceased, invoking the power of deities associated with life and breath.

The Sem Priest would recite specific prayers and incantations, beseeching the gods to restore the faculties of the deceased. The adze and the pesesh-kef would be used to touch and symbolically "open" the mouth of the deceased, enabling them to speak and partake in the offerings and sustenance provided by their loved ones. This symbolic act ensured that the deceased could communicate and receive the necessary nourishment for their journey in the afterlife.

The "Opening of the Mouth" spell held great significance as it enabled the deceased to actively participate in the ongoing rituals and offerings made by their family and loved ones. It allowed the deceased to maintain a connection with the living world and receive the sustenance and support needed for their eternal journey.

This spell exemplifies the ancient Egyptian belief in the importance of maintaining the spiritual and physical well-being of the deceased in the afterlife. It highlights the role of rituals and incantations in facilitating the transition of the deceased into the realm of the dead and ensuring their continued existence and participation in the spiritual realm. The "Opening of the Mouth" spell provides valuable insights into the religious practices and customs surrounding death and the afterlife in ancient Egypt.

Spell 148: This spell, commonly referred to as the "Weighing of the Heart," depicts the judgment scene in the afterlife, where the heart of the deceased is weighed against the feather of Ma'at, the goddess of truth and justice. If the heart was found to be pure and free from sin, the deceased would be granted eternal life. If the heart was heavy with wrongdoing, it would be devoured by a monstrous creature, resulting in eternal annihilation.

Spell 148, commonly referred to as the "Weighing of the Heart," is one of the most iconic and significant spells found in the ancient Egyptian funerary texts, specifically the Book of the Dead. This spell vividly portrays the judgment scene in the afterlife, where the heart of the deceased is subjected to a meticulous examination to determine their fate in eternity.

According to ancient Egyptian belief, the heart was considered the seat of consciousness, morality, and the essence of a person's character. In the afterlife, the heart of the deceased would be weighed against the feather of Ma'at, the goddess of truth, justice, and cosmic order. This symbolic weighing process was overseen by the divine tribunal, including the gods Osiris, Thoth, and Anubis.

The judgment scene would unfold in the Hall of Ma'at, a sacred space where the divine tribunal gathered. The heart of the deceased, represented as a small vessel or an amulet, would be placed on one side of a scale, while the feather of Ma'at, representing truth and righteousness, would be placed on the other side. The scale itself was believed to be balanced and perfectly calibrated, symbolizing the harmony and balance of the cosmic order.

As the weighing took place, the deceased would recite prayers and declarations of innocence, affirming their righteousness and adherence to Ma'at's principles during their earthly life. The god Thoth, often depicted as a scribe with the head of an ibis, would meticulously record the results of the weighing, ensuring fairness and accuracy in the judgment.

If the heart of the deceased was found to be pure and free from sin, perfectly balanced with the feather of Ma'at, it would signify that the individual had led a virtuous and righteous life. In this case, the deceased would be granted eternal life and admitted into the blessed realm of the afterlife, joining the company of the gods and ancestors.

However, if the heart was found to be heavy with wrongdoing, if it failed to balance with the feather of Ma'at, it would indicate moral and ethical transgressions committed during the earthly life. In this scenario, the heart would be devoured by a monstrous creature known as Ammit, who possessed the head of a crocodile, the front body of a lion, and the hindquarters of a hippopotamus. The devouring of the heart resulted in eternal annihilation, effectively ceasing the existence of the individual.

The "Weighing of the Heart" spell encapsulates the ancient Egyptian belief in the divine judgment and the importance of leading a morally upright life. It serves as a reminder that one's actions and intentions are ultimately weighed against the principles of truth, justice, and cosmic order. This spell reflects the Egyptians' aspiration for an eternal existence in harmony with the gods and the cosmic forces that governed their world.

The "Weighing of the Heart" spell continues to capture the imagination and curiosity of scholars and enthusiasts alike, offering profound insights into ancient Egyptian beliefs about morality, judgment, and the afterlife.

Spell 335: This spell, known as the "Negative Confession," was a declaration of innocence and a list of forty-two sins that the deceased vowed not to have committed during their lifetime. By reciting this confession, the deceased sought to assert their purity and righteousness before the gods.

Spell 335, commonly referred to as the "Negative Confession," holds great significance within the ancient Egyptian funerary texts, particularly in the Book of the Dead. It is a powerful declaration of innocence, in which the deceased proclaims their moral uprightness and vows not to have committed a list of forty-two sins during their lifetime. By reciting this confession, the deceased seeks to assert their purity and righteousness before the divine tribunal.

The "Negative Confession" is a solemn and sacred recitation that takes place during the judgment scene in the Hall of Ma'at, where the heart of the deceased is weighed against the feather of Ma'at, the goddess of truth and justice. As part of this process, the deceased recites the confession as a testament to their virtuous conduct and adherence to the principles of Ma'at.

The recitation begins with the declarative statement, "I have not committed sin," followed by a series of negative assertions, each expressing the negation of a specific transgression. The forty-two sins listed in the confession cover a broad range of moral and ethical violations, encompassing actions, thoughts, and intentions that would disrupt the harmony and order of the cosmic balance.

Some of the sins mentioned in the "Negative Confession" include:

"I have not committed theft."
"I have not told lies."
"I have not cheated or deceived."
"I have not harmed others unjustly."
"I have not committed acts of violence."
"I have not polluted the waters or land."
"I have not acted with arrogance."
"I have not neglected my duties and obligations."

These statements serve as a testament to the deceased's moral character and their commitment to upholding the principles of Ma'at. By expressly denying involvement in these transgressions, the deceased seeks to establish their innocence and purity before the divine tribunal.

The "Negative Confession" holds great significance as it reflects the ancient Egyptian belief in personal responsibility, accountability, and the pursuit of righteousness. By reciting this confession, the deceased presents themselves as virtuous and deserving of a favorable judgment in the afterlife. It is an opportunity for the individual to assert their moral integrity and demonstrate their alignment with the divine order.

The inclusion of the "Negative Confession" in the funerary texts highlights the importance of ethical conduct and the concept of judgment in ancient Egyptian religious beliefs. It underscores the belief that a righteous life, free from moral transgressions, was essential for achieving eternal bliss and joining the realm of the gods in the afterlife.

The "Negative Confession" continues to captivate scholars and researchers, offering valuable insights into the moral framework and religious beliefs of ancient

Egyptians. Its presence in the funerary texts exemplifies the significance of personal integrity and the pursuit of righteousness in the quest for a favorable judgment and eternal salvation.

Spell 410: This spell, called the "Book of Two Ways," describes the various paths and routes the deceased could take in the afterlife. It provides instructions and guidance on how to navigate the dangerous realms and reach the ultimate destination of eternal life.

Spell 410, the "Book of Two Ways," is a fascinating funerary spell found in ancient Egyptian texts, particularly in the coffins and tombs of the Middle Kingdom. This spell serves as a guidebook for the deceased, providing detailed instructions and insights into the multiple paths and routes they could take in the afterlife. It offers invaluable guidance on how to navigate the perilous realms of the underworld and successfully reach the ultimate destination of eternal life.

The "Book of Two Ways" presents the deceased with a choice between two primary paths or ways: the land-based path and the water-based path. Each path represents a distinct route to the realm of the gods, where the deceased would find eternal bliss and union with the divine. The spell outlines the various stages, landmarks, and challenges that the deceased would encounter on their chosen journey.

In the land-based path, the deceased would traverse a series of landscapes, encountering gates, caverns, fields, and divine beings along the way. The spell describes specific actions and rituals that the deceased must perform at each stage, ensuring safe passage and protection from malevolent forces. The detailed instructions provide a sense of order and guidance, helping the deceased navigate the complex underworld terrain.

The water-based path, on the other hand, involves a journey through a mystical river or waterway. The spell highlights the importance of boats and navigation in this path, emphasizing the significance of understanding the currents, tides, and hazards of the water. It provides instructions on the proper rituals and offerings to be made to river deities and guardians, ensuring a smooth passage and avoiding any dangers that may lie in wait.

The "Book of Two Ways" goes beyond mere directional guidance. It also includes protective spells, invocations, and magical formulas that the deceased could use to ward off evil spirits, gain favor from benevolent deities, and overcome obstacles along their chosen path. The inclusion of these spells underscores the ancient Egyptians' belief in the power of ritual actions and magical utterances to influence the afterlife journey.

By offering detailed descriptions of the paths and providing instructions on how to navigate them, the "Book of Two Ways" offers a comprehensive framework for the deceased to embark on their journey to the divine realms. It serves as a practical and spiritual guide, ensuring that the deceased are equipped with the knowledge and tools necessary to navigate the complex and treacherous landscapes of the afterlife.

The "Book of Two Ways" not only reflects the ancient Egyptians' beliefs and expectations regarding the afterlife but also offers insights into their worldview, understanding of cosmology, and the importance they placed on proper preparation for the journey to eternity. It exemplifies the meticulousness and depth of their funerary beliefs and rituals, emphasizing the need for guidance and protection in the perilous realms beyond death.

In conclusion, Spell 410, the "Book of Two Ways," is a significant funerary text that provides the deceased with essential instructions and guidance on their journey through the afterlife. By presenting the choice between land and water paths, describing the various stages and challenges, and offering protective spells and rituals, this spell served as a valuable guidebook for the deceased, ensuring their successful navigation of the realms beyond and the attainment of eternal life in the divine presence.

These are just a few examples of the Coffin Texts from the Middle Kingdom. Each spell and text within this collection serves a specific purpose in facilitating the journey of the deceased and ensuring their successful transition into the afterlife. The Coffin Texts provide valuable insights into the ancient Egyptian concept of the afterlife and the rituals and beliefs surrounding death, offering a glimpse into the religious worldview and spiritual practices of this ancient civilization.

Part 5: New Kingdom (c. 1550 BCE - 1069 BCE)

The New Kingdom period of ancient Egypt, spanning from approximately 1550 BCE to 1069 BCE, represents a significant era of political, social, and religious transformation. It was a time of great expansion, military conquests, and cultural achievements, marking a renaissance in ancient Egyptian history. In this chapter, we will delve into the religious beliefs and practices of the New Kingdom, examining the key deities, rituals, and magical traditions that shaped the spiritual landscape of this period.

Historical Context:

The New Kingdom era emerged following a period of political instability known as the Second Intermediate Period. The early New Kingdom saw the rise of the powerful Eighteenth Dynasty, with pharaohs such as Ahmose I, Hatshepsut, and Tutankhamun making significant contributions to the religious and cultural developments of the time. The period also witnessed the establishment of an empire, with Egypt expanding its influence and engaging in diplomatic relations with neighboring civilizations.

Religious Continuity and Evolution:

The religious beliefs and practices of the New Kingdom built upon the foundations laid in previous eras, while also introducing new elements and cults. The pantheon of gods remained diverse and extensive, with Amun-Ra, the sun god, rising to prominence and becoming the state deity. The role of the pharaoh as the intermediary between the divine and mortal realms continued to be emphasized, and temples grew in importance as centers of religious and economic activity.

Cults and Deities:

The New Kingdom witnessed the flourishing of various cults and the veneration of specific deities. Amun-Ra, associated with kingship, power, and fertility, enjoyed great popularity and was often syncretized with other deities. The worship of Osiris, god of the afterlife, and his consort Isis gained prominence, emphasizing the importance of personal salvation and the belief in an afterlife.

Other deities, such as Hathor, Horus, and Set, also played significant roles in religious practices during this period.

Rituals and Temples:

The New Kingdom saw the construction of grand temples dedicated to the worship of the gods. These temples served as centers of religious and economic activity, where rituals, processions, and offerings took place. The rituals performed within these temples aimed to maintain cosmic order, ensure divine favor, and sustain the prosperity of the kingdom. Festivals and religious processions were held regularly, allowing the public to participate in the religious life of the community.

Magic and Ritual Practices:

Magic and ritual practices continued to be an integral part of religious life in the New Kingdom. The use of amulets, spells, and protective rituals was prevalent, serving various purposes such as healing, protection against malevolent forces, and enhancing personal well-being. The practice of divination, the interpretation of omens, dreams, and oracles, also played a significant role in seeking guidance and insight from the divine realm.

Interactions with Other Cultures:

The New Kingdom era witnessed increased contact and cultural exchange with other civilizations, including the Near East and the Mediterranean world. These interactions influenced religious beliefs and practices, resulting in syncretism and the adoption of foreign deities and rituals. The Amarna period, during the reign of Akhenaten, stands out as a unique phase characterized by the introduction of a monotheistic cult centered on the worship of the Aten, the sun-disk.

In this chapter, we will explore the religious landscape of the New Kingdom in detail, examining the diverse cults, rituals, and magical traditions that defined this period. Through the analysis of textual sources, archaeological evidence, and comparative studies, we will gain a comprehensive understanding of the religious beliefs and practices that shaped the lives of ancient Egyptians during this transformative era.

Exploring the Rituals, Beliefs, and Syncretism of Ancient Egyptian Religion

Pharaoh	Queen	Children	Notable Information	Years of Reign
Ahmose I	Nefertari		Founder of 18th Dynasty	1550-1525 BCE
Hatshepsut		Neferure	One of the few female pharaohs	1479-1458 BCE
Thutmose III			Known as the "Napoleon of Egypt"	1479-1425 BCE
Amenhotep III	Tiye	Akhenaten (son)	Known for opulent reign and building projects	1386-1353 BCE
Akhenaten	Nefertiti	Tutankhamun (possible son)	Introduced worship of Aten, monotheism	1353-1336 BCE
Tutankhamun			Boy pharaoh, tomb discovery	1332-1323 BCE
Ramesses II	Nefertari	Merneptah (son)	Prolific builder, Battle of Kadesh	1279-1213 BCE
Merneptah			Known for military campaigns, Merneptah Stele inscription	1213-1203 BCE

Please note that this graph only includes selected individuals and their immediate family members, and there were other pharaohs and queens who ruled during this period as well. The notable information provided here is a brief summary, and each pharaoh and queen had a more extensive reign with various accomplishments and historical significance.

Chapter 13: The Peak of Ancient Egyptian Civilization and Religious Practices

The New Kingdom period marks a significant era in ancient Egyptian history, characterized by political stability, territorial expansion, and cultural flourishing. It followed the Second Intermediate Period and was succeeded by the Third Intermediate Period. The New Kingdom witnessed remarkable achievements in various aspects of Egyptian society, including art, architecture, literature, and religious practices.

Significance of the New Kingdom as the peak of ancient Egyptian civilization

The New Kingdom is widely regarded as the peak of ancient Egyptian civilization due to its military conquests, diplomatic relations, economic prosperity, and cultural achievements. It was a time of great power and influence for Egypt, as it expanded its empire, established trade networks, and solidified its position as a dominant force in the ancient Near East. The New Kingdom pharaohs, such as Thutmose III, Amenhotep III, and Ramses II, left a lasting legacy through their military campaigns, monumental construction projects, and patronage of the arts.

Importance of religious practices during this period

Religion played a central role in ancient Egyptian society, and this was particularly true during the New Kingdom period. The Egyptians believed that their pharaohs were divine rulers, closely connected to the gods and responsible for maintaining ma'at, the cosmic order. Therefore, religious practices were integral to both the state and individual life. Temples were centers of religious activities, and offerings, rituals, and festivals were conducted to appease the gods, seek their blessings, and ensure the prosperity and stability of Egypt. The New Kingdom witnessed the proliferation of new cults and the prominence of certain deities, such as Amun, who became a supreme deity, and Aten, during the brief period of Atenism under Akhenaten.

Moreover, religious beliefs and practices were intertwined with other aspects of Egyptian culture, including art, architecture, and funerary customs. The construction of monumental temples and tombs, the production of elaborate religious artwork, and the development of funerary texts and rituals all reflected the deep-rooted religious convictions of the New Kingdom Egyptians. The religious sphere provided a framework for understanding the world, expressing devotion, and seeking divine guidance and protection.

Understanding the religious practices of the New Kingdom offers invaluable insights into the beliefs, values, and societal structures of ancient Egypt. It sheds light on the complex relationship between the state, the individual, and the divine, and provides a glimpse into the worldview and spiritual aspirations of the ancient Egyptians.

By examining the New Kingdom period and its religious practices in depth, we can gain a deeper appreciation for the peak of ancient Egyptian civilization and the profound impact of religious beliefs on the lives of its people. This chapter will delve into the historical, cultural, and religious dimensions of the New Kingdom, exploring its significance, achievements, and the rich tapestry of religious practices that defined this remarkable era.

Historical Context

The New Kingdom period witnessed significant political developments and major events that shaped the course of ancient Egyptian history. It began with the expulsion of the Hyksos, a foreign group that had ruled Egypt during the Second Intermediate Period. Ahmose I, the founder of the Eighteenth Dynasty, initiated a successful military campaign to drive out the Hyksos and reunify Egypt. This marked the beginning of the New Kingdom, a period characterized by strong central authority and ambitious expansionist policies.

Under the rule of powerful pharaohs, such as Thutmose III, Amenhotep III, and Ramses II, the New Kingdom experienced unprecedented military conquests and territorial expansion. Thutmose III conducted numerous successful military campaigns, extending Egyptian influence deep into Syria and the Levant. Amenhotep III focused on diplomatic relations, forming alliances through marriage alliances and establishing trade networks that brought wealth and exotic goods to Egypt. Ramses II, often referred to as Ramses the Great, engaged in military conflicts with various neighboring powers and was known for his extensive building projects, including the grand temples at Abu Simbel and Karnak.

The New Kingdom was not without challenges and periods of turmoil. The reign of Amenhotep IV, later known as Akhenaten, witnessed a radical religious reform that emphasized the worship of a single deity, the Aten. This brief period, known as Atenism, saw the neglect of traditional gods and the establishment of a new capital city, Amarna. However, after Akhenaten's death, the traditional religious practices were restored, and the capital returned to Thebes.

Role of pharaohs and their divine status in religious practices

The pharaohs held a central role in ancient Egyptian religious practices, particularly during the New Kingdom. They were considered the intermediaries between the gods and the mortal realm, serving as the link between the divine and human spheres. The pharaohs were believed to be the sons of gods, and their divine status endowed them with immense power and authority. They were not only political leaders but also the high priests and spiritual guides of the nation.

As divine rulers, the pharaohs were responsible for upholding ma'at, the cosmic order that governed the universe. They conducted rituals, made offerings, and performed sacred duties to ensure the harmony between the human realm and the gods. The temples served as the locus of religious activities, and the pharaohs played a vital role in their construction, endowment, and maintenance.

The divine status of the pharaohs was evident in various religious ceremonies and rituals. They performed the Sed festival, a jubilee celebration that symbolized their rejuvenation and eternal kingship. They also conducted the Heb Sed ritual, which reinforced their power and authority. Through these rituals, the pharaohs sought to establish their divine legitimacy and ensure the continuity of their rule.

The divine status of the pharaohs had profound implications for the religious practices of the New Kingdom. It shaped the beliefs, rituals, and social structures of ancient Egyptian society. The pharaohs' association with the gods and their role as divine rulers created a close relationship between the state and religion, with the pharaohs acting as the chief patrons and protectors of the gods and their cults.

Understanding the role of pharaohs and their divine status in religious practices is crucial for comprehending the religious and political dynamics of the New Kingdom period. It highlights the interplay between political power and religious authority and provides insights into the complex relationship between the divine and mortal realms in ancient Egyptian civilization.

Religious Beliefs and Concepts

Despite the political and social changes of the New Kingdom, traditional religious beliefs and deities remained integral to Egyptian society. The worship of Osiris, Isis, Horus, Hathor, and other ancient gods continued, and their cults remained prominent. These deities represented various aspects of nature, fertility, protection, and divine power. Their worship was deeply ingrained in the religious and cultural fabric of Egypt, and temples dedicated to these gods were centers of religious activity.

Role of the cult of Amun and the expansion of his worship

One notable development during the New Kingdom was the rise of the cult of Amun. Originally a local deity of Thebes, Amun gradually rose in prominence and became associated with the sun god, Ra, to form Amun-Ra. The priesthood of Amun gained significant power and influence, both religiously and politically, as Amun-Ra was increasingly regarded as the supreme deity of the pantheon. The expansion of Amun's worship led to the construction of grand temples, such as the Karnak Temple Complex, which became the largest religious complex in ancient Egypt.

Influence of Atenism and the reign of Akhenaten

Atenism, introduced by Akhenaten, represents a unique religious experiment during the New Kingdom. Akhenaten promoted the worship of a single deity, the Aten, the solar disc, and attempted to establish a monotheistic belief system. The Aten was believed to be the sole creator and sustainer of the universe. As a result, the traditional gods were neglected, and their cults were suppressed.

Akhenaten's religious reforms had a profound impact on the artistic and religious landscape of the time. Artistic representations shifted from the idealized and stylized forms of traditional Egyptian art to a more naturalistic style that emphasized the Aten's life-giving rays. Temples were built in honor of the Aten in the new capital city of Amarna, and the pharaoh himself became the sole intermediary between the Aten and the people.

Importance of ma'at (truth, balance, and justice) in religious and moral framework

Ma'at, the concept of truth, balance, and justice, played a central role in Egyptian religious and moral thought. It represented the cosmic order that governed the universe and provided the ethical foundation for human behavior. The pharaohs were responsible for upholding ma'at and ensuring its preservation in society. The rituals, prayers, and offerings performed by the pharaohs and the general population aimed to maintain ma'at and restore any imbalances that might occur.

Ma'at influenced various aspects of Egyptian life, including law, morality, social relationships, and even the afterlife. The weighing of the heart in the judgment scene depicted in Spell 148 of the Book of the Dead exemplifies the belief that one's adherence to ma'at determined their fate in the afterlife. Living in accordance with ma'at was considered virtuous and ensured a favorable judgment in the afterlife.

Interactions between Egyptian religion and other cultural and religious influences

The New Kingdom period witnessed interactions between Egyptian religion and other cultural and religious influences, particularly through trade and diplomatic relations. Egypt had contact with various Near Eastern and Mediterranean civilizations, such as the Hittites, Mitanni, and Mycenaeans. These interactions led to the exchange of ideas, beliefs, and religious practices.

For example, the worship of the goddess Hathor, known for her nurturing and protective attributes, bore similarities to the worship of the Near Eastern goddess Ishtar. Likewise, the identification of Amun with the sun god Ra reflected the syncretism of Egyptian and solar deities. These exchanges highlight the dynamic nature of ancient religions and the potential influences and adaptations that occurred during the New Kingdom.

Understanding the continuation of traditional beliefs, the role of cults like Amun, the influence of Atenism, the significance of ma'at, and the interactions with other cultures provides a comprehensive understanding of the religious beliefs and concepts during the peak of ancient Egyptian civilization in the New Kingdom. These religious beliefs shaped the lives of the ancient Egyptians, influencing their daily practices, rituals, and worldview.

Rituals and Ceremonies

Temple rituals were an essential part of religious practices in ancient Egypt during the New Kingdom. Temples served as sacred spaces where the gods were believed to reside, and the rituals conducted within them aimed to maintain the gods' favor and ensure the well-being of the community. These rituals included daily offerings of food, drink, incense, and precious objects to the statues or representations of the gods.

The priests and priestesses played a crucial role in performing these rituals and overseeing the offerings. They acted as intermediaries between the divine and human realms, ensuring the correct performance of the rituals and the proper presentation of offerings. The rituals often involved purification, prayers, hymns, and recitations of sacred texts, creating a solemn and spiritually charged atmosphere.

Role of priests and priestesses in religious ceremonies

The priests and priestesses held significant influence and authority within the religious hierarchy of ancient Egypt. They were responsible for maintaining the temples, performing the rituals, and interpreting the divine will. The priests underwent rigorous training and were knowledgeable in religious texts, rituals, and the proper conduct of ceremonies. They were often organized into different ranks and specialized roles based on their duties and responsibilities.

The priestesses also played an important role in religious ceremonies. They served in various capacities, including as temple musicians, singers, oracles, and participants in rituals dedicated to specific goddesses. The priestesses of Hathor, for example, were renowned for their musical performances and dance rituals, which were believed to bring joy and fertility to the land.

Festivals and celebrations dedicated to various deities

Festivals and celebrations held throughout the year were an integral part of religious life in ancient Egypt. These festivals were dedicated to specific deities and commemorated important events, such as the gods' birthdays, their sacred unions, or their victorious battles against chaos and disorder.

One of the most renowned festivals was the Opet Festival, which took place in Thebes and honored the Theban triad of Amun, Mut, and Khonsu. The festival involved elaborate processions, rituals, and offerings, where the statues of the deities were carried from their temples to the Karnak Temple Complex. The procession symbolized the gods' renewal and rejuvenation and allowed the people to connect with their divine protectors.

The importance of mortuary rituals and practices

Mortuary rituals and practices held great significance in ancient Egyptian religion, reflecting the belief in the afterlife and the journey of the soul. The preservation and proper burial of the deceased were essential to ensure a successful transition to the afterlife.

The rituals included the Opening of the Mouth ceremony, where the deceased's faculties were symbolically restored to enable them to partake in the offerings and rituals performed by their loved ones. The Book of the Dead, a collection of spells and prayers, was also crucial in guiding the deceased through the dangers and challenges of the afterlife.

Tombs, such as the Valley of the Kings, were carefully constructed and decorated to provide a comfortable and eternal resting place for the deceased. These tombs included various chambers and funerary equipment, such as coffins, canopic jars, and shabti figurines, to assist the deceased in their journey.

The mortuary rituals and practices reflected the Egyptians' belief in the continuity of life after death and the importance of preserving the physical and spiritual aspects of the deceased. They also provided a sense of continuity and connection between the living and the dead, ensuring that the deceased remained a part of the community even in the afterlife.

Temples and Cult Centers

The New Kingdom witnessed the construction and expansion of numerous temples and cult centers throughout Egypt. These sacred sites served as focal points for religious activities and played a vital role in the spiritual and social life of the people. Some of the most significant temples and cult centers during this period include the Karnak Temple Complex in Thebes, the Luxor Temple, the Temple of Amun at Soleb, and the Temple of Seti I at Abydos.

Architectural features and symbolism in temple design

The architecture of the temples in the New Kingdom displayed a remarkable grandeur and intricate design, reflecting the Egyptians' devotion to their gods and their understanding of cosmology. The temples were characterized by massive pylons, expansive courtyards, hypostyle halls with towering columns, and sanctuaries housing the cult statues of the deities.

Symbolism played a crucial role in temple design. For instance, the pylons represented the gateway between the mortal world and the divine realm, while the hypostyle halls symbolized the primordial marsh from which creation emerged. The alignment of temple axes with celestial bodies, such as the rising sun or specific stars, emphasized the connection between the gods, the pharaoh, and the cosmic order.

Role of temples as economic and administrative centers

Temples in ancient Egypt, particularly during the New Kingdom, served not only as places of worship but also as centers of economic and administrative activities. They owned extensive land holdings, agricultural estates, and livestock, which provided them with considerable wealth and resources. The temples played a crucial role in the redistribution of goods, as they received offerings from the population and distributed them among the temple staff, the priests, and the wider community.

Temples also served as administrative centers, where scribes and officials managed the temple's estates, recorded transactions, and maintained detailed accounts. They oversaw the collection of taxes, the organization of labor for construction projects, and the administration of justice within the temple jurisdiction.

Furthermore, temples acted as educational institutions, training scribes and craftsmen, and contributing to the cultural and intellectual development of society. They were repositories of knowledge, housing libraries and archives that preserved important texts and records.

The economic and administrative functions of the temples demonstrated their significant influence and power in ancient Egyptian society, as they not only played a central role in religious practices but also had a profound impact on the economy, governance, and education of the time.

Royal Funerary Practices

The New Kingdom witnessed a significant evolution in royal burial practices compared to earlier periods. The pharaohs of this era sought to create elaborate and monumental tombs that would serve as eternal resting places for their bodies and ensure their successful transition into the afterlife. These developments reflected the pharaoh's increasing desire to assert their divine status and secure their eternal existence.

Tombs and burial complexes of the pharaohs

The tombs and burial complexes of the pharaohs in the New Kingdom were architectural marvels, designed to embody the pharaoh's grandeur and provide them with a secure and opulent final resting place. The Valley of the Kings, located on the west bank of Thebes, became the principal royal burial site during this period. Pharaohs such as Tutankhamun, Ramesses II, and Seti I constructed elaborate tombs within the valley, adorned with intricate wall paintings, texts, and burial goods.

These tombs consisted of a series of chambers and corridors, often hidden and protected to deter tomb robbers. The burial chambers held the sarcophagus containing the pharaoh's mummified body, surrounded by valuable funerary objects and offerings. The walls of the tombs were adorned with scenes from the Book of the Dead, depicting religious and mythological motifs, and providing guidance and protection for the deceased in the afterlife.

Significance of the Book of the Dead and funerary texts

The Book of the Dead and other funerary texts played a vital role in royal funerary practices during the New Kingdom. These texts, written on papyrus or inscribed on tomb walls, contained spells, prayers, and rituals that aimed to guide and assist the deceased pharaoh in the afterlife. They provided instructions on how to navigate the perilous journey through the underworld, overcome obstacles, and attain eternal life.

The Book of the Dead, in particular, was a compilation of spells and incantations intended to ensure the pharaoh's successful judgment and resurrection. It contained spells for the protection of the deceased's body, the awakening of their senses, and the restoration of their bodily functions in the afterlife. The inclusion of these texts in the royal tombs emphasized the pharaoh's divine nature and their aspiration for immortality.

Importance of the afterlife beliefs and rituals

The afterlife held immense significance in ancient Egyptian religious beliefs, particularly during the New Kingdom. The pharaohs believed that they would continue their existence in a realm beyond death, where they would be reunited with their ancestors and the gods. Achieving a successful afterlife required proper burial, preservation of the body, and the performance of rituals and offerings.

Rituals and offerings played a crucial role in the pharaoh's journey to the afterlife. Priests conducted ceremonies in the temples and tombs, offering food, drink, and other goods to sustain the deceased pharaoh's ka (spirit) in the afterlife. These rituals aimed to nourish and satisfy the spiritual needs of the pharaoh, ensuring their continued existence and divine favor.

The funerary practices and beliefs of the New Kingdom pharaohs reflected their aspirations for immortality and their desire to perpetuate their royal lineages. The grandeur and complexity of their tombs, the inclusion of funerary texts, and the performance of rituals demonstrated their commitment to securing a prosperous afterlife and maintaining their divine status even in death.

Interaction with the Divine

The New Kingdom witnessed a rich tradition of prayers, hymns, chants, and spells as integral components of religious practices. These sacred texts were recited or sung during rituals and ceremonies as a means of communicating with the gods and expressing devotion. Prayers and hymns praised the deities, sought their favor, and acknowledged their powers. Chants and spells were recited to invoke divine assistance, ward off evil, and ensure the success of religious rituals.

Devotional practices and personal piety

The New Kingdom period saw a heightened emphasis on personal piety and individual devotion to the gods. While the pharaohs played a central role in religious practices, ordinary individuals also engaged in acts of worship and sought a personal connection with the divine. Devotional practices included making offerings at household shrines, participating in temple rituals, and reciting prayers or hymns in private settings. These acts of piety aimed to establish a personal relationship with the gods, seek their guidance, and gain their protection.

Oracles, divination, and communication with the gods

Ancient Egyptians believed in the power of oracles and divination as methods of communication with the gods. Oracles, often located in temples, were sacred spaces where individuals could seek divine guidance and receive messages from the gods. Priests, acting as intermediaries, would interpret signs and symbols to provide insight into future events or divine will. Divination practices such as interpreting dreams, reading animal entrails, or using oracular instruments were employed to gain knowledge of the gods' intentions and seek their advice.

Use of magic and amulets in religious and everyday life

Magic held a significant place in ancient Egyptian religious practices, both in the New Kingdom and throughout their history. Magic was believed to harness supernatural forces and manipulate them to achieve desired outcomes. Amulets, small objects imbued with magical properties, were commonly worn or carried by individuals for protection and good fortune. They were often inscribed with spells or images of protective deities. Magical spells and rituals were also used for healing, fertility, and other practical purposes. While magic was closely tied to religious beliefs, it also permeated everyday life and was employed by individuals from various social strata.

The interaction between humans and the divine in the New Kingdom was multifaceted, encompassing prayers, hymns, chants, and spells as means of communication, devotional practices that reflected personal piety, divination methods to seek divine guidance, and the use of magic and amulets for spiritual and practical purposes. These practices provided individuals with a sense of connection to the gods, guidance in navigating life's challenges, and a means of expressing their devotion and seeking divine favor.

Legacy and Influence

The religious practices of the New Kingdom period had a profound and lasting impact on subsequent eras of ancient Egyptian civilization. Many of the rituals, beliefs, and deities that emerged during this time continued to be central to Egyptian religious life in the later periods. The cult of Amun, for example, which gained prominence during the New Kingdom, remained a dominant religious force well into the Late and Greco-Roman periods. The emphasis on personal piety, the use of prayers and hymns, and the importance of mortuary rituals were also perpetuated and evolved in subsequent Egyptian religious practices.

Influence on neighboring civilizations and cultural exchanges

The New Kingdom period witnessed significant cultural exchanges and interactions with neighboring civilizations, such as the Nubians, Assyrians, and Hittites. These interactions had a reciprocal influence on religious beliefs and practices. The Amarna Period, particularly the religious revolution initiated by Akhenaten, had an impact on the monotheistic traditions that emerged in the Near East. The Atenist concept of a single deity represented a departure from the polytheistic norms of the time and influenced religious thought in neighboring cultures.

Continuity and transformation of religious beliefs and practices in later periods

Despite the political and cultural changes that occurred after the New Kingdom, elements of the religious beliefs and practices from this period persisted and underwent transformations in subsequent eras. The concepts of ma'at, truth, balance, and justice, continued to be revered as fundamental principles in Egyptian religious and moral frameworks. The Book of the Dead and funerary texts remained influential in guiding the deceased's journey into the afterlife, even as new texts and rituals emerged in later periods.

The religious practices of the New Kingdom left a lasting legacy on Egyptian civilization. They shaped the religious landscape of ancient Egypt in the subsequent eras, influenced neighboring civilizations through cultural exchanges, and provided a foundation for the continuity and transformation of religious beliefs and practices in later periods. The impact of the New Kingdom's religious practices can still be observed in the religious traditions of ancient Egypt and their enduring influence on subsequent cultures.

Conclusion

Throughout this chapter, we have explored the religious practices of the New Kingdom period in ancient Egypt, spanning from approximately 1550 BCE to 1069 BCE. We examined the political context, the role of pharaohs in religious practices, the continuation of traditional beliefs and deities, the cult of Amun and Atenism, the concept of ma'at, and the interactions between Egyptian religion and other cultural influences. We also delved into rituals, temple worship, royal funerary practices, and the various ways in which the ancient Egyptians interacted with the divine.

Significance of the New Kingdom religious practices in understanding ancient Egyptian spirituality

The religious practices of the New Kingdom period hold great significance in our understanding of ancient Egyptian spirituality. They provide valuable insights into the beliefs, rituals, and concepts that shaped the religious worldview of the ancient Egyptians. Through the study of prayers, hymns, chants, spells, and temple ceremonies, we gain a deeper understanding of how the ancient Egyptians sought to connect with the divine, maintain cosmic order, and ensure their well-being in this world and the afterlife.

Relevance and impact of these practices on modern perceptions and interpretations of ancient Egypt

The religious practices of the New Kingdom continue to captivate the imagination and curiosity of scholars, historians, and enthusiasts of ancient Egypt. They form a foundational part of our modern perceptions and interpretations of ancient Egyptian civilization. The rituals, beliefs, and cultural exchanges of this period have shaped the way we view and study ancient Egyptian religion, offering valuable insights into the complexities of their spiritual beliefs and the interplay between religious, political, and social aspects of their society.

Studying the religious practices of the New Kingdom period provides a window into the rich and diverse spiritual landscape of ancient Egypt. It allows us to appreciate the intricacies of their religious rituals, the significance of their deities, and the profound influence of their beliefs on various aspects of their lives. By exploring and understanding these practices, we gain a deeper appreciation for the ancient Egyptian civilization and its enduring legacy.

Chapter 14: Temples, Festivals, and Tools used c. 1550 BCE - 1069 BCE

In Chapter 14, we will delve into the fascinating world of temples, festivals, and tools used in ancient Egyptian religious practices during the period of c. 1550 BCE - 1069 BCE. This era, known as the New Kingdom, marked the peak of ancient Egyptian civilization and witnessed significant developments in religious beliefs and rituals. By exploring the temples, festivals, and the tools employed in religious ceremonies, we gain valuable insights into the profound spiritual beliefs and practices of this remarkable civilization.

Significance of Temples and Festivals in Ancient Egyptian Religious Practices

Temples held immense significance in ancient Egyptian religious practices. They were considered sacred spaces where the gods resided and where humans could communicate with the divine. These magnificent structures were not merely places of worship but served as centers of spiritual, economic, and administrative activities. The New Kingdom saw the construction of grand temples that reflected the wealth, power, and religious devotion of the pharaohs and the Egyptian society as a whole.

Festivals were integral to ancient Egyptian religious life. They were vibrant and communal celebrations dedicated to various deities, providing opportunities for the people to express their devotion and seek blessings from the gods. These festivals were marked by elaborate rituals, processions, music, dance, and feasting, creating a sense of unity and reinforcing the social fabric of the community. Festivals were also occasions for the renewal of cosmic order and the reaffirmation of the divine kingship.

Importance of Understanding the Tools and Materials Used in Religious Rituals

To fully comprehend ancient Egyptian religious practices, it is crucial to examine the tools and materials employed in their rituals. The ancient Egyptians meticulously crafted and utilized a wide array of objects and implements, each with its own symbolic significance and purpose. These tools played essential roles in facilitating communication with the divine, performing rituals, and conveying religious messages.

Studying the tools used in religious rituals offers us valuable insights into the ancient Egyptians' profound spiritual beliefs and their relationship with the gods. From statues and altars to offering tables and vessels, these objects were crafted with precision and imbued with symbolism. Understanding the materials used, such as precious metals, stones, and organic substances, helps us appreciate the cultural, economic, and spiritual contexts within which these rituals took place.

By comprehending the tools and materials used in religious rituals, we gain a deeper understanding of the complex interplay between the physical and the spiritual in ancient Egyptian religious practices. Moreover, it allows us to appreciate the craftsmanship and artistry of the ancient Egyptians, showcasing their dedication to creating objects that bridged the gap between the mortal and the divine.

In the subsequent sections of this chapter, we will explore the temples and their functions, delve into the significance of festivals, and examine the tools and materials utilized in ancient Egyptian religious rituals. Through a comprehensive analysis of these topics, we aim to unravel the intricacies of religious life in ancient Egypt and shed light on the profound spiritual beliefs and practices that shaped this extraordinary civilization.

Temples and Their Functions

During the New Kingdom period, temple architecture reached its pinnacle in terms of grandeur and sophistication. The temples were meticulously designed and constructed to reflect the power, wealth, and religious devotion of the pharaohs and the Egyptian society. These architectural marvels were not only places of worship but also served as symbolic representations of the cosmos, bridging the mortal world with the divine realm.

The temples were typically constructed using durable materials such as limestone or sandstone, showcasing intricate carvings, colorful reliefs, and hieroglyphic inscriptions. The layout of the temples followed a standardized plan, consisting of various sections and chambers that played distinct roles in religious rituals and practices.

Role of Temples as Centers of Religious, Economic, and Administrative Activities

Temples held a central position in ancient Egyptian society, serving as multifunctional centers for religious, economic, and administrative activities. They were not only places of worship but also economic powerhouses and administrative hubs. The temples owned vast lands, livestock, and estates, and received offerings and tributes from the populace. These resources were utilized to support the temple staff, fund religious rituals, and contribute to the overall prosperity of the community.

Furthermore, the temples served as important administrative centers, with priests and temple officials playing key roles in governing and managing the affairs of the local communities. The temples were involved in matters such as tax collection, land distribution, legal proceedings, and the storage of records and documents.

Functions of Different Areas within the Temple Complex

The temple complex comprised various areas, each serving specific functions in religious rituals and practices. The sanctuary, located at the heart of the temple, was the most sacred area and housed the cult statue of the deity. It was accessible only to the high priests and pharaohs, symbolizing the intimate connection between the divine and the ruling elite.

The offering halls and courtyards were important spaces where priests and devotees performed rituals and made offerings to the gods. These areas were adorned with elaborate reliefs depicting scenes of offerings, processions, and interactions between the divine and the mortal. The courtyards also served as gathering places for the community during festivals and other religious events.

Examples of Notable Temples and Their Significance

Several temples from the New Kingdom period stand as remarkable examples of ancient Egyptian architectural and religious achievements. One such temple is the Temple of Karnak in Thebes, dedicated to the god Amun-Ra. This vast complex underwent continuous construction and expansion, spanning several centuries. It showcases the evolving architectural styles and religious practices of the New Kingdom, with its monumental pylons, obelisks, colossal statues, and hypostyle halls.

Another notable temple is the Mortuary Temple of Hatshepsut at Deir el-Bahari. This temple, dedicated to the female pharaoh Hatshepsut, is a striking example of innovative architectural design. It features a terraced structure, statues, and reliefs depicting the divine birth and accomplishments of Hatshepsut.

The Temple of Luxor, dedicated to the gods Amun-Ra, Mut, and Khonsu, is yet another remarkable example. It is known for its stunning avenue of sphinxes, colossal statues, and beautifully decorated hypostyle halls.

The significance of these temples lies not only in their architectural splendor but also in their role as religious and cultural centers. They served as focal points of worship, contributed to the prosperity of the community, and reflected the ancient Egyptians' deep-seated spiritual beliefs and practices.

In the subsequent sections of this chapter, we will delve deeper into the architectural features, symbolism, and specific functions of temples, exploring how these monumental structures played a crucial role in ancient Egyptian religious life and societal dynamics.

Festivals and Celebrations

Festivals held a significant place in the ancient Egyptian religious calendar, playing a crucial role in the expression of religious devotion and the reinforcement of communal bonds. These festive occasions were eagerly anticipated by the Egyptian populace and were celebrated with great enthusiasm and reverence. Festivals provided a platform for the community to come together, honor the deities, and partake in religious rituals and festivities.

Overview of Major Festivals and their Associated Deities

The ancient Egyptian religious calendar was rich with a multitude of festivals dedicated to various deities. Each deity had their own special festival, usually commemorating an important event or aspect of their mythological narrative. Some of the major festivals during the New Kingdom period include:

The Festival of Opet: This festival was celebrated in Thebes and was dedicated to the Theban triad of gods—Amun, Mut, and Khonsu. It involved processions, offerings, and rituals, with the statues of the deities being paraded from the Karnak Temple to the Luxor Temple.

The Feast of the Valley: This festival was held annually in the Theban Necropolis and was dedicated to the god Amun-Ra. It involved ceremonies to honor the deceased pharaohs, with priests and mourners visiting the tombs, making offerings, and reciting prayers.

Exploring the Rituals, Beliefs, and Syncretism of Ancient Egyptian Religion

The Festival of Bastet: Bastet, the feline goddess, was celebrated in her temple in the city of Bubastis. This festival was known for its vibrant processions, music, dance, and revelry. It attracted both Egyptians and foreigners, becoming a lively and joyous celebration.

Rituals, Processions, and Activities during Festivals

Festivals were marked by a variety of rituals, processions, and activities that added to the festive atmosphere and reinforced the connection between the mortal realm and the divine. These included:

Ritual Offerings: Festivals provided an opportunity for priests and devotees to make lavish offerings to the deities, including food, drink, incense, and floral arrangements. These offerings were believed to sustain and please the gods.

Processions: Processions were a central element of festivals, involving the ceremonial movement of the cult statues of the deities from their temples to various designated locations. The statues were carried on sacred barques and accompanied by priests, musicians, dancers, and devotees. The processions showcased the magnificence of the deities and allowed the community to express their devotion.

Sacred Drama: Some festivals incorporated dramatic reenactments of mythological events or symbolic rituals. These performances engaged the community and brought the myths and beliefs to life, deepening the religious experience.

Significance of Festivals in Community Cohesion and Religious Devotion

Festivals played a crucial role in fostering community cohesion and reinforcing religious devotion among the ancient Egyptians. These festive occasions provided opportunities for social interaction, allowing people from various social strata to come together in shared religious experiences. Festivals served as platforms for people to express their faith, gratitude, and reverence towards the gods, fostering a sense of unity and collective identity.

Moreover, festivals provided a break from the daily routine and offered moments of joy, celebration, and cultural expression. They allowed the community to temporarily set aside their concerns and immerse themselves in the sacred and festive atmosphere. Festivals also served as a means of education, as they provided opportunities for the transmission of religious knowledge, myths, and moral teachings.

In the subsequent sections of this chapter, we will delve deeper into the specific rituals, processions, and activities associated with major festivals, exploring their cultural significance, religious symbolism, and the ways in which they contributed to the religious and social fabric of ancient Egyptian society. Through our exploration, we will gain a comprehensive understanding of the role of festivals in ancient Egyptian religious practices, further enriching our appreciation of this remarkable civilization.

Tools and Implements in Rituals

Religious rituals in ancient Egypt were accompanied by a variety of tools and implements that were essential for their proper execution. These tools served both practical and symbolic purposes, facilitating the communication between the human and divine realms. Understanding the significance of these tools provides valuable insights into the religious practices of the time.

Ritual Objects, such as Statues, Altars, and Offering Tables

Statues: Statues played a prominent role in Egyptian religious rituals. They served as physical representations of deities and were believed to house the divine essence. These statues were carefully crafted and consecrated, and during rituals, they were invoked and honored as the embodiment of the gods.

Altars: Altars were platforms or raised structures specifically designated for making offerings to the gods. They were usually made of stone or wood and were considered sacred spaces. Altars provided a focal point for rituals, allowing the priests and devotees to present offerings and perform rituals in a designated area.

Offering Tables: Offering tables were another important component of religious rituals. These tables were used to display and arrange various offerings, such as food, drink, flowers, and incense. The act of placing offerings on the table was a symbolic gesture of providing sustenance and nourishment to the deities.

Symbols and Symbolism in Religious Artifacts

Ancient Egyptian religious artifacts were rich in symbolism, conveying deeper meanings and concepts associated with the religious beliefs and practices of the time. Some common symbols and their meanings include:

Ankh: The ankh, a symbol resembling a cross with a loop at the top, represented life and immortality. It was often depicted being held by gods and pharaohs, emphasizing their divine authority and eternal nature.

Djed Pillar: The djed pillar symbolized stability, endurance, and the resurrection of Osiris. It was associated with the renewal and perpetuation of life, particularly in the afterlife.

Scarab Beetle: The scarab beetle, often depicted in amulets and jewelry, symbolized rebirth and regeneration. It represented the sun and its daily journey across the sky, as well as the concept of eternal life and transformation.

Materials and Techniques Used in Crafting Religious Tools

Crafting religious tools in ancient Egypt required skilled artisans and the use of various materials and techniques. Some commonly used materials included:

Stone: Stone, particularly limestone, sandstone, and granite, was widely used for carving statues, altars, and offering tables. The durability and symbolism of stone made it a favored material for creating enduring religious artifacts.

Wood: Wood, such as cedar and acacia, was used to construct altars, offering tables, and ceremonial objects. Wood was also employed in the production of statues, although stone was more commonly used for this purpose.

Metals: Precious metals, including gold and silver, were used in the creation of statues, sacred vessels, and ornamental details. These metals symbolized the divine and were associated with the sun and its radiant power.

Craftsmen utilized various techniques such as carving, sculpting, inlaying, and gilding to enhance the aesthetic appeal and symbolic significance of the religious tools. Their craftsmanship, combined with the choice of materials, contributed to the sacredness and efficacy of the ritual objects.

By studying the tools and implements used in ancient Egyptian religious rituals, we gain a deeper understanding of the intricate and meaningful practices that were integral to their religious beliefs and observances. In the subsequent sections of this chapter, we will explore specific examples of these tools and their role in various rituals and ceremonies, providing a comprehensive perspective on the religious practices of the New Kingdom period.

Magical and Ritual Objects

In addition to the tools and implements used in religious rituals, ancient Egyptian religious practices also involved the use of magical and ritual objects. These objects were imbued with symbolic and supernatural qualities and were believed to have protective, healing, or transformative powers. They played a crucial role in connecting the human and divine realms and were employed to influence the outcome of events, ward off evil, and enhance spiritual well-being.

Overview of Amulets, Charms, and Talismans and Their Protective and Symbolic Functions

Amulets: Amulets were small objects typically worn or carried by individuals as personal protection. They were believed to possess magical properties and were associated with specific deities or concepts. Amulets ranged from simple symbols, such as the ankh or the Eye of Horus, to intricate figurines representing deities or sacred animals.

Charms: Charms were similar to amulets but often had a specific purpose, such as attracting good fortune, promoting fertility, or warding off specific dangers. Charms were usually inscribed with protective spells or symbols and were worn or carried by individuals seeking their desired outcome.

Talismans: Talismans were objects believed to have inherent magical powers and were used to bring about a desired effect or outcome. They were often inscribed with magical spells, symbols, or religious texts and were utilized in various rituals and ceremonies.

These magical objects served as tangible expressions of divine protection and guidance, offering a sense of security and empowerment to those who possessed or interacted with them.

Use of Magical Spells and Incantations in Religious Rituals

Magical spells and incantations were an integral part of ancient Egyptian religious rituals. These spells, known as heka, were recited or performed by priests, magicians, or individuals seeking to access the supernatural forces and influence events in their favor. The recitation of spells involved the use of specific words, sounds, gestures, and ritual actions to activate the desired magical effect.

Magical spells encompassed a wide range of purposes, including healing, protection, divination, love, fertility, and even control over natural elements. They were believed to harness the power of the gods and other divine forces, channeling their energy into the physical world.

Examples of Magical and Ritual Objects and Their Significance

Heart Scarab: The heart scarab was a type of amulet in the shape of a scarab beetle, often inscribed with spells from the Book of the Dead. It was placed on the chest of the deceased during the mummification process and served as a protective amulet, ensuring the heart's purity during the judgment in the afterlife.

Wand: The wand, known as the hekat stick, was a magical tool used in various rituals and spellcasting. It was often inscribed with sacred symbols and held by priests or magicians during rituals to channel divine energy and invoke the gods.

Magical Stelae: Magical stelae were stone slabs inscribed with spells and protective texts. They were placed in temples, tombs, or other sacred spaces to invoke divine protection and ward off evil. These stelae acted as focal points for ritual activities and were believed to have the power to influence the supernatural realm.

The significance of these magical and ritual objects lies in their ability to bridge the gap between the physical and spiritual worlds, offering individuals a means to connect with the divine, seek protection, and manipulate the forces of the universe in their favor.

Purification and Ritualistic Practices

Purification played a crucial role in ancient Egyptian religious rituals, as it was believed to cleanse individuals, objects, and sacred spaces from impurities and negative influences. The concept of purity was highly valued in Egyptian religious and moral frameworks, as it reflected the ideal state of being in alignment with ma'at, the cosmic order and harmony.

Rituals of Cleansing and Purification, such as Ablutions and Fumigation

Ablutions: Ablutions were ritualistic acts of cleansing through the use of water. These rituals involved washing hands, face, and body as a means of purifying oneself before engaging in religious activities. Ablutions were often performed at designated purification basins or sacred pools within temple complexes.

Fumigation: Fumigation rituals involved the burning of aromatic substances, such as incense or herbs, to create fragrant smoke. The smoke was believed to purify the atmosphere, ward off evil spirits, and create a conducive environment for divine presence. Fumigation was commonly practiced in temples and during religious ceremonies.

Role of Priests and Priestesses in Performing Purification Rituals

Priests and priestesses held a significant role in performing purification rituals. They were responsible for conducting the necessary rites and ceremonies to ensure the sanctity and purity of individuals, sacred objects, and temple spaces. The priests would undergo their own purification rituals before engaging in their sacred duties, emphasizing the importance of personal purity in facilitating a connection with the divine.

Symbolism and Spiritual Significance of Purification Practices

Purification rituals held deep symbolic and spiritual significance in ancient Egyptian religious beliefs. The act of cleansing represented the removal of physical and spiritual impurities, allowing individuals to approach the divine in a state of purity and reverence. It served as a means of preparing oneself for spiritual communion, ensuring that one's intentions and offerings were sincere and worthy.

Symbolically, purification rituals represented the restoration of ma'at, the cosmic balance, within oneself and the world. By purifying oneself, individuals sought to align their inner being with the divine order, seeking harmony and balance in their relationship with the gods and the natural forces around them.

The practice of purification also served as a means of transformation and renewal. Through the ritualistic acts of ablutions and fumigation, individuals sought to shed their previous state and emerge spiritually renewed, ready to engage in religious practices and receive the blessings and guidance of the gods.

In conclusion, purification held great importance in ancient Egyptian religious rituals, serving as a means of cleansing and preparing individuals for spiritual communion with the divine. Through ablutions, fumigation, and the guidance of priests and priestesses, the ancient Egyptians sought to uphold the ideals of purity and ma'at in their religious practices, seeking spiritual alignment and connection with the gods. The symbolism and spiritual significance of purification rituals emphasized the restoration of balance and harmony within oneself and the cosmic order. By engaging in these practices, individuals sought not only to purify themselves but also to create an environment conducive to divine presence and to establish a deeper connection with the spiritual realm.

Offerings and Sacrifices

Offerings held a profound meaning and purpose in ancient Egyptian religious practices. They were an integral part of establishing and maintaining a reciprocal relationship between humans and the gods. Offerings were seen as a means of sustenance and nourishment for the divine entities, demonstrating reverence, gratitude, and devotion to the gods.

Types of Offerings, Including Food, Beverages, and Incense

Food Offerings: Food offerings were among the most common types of offerings in ancient Egypt. These offerings included a variety of foods such as bread, fruits, vegetables, meat, and dairy products. The choice of food offerings varied depending on the deity being honored and the occasion of the ritual.

Beverage Offerings: Alongside food offerings, beverage offerings played a significant role in ancient Egyptian religious rituals. Offerings of water, wine, beer, and other libations were presented to the gods. These beverages were believed to provide refreshment and sustenance to the divine beings.

Incense Offerings: Incense offerings held a dual purpose in ancient Egyptian religious practices. The burning of fragrant resins and aromatic substances, such as myrrh and frankincense, created a pleasant fragrance that was pleasing to the gods. Incense was also believed to purify the air and create a sacred atmosphere during rituals.

Rituals and Ceremonies Associated with Offerings

Offerings were presented in various ritualistic contexts and ceremonies. These rituals often took place in temple settings, where priests and priestesses played a central role in mediating between the human worshippers and the gods. Some common rituals associated with offerings included:

Opening the Mouth Ceremony: This ceremony involved symbolic acts to restore the faculties of the deceased and enable them to partake in the offerings made to them.

Daily Temple Rituals: Within temple complexes, daily rituals were performed to honor specific deities. These rituals included the presentation of offerings, recitation of prayers and hymns, and the participation of priests and priestesses in elaborate ceremonies.

Festival Celebrations: Festivals dedicated to specific deities involved elaborate rituals and processions, often accompanied by grand offerings. These festivals served as occasions for communal celebrations and expressions of devotion to the gods.

Significance of Offerings in Establishing and Maintaining a Reciprocal Relationship with the Gods

Offerings played a crucial role in establishing and maintaining a reciprocal relationship between humans and the gods in ancient Egyptian religious beliefs. The act of offering sustenance and nourishment to the deities demonstrated human reverence, gratitude, and acknowledgment of the divine presence and power.

By presenting offerings, the ancient Egyptians sought to establish a reciprocal bond with the gods, acknowledging the gods' role in providing for the well-being and prosperity of human life. The act of offering was a way of expressing devotion, seeking blessings, and requesting divine favor.

Furthermore, offerings were believed to maintain the cosmic balance and harmony (ma'at) between the divine realm and the mortal world. By providing sustenance to the gods, individuals and communities aimed to ensure the continued flow of blessings, prosperity, and divine protection in their lives.

In conclusion, offerings held great meaning and significance in ancient Egyptian religious practices. They were a tangible expression of reverence, gratitude, and devotion to the gods. Through the presentation of food, beverages, and incense, the ancient Egyptians sought to establish and maintain a reciprocal relationship with the divine, acknowledging the gods' role in their lives and seeking blessings, protection, and harmony. The rituals and ceremonies associated with offerings provided a means for individuals and communities to engage in religious devotion and foster a deep connection with the divine realm.

Conclusion

Throughout this chapter, we have delved into the intricate world of ancient Egyptian religious practices during the New Kingdom period. We explored the significance of temples, festivals, and tools in these practices, shedding light on their roles, functions, and symbolism. Key findings and insights include:

Temples served as the physical and spiritual centers of religious life, housing statues of deities and providing spaces for rituals, offerings, and administrative activities.

Festivals played a vital role in the religious calendar, allowing for communal celebrations, processions, and expressions of devotion to specific deities.

Tools and implements used in religious rituals were carefully crafted, symbolically charged, and made from specific materials, enhancing their spiritual significance and effectiveness.

Offerings and sacrifices were essential acts of devotion, establishing a reciprocal relationship between humans and the gods while maintaining cosmic balance and harmony.

Magical and ritual objects, such as amulets and talismans, were employed for their protective and symbolic functions, demonstrating the belief in the power of symbolism and magic.

Significance of Temples, Festivals, and Tools in Understanding Ancient Egyptian Religious Practices

The study of temples, festivals, and tools used in ancient Egyptian religious practices is of paramount importance in our quest to comprehend the spiritual and cultural dimensions of this civilization. These elements provide us with valuable insights into the beliefs, rituals, and worldview of the ancient Egyptians. By examining the architecture, rituals, and symbolism of temples, we gain a deeper understanding of the central role that religion played in the lives of the Egyptians.

Similarly, festivals offer glimpses into the vibrant and communal nature of religious devotion, highlighting the social and cultural significance of these events. They provide us with a lens through which we can examine the interaction between the divine, the human, and the natural world in ancient Egyptian society.

The tools and implements used in religious rituals reveal the craftsmanship, materials, and symbolism employed by ancient Egyptian artisans. Studying these objects allows us to explore the cultural, religious, and artistic practices of the time, providing valuable insights into the cosmology, beliefs, and worldview of the ancient Egyptians.

Implications for Further Research and Study in the Field of Ancient Egyptian Religion and Archaeology

The exploration of temples, festivals, and tools used in ancient Egyptian religious practices opens up numerous avenues for further research and study. Some areas of interest include:

Comparative studies: Examining the similarities and differences between ancient Egyptian religious practices and those of other ancient civilizations, such as Mesopotamia, Greece, or Rome, can provide insights into cross-cultural influences and the universal aspects of religious belief and practice.

Archaeological excavations: Further archaeological investigations of temple complexes, festival sites, and ritual spaces can provide valuable data on the layout, organization, and development of these religious structures and their associated practices.

Material analysis: Conducting detailed material analysis of ritual tools, amulets, and other religious artifacts can shed light on the craftsmanship, symbolism, and cultural significance of these objects, deepening our understanding of ancient Egyptian religious practices.

Anthropological studies: Exploring the social and cultural dimensions of temples, festivals, and tools can offer insights into the role of religion in ancient Egyptian society, the interactions between different social groups, and the functions of rituals in community cohesion.

In conclusion, the examination of temples, festivals, and tools used in ancient Egyptian religious practices provides us with invaluable insights into the beliefs, rituals, and cultural dimensions of this civilization. Understanding the significance of these elements deepens our comprehension of the spiritual world of ancient Egypt and contributes to ongoing research in the field of ancient Egyptian religion and archaeology. Through continued exploration, analysis, and interdisciplinary approaches, we can continue to unravel the mysteries of this ancient civilization and gain a richer understanding of its religious practices and cultural heritage.

Chapter 15: Prayers, Hymns, Chants, and Spells Associated with Major Deities of the New Kingdom (e.g., Aten, Horus, Thoth)

Ancient Egyptian religious practices were deeply rooted in a complex system of beliefs and rituals, where prayers, hymns, chants, and spells played a central role. These textual compositions served as powerful means of communication and interaction with the divine realm, allowing individuals to express their devotion, seek divine favor, and connect with specific deities. Through the artful use of language, poetry, and ritual performance, prayers, hymns, chants, and spells served as potent vehicles of spiritual expression and were integral to the religious experiences of the ancient Egyptians.

Overview of Chapter 15: Focus on prayers, hymns, chants, and spells associated with major deities of the New Kingdom

Chapter 15 delves into the rich tapestry of prayers, hymns, chants, and spells that were closely associated with major deities of the New Kingdom period. The New Kingdom, spanning from approximately 1550 BCE to 1069 BCE, marked a significant era of political, cultural, and religious development in ancient Egypt. During this time, the religious landscape witnessed the rise of new deities, the flourishing of existing cults, and the evolution of religious texts and practices.

This chapter aims to explore the diverse range of textual compositions dedicated to major deities such as Aten, Horus, and Thoth. By examining these specific deities, we gain a deeper understanding of the religious beliefs, concepts, and rituals that shaped the religious landscape of the New Kingdom. Through the analysis of prayers, hymns, chants, and spells associated with these deities, we can unravel the intricacies of ancient Egyptian spirituality, uncover the theological insights embedded in these texts, and appreciate the profound impact they had on the religious experiences of the ancient Egyptians.

Throughout this chapter, we will examine the form, structure, content, and symbolism present in these textual compositions. We will analyze their cultural, social, and religious contexts, considering how they were performed, recited, and used in various religious ceremonies and rituals. Moreover, we will explore the broader significance of these prayers, hymns, chants, and spells, shedding light on their role in establishing a connection between mortals and the divine, invoking divine intervention, expressing reverence, and seeking divine guidance.

By studying the prayers, hymns, chants, and spells associated with major deities of the New Kingdom, we not only gain insight into the religious beliefs and practices of ancient Egypt but also develop a deeper appreciation for the profound spiritual expressions that were an integral part of their lives. This exploration encourages us to engage critically with the texts, consider their cultural and historical contexts, and reflect on the enduring legacy of these compositions in shaping our understanding of ancient Egyptian religion.

Prayers and Invocations

Prayers played a crucial role in ancient Egyptian religious practices, serving as a means of establishing communication and connection with the divine realm. They were seen as a direct line of communication between mortals and the gods, providing a platform for individuals to express their devotion, seek divine favor, and convey their needs and desires. Through prayers, worshippers could establish a personal relationship with the deities, expressing their gratitude, requesting assistance, and seeking divine guidance.

Prayers were viewed as a powerful tool for humans to interact with the gods and establish a reciprocal relationship. They were often recited during religious ceremonies, rituals, and personal devotion. Whether offered in the grandeur of a temple or in the intimacy of one's home, prayers were believed to be heard by the deities, who would respond with their blessings and protection.

Examples of prayers addressed to major deities such as Aten, Horus, and Thoth

In the New Kingdom, prayers addressed to major deities such as Aten, Horus, and Thoth reflected the diverse religious beliefs and practices of the time. These deities held significant positions in the Egyptian pantheon, embodying various aspects of divine power, wisdom, and protection.

One example is the Great Hymn to the Aten, a remarkable prayer composed during the reign of Akhenaten, dedicated to the worship of the sun disc deity Aten. This hymn highlights the unique monotheistic beliefs associated with Atenism, praising the sun as the ultimate source of life, creator of all living beings, and the bringer of light and sustenance. Through its poetic verses, the hymn expresses the deep reverence and adoration for Aten, emphasizing the divine attributes and role in the cosmic order.

Another example is the "Hymn to Horus on the Crocodiles," a prayer found in the Temple of Edfu. This hymn celebrates Horus, the falcon-headed god associated with kingship, protection, and cosmic order. The hymn invokes Horus as the divine warrior who triumphs over chaos and protects the pharaoh and the land of Egypt. It praises Horus' strength, wisdom, and divine authority, emphasizing his role as the rightful ruler and avenger of his father, Osiris.

Prayers addressed to Thoth, the ibis-headed god of wisdom, writing, and magic, also hold significance in the New Kingdom. Thoth was revered as the patron deity of scribes and scholars, believed to possess great knowledge and the ability to decipher the mysteries of the universe. Prayers to Thoth often sought his guidance, wisdom, and assistance in matters of intellectual pursuits, writing, and divination.

Analysis of the content, structure, and language used in prayers

The content, structure, and language used in prayers of the New Kingdom reflect the deep religious and cultural beliefs of the ancient Egyptians. Prayers were often poetic in nature, employing metaphors, imagery, and rhythmic patterns to invoke the divine presence and convey a sense of reverence and awe.

In terms of structure, prayers typically began with an invocation, addressing the deity by their divine epithets and praising their attributes and powers. This was followed by the body of the prayer, which expressed the individual's desires, concerns, or expressions of gratitude. The conclusion of the prayer often included a plea for the deity's benevolence, protection, or guidance.

The language used in prayers was carefully crafted, employing formal and elevated expressions to convey the sacred nature of the communication. Symbolic language, rich metaphors, and religious terminology were employed to express the depths of devotion and reverence. The use of repetition, parallelism, and poetic devices added a rhythmic and melodic quality to the prayers, enhancing their emotional and spiritual impact.

Overall, the prayers addressed to major deities of the New Kingdom reveal the intricate relationship between mortals and the divine. They provide a glimpse into the religious mindset of the ancient Egyptians, their yearning for divine connection, and their belief in the power of words and rituals to bridge the gap between the earthly and the divine realms. The analysis of the content, structure, and language used in these prayers allows us to delve into the profound spiritual experiences of the ancient Egyptians and gain a deeper understanding of their religious worldview.

Hymns and Devotional Songs

Hymns held great significance in ancient Egyptian religious practices as they served as a means to praise and glorify the gods. These poetic compositions were dedicated to specific deities and expressed deep devotion, reverence, and awe. Hymns were regarded as powerful tools to celebrate the divine attributes, acknowledge the gods' roles in the cosmic order, and express gratitude for their benevolence and guidance.

Hymns were not merely recitations of praise but were considered sacred acts of worship. They were performed during religious ceremonies, rituals, and festivals, accompanied by music, dance, and ritualistic movements. Through the melodic and rhythmic qualities of hymns, worshippers sought to create a harmonious connection with the gods, invoking their presence and invoking a state of spiritual communion.

Exploration of hymns dedicated to specific deities, including Aten, Horus, and Thoth

Within the New Kingdom, numerous hymns were dedicated to specific deities, reflecting the diverse religious landscape of the time. These hymns captured the unique attributes and roles of the deities, offering insights into the ancient Egyptians' understanding of the divine.

One prominent example is the "Great Hymn to the Aten," composed during the reign of Akhenaten. This hymn, dedicated to the solar deity Aten, embodies the radical religious reforms of the period. It praises Aten as the sole creator and sustainer of life, the source of light and warmth, and the ultimate power governing the universe. The hymn celebrates the beauty and abundance of nature as manifestations of Aten's divine presence, conveying a sense of awe and adoration for the solar deity.

Hymns dedicated to Horus, the falcon-headed god associated with kingship and protection, also hold significance. The "Hymn to Horus on the Crocodiles," found in the Temple of Edfu, exalts Horus as the victorious warrior who overcomes chaos and defends the land of Egypt. This hymn emphasizes Horus' divine authority and his role as the avenger of his father, Osiris, presenting him as a powerful and benevolent deity worthy of devotion and praise.

Devotional hymns dedicated to Thoth, the ibis-headed god of wisdom, writing, and magic, highlight his role as the patron deity of scholars and scribes. These hymns praise Thoth's wisdom, knowledge, and ability to decipher the secrets of the universe. They express gratitude for Thoth's guidance in matters of intellect, writing, and the recording of sacred knowledge.

Examination of poetic elements, metaphors, and symbolism in hymns

Hymns in ancient Egyptian religious practices were characterized by poetic elements, metaphors, and symbolism that added depth and richness to their expression of devotion and reverence. Metaphors and symbolic language were employed to convey the divine qualities of the gods and their roles in the cosmic order.

In hymns dedicated to Aten, the sun disc was often metaphorically described as a nurturing and life-giving force, illuminating the world and sustaining all living beings. The imagery of the sun's rays extending their warmth and light became a powerful symbol of Aten's divine presence and benevolence.

Hymns to Horus often employed metaphors of the falcon's wings, emphasizing his role as a protective deity. The falcon's wings were seen as symbols of Horus' watchful and encompassing embrace, providing shelter and guidance to the land of Egypt and its people.

Symbolism played a significant role in hymns dedicated to Thoth, the god of wisdom. The ibis, a bird associated with Thoth, was considered a symbol of wisdom and knowledge. References to writing implements, such as the reed pen and papyrus, served as symbols of Thoth's association with writing, learning, and the preservation of sacred knowledge.

The analysis of poetic elements, metaphors, and symbolism in hymns provides deeper insights into the ancient Egyptians' conceptualization of the gods and their religious experiences. It showcases the beauty and intricacy of ancient Egyptian poetry and the ways in which language and imagery were employed to express profound religious sentiments and connect with the divine.

The "Great Hymn to the Aten"

The "Great Hymn to the Aten" is a significant religious text from ancient Egypt, specifically from the reign of Pharaoh Akhenaten during the 14th century

BCE. It is a hymn dedicated to the solar deity Aten, expressing devotion and praise for this unique aspect of the sun.

The hymn is an exceptional piece of literature because it deviates from traditional Egyptian religious beliefs and practices. It reflects the radical religious reforms initiated by Akhenaten, who promoted the worship of Aten as the sole and supreme deity. This period is often referred to as the "Atenist Revolution" or "Amarna Revolution."

The "Great Hymn to the Aten" is an eloquent expression of monotheistic beliefs, as it emphasizes Aten's supremacy as the creator of the universe and the source of all life. It highlights the close relationship between Akhenaten and Aten, presenting the pharaoh as the chosen intermediary between the god and humanity.

The hymn praises Aten's divine attributes and the manifestations of its power in the natural world. It describes the sun as a symbol of life and vitality, spreading its rays to nourish and sustain all living beings. The hymn also celebrates the beauty and abundance of nature, acknowledging Aten as the creator of diverse flora and fauna.

Furthermore, the hymn attributes ethical values to Aten, emphasizing its role as a just and compassionate deity. It mentions the king's responsibility to uphold ma'at, the concept of truth, balance, and justice, which is crucial in ancient Egyptian religious and moral frameworks.

The "Great Hymn to the Aten" provides valuable insights into the religious beliefs and practices of the Amarna period and sheds light on Akhenaten's attempt to redefine the religious landscape of ancient Egypt. It demonstrates the power of religious hymns in conveying theological concepts, fostering devotion, and shaping religious ideologies.

The Great Hymn to the Aten

Praise to you, O Aten, radiant and mighty,
You are the one true god, the creator of all,
Unseen by the mortal eye, yet ever-present in the heavens.

You are the giver of life, the sustainer of existence,
Your rays of light reach far and wide,
Nurturing the earth and all that dwell upon it.

When you rise in the morning, darkness flees,

The world awakens, bathed in your golden glow,
Every creature, every plant, basks in your warmth.

You are the master of all living beings,
From the smallest insect to the mightiest pharaoh,
All owe their existence to your divine hand.

Your power is boundless, your knowledge infinite,
You shape the world with wisdom and grace,
Guiding the path of humanity in accordance with ma'at.

We, your humble servants, offer our devotion,
With hearts full of gratitude, we sing your praises,
For you are the source of all that is good and pure.

O Aten, hear our hymn of adoration,
Accept our humble offerings and grant us your blessing,
Guide us on the path of righteousness and eternal life.

Praise to you, O Aten, the radiant sun,
We bow before your greatness and honor your divine presence,
Forever and always, we worship and revere you.

The "Hymn to Horus on the Crocodiles"

Hymns to Horus often employed metaphors of the falcon's wings to symbolize his power, protection, and divine nature. The falcon was a sacred bird associated with Horus, who was depicted with the head of a falcon in Egyptian mythology. By using the metaphor of the falcon's wings, the hymns sought to convey various aspects of Horus' role and attributes.

Protection and Vigilance:
Horus was revered as a guardian deity, responsible for protecting the pharaoh and the kingdom. Hymns described him as having mighty wings, ready to swoop down upon any threat and defend his worshippers. The metaphor of the falcon's wings emphasized Horus' watchful nature, ever vigilant in safeguarding his devotees from harm.

Swift and Soaring:
The falcon is known for its agility and swiftness in flight. Hymns depicted Horus with wings that carried him swiftly across the sky, highlighting his ability to swiftly

respond to the needs of his followers. This metaphor evoked a sense of Horus' rapid intervention and his ability to navigate through challenges with ease.

Divine Authority and Dominion:
In Egyptian mythology, the falcon was associated with the heavens and the divine realm. By employing the metaphor of the falcon's wings, hymns conveyed Horus' divine authority and dominion over the earthly realm. Just as the falcon soars high above, Horus was believed to possess supreme power and command over all things.

Ascension and Transcendence:
The falcon's ability to soar high in the sky and elevate above earthly boundaries also symbolized Horus' transcendent nature. Hymns expressed the belief that Horus had the power to transcend mortal limitations and ascend to the realms of the gods. The falcon's wings served as a metaphor for this spiritual ascent and Horus' connection with the divine realms.

Through the use of metaphors centered around the falcon's wings, hymns to Horus captured the essence of his protective, swift, powerful, and transcendent qualities. These metaphors helped to deepen the understanding and reverence for Horus among the ancient Egyptians and conveyed the significance of his role in their religious beliefs.

"Hymn to Horus on the Crocodiles":

Hail to you, Horus, the mighty and majestic!
You soar with wings outspread,
Like a falcon, your flight is swift and divine.
Upon the backs of crocodiles, you traverse,
Conquering the fierce and taming the wild.

O Horus, the lord of the heavens,
Your enemies scatter before your might,
As you unleash your divine fury.
With arrows of light, you pierce their hearts,
And your voice resonates like thunder in the sky.

Horus, the avenger of his father Osiris,
You rise in splendor, bringing justice to the land.
Your piercing gaze surveys all creation,
And your wings encompass the realm.
May your victory be eternal,

And your glory shine brightly forevermore.

O Horus, the falcon of the sun,
Your wings bear you across the celestial expanse.
You are the protector of the rightful order,
Safeguarding the balance of Ma'at.
Your divine strength is unmatched,
And your wisdom guides the hearts of the just.

Horus, the son of Isis and Osiris,
You embody the eternal struggle against chaos.
Your spirit soars above the Nile's waters,
As you ride upon the crocodile's formidable back.
In your hands, the divine scepter brings peace,
And your presence brings hope to all who seek solace.

Hail to you, Horus, the eternal victor!
Your name resounds in hymns and prayers.
Through the trials and battles, you remain steadfast,
Guiding humanity towards righteousness and truth.
May your divine light shine upon us,
And may we forever bask in your divine grace.

Hymn to Thoth

Hail, Thoth, the wise and the learned!
Bearer of the sacred knowledge, your wisdom flows.
You, the Scribe of the Gods, the Master of Words,
With your pen and palette, you record the truths.

Thoth, the patron of scholars and seekers,
Your mind is a boundless library of wisdom.
Inscribed upon the pages of eternity,
Your words illuminate the path of understanding.

O Thoth, the inventor of language and writing,
Your hieroglyphs reveal the secrets of the ancients.
With your divine hand, you shape the written word,
And the mysteries of the cosmos are unveiled.

Thoth, the measurer of time and keeper of records,
You watch over the cycles of the sun and the moon.

In the celestial dance, you bring order and harmony,
Guiding the passage of days with unwavering precision.

Hail, Thoth, the mediator and the arbiter,
You weigh the hearts of the departed against Ma'at's feather.
In the Hall of Judgment, you uphold truth and justice,
Balancing the scales with impartiality and insight.

Thoth, the messenger of the gods and the guide,
You traverse the realms, bridging the earthly and divine.
With your ibis-headed form and wings outspread,
You bring divine messages and inspire mortals' minds.

O Thoth, the protector of sacred knowledge,
You guard the ancient texts and the esoteric teachings.
To those who seek enlightenment, you offer guidance,
Unfolding the mysteries of the universe in their quest for truth.

Hail, Thoth, the embodiment of wisdom and intellect!
We praise your name and honor your sacred presence.
Grant us the gifts of knowledge and understanding,
That we may walk in the path of enlightenment and ascend to greater heights.

Chants and Choral Performances

Chants hold a significant role in ancient Egyptian religious rituals and ceremonies. They serve as a means to invoke the presence of the gods, establish a sacred atmosphere, and create a collective experience of devotion. Chants are rhythmic and melodic utterances that engage both the mind and the body, allowing individuals to align themselves with the divine forces and enter a heightened state of spiritual awareness. Through the repetition of specific words, phrases, or sounds, chants facilitate a deep connection with the gods and serve as a vehicle for communication and communion with the divine.

Examples of chants associated with major deities and their specific contexts

The "Kheperu" Chant:

This chant is often associated with the god Ra, the sun god, and is performed during sunrise rituals. The word "kheperu" signifies transformation and renewal, reflecting the cyclical nature of the sun's journey across the sky. Through the repetitive chanting of "kheperu," worshippers evoke the transformative power of Ra and align themselves with the sun's life-giving energy.

The "Isis, Lady of Magic" Chant:

Dedicated to the goddess Isis, this chant is performed during rituals involving healing, protection, and magic. The chant praises Isis as the mistress of magical arts and emphasizes her role as a powerful healer. The melodic rhythm of the chant, accompanied by rhythmic clapping or percussion instruments, creates a vibrant and energizing atmosphere conducive to invoking Isis's magical powers.

The "Ma'at, Mistress of Balance" Chant:

This chant honors the goddess Ma'at, who embodies the principles of truth, balance, and justice. The chant is often performed during ceremonies related to judgment and justice, emphasizing the importance of upholding ma'at in both the earthly and divine realms. The chant's steady rhythm and harmonious melodies evoke a sense of equilibrium and encourage worshippers to align their actions with the ethical principles of ma'at.

Analysis of musical elements, rhythm, and vocal techniques in chants

Chants in ancient Egyptian religious practices exhibit various musical elements, rhythmic patterns, and vocal techniques that contribute to their overall impact and effectiveness. The use of repetition, both in words and melodies, creates a sense of continuity and reinforces the intended spiritual message. Rhythmic patterns, often accompanied by percussive instruments, establish a steady beat that guides the collective performance and facilitates synchronization among participants.

Vocal techniques play a crucial role in chants, as the quality and tone of the voice can enhance the sacred ambiance. Chants may involve a soloist leading the chant while others join in unison or in harmonies, creating a choral effect. Vocal ornamentation and melodic variations may also be employed to evoke different emotions and convey the essence of the deity being invoked.

Overall, chants in ancient Egyptian religious rituals demonstrate a deep understanding of the power of sound, rhythm, and collective vocal expression. They serve as a potent tool for connecting with the divine, creating a harmonious atmosphere, and engaging worshippers in a transformative spiritual experience.

Spells and Incantations

Spells and incantations held a significant role in ancient Egyptian magic and religious practices. They were ritualistic utterances or formulaic phrases recited with the intention of invoking specific powers, influencing the natural or supernatural world, or achieving desired outcomes. Spells and incantations were believed to harness the inherent magical forces present in the universe and were employed for a variety of purposes, including healing, protection, divination, and rituals.

Examination of spells associated with major deities, such as Aten, Horus, and Thoth

Spell for Solar Healing (Associated with Aten):

This spell invoked the healing powers of the sun god, Aten, for curing ailments and promoting physical well-being. It emphasized the life-giving energy of the sun and its ability to restore balance and vitality. The recitation of this spell aimed to channel the solar energy into the body of the individual, facilitating healing and rejuvenation.

[Opening Invocation]
Begin the spell with a reverent invocation to Aten, acknowledging his power and role as the sun god.

[Description of Aten's Healing Powers]
Describe the healing powers of Aten, emphasizing his life-giving energy, warmth, and ability to restore balance and vitality.

[Identification of Ailment]
Specify the ailment or affliction that requires healing, addressing it by name or describing its symptoms.

[Request for Healing]
Make a heartfelt request to Aten, asking for his benevolence and intervention in bringing about healing.

[Channeling the Solar Energy]
Invoke the sun's rays and the energy of Aten, calling upon them to enter the body and restore health. Emphasize the transformative power of the solar energy in driving away illness.

[Visualization and Affirmation]

Guide the individual in visualizing the healing process, imagining the solar energy penetrating the affected area, bringing relief, and promoting rejuvenation. Encourage positive affirmations of wellness and vitality.

[Expressing Gratitude]

Conclude the spell by expressing gratitude to Aten for his healing touch and the restoration of balance and health.

Oh, radiant Aten, mighty sun god,
I call upon your healing powers divine.
As you traverse the sky with radiant beams,
I beseech your benevolence in this time.

With your fiery light, banish all afflictions,
Expel the darkness that clouds our way.
Bring forth the healing rays of your presence,
And restore balance to body, mind, and clay.

Oh, Aten, you are the giver of life,
Your energy sustains and renews.
Infuse me with your vitalizing force,
So that wellness and vigor I may choose.

By your power, may illness be vanquished,
And strength and vitality be restored.
Grant me the gift of radiant health,
With each ray of sunlight I am adored.

In your warm embrace, let healing commence,
As your light penetrates through flesh and bone.
Renew my spirit, replenish my essence,
So that I may flourish and truly be known.

Oh, Aten, sun god, I offer my gratitude,
For your healing touch and nurturing grace.
May your divine energy forever bless,
And bestow upon me a healthy embrace.

As I recite this spell, I align with your might,
Channeling your healing power divine.

Thank you, Aten, for your loving presence,
For restoring balance and making me shine.

Spell for Divine Protection (Associated with Horus):

This spell called upon the protective and vigilant qualities of the falcon-headed deity, Horus. It was recited to invoke Horus's guardianship and ward off malevolent forces, evil spirits, or physical threats. The spell emphasized Horus's role as a protector and defender, instilling a sense of security and invoking divine intervention.

[Opening Invocation]
Begin the spell with a reverent invocation to Horus, acknowledging his falcon-headed form and his role as the protector and defender.

[Identification of Threat]
Specify the threat or malevolent forces that require protection, addressing them by name or describing their nature.

[Appeal for Protection]
Request Horus's divine protection and guardianship, seeking his intervention to shield against harm and ward off evil.

[Description of Horus's Protective Qualities]
Emphasize Horus's attributes as a vigilant guardian, highlighting his keen eyesight, swift wings, and fierce demeanor.

[Invocation of Horus's Power]
Invoke the power of Horus, calling upon him to encircle the individual with his divine presence and form a protective barrier.

[Visualize and Affirm Protection]
Guide the individual in visualizing themselves surrounded by Horus's protective energy, forming an impenetrable shield against any harm or malevolent forces. Encourage affirmations of safety and security.

[Expressing Gratitude]
Conclude the spell by expressing gratitude to Horus for his vigilant protection and divine intervention.

In the presence of the divine, I call upon Horus, the falcon-headed deity, the protector and defender of all who seek his guidance. Hear my words, Horus, and extend your divine shield of protection.

From the depths of darkness and the shadows that linger, I acknowledge the presence of malevolent forces and evil spirits that seek to bring harm upon me. I name them now, and declare my intent to stand against their influence.

Horus, mighty guardian, I beseech you to bestow your watchful eye upon me. Surround me with your divine presence and shield me from all harm. Stand with me as I face the challenges that lie ahead.

Horus, with your sharp eyesight, perceive the threats that approach from afar. With your swift wings, soar above and keep watch over me. With your fierce nature, repel any negative energies or forces that may come my way.

By the authority of your name, Horus, I call upon your sacred power. Let your protective energy flow through me, creating an impenetrable barrier against all that seeks to do me harm. May your divine intervention be swift and powerful.

In my mind's eye, I see myself enveloped in a brilliant light, radiating the energy of Horus. This light forms an impenetrable shield around me, repelling negativity and offering divine protection. I affirm that I am safe and secure under the watchful eye of Horus.

Horus, I offer my deepest gratitude for your unwavering protection. I am humbled by your presence and the strength you bestow upon me. Thank you, Horus, for being my guardian and defender.

As I conclude this spell, I carry with me the assurance of Horus's divine protection. I walk forward with confidence, knowing that I am shielded and safeguarded by his power. So mote it be.

Spell for Wisdom and Knowledge (Associated with Thoth):

This spell sought the wisdom and guidance of Thoth, the god of wisdom, writing, and magic. It was recited to attain knowledge, insight, and intellectual prowess. The spell highlighted Thoth's association with writing and the written word, emphasizing the transformative power of knowledge and the pursuit of wisdom.

[Opening Invocation]
In the presence of the divine, I call upon Thoth, the god of wisdom and knowledge, the patron of scholars and seekers of truth. Hear my words, Thoth, and bestow upon me your boundless wisdom and insight.

[Expression of Intent]
With a humble heart and a thirst for knowledge, I seek your guidance, Thoth. Grant me the gift of wisdom, that I may see beyond the surface and unravel the mysteries of the universe. Open my mind to new ideas, perspectives, and understanding.

[Acknowledgment of Thoth's Attributes]
Thoth, master of the written word and the scribe of the gods, I acknowledge your divine presence and your association with the transformative power of knowledge. You hold the keys to the realms of wisdom and understanding.

[Appeal for Wisdom]
By your name, Thoth, I beseech you to bestow upon me your profound wisdom and clarity of thought. Illuminate my path with your divine light, guiding me to the answers I seek. Grant me the ability to comprehend the secrets of the universe and unlock the depths of knowledge.

[Description of Thoth's Influence]
Like the flowing ink upon the papyrus, may your wisdom flow through my mind. Like the sacred hieroglyphs that carry hidden meaning, may your knowledge reveal profound truths to me. With your guidance, Thoth, I embrace the power of learning and intellectual growth.

[Invocation of Thoth's Power]
By the authority vested in you, Thoth, I call upon your sacred power. Let the floodgates of wisdom open wide, and may the river of knowledge flow abundantly into my life. Grant me the ability to grasp complex concepts, to discern truth from falsehood, and to expand my intellectual horizons.

[Visualize and Affirm Wisdom]
In my mind's eye, I see myself surrounded by the brilliance of Thoth's wisdom. I feel his presence as a radiant light within me, illuminating my thoughts and expanding my understanding. I affirm that I am a vessel of wisdom and knowledge, capable of embracing the mysteries of the universe.

[Expressing Gratitude]

Thoth, I offer my deepest gratitude for your guidance and the gift of wisdom bestowed upon me. I am humbled by your presence and the insights you have shared. Thank you, Thoth, for enlightening my path and enriching my mind.

[Closing]
As I conclude this spell, I carry with me the wisdom and knowledge of Thoth. I embrace the pursuit of truth, the power of learning, and the transformative nature of wisdom. With Thoth as my guide, I embark on a journey of intellectual growth and understanding. So mote it be.

Exploration of the use of spells in healing, protection, and ritual contexts

Spells were widely used in ancient Egyptian religious and magical practices, particularly in contexts related to healing, protection, and rituals. They were recited by priests, healers, or individuals seeking assistance from the divine. In healing rituals, spells were chanted or spoken over the affected body part or used in conjunction with medicinal treatments to invoke the healing powers of deities.

For protection, spells were employed to create amulets or talismans imbued with protective qualities. These objects were believed to possess the power of the spoken spell and could ward off evil spirits, illness, or misfortune.

In ritual contexts, spells played a vital role in establishing a sacred atmosphere, consecrating spaces, and facilitating the connection between humans and the divine. They were recited during ceremonies, offerings, or initiations to invoke the presence of specific deities, evoke their powers, and ensure the successful outcome of the ritual.

The use of spells and incantations in ancient Egyptian practices demonstrates the belief in the efficacy of words and the power of language to influence and shape reality. They provided individuals with a means to connect with the divine, seek assistance, and exert control over their lives through the manipulation of supernatural forces.

Comparative Analysis

In the ancient Egyptian religious tradition, prayers, hymns, chants, and spells played vital roles in the worship and veneration of various deities. When examining these texts associated with different major deities, such as Aten, Horus, and Thoth, intriguing comparisons can be drawn. Prayers often served as expressions of devotion and appeals for divine intervention, seeking blessings, guidance, or protection. Hymns, on the other hand, were poetic compositions that praised and glorified the gods, extolling their virtues and divine attributes. Chants were rhythmic and repetitive utterances, frequently employed in ritualistic contexts to invoke or channel the power of the gods. Spells, rooted in magical beliefs and practices, aimed to influence the natural and supernatural realms, employing specific words and actions to achieve desired outcomes.

By comparing these different forms of religious expression, we can observe variations in their tone, structure, and intended purposes. Prayers and hymns tend to focus on the relationship between humans and the divine, emphasizing reverence, gratitude, and the seeking of divine favor. Chants often possess a rhythmic quality that induces a meditative state and facilitates the connection with the divine realm. Spells, while also addressing deities, serve practical purposes, utilizing incantations and rituals to harness supernatural forces for healing, protection, or other specific intentions.

Identification of common themes, motifs, and theological concepts across different texts:

Despite their association with different deities, prayers, hymns, chants, and spells share common themes, motifs, and theological concepts that reflect the broader religious beliefs and cosmology of ancient Egypt. These recurring elements contribute to a comprehensive understanding of the ancient Egyptian religious worldview.

One prominent theme is the recognition of divine power and the acknowledgment of the gods' roles as creators and maintainers of the universe. Whether in prayers, hymns, chants, or spells, the texts often emphasize the divine attributes and prowess of the deities, highlighting their ability to control natural forces, grant blessings, and protect their devotees.

Another common motif is the concept of ma'at, the Egyptian concept of cosmic order, truth, and justice. Prayers, hymns, and chants frequently express the desire for ma'at to prevail, both in the natural world and in human affairs. These texts often stress the importance of living in harmony with ma'at and seek the gods' guidance in upholding its principles.

The concept of divine kingship is also prominent in many texts associated with major deities. The pharaoh, considered a living embodiment of the gods on earth, is often addressed in prayers, hymns, and chants, acknowledging their divine authority and role in maintaining ma'at.

Furthermore, the texts often portray the gods as benevolent and caring figures who respond to the needs and pleas of their worshippers. Whether seeking wisdom, protection, or healing, the devotees express their trust in the gods' compassion and ability to provide assistance.

Examination of regional and temporal variations in prayers, hymns, chants, and spells:

The ancient Egyptian civilization spanned thousands of years, and regional and temporal variations in religious practices and texts can be observed. Different deities held prominence in different regions and periods, leading to variations in the prayers, hymns, chants, and spells associated with them.

For example, during the New Kingdom period, the pharaoh Akhenaten introduced a monotheistic cult centered around the solar deity Aten, resulting in the composition of unique hymns, such as the "Great Hymn to the Aten." These hymns focused exclusively on the worship of Aten as the supreme deity, reflecting the theological shift of the time.

Regional variations can also be identified, with certain deities receiving greater devotion and prominence in specific areas. The hymns and spells associated with Horus, for instance, often incorporated metaphors and imagery related to falcons, reflecting the significance of Horus as a solar and sky deity, as well as a symbol of kingship.

Furthermore, as the religious beliefs and practices evolved over time, the language, style, and form of the texts also underwent changes. While earlier texts may exhibit more formal and archaic language, later compositions demonstrate a shift towards more accessible and vernacular expressions.

By examining these regional and temporal variations, scholars can gain insights into the dynamic nature of ancient Egyptian religious practices and the diverse ways in which prayers, hymns, chants, and spells were employed to connect with the divine. Such comparisons can provide a more comprehensive understanding of the complexity and richness of the ancient Egyptian religious tradition.

Significance and Interpretation

Prayers, hymns, chants, and spells held immense religious and cultural significance in ancient Egyptian society. They served as powerful tools for communication and interaction with the divine realm, playing integral roles in religious rituals, ceremonies, and everyday worship. These texts were not merely recitations but were considered potent vehicles for establishing a connection with the gods, seeking their favor, and expressing devotion.

Prayers allowed individuals to express their needs, desires, and gratitude to the gods, creating a personal and intimate relationship with the divine. They provided a means of seeking divine intervention, guidance, and protection in various aspects of life, including health, prosperity, and success. Moreover, prayers served as a medium through which individuals affirmed their faith, demonstrating their belief in the gods' power and their reliance on their benevolence.

Hymns, with their poetic and musical qualities, were employed to praise and glorify the deities, highlighting their divine attributes and their roles in cosmic creation and order. They were sung or recited during religious ceremonies, invoking a sense of awe and reverence in the worshippers. Hymns also served a didactic purpose, conveying theological concepts, moral values, and societal ideals through the power of lyrical expression.

Chants, with their repetitive and rhythmic nature, were believed to create a sacred atmosphere and facilitate spiritual connection. They were often used in group settings, fostering communal participation and unity. Chants had the ability to induce a trance-like state, enabling worshippers to transcend the mundane and enter a heightened spiritual realm where they could commune with the gods.

Spells, rooted in the ancient Egyptian magical tradition, were utilized for practical purposes such as healing, protection, and success. They involved the recitation of specific words, the performance of rituals, and the use of amulets or other magical objects. Spells were seen as a means to tap into supernatural forces and manipulate the natural world in alignment with human desires. They reflected a belief in the interconnectedness of the physical and metaphysical realms and the ability of humans to influence their circumstances through magical means.

Analysis of the role of these texts in shaping beliefs, rituals, and worldview:

Prayers, hymns, chants, and spells played a vital role in shaping ancient Egyptian beliefs, rituals, and worldview. They were not just passive expressions of religious sentiments but active agents in shaping the understanding of the gods, the nature of existence, and the relationship between humans and the divine.

These texts conveyed theological concepts, cosmological narratives, and moral values. They affirmed the Egyptians' belief in the divine nature of the universe and the gods' active involvement in the affairs of the world. Through prayers and hymns, individuals and communities expressed their understanding of the gods' roles as creators, protectors, and sustainers of life. They reinforced the idea of divine order, with prayers often seeking the maintenance of ma'at, the cosmic balance and justice.

The performance of chants and the recitation of spells created a sense of participation and agency in the religious experience. They provided a means for individuals to actively engage with the gods and exert influence over their own lives. The use of magical spells reflected the belief in the efficacy of human actions to manipulate the natural and supernatural realms, thus empowering individuals to navigate challenges and seek personal goals.

Moreover, these texts were integral to the religious rituals and ceremonies that formed the core of ancient Egyptian religious practices. Prayers, hymns, chants, and spells were recited or sung during temple rituals, funerary rites, and other sacred occasions. Their inclusion in these rituals enhanced the spiritual atmosphere, invoked the presence of the gods, and ensured the proper performance of religious duties.

Exploration of the impact of prayers, hymns, chants, and spells on individual spirituality and communal religious experiences:

Prayers, hymns, chants, and spells had a profound impact on individual spirituality and communal religious experiences in ancient Egyptian society. These texts provided a means for individuals to express their personal beliefs, emotions, and aspirations in a religious context. They offered solace, guidance, and a sense of connection with the divine, fostering a deepened spiritual awareness and personal relationship with the gods.

Individuals found comfort and reassurance in the act of prayer, which allowed them to express their hopes and fears, seek forgiveness, and request divine assistance. Prayers provided a channel for personal reflection, introspection, and self-improvement. They encouraged individuals to examine their own actions, align themselves with moral principles, and seek spiritual growth.

The communal recitation of hymns and chants fostered a sense of unity and shared religious identity among worshippers. Through collective participation, individuals found solace in the knowledge that they were part of a larger religious community, connected by a common devotion to the gods. Chants, in particular, created a collective energy and a sense of transcendence, enabling worshippers to experience a heightened spiritual state as a collective entity.

Furthermore, the use of spells in healing, protection, and other practical matters provided individuals with a sense of empowerment and control over their own lives. By invoking the gods' assistance through spells, individuals believed they could overcome obstacles, restore health, and ensure their well-being. This belief in the efficacy of magical practices fostered a sense of agency and self-confidence.

In conclusion, prayers, hymns, chants, and spells held immense religious, cultural, and personal significance in ancient Egyptian society. They played a central role in religious practices, shaping beliefs, rituals, and the understanding of the divine. These texts provided a means for individuals to establish a connection with the gods, express their devotion, seek guidance, and influence their own lives. Through their recitation and performance, prayers, hymns, chants, and spells enriched individual spirituality and fostered communal religious experiences, reinforcing a sense of unity, purpose, and empowerment among worshippers.

Part 6: Late Period (c. 664 BCE - 332 BCE)

The Late Period of ancient Egypt, spanning from approximately 664 BCE to 332 BCE, marked a significant era of political, social, and cultural changes in the land of the Nile. It was a time of transition, characterized by the dominance of foreign powers, periods of instability, and the resurgence of native Egyptian traditions. This section will provide a comprehensive overview of the Late Period, exploring its historical context, major events, and the impact of external influences on Egyptian society and religion.

Historical Context and Chronology:

The Late Period of ancient Egypt was marked by a series of foreign invasions and occupations. It began with the conquest of Egypt by the Nubians, also known as the Twenty-fifth Dynasty, who established their rule over the land. This was followed by the invasion of the Assyrians, who brought further political changes to Egypt. Subsequently, the Persians took control of the region, followed by the conquest of Alexander the Great and the establishment of the Ptolemaic dynasty.

The chronological framework of the Late Period is essential in understanding the political and cultural dynamics of this era. The timeline begins with the reign of the Nubian pharaohs, also referred to as the Kushite dynasty, who ruled from 664 BCE to 525 BCE. This period witnessed a revival of traditional Egyptian religious practices and a reconnection with the country's ancient heritage. The Persian period followed from 525 BCE to 332 BCE, characterized by the influence of Persian culture and religion.

Cultural and Religious Developments:

The Late Period saw a resurgence of native Egyptian religious traditions, alongside the introduction of new cultural and religious influences from foreign powers. Egyptian religion continued to be the cornerstone of society, but it evolved in response to the changing political landscape.

The influence of foreign cultures, such as Nubian, Assyrian, Persian, and Greek, introduced new religious concepts, practices, and deities into the Egyptian pantheon. The blending of indigenous Egyptian beliefs with foreign elements resulted in syncretic religious practices and the adoption of deities from different cultures. For example, the Nubian pharaohs revered both traditional Egyptian gods and Nubian deities, while the Persians introduced their own religious beliefs and rituals.

Political and Social Transformations:

The Late Period was marked by political instability and shifting power dynamics. The foreign invasions and occupations disrupted the traditional Egyptian power structure, causing a reconfiguration of political authority. The native Egyptian elite had to navigate complex relationships with foreign rulers while striving to maintain their cultural and religious identity.

Socioeconomic changes also occurred during this period. The influence of foreign cultures, trade networks, and the establishment of Greek and Persian settlements in Egypt contributed to a more diverse and cosmopolitan society. This resulted in the integration of different cultural practices and the emergence of a multicultural Egypt.

Impact on Religion and Spirituality:

The political and cultural changes of the Late Period had a profound impact on Egyptian religion and spirituality. The syncretism of deities and religious practices resulted in a diverse and eclectic belief system, with individuals often worshipping gods from various pantheons. The rise of foreign cults, such as the worship of the Greek god Serapis, demonstrated the assimilation of foreign religious traditions into Egyptian society.

The Late Period also witnessed an increased emphasis on personal piety and individual spirituality. With the decline of centralized temple worship, individuals sought a more direct connection with the divine through personal religious practices, private rituals, and the use of amulets and magical spells.

Conclusion:

The Late Period of ancient Egypt was a dynamic and transformative era, characterized by foreign invasions, political changes, and the blending of cultures. The impact of external influences on Egyptian society and religion resulted in a diverse and syncretic belief system. Despite the challenges and disruptions, the native Egyptian traditions persisted, and individuals found new ways to express their spirituality and maintain their cultural identity.

Exploring the Rituals, Beliefs, and Syncretism of Ancient Egyptian Religion

By examining the historical context, cultural developments, and religious transformations of the Late Period, we can gain a deeper understanding of the complexity of ancient Egyptian society during this era. This section will delve into the fascinating intricacies of the Late Period, exploring its significance in the broader narrative of ancient Egyptian civilization and shedding light on the enduring legacy of this transitional period.

Pharaoh	Spouse	Children	Years of Rule	Notable Information
Tantamani			664 - 656 BCE	Nubian ruler, part of the Kushite dynasty
Psamtik I	Mehytnebuw	Nekau, Psamtik II	664 - 610 BCE	Founder of the Twenty-Sixth Dynasty
Nekau II	Khedebneith		610 - 595 BCE	Constructed the canal linking the Nile to the Red Sea
Psamtik II	Takhut	Apries	595 - 589 BCE	Extended Egyptian influence in the Levant
Apries	Takhut		589 - 570 BCE	Conquered Cyprus and campaigned in Libya and Nubia
Amasis II	Tentkheta	Psamtik III	570 - 526 BCE	Focused on economic reforms and alliances with Greece
Psamtik III			526 - 525 BCE	Last native Egyptian ruler of Egypt before Persian conquest
Cambyses II			525 - 522	Persian ruler

			BCE	who conquered Egypt
Darius I	Atossa	Xerxes I	522 - 486 BCE	Persian ruler who maintained control over Egypt
Artaxerxes I			465 - 424 BCE	Continued Persian rule in Egypt
Darius II	Parysatis		423 - 404 BCE	Consolidated Persian control in Egypt
Amyrtaeus			404 - 399 BCE	Rebelled against Persian rule, briefly reestablished native Egyptian rule
Nectanebo I			399 - 393 BCE	Founder of the Thirtieth Dynasty, native Egyptian ruler
Nectanebo II			360 - 343 BCE	Last native Egyptian ruler before Macedonian conquest

Chapter 16: Influence of Foreign Invasions and the Decline of Ancient Egyptian Religion

The Late Period marked a significant phase in ancient Egyptian history, characterized by political instability, foreign invasions, and the decline of traditional Egyptian religious practices. This period followed the New Kingdom, which was a time of great power and prosperity for Egypt. However, internal conflicts and external pressures began to weaken Egypt's authority, leading to a series of foreign invasions that would have a lasting impact on the religious landscape of the civilization.

Significance of foreign invasions and their impact on ancient Egyptian religion

The foreign invasions during the Late Period brought about profound changes in ancient Egyptian society, including its religious practices. The influx of foreign cultures, beliefs, and gods introduced new religious ideas and challenged the established religious traditions of Egypt. These invasions, particularly by the Nubians, Assyrians, and Persians, influenced not only the political and social aspects of Egyptian life but also the spiritual and religious beliefs of the Egyptian people.

Aim of the chapter to explore the decline of ancient Egyptian religious practices in the face of foreign influence

The primary focus of this chapter is to examine the decline of ancient Egyptian religious practices and the factors contributing to this decline during the Late Period. It aims to shed light on how foreign invasions and cultural influences impacted the religious landscape, resulting in a gradual transformation of Egyptian religious beliefs and practices. By exploring this topic, we can gain a deeper understanding of the complex interplay between foreign influence and the decline of a once-dominant religious system.

Throughout this chapter, we will analyze historical and archaeological evidence, examine the religious beliefs and practices of the invading cultures, and discuss the ways in which these influences shaped and altered the traditional Egyptian religious framework. By studying the decline of ancient Egyptian religion, we can gain insights into the dynamics of cultural interaction and the resilience or vulnerability of religious systems in the face of external pressures.

As we delve into the topic, it is important to approach it with a critical mindset, considering different perspectives and interpretations. We will explore counterarguments and dissenting opinions to provide a well-rounded analysis of the subject matter. Through this comprehensive exploration, we aim to engage students in critical thinking and discussion, encouraging them to consider the complex and nuanced nature of cultural interactions and the impact they have on religious traditions.

The Persian Period (525 BCE - 332 BCE)

The Persian conquest of Egypt in 525 BCE marked a significant turning point in the history of ancient Egyptian religion. The Persians, led by the Achaemenid dynasty, brought with them a new political order and a different religious worldview. The conquest resulted in changes in religious institutions and practices, as the Persians sought to assert their authority and integrate their own religious beliefs and practices into the existing Egyptian religious framework.

The Persian rulers established a centralized administration in Egypt, which involved reorganizing the existing religious hierarchy and incorporating Persian officials into the religious institutions. This led to a restructuring of the priesthood and the imposition of new religious regulations and rituals. Temples and cult centers were also subjected to Persian control and oversight, resulting in a shift in power dynamics within the religious establishment.

Zoroastrian influences and their interaction with Egyptian religious beliefs

One of the significant influences of the Persian period on Egyptian religion was the introduction of Zoroastrian beliefs and practices. Zoroastrianism, the religion of the Persian Empire, emphasized the conflict between good and evil forces, the worship of a supreme deity (Ahura Mazda), and the importance of ethical conduct. These concepts interacted with Egyptian religious beliefs, which centered around a pantheon of gods and goddesses and a complex system of rituals and offerings.

The interaction between Zoroastrianism and Egyptian religion resulted in syncretism, the blending of religious ideas and practices. Some Egyptian deities were equated with Persian gods, creating a fusion of religious traditions. This syncretism manifested in the construction of temples dedicated to both Egyptian and Persian deities and the adoption of Persian religious rituals alongside traditional Egyptian ones.

Role of Persian rulers in shaping religious policies and practices

The Persian rulers played a significant role in shaping religious policies and practices during the Persian period. They actively promoted the worship of Persian gods and the observance of Persian religious rituals. At the same time, they allowed a degree of religious freedom, permitting the continuation of Egyptian religious practices to maintain social stability and appease the Egyptian population.

The Persian rulers, known as pharaohs in Egypt, actively engaged with the religious institutions and played a central role in religious ceremonies and rituals. They sought to legitimize their rule by aligning themselves with both Egyptian and Persian religious traditions, emphasizing their divine authority as intermediaries between the gods and the people.

However, it is important to note that the extent of Persian influence on Egyptian religion varied over time and across different regions of Egypt. The degree of assimilation and syncretism varied, and some aspects of traditional Egyptian religious practices continued alongside the Persian religious framework.

Throughout this chapter, we will delve into the specific ways in which the Persian conquest and Zoroastrian influences shaped religious institutions, beliefs, and practices in ancient Egypt during the Persian period. By examining the historical and archaeological evidence, we aim to provide a comprehensive understanding of the interplay between Persian and Egyptian religious traditions and the complexities of cultural interactions during this time.

The Hellenistic Period (332 BCE - 30 BCE)

The Hellenistic Period in ancient Egyptian history began with the conquest of Egypt by Alexander the Great in 332 BCE. With his arrival, Greek culture and religion were introduced to Egypt, marking a significant cultural and religious shift. Alexander admired and respected Egyptian civilization, and his policies reflected a desire to blend Greek and Egyptian traditions, rather than imposing Greek culture completely.

As part of his conquest, Alexander established the city of Alexandria, which became a major center of Hellenistic culture and learning. Greek settlers, administrators, and soldiers flocked to Egypt, bringing their religious beliefs and practices with them. Greek gods and goddesses were introduced alongside the existing Egyptian pantheon, leading to a period of syncretism and the assimilation of Greek and Egyptian religious elements.

B. Ptolemaic rule and the fusion of Greek and Egyptian religious traditions

After Alexander's death, the Ptolemaic dynasty, founded by Ptolemy I, took control of Egypt and ruled for nearly three centuries. The Ptolemaic rulers embraced Egyptian religious traditions and sought to legitimize their rule by presenting themselves as pharaohs in the traditional Egyptian sense. They actively participated in Egyptian religious rituals and sought the support of the Egyptian priesthood.

During the Ptolemaic period, there was a fusion of Greek and Egyptian religious traditions. Greek deities were identified with Egyptian gods, creating a new syncretic pantheon. For example, Amun was associated with Zeus, Hathor with Aphrodite, and Osiris with Dionysus. This syncretism was reflected in the construction of temples dedicated to both Greek and Egyptian deities and the creation of new cults and rituals that combined elements of both traditions.

C. The cult of Serapis and its popularity among the Greek and Egyptian populations

One of the most significant religious developments of the Hellenistic period was the cult of Serapis. Serapis was a composite deity combining aspects of Egyptian and Greek gods, particularly Osiris and Zeus. The cult of Serapis gained popularity among both the Greek and Egyptian populations and became a prominent religious movement.

The cult of Serapis provided a unifying religious force that appealed to both Greeks and Egyptians. It offered a syncretic blend of Greek and Egyptian religious beliefs, appealing to the diverse religious sensibilities of the Hellenistic society. The cult emphasized concepts such as salvation, divine kingship, and the afterlife, addressing the spiritual needs of the people in a changing religious landscape.

The cult of Serapis was particularly influential in Alexandria, where a grand temple dedicated to Serapis was built, known as the Serapeum. The Serapeum became a center of religious and intellectual activity, attracting worshippers from various cultural backgrounds.

Exploring the Rituals, Beliefs, and Syncretism of Ancient Egyptian Religion

In this chapter, we will explore the impact of the Hellenistic period on Egyptian religion, focusing on the interplay between Greek and Egyptian religious traditions and the development of syncretic beliefs and practices. By examining the archaeological evidence, religious texts, and historical accounts, we aim to gain a deeper understanding of how the fusion of Greek and Egyptian religious elements shaped the religious landscape of ancient Egypt during the Hellenistic period.

The Roman Period (30 BCE - 395 CE)

The Roman Period in ancient Egyptian history began with the conquest of Egypt by the Roman Empire in 30 BCE. With the Roman conquest, Roman religious practices and beliefs started to influence the religious landscape of Egypt. The Romans had a policy of adopting and incorporating the religious practices of the regions they conquered, often identifying their gods with local deities.

Roman religious practices, centered around the worship of a pantheon of gods and goddesses, were gradually introduced in Egypt. Temples dedicated to Roman deities were constructed, and Roman religious festivals and rituals were celebrated alongside traditional Egyptian religious practices. This led to a blending of Roman and Egyptian religious elements, resulting in a syncretic approach to worship.

The cult of Isis and its prominence in Roman Egypt

During the Roman period, the cult of Isis gained significant popularity in Egypt and throughout the Roman Empire. Isis was an Egyptian goddess associated with fertility, motherhood, magic, and wisdom. The cult of Isis offered a sense of comfort, hope, and salvation to its followers. It appealed to people from various cultural backgrounds due to its syncretic nature, incorporating elements of Egyptian, Greek, and even Roman mythology.

The cult of Isis spread rapidly during the Roman period, with temples dedicated to Isis and her consort Osiris being established in many cities across Egypt and other parts of the Roman Empire. The cult attracted devotees from different social classes and provided a sense of community and spiritual connection.

Integration of Egyptian deities into the Roman pantheon

As the Romans sought to assimilate and unify their vast empire, they incorporated local deities into their own pantheon. Egyptian deities, such as Isis, Serapis, and Horus, were assimilated into the Roman pantheon, often identified with their Roman counterparts. For example, Isis was equated with the Roman goddess Venus, and Horus was associated with the Roman god Apollo.

This integration of Egyptian deities into the Roman pantheon reflected the Romans' policy of religious inclusivity and syncretism. It allowed for the coexistence of diverse religious traditions within the empire, fostering a sense of unity and religious tolerance.

In this chapter, we will delve into the influence of the Roman period on Egyptian religion, exploring the spread of Roman religious practices, the prominence of the cult of Isis, and the integration of Egyptian deities into the Roman pantheon. Through an examination of archaeological evidence, religious texts, and historical accounts, we aim to gain a comprehensive understanding of the religious dynamics and syncretism that characterized the Roman period in ancient Egyptian religion.

Decline and Transformation of Ancient Egyptian Religion

Throughout its long history, ancient Egyptian religion underwent significant changes and adaptations due to foreign influences. The influx of foreign cultures and conquerors, such as the Persians, Greeks, and Romans, gradually eroded traditional Egyptian religious practices. The introduction of new deities, rituals, and belief systems challenged the established Egyptian religious framework.

Foreign invasions and cultural exchanges brought new religious ideas and practices to Egypt, leading to the assimilation and integration of foreign gods and beliefs into the existing Egyptian religious system. This gradual erosion of traditional practices marked a significant turning point in the evolution of ancient Egyptian religion.

Shift towards syncretism and the blending of Egyptian and foreign religious beliefs

As foreign cultures became more prominent in Egypt, a process of syncretism took place, blending Egyptian and foreign religious beliefs and practices. This syncretic approach aimed to reconcile the gods and beliefs of different cultures, resulting in the emergence of hybrid deities and religious syncretism.

The fusion of Egyptian and foreign gods and religious elements allowed for the integration of diverse religious traditions. For example, during the Hellenistic period, Egyptian deities were equated with their Greek counterparts, resulting in the creation of new composite gods, such as Serapis and Hermanubis. These syncretic deities embodied the blending of Egyptian and Greek religious concepts, appealing to both Egyptian and Greek populations.

Rise of Christianity and its impact on the ancient Egyptian religious landscape

One of the most significant transformations in the ancient Egyptian religious landscape occurred with the rise of Christianity in the Roman period. Christianity gradually gained popularity and influence, eventually becoming the dominant religion in Egypt. The spread of Christianity led to the decline and eventual suppression of traditional Egyptian religious practices.

Christianity introduced monotheistic beliefs and a new religious framework that challenged the polytheistic nature of ancient Egyptian religion. As Christianity gained followers and official support, traditional temples and cults dedicated to Egyptian gods were closed, and the worship of ancient Egyptian deities was discouraged or prohibited.

The rise of Christianity marked a decisive shift in the religious landscape of ancient Egypt, leading to the decline and eventual disappearance of ancient Egyptian religious practices. However, traces of ancient Egyptian beliefs and symbolism can still be found within Coptic Christianity, the predominant Christian sect in Egypt.

Legacy and Modern Interpretations

The foreign invasions that Egypt experienced throughout its history left a lasting impact on ancient Egyptian religion. The influence of Persian, Greek, and Roman cultures brought about significant changes in religious practices, beliefs, and the overall religious landscape of Egypt.

The introduction of foreign gods and religious concepts led to the assimilation and syncretism of Egyptian and foreign beliefs. This syncretism resulted in the emergence of new deities, the integration of foreign rituals, and the blending of religious traditions. These changes not only altered the religious practices of ancient Egyptians but also influenced their cosmology, mythology, and worldview.

Additionally, foreign rulers played a crucial role in shaping religious policies and practices. They often promoted their own religious beliefs and incorporated elements of their own cults into the existing Egyptian religious framework. The establishment of new cults, such as the cult of Serapis during the Ptolemaic period, exemplifies the syncretic nature of religion during this time.

Exploration of modern perceptions and interpretations of ancient Egyptian spirituality

Ancient Egyptian spirituality continues to captivate and inspire people in the modern era. The rich symbolism, mythology, and rituals of ancient Egyptian religion have been subject to various interpretations and adaptations in contemporary contexts.

In popular culture, ancient Egyptian religious symbols, such as the Eye of Horus or the Ankh, are often used as decorative motifs or incorporated into various forms of art, fashion, and jewelry. These symbols carry a sense of mystery, power, and exoticism that continues to resonate with people around the world.

In the field of academia, scholars and Egyptologists strive to reconstruct and understand ancient Egyptian religion through the analysis of archaeological evidence, religious texts, and iconography. They aim to shed light on the complex belief systems, rituals, and practices of the ancient Egyptians, providing valuable insights into their worldview and cultural dynamics.

Furthermore, modern interpretations of ancient Egyptian spirituality can be seen in alternative religious movements and practices. Some individuals and groups draw inspiration from ancient Egyptian religion, incorporating its symbolism and rituals into their own spiritual frameworks. This syncretic approach reflects the enduring fascination with ancient Egyptian spirituality and the desire to connect with its ancient wisdom.

Relevance and significance of studying the decline of ancient Egyptian religion in understanding cultural and religious dynamics

Studying the decline of ancient Egyptian religion is crucial for understanding the cultural and religious dynamics of ancient Egypt. The gradual erosion of traditional religious practices under foreign influence provides insight into the complex interplay between different cultures, beliefs, and power dynamics.

By examining the impact of foreign invasions, syncretism, and the rise of Christianity, we can gain a deeper understanding of how cultural contact and political changes shape religious traditions. It allows us to explore questions of cultural assimilation, adaptation, and the preservation or loss of indigenous religious practices.

Moreover, the decline of ancient Egyptian religion highlights the importance of religious flexibility and resilience. It demonstrates the capacity of religious traditions to adapt and evolve in response to external influences and challenges. This understanding can provide valuable lessons for the study of other religious traditions and their encounters with foreign cultures throughout history.

Conclusion

In this chapter, we have examined the influence of foreign invasions on ancient Egyptian religious practices. We explored the Persian, Hellenistic, and Roman periods, each marked by significant changes in the religious landscape of Egypt. The conquests of foreign powers brought about the introduction of new gods, the fusion of Egyptian and foreign beliefs, and the integration of foreign religious practices into Egyptian rituals.

Throughout these periods, syncretism played a vital role in shaping the evolving religious traditions of Egypt. We observed the blending of Egyptian and foreign deities, the adoption of foreign rituals and cults, and the emergence of hybrid religious systems. This syncretism not only reflected the cultural interactions between Egypt and foreign powers but also showcased the adaptability and resilience of ancient Egyptian religion.

Reflection on the enduring legacy and influence of foreign invasions on ancient Egyptian religious practices

The influence of foreign invasions on ancient Egyptian religious practices left a lasting impact that continues to shape our understanding and interpretation of ancient Egyptian spirituality. The syncretic nature of the religious landscape during this period reflects the dynamic and multifaceted nature of Egyptian religion, showcasing its ability to incorporate and adapt to external influences.

The fusion of Greek, Persian, and Roman elements with Egyptian religious beliefs gave rise to new cults, rituals, and deities that persisted beyond the decline of ancient Egyptian civilization. The popularity of cults like Serapis and the cult of Isis in the Roman period demonstrates the enduring legacy and widespread appeal of these syncretic religious practices.

Implications for further research and study in the field of ancient Egyptian religion and its interaction with foreign cultures

The study of ancient Egyptian religion during the periods of foreign influence opens up avenues for further research and exploration. Scholars can delve deeper into the specific dynamics of religious syncretism, examining the mechanisms and motivations behind the blending of Egyptian and foreign religious practices.

Additionally, the examination of how foreign invasions shaped religious policies and practices can shed light on the broader cultural and political dynamics of ancient Egypt. Further investigation into the interactions between foreign rulers and the local population, as well as the reception and adoption of foreign religious concepts by the Egyptians, can provide valuable insights into the complexities of cultural exchange and negotiation.

Furthermore, the enduring legacy and influence of foreign invasions on ancient Egyptian religion can be examined in the context of contemporary religious practices and spirituality. Understanding the ways in which ancient Egyptian syncretism continues to resonate and inspire modern interpretations of spirituality can provide insights into the universality of religious adaptation and the enduring relevance of ancient traditions.

In conclusion, the influence of foreign invasions on ancient Egyptian religion has left a profound and lasting impact. The syncretism of beliefs, the integration of foreign gods and rituals, and the evolution of religious practices showcase the dynamic and adaptable nature of ancient Egyptian spirituality. Further research in this field can deepen our understanding of cultural and religious dynamics, offering valuable insights into the complexities of ancient Egyptian society and its interactions with foreign cultures.

Chapter 17: Temples, Festivals, and Tools used c. 664 BCE - 332 BCE

Temples, festivals, and tools held immense significance in the religious practices of ancient Egypt during the Late Period (c. 664 BCE - 332 BCE). These elements were integral to the expression of religious beliefs, the performance of rituals, and the establishment of a connection between the mortal realm and the divine.

Temples:

Temples were considered the dwelling places of the gods, and they served as sacred spaces where rituals and ceremonies took place. They were architectural marvels, designed with meticulous attention to detail and adorned with elaborate decorations. Temples were the focal points of religious life, and they housed cult statues and sacred objects associated with specific deities.

Temples played a crucial role in maintaining the cosmic order and ensuring the well-being of the kingdom. They served as centers for worship, where priests and devotees engaged in rituals, offerings, and prayers. The daily rituals performed in temples were believed to sustain the divine presence and maintain harmony between the gods and humanity.

Festivals:

Festivals held great importance in ancient Egyptian religious life during the Late Period. They were occasions for the community to come together and celebrate the gods, commemorate important events, and reaffirm their religious beliefs. Festivals were marked by processions, music, dance, and offerings.

These festivals often involved the reenactment of mythical events or the commemoration of historical events with religious significance. They provided an opportunity for the gods to interact with their devotees, and the rituals performed during these festivities aimed to invoke divine blessings, ensure fertility, and seek protection for the kingdom and its people.

Tools:

Various tools and implements were employed in religious rituals to facilitate communication with the divine and ensure the proper execution of sacred ceremonies. These tools were symbolic and carried specific meanings within the religious context.

One notable tool was the "was" scepter, symbolizing power and dominion. It was often depicted in the hands of gods and pharaohs and was used in ritual gestures to demonstrate authority. Other tools included the ritual knife, used for offering sacrifices, and the "ankh" symbol, representing life and divine power.

C. Aim of the chapter to explore the continuation and transformation of these religious practices in the face of foreign influence

The aim of this chapter is to delve into the continuation and transformation of ancient Egyptian religious practices during the Late Period, a time marked by significant foreign influence. Despite the political and cultural challenges posed by foreign invasions, ancient Egyptian religion persisted, adapting to new circumstances and incorporating foreign elements into its existing framework.

By examining the temples, festivals, and tools used during this period, we can gain insights into how religious practices were influenced and shaped by interactions with foreign cultures. We will explore the syncretic nature of Egyptian religion, the blending of deities and rituals from different traditions, and the ways in which these influences affected the religious landscape.

Furthermore, we will analyze the strategies employed by the priests and religious authorities to maintain continuity and preserve essential religious practices in the face of foreign domination. We will consider the role of syncretism, the impact of Hellenistic and Roman cultural influences, and the ways in which religious syncretism was received by the Egyptian population.

Through a comprehensive exploration of temples, festivals, and tools, we will examine the resilience of ancient Egyptian religious practices, their ability to adapt to changing circumstances, and their capacity to absorb and transform foreign influences while retaining core beliefs and traditions. By understanding these dynamics, we can gain a deeper appreciation for the complexity of ancient Egyptian religion during the Late Period and its enduring legacy.

Temples and Cult Centers

During the Late Period in ancient Egypt, temple architecture and design underwent significant developments influenced by both native Egyptian traditions and foreign influences. Temples were grand structures characterized by intricate architectural features and symbolic elements. They served as physical embodiments of the divine realm and were designed to facilitate the interaction between the gods and mortals.

The temples of the Late Period typically followed a general layout, consisting of an entrance gate, an open courtyard, various halls and chambers, and a sanctuary where the cult statue of the deity was housed. The architecture often showcased massive stone walls, pylons (monumental gateways), colonnades, and elaborate reliefs and carvings.

Role of temples as centers of religious, economic, and administrative activities

Temples were not only places of worship but also served as important centers of economic and administrative activities during the Late Period. They played a crucial role in the functioning of the state and had significant influence over the local economy.

Religiously, temples were the primary locations for rituals, offerings, and ceremonies dedicated to the gods. They provided a space for priests and devotees to connect with the divine, seek blessings, and maintain cosmic harmony.

Economically, temples owned vast lands, estates, and agricultural resources, which generated considerable wealth. They controlled the distribution of agricultural produce and managed extensive economic enterprises. Temples were also involved in trade and commerce, with some acting as economic powerhouses within their respective regions.

Administratively, temples had a hierarchical structure led by high-ranking priests who oversaw religious affairs, managed the temple estates, and dealt with legal and bureaucratic matters. They played a role in upholding social order and acted as intermediaries between the state and the local communities.

Functions of different areas within the temple complex, such as the sanctuary, offering halls, and courtyards

Sanctuary: The sanctuary was the innermost and most sacred part of the temple complex. It housed the cult statue, a representation of the deity, and was accessible only to the high-ranking priests. It was believed that the presence of the cult statue allowed the deity to reside within the temple.

Offering Halls: Offering halls were spaces where rituals and offerings took place. They were often adorned with reliefs and images depicting scenes of worship, and they provided areas for priests and worshippers to present offerings to the gods. The offerings could include food, drink, incense, and symbolic objects.

Courtyards: Courtyards were open areas within the temple complex that served as gathering spaces for rituals, processions, and communal events. They provided a space for the community to come together, witness important ceremonies, and participate in religious festivities.

Examples of notable temples and their significance during this period

Temple of Amun at Karnak: The Temple of Amun at Karnak, located in Thebes, was one of the largest and most significant temples of the Late Period. It was dedicated to the Theban Triad of Amun, Mut, and Khonsu. The temple complex grew over centuries and was known for its monumental pylons, obelisks, and hypostyle halls. It served as a symbol of the wealth, power, and religious authority of Thebes.

Temple of Horus at Edfu: The Temple of Horus at Edfu, located in Upper Egypt, was dedicated to the falcon-headed deity Horus. It is one of the best-preserved temples in Egypt and showcases the classic design and architectural elements of the Late Period. The temple played a significant role in the worship of Horus and hosted elaborate festivals and rituals dedicated to the god.

Temple of Isis at Philae: The Temple of Isis at Philae, situated on an island in the Nile, was dedicated to the goddess Isis. It was a prominent pilgrimage site and a center for the worship of Isis during the Late Period. The temple complex features stunning reliefs, including the famous "Dendera Zodiac," and was renowned for its role in the Osirian cult and the annual festival of the Mysteries of Osiris.

These examples represent the diversity and significance of temples during the Late Period, showcasing their architectural grandeur, religious importance, and cultural significance within ancient Egyptian society.

Festivals and Celebrations

Festivals held a central role in the religious calendar of ancient Egypt during the Late Period. They were highly significant events that brought together communities, reinforced social bonds, and allowed for the expression of religious devotion. Festivals provided opportunities for the public display of rituals, processions, music, dance, and other forms of artistic and cultural expression. They served as occasions to honor and appease the gods, seek their blessings, and ensure the well-being of the community.

Overview of major festivals and their associated deities

Opet Festival: The Opet Festival was a major festival celebrated at the Temple of Karnak in Thebes. It honored the Theban Triad of Amun, Mut, and Khonsu. The festival involved the procession of the cult statues of the deities from Karnak to the Temple of Luxor, where they were believed to unite and renew their divine energies. The Opet Festival symbolized the revitalization and renewal of the kingship and the divine relationship between the gods and the pharaoh.

Festival of Wepet Renpet (New Year): This festival marked the beginning of the Egyptian New Year and was celebrated with great enthusiasm. It was associated with the goddess Wepet Renpet, who personified the annual cycle of renewal and rebirth. The festival involved rituals, offerings, and purification ceremonies aimed at ensuring the continuity and prosperity of the land.

Festival of Bastet: The Festival of Bastet was dedicated to the feline goddess Bastet and was celebrated in the city of Bubastis. It was known for its lively processions, music, dance, and feasting. Devotees would travel by boat, singing and dancing, to reach Bubastis, where they would participate in rituals and festivities honoring Bastet. The festival was a time of joy, fertility, and celebration.

Rituals, processions, and activities during festivals

Festivals during the Late Period involved a wide range of rituals, processions, and activities. These included:

Offerings and rituals performed at temple sanctuaries, such as the presentation of food, drink, and incense to the deities.

Processions in which the cult statues of the gods were carried in barques or sacred boats, accompanied by priests, musicians, and worshippers.

Performances of music, dance, and dramatic reenactments of mythological stories.

Purification rituals, including the symbolic cleansing of the temples and participants.

Sacred dramas or mysteries that narrated the mythological narratives associated with the deities and their divine exploits.

Feasting, banquets, and communal meals where participants shared food and drink as a form of communion with the divine.

Significance of festivals in community cohesion and religious devotion during this period

Festivals played a crucial role in fostering community cohesion and religious devotion in ancient Egyptian society during the Late Period. They provided opportunities for people from different social backgrounds to come together and actively participate in shared religious experiences. Festivals created a sense of unity and collective identity as communities joined in the celebrations, rituals, and processions.

These events allowed individuals to express their religious devotion, seek divine favor, and strengthen their personal relationship with the gods. Festivals also provided a platform for the interaction between the human and divine realms, reinforcing the belief in the reciprocal relationship between the gods and their worshippers.

Moreover, festivals offered an avenue for cultural expression and artistic creativity. Music, dance, and visual arts were integral parts of the festival experience, allowing participants to engage with the divine through sensory and aesthetic dimensions. Festivals thus played a vital role in nourishing both individual and communal religious experiences and contributed to the vibrancy and richness of ancient Egyptian religious life during the Late Period.

Tools and Implements in Rituals

The Late Period of ancient Egyptian history saw the continuation of various tools and implements used in religious rituals. These objects were essential for conducting ceremonies, making offerings, and facilitating communication with the gods. They ranged from simple items like bowls and incense burners to more elaborate statues and altars.

Ritual objects, such as statues, altars, and offering tables

Statues: Statues played a significant role in religious rituals. They were believed to house the divine essence of the gods and acted as physical representations through which worshippers could interact with the divine. The statues of deities were often made of stone or wood and were placed in temple sanctuaries or carried in processions during festivals.

Altars: Altars were platforms or raised structures used for making offerings to the gods. They could be made of stone, wood, or clay and were typically located in temple courtyards or designated sacred spaces. Altars served as focal points for rituals, where priests and devotees would present offerings of food, drink, incense, and other symbolic items.

Offering Tables: Offering tables were small tables or pedestals used for presenting offerings. They were often decorated with inscriptions or symbols associated with the particular deity being honored. Offering tables could be found both within temple complexes and in private homes, where individuals would make offerings to their personal household gods.

Symbols and symbolism in religious artifacts

Religious artifacts in ancient Egyptian rituals were imbued with symbolic meanings that connected them to the realm of the divine. These symbols conveyed specific concepts, attributes, or relationships associated with the gods and their interactions with humans. Some common symbols found in religious artifacts during the Late Period include:

Ankh: The ankh symbol, often referred to as the "key of life," represented eternal life and was associated with deities and the pharaoh. It was frequently depicted in reliefs, amulets, and other religious objects.

Djed: The djed symbolized stability and endurance. It represented the backbone of the god Osiris and was often depicted on amulets and temple walls.

Shen: The shen symbol, resembling a looped rope, symbolized eternity and encirclement. It was commonly used in amulets and as a decorative motif on ritual objects.

Solar Disc: The solar disc, with or without wings, represented the sun god Ra or other solar deities. It symbolized divine power, enlightenment, and the eternal cycle of the sun.

Materials and techniques used in crafting religious tools during this period

The materials and techniques employed in crafting religious tools during the Late Period varied depending on the object and its purpose. Common materials included:

Stone: Various types of stone, such as limestone, granite, and basalt, were used to create statues, altars, and stelae. Stone carving techniques allowed for intricate details and durable craftsmanship.

Wood: Wood, particularly cedar, cypress, and sycamore, was used for the construction of statues, furniture, and smaller ritual objects. Woodcarving techniques allowed for greater flexibility in design and decoration.

Clay: Clay was widely used for creating pottery vessels, offering bowls, and incense burners. These objects were often shaped by hand or made using molds and then fired in kilns.

Metals: Metals like bronze and gold were used to create more luxurious and elaborate religious objects. Gold, in particular, was associated with divine attributes and was used in the gilding of statues and decoration of temple furniture.

Craftsmen employed various techniques such as carving, sculpting, casting, and inlaying to create religious tools. These techniques required a high level of skill and precision, and the resulting artifacts were not only functional but also aesthetically pleasing, reflecting the religious and artistic ideals of the time.

In conclusion, the Late Period of ancient Egyptian history witnessed the use of a variety of tools and implements in religious rituals. Statues, altars, and offering tables played crucial roles in facilitating communication with the gods and making offerings. These objects were often rich in symbolism, conveying deeper meanings associated with the divine. Crafted from materials such as stone, wood, clay, and metals, these religious tools showcased the craftsmanship and artistic abilities of ancient Egyptian artisans. Their creation involved intricate techniques that resulted in objects of both practical and aesthetic value.

Transformation and Syncretism

The Late Period of ancient Egyptian history witnessed significant foreign influence on temple architecture and design. As foreign powers, such as the Persians and Greeks, exerted their control over Egypt, their architectural styles and preferences found their way into temple construction. The Persian influence can be seen in the use of columned halls and elevated platforms in temple complexes, while the Greek influence introduced elements like porticoes, colonnades, and decorative motifs such as acanthus leaves and floral designs. These architectural innovations reflected the blending of Egyptian and foreign aesthetics, creating a unique fusion of styles.

Integration of foreign deities and practices into Egyptian festivals and celebrations

During the Late Period, as foreign cultures and religions infiltrated Egypt, there was a growing trend of integrating foreign deities and practices into Egyptian festivals and celebrations. The arrival of the Greeks, for example, led to the identification of Egyptian gods with their Greek counterparts through syncretism. This resulted in the creation of new hybrid deities, such as Serapis, who combined aspects of Egyptian and Greek gods. Festivals and celebrations became opportunities for cultural exchange and religious syncretism, allowing for the coexistence of Egyptian and foreign religious traditions.

Shifts in religious symbolism and the use of tools and implements

With the influx of foreign cultures and religious practices, there were notable shifts in religious symbolism and the use of tools and implements during the Late Period. The integration of foreign deities often necessitated the creation of new religious artifacts and symbols that represented the combined beliefs and rituals of different cultures. For example, statues and reliefs began to depict Egyptian gods with Greek-influenced iconography, showcasing a blending of visual symbolism. Additionally, the use of tools and implements in rituals underwent modifications to accommodate new religious practices and beliefs brought in by foreign cultures.

Impact of syncretism on the overall religious landscape of ancient Egypt during this period

The process of syncretism, where Egyptian and foreign religious beliefs and practices merged, had a profound impact on the overall religious landscape of ancient Egypt during the Late Period. Syncretism allowed for the adaptation and incorporation of foreign gods into the Egyptian pantheon, resulting in a broader range of deities and increased diversity in religious practices. This blending of traditions and beliefs fostered a sense of religious tolerance and openness to cultural exchange. Syncretism also played a role in the preservation of certain aspects of ancient Egyptian religion, as foreign rulers and communities sought to align themselves with the ancient Egyptian religious heritage.

In conclusion, the Late Period of ancient Egyptian history witnessed a transformation and syncretism of religious practices due to the influence of foreign cultures. Temple architecture and design incorporated elements from Persian and Greek cultures, creating a unique fusion of styles. Festivals and celebrations became platforms for the integration of foreign deities and practices into the Egyptian religious calendar. Religious symbolism and the use of tools and implements underwent changes to accommodate these new influences. Syncretism had a profound impact on the overall religious landscape, fostering religious tolerance and preserving aspects of ancient Egyptian religion in the face of foreign influence.

Preservation and Destruction

During the Late Period, despite foreign rule and influences, there were notable preservation efforts made to protect temples and religious sites. The rulers of the time recognized the importance of these sacred spaces as centers of power and community cohesion. They invested resources in maintaining and renovating temples, ensuring that the religious structures remained functional and visually impressive. These preservation efforts aimed to uphold the religious traditions and the divine authority associated with the temples. It is through these efforts that many temples from the Late Period have survived to the present day, allowing us to study and understand ancient Egyptian religious practices.

Destruction and repurposing of temples under foreign rule

While there were preservation efforts, the foreign rulers of Egypt also had their own religious and political agendas that sometimes led to the destruction and repurposing of temples. The Persians, for instance, often viewed religious structures as symbols of power and authority. They would occasionally dismantle or modify existing temples to suit their own religious beliefs and practices. Similarly, the Greeks, while introducing their own architectural styles and deities, sometimes repurposed Egyptian temples for their own religious ceremonies. This resulted in a gradual alteration of the original religious intent and purpose of these temples.

Rediscovery and archaeological study of temples and religious artifacts from this period

In modern times, the rediscovery and archaeological study of temples and religious artifacts from the Late Period have greatly contributed to our understanding of ancient Egyptian religion. The efforts of archaeologists and scholars have unearthed significant temple complexes, providing valuable insights into the religious practices, rituals, and beliefs of the time. Through meticulous excavations, researchers have uncovered statues, reliefs, and inscriptions that shed light on the syncretism and blending of cultures during this period. These discoveries have allowed for a deeper examination of the impact of foreign influences on Egyptian religious practices and the transformation of ancient Egyptian spirituality.

In conclusion, the Late Period witnessed a combination of preservation and destruction of temples and religious sites under foreign rule. While preservation efforts were made to maintain the sacred spaces and uphold religious traditions, foreign rulers also repurposed and modified temples to align with their own religious and political agendas. Nonetheless, the rediscovery and archaeological study of temples and religious artifacts from this period have provided invaluable insights into the religious practices and beliefs of ancient Egypt, allowing us to piece together the complex interactions between indigenous and foreign influences during this transformative era.

Chapter 18: Prayers, Hymns, Chants, and Spells Reflecting Syncretism with Foreign Gods and Religious Practices

The Late Period of ancient Egypt witnessed significant political and cultural changes, including foreign invasions and the subsequent influence of foreign cultures on Egyptian society. As a result, the religious landscape of this period became increasingly syncretic, marked by the blending and integration of Egyptian deities and practices with those of foreign gods and religious traditions. This chapter aims to explore the syncretic nature of prayers, hymns, chants, and spells during the Late Period, shedding light on the dynamic interplay between indigenous Egyptian beliefs and the religious concepts introduced by foreign cultures.

Significance of prayers, hymns, chants, and spells in reflecting the influence of foreign gods and religious practices

Prayers, hymns, chants, and spells held immense significance in ancient Egyptian religious practices. They were considered powerful means of communication with the divine and were employed in various contexts, including daily rituals, temple ceremonies, and personal devotions. During the Late Period, as foreign deities and religious practices were introduced to Egypt, these texts played a crucial role in reflecting the syncretic nature of the religious beliefs and practices of the time.

The syncretism seen in prayers, hymns, chants, and spells is evident in the invocation and acknowledgment of both Egyptian and foreign gods. These texts often combined elements from different religious traditions, merging Egyptian concepts with those of the foreign deities. Through the use of syncretic language and imagery, they aimed to establish a connection between diverse religious systems and foster a sense of unity among worshippers.

Aim of the chapter to explore the syncretic nature of these texts and their role in the religious beliefs and practices of the time

The aim of this chapter is to delve into the syncretic nature of prayers, hymns, chants, and spells during the Late Period and examine their role in shaping religious beliefs and practices. By studying these texts, we can gain insights into the ways in which the ancient Egyptians navigated the complexities of religious syncretism, adapting their traditional beliefs to incorporate foreign concepts and deities. This analysis will shed light on the dynamic and ever-evolving nature of ancient Egyptian spirituality and its response to cultural exchanges and influences.

To facilitate a comprehensive understanding, the chapter will present a range of examples, problems, and exercises to illustrate the syncretic aspects of prayers, hymns, chants, and spells. These examples will draw from various fields, such as Witchcraft, Divination, Herbalism, Shamanism, Ecospirituality, and Magic in Ancient Egypt, allowing students to explore the diverse manifestations of syncretism in ancient Egyptian religious texts. By engaging in critical thinking and discussion, students will deepen their understanding of the complexities surrounding the fusion of Egyptian and foreign religious beliefs, while also considering counterarguments and dissenting opinions within the scholarly discourse.

In conclusion, the syncretic religious landscape of ancient Egypt during the Late Period provided fertile ground for the integration of foreign gods and religious practices with the indigenous Egyptian traditions. Prayers, hymns, chants, and spells played a crucial role in reflecting this syncretism, offering glimpses into the religious beliefs and practices of the time. Through a thorough examination of these texts, this chapter aims to unravel the intricacies of religious syncretism and its impact on the ancient Egyptian worldview, inviting students to explore the dynamic nature of religious evolution and adaptation in a multicultural society.

Syncretism and Foreign Influence

Syncretism refers to the merging or blending of different religious beliefs and practices, often resulting in the incorporation of foreign elements into existing religious systems. In the context of ancient Egypt during the Late Period, syncretism played a significant role in shaping the religious landscape. As Egypt experienced foreign invasions and cultural exchanges, the interaction with diverse cultures led to the assimilation of foreign gods, rituals, and religious concepts into the Egyptian pantheon.

Syncretism in ancient Egyptian religion was not a sudden phenomenon but rather a gradual process that occurred over centuries. It reflected the cultural exchanges, political alliances, and trade networks established with neighboring regions, such as Persia, Greece, and Rome. The syncretic nature of religious beliefs during this period highlights the adaptability and flexibility of ancient Egyptian spirituality in response to external influences.

Overview of the foreign gods and religious practices that influenced Egyptian belief systems

The foreign gods and religious practices that influenced Egyptian belief systems during the Late Period were diverse and varied. The Persian conquest of Egypt introduced elements of Zoroastrianism, such as the worship of Ahura Mazda and the concept of cosmic dualism. Greek and Hellenistic influences brought deities such as Dionysus, Hercules, and Serapis into the Egyptian pantheon, while Roman rule further expanded the integration of foreign gods, including Isis and Osiris.

These foreign gods often found their counterparts in the Egyptian pantheon, with syncretic deities being formed as a result. For example, the Egyptian god Amun was associated with the Greek deity Zeus-Ammon, forming the syncretic deity Amun-Zeus. Similarly, the goddess Isis became associated with the Greek goddess Demeter, giving rise to the syncretic deity Isis-Demeter.

Examination of the reasons behind the assimilation of foreign deities into the Egyptian pantheon

The assimilation of foreign deities into the Egyptian pantheon can be attributed to several factors. Firstly, it served political and diplomatic purposes, as Egyptian rulers sought to establish alliances and foster cultural integration with foreign powers. By incorporating foreign deities, they aimed to legitimize their rule and create a sense of unity among their diverse subjects.

Secondly, the assimilation of foreign deities was also driven by religious syncretism, which allowed for the integration of different religious concepts and practices. This syncretism facilitated a sense of religious harmony, enabling worshippers to find common ground and celebrate shared religious values.

Furthermore, the assimilation of foreign deities into the Egyptian pantheon also catered to the needs and beliefs of the multicultural population within Egypt. As the country became a melting pot of cultures, syncretism provided a means to accommodate diverse religious practices and create a cohesive social fabric.

In conclusion, the Late Period of ancient Egypt witnessed the emergence of a syncretic religious landscape characterized by the assimilation of foreign gods and religious practices into the Egyptian pantheon. This process of syncretism reflected the cultural exchanges and political dynamics of the time. The integration of foreign deities allowed for the formation of syncretic gods and the development of new rituals, prayers, hymns, chants, and spells that blended elements from different religious traditions. By exploring these syncretic texts, this chapter aims to provide students with a deeper understanding of the complex interplay between indigenous Egyptian beliefs and the religious concepts introduced by foreign cultures. Through the examination of examples, problems, and exercises, students will engage in critical thinking and discussion, exploring the implications and significance of syncretism in ancient Egyptian spirituality.

Prayers Reflecting Syncretism

During the Late Period, prayers reflecting syncretism emerged as a result of the assimilation of foreign gods and religious practices into the Egyptian pantheon. These prayers demonstrate the blending of indigenous Egyptian beliefs with concepts and imagery from foreign cultures. By analyzing these syncretic prayers, we gain insight into the complex interplay between different religious traditions and the evolving spiritual landscape of ancient Egypt.

One example of syncretic prayers can be found in the worship of the syncretic deity Isis-Demeter. These prayers often include references to both Egyptian and Greek mythologies, invoking the protective and nurturing qualities of Isis as well as the fertility and agricultural aspects associated with Demeter. Through the combination of Egyptian and Greek symbolism, these prayers provide a unique expression of devotion that resonated with individuals from both cultures.

Identification of common themes, motifs, and theological concepts in these syncretic prayers

Syncretic prayers often exhibit common themes, motifs, and theological concepts that reflect the merging of Egyptian and foreign religious traditions. One recurring theme is the emphasis on divine protection and guidance, drawing upon the Egyptian belief in the protective role of deities and combining it with elements of foreign traditions. These prayers seek the benevolence of the syncretic deities, invoking their powers to ensure safety, prosperity, and spiritual enlightenment.

Another prominent motif is the focus on divine healing and fertility. Syncretic prayers frequently incorporate elements of Egyptian healing rituals and magical practices alongside influences from other cultures. These prayers invoke the syncretic deities to restore health, provide solace, and bless individuals with abundance and fertility.

Theological concepts present in syncretic prayers include the idea of divine intercession and the concept of a universal deity encompassing multiple aspects and identities. These prayers often acknowledge the interconnectedness of different gods and goddesses, highlighting their complementary roles and the harmony that can be found in their combined worship.

Exploration of the language, structure, and purpose of these prayers in the context of syncretism

The language, structure, and purpose of syncretic prayers reflect the fusion of Egyptian and foreign religious traditions. In terms of language, syncretic prayers often incorporate both Egyptian and foreign words, invoking deities using their respective names from different pantheons. This linguistic blending serves to honor and unite the diverse spiritual influences present in the syncretic context.

The structure of syncretic prayers may follow traditional Egyptian prayer formats, such as invocations, praises, and petitions, while incorporating new elements influenced by foreign practices. These prayers may incorporate hymnic elements, poetic verses, or formulaic phrases that draw upon both Egyptian and foreign religious traditions.

The purpose of syncretic prayers is multifaceted. They seek to establish a connection with the syncretic deities, express devotion, and seek divine assistance and blessings. Additionally, syncretic prayers often serve as a means of affirming the cultural and religious identity of individuals living in a diverse and changing religious landscape.

By exploring the language, structure, and purpose of syncretic prayers, students can gain a deeper understanding of how these texts reflect the syncretic nature of ancient Egyptian religion during the Late Period. Through examples, problems, and exercises, students will engage in critical analysis, examining the theological implications, cultural significance, and individual spiritual experiences conveyed in these syncretic prayers. This exploration will foster a broader appreciation for the complexities of religious syncretism and its role in shaping the religious beliefs and practices of ancient Egypt.

Hymns Reflecting Syncretism

In the syncretic religious landscape of ancient Egypt during the Late Period, hymns emerged as a significant form of religious expression that blended elements of both indigenous Egyptian beliefs and foreign religious traditions. These syncretic hymns represent a fascinating fusion of diverse cultural influences and offer valuable insights into the evolving religious beliefs and practices of the time.

One notable example of syncretic hymns is found in the worship of the deity Serapis. Serapis was a syncretic god combining attributes of the Egyptian deity Osiris and the Greek god Zeus, among others. Hymns dedicated to Serapis often incorporate references to Egyptian concepts of resurrection, the afterlife, and divine kingship, while also incorporating Greek motifs of power, wisdom, and cosmic harmony. Through the blending of Egyptian and Greek themes, these hymns create a unique poetic expression that resonated with individuals from both cultural backgrounds.

Analysis of poetic elements, metaphors, and imagery used in syncretic hymns

Syncretic hymns often employ a rich array of poetic elements, metaphors, and imagery to convey the complex interplay between different religious traditions. These poetic devices serve to bridge the cultural and theological gaps between the Egyptian and foreign elements, creating a harmonious blend of symbolism.

Metaphors play a vital role in syncretic hymns, enabling the expression of abstract concepts and the forging of connections between different religious ideas. Metaphorical language is used to describe the syncretic deities and their attributes, drawing upon both Egyptian and foreign mythological imagery. For example, a syncretic hymn may describe a deity as "the winged protector, soaring like the falcon, embodying the divine justice of Ma'at and the swift messenger of the Greek pantheon." Such metaphors unite diverse cultural symbols and evoke a vivid imagery that resonates with worshippers.

Imagery in syncretic hymns often draws upon the iconography of both Egyptian and foreign deities, merging visual representations to create a new symbolic language. These hymns may describe the syncretic gods as having the head of one deity and the body of another, symbolizing the blending of their powers and characteristics. Additionally, natural and cosmic imagery are frequently employed to convey the grandeur and universality of the syncretic deities, evoking images of starry skies, flowing rivers, and fertile landscapes.

Discussion of the role of syncretic hymns in expressing devotion and establishing a connection with the divine

Syncretic hymns serve as powerful tools for expressing devotion and establishing a profound connection with the divine in the syncretic religious context. Through the blending of Egyptian and foreign religious themes, these hymns offer worshippers a means to engage with and honor the diverse spiritual influences present in their religious lives.

These hymns enable individuals to articulate their religious experiences and aspirations in a way that bridges cultural boundaries. By incorporating elements from multiple traditions, syncretic hymns foster a sense of inclusivity and universality, inviting worshippers from different backgrounds to unite in their devotion to the syncretic deities.

Furthermore, syncretic hymns provide a channel for worshippers to connect with the divine on a personal and emotional level. The poetic language, metaphors, and imagery employed in these hymns evoke a sense of awe, wonder, and reverence. They inspire worshippers to contemplate the divine mysteries, seek divine guidance, and express gratitude for the blessings bestowed upon them.

Through examples, problems, and exercises, students will delve into the analysis of syncretic hymns, examining the poetic elements, metaphors, and imagery used to convey the blending of Egyptian and foreign religious themes. Students will also explore the emotional and spiritual impact of syncretic hymns, reflecting on the role of these hymns in fostering a sense of devotion, unity, and connection with the divine. This exploration will facilitate critical thinking and discussion, allowing students to appreciate the complex beauty and profound spiritual significance of syncretic hymns in ancient Egyptian religious practices during the Late Period.

Chants Reflecting Syncretism

Within the syncretic religious landscape of ancient Egypt during the Late Period, chants emerged as a distinct form of religious expression that integrated elements of both Egyptian and foreign religious practices and beliefs. These syncretic chants reflect the cultural exchange and assimilation of diverse religious traditions, offering valuable insights into the evolving religious landscape of the time.

One example of chants reflecting syncretism is found in the worship of the goddess Isis. As the popularity of the cult of Isis spread throughout the Mediterranean, chants dedicated to Isis incorporated elements from various cultures and traditions. These chants often blended Egyptian invocations and praises with Greek and Roman musical styles and linguistic patterns. The result was a harmonious fusion of vocal expressions that resonated with worshippers from different cultural backgrounds.

Analysis of the rhythmic patterns, vocal techniques, and musical elements in syncretic chants

Syncretic chants exhibit distinct rhythmic patterns, vocal techniques, and musical elements that contribute to their unique character and spiritual significance. The rhythmic patterns employed in these chants often draw from both Egyptian and foreign musical traditions. They may incorporate the steady and cyclic rhythms of ancient Egyptian music with the melodic and rhythmic complexity of Greek or Roman musical styles. This blending of rhythmic elements creates a dynamic and engaging sonic experience during communal worship and ritual practices.

Vocal techniques play a crucial role in syncretic chants, conveying the emotional and spiritual content of the religious expressions. These techniques may include melodic ornamentation, vocal improvisation, and harmonic interplay. By combining vocal techniques from different cultural traditions, syncretic chants evoke a sense of unity in diversity, celebrating the fusion of various religious practices and beliefs.

Musical elements, such as instrumentation and accompanying sounds, also contribute to the richness of syncretic chants. Depending on the cultural influences, these chants may be accompanied by traditional Egyptian instruments like the sistrum or harp, as well as instruments introduced through foreign contacts, such as the lyre or tambourine. The interplay of these musical elements adds depth and texture to the chants, enhancing the spiritual experience and fostering a sense of collective worship.

Exploration of the performative aspects of these chants and their role in communal worship and ritual practices

Syncretic chants hold a significant role in communal worship and ritual practices, serving as a unifying force and facilitating a shared religious experience. These chants are often performed by a group of worshippers, creating a collective voice that resonates with the divine and strengthens the bonds of the community.

The performative aspects of syncretic chants involve not only the vocal delivery but also bodily movements and gestures. Worshippers may sway, dance, or engage in synchronized movements during the chanting, enhancing the spiritual atmosphere and fostering a sense of connection with the divine and fellow worshippers.

Syncretic chants function as a means to invoke and honor the syncretic deities, establishing a sacred space and inviting the presence of the divine. Through the rhythmic patterns, vocal techniques, and musical elements, these chants evoke a sense of reverence, devotion, and transcendence. They create a collective energy and emotional resonance that binds worshippers together in their shared religious journey.

Through examples, problems, and exercises, students will have the opportunity to analyze and interpret syncretic chants, exploring the rhythmic, vocal, and musical elements that reflect the fusion of Egyptian and foreign religious practices. They will also reflect on the performative aspects of these chants, considering their role in fostering communal worship, spiritual connection, and the expression of syncretic religious beliefs. This analysis will encourage critical thinking and provide students with a deeper understanding of the diverse and dynamic nature of ancient Egyptian religious practices during the Late Period.

Spells Reflecting Syncretism

In the syncretic religious landscape of ancient Egypt during the Late Period, spells played a significant role in the integration of Egyptian and foreign magical traditions and practices. These syncretic spells exemplify the cultural exchange and assimilation of diverse magical beliefs and techniques, offering valuable insights into the evolving nature of magical practices during this period.

One notable example is the combination of Egyptian and Greek magical traditions in the form of magical papyri, such as the Greek Magical Papyri. These papyri contain a collection of spells and rituals that blend elements of both Egyptian and Greek magical systems. They reflect the influences of Greek magical practices, including the use of invocations, incantations, and magical formulas, combined with Egyptian concepts of divine power, deities, and ritual symbolism.

"The Charm of Opening":

"Place a beetle between the rays of the sun and the light of the moon, then read the charm: 'I invoke you, the great god, the one who holds sway over the heavens and the earth, the one who brings forth the power of the gods, the one who possesses the knowledge of the hidden secrets. By your divine authority, I command the gatekeeper to open the doors and reveal the hidden treasures.'"

This spell demonstrates the syncretic nature of the Greek Magical Papyri, incorporating elements of Egyptian symbolism (the beetle, associated with the sun god Khepri) and Greek invocations and concepts (the great god who holds sway over the heavens and the earth). The purpose of this spell is to open doors and access hidden treasures, utilizing the combined power of Egyptian and Greek magical beliefs and practices.

This excerpt showcases the linguistic blend, ritual structure, and syncretic approach found in the Greek Magical Papyri, as it draws upon both Egyptian and Greek magical traditions to achieve its desired effect.

Analysis of the language, structure, and symbols used in syncretic spells

Syncretic spells exhibit distinctive features in terms of language, structure, and symbols, reflecting the amalgamation of Egyptian and foreign magical traditions. The language used in these spells often demonstrates a blend of Egyptian and foreign words, phrases, and incantations. For instance, an Egyptian spell invoking the power of an Egyptian deity may incorporate Greek or Demotic words for specific magical actions or concepts.

The structure of syncretic spells may follow a hybrid format, combining elements from Egyptian ritual texts and foreign magical formulae. This fusion results in a unique structure that accommodates the incorporation of foreign concepts while maintaining the core principles of Egyptian magical practices.

Symbols used in syncretic spells represent a fusion of Egyptian and foreign deities, magical creatures, and divine forces. These symbols serve as conduits for the desired magical effects, bridging the gap between different religious traditions and unlocking the power of the syncretic spell.

Discussion of the intended purposes and effects of these spells in the context of syncretism

Syncretic spells were employed for a variety of purposes, including healing, protection, divination, love, and fertility. Their intended effects were achieved through the harmonious blending of Egyptian and foreign magical techniques and belief systems. For example, a syncretic love spell might combine Egyptian love deities with Greek love charms and rituals to attract affection or strengthen romantic relationships.

The syncretic nature of these spells allowed individuals to tap into a broader range of magical resources and belief systems. It provided practitioners with a more versatile toolkit, drawing on the strengths and attributes of various deities and magical practices. The syncretic spells aimed to leverage the combined power and effectiveness of multiple traditions, offering a comprehensive and inclusive approach to magic.

Through the analysis of examples, problems, and exercises, students will gain a deeper understanding of syncretic spells and their role in ancient Egyptian religious practices. They will explore the blending of Egyptian and foreign magical traditions, decipher the language, structure, and symbols used in syncretic spells, and contemplate the intended purposes and effects of these spells in the context of syncretism. This exploration will foster critical thinking and appreciation for the complex interplay of cultural and magical influences in ancient Egypt.

Title: Spell for Harmony and Protection

Purpose: This syncretic spell combines Egyptian and Roman elements to invoke harmony and protection in daily life.

Ingredients:

A small amulet or charm representing the deity of harmony (e.g., Ma'at in Egyptian mythology)
An incense blend combining traditional Egyptian herbs (such as myrrh and frankincense) with Roman herbs (such as lavender and rosemary)
A white candle
A piece of parchment or paper
A writing utensil
Instructions:

Exploring the Rituals, Beliefs, and Syncretism of Ancient Egyptian Religion

Begin by preparing your sacred space. Light the white candle and the blended incense, allowing their fragrances to fill the air.

Take the amulet or charm in your hands and close your eyes. Visualize a harmonious energy surrounding you, emanating from the amulet and spreading throughout your being.

On the parchment or paper, write the following incantation, combining Egyptian and Roman elements:

"By the power of Ma'at, the embodiment of balance,
And by the grace of Venus, the goddess of love,
I call upon the forces of harmony and protection.
May the balance of Ma'at guide my actions,
And may the love of Venus shield me from harm.
As I carry this amulet, I am in harmony with the cosmos,
And I am protected from all negativity and discord."

Fold the parchment or paper, symbolizing the sealing of the spell's intention. Hold it close to the flame of the white candle, allowing the fire to purify and activate the written words.

Place the folded parchment or paper near the amulet or charm, infusing it with the energy of the spell. Keep it in a safe place or carry it with you as a talisman of harmony and protection.

As you conclude the spell, express your gratitude to the deities and forces invoked. Extinguish the candle and let the incense burn out naturally.

Note: It is essential to approach syncretic spells with respect and understanding of the deities and traditions involved. It is also recommended to adapt and personalize the spell according to your own beliefs and practices, ensuring that you work with cultural and spiritual sensitivity.

Remember, this example is a general outline, and it is important to conduct further research and adapt the spell to align with specific deities or belief systems that resonate with you.

Title: Spell for Abundance and Prosperity

Purpose: This spell combines elements from ancient Egyptian and Celtic traditions to attract abundance and prosperity into one's life.

Ingredients:

Green candle
A small bowl of earth or soil
A handful of coins or small gemstones
A sprig of fresh mint
A small piece of paper or parchment
A writing utensil
Instructions:

Begin by finding a quiet and sacred space where you can focus on the spell. Light the green candle, representing growth, abundance, and prosperity.

Take the bowl of earth or soil and hold it in your hands. Close your eyes and visualize fertile land, symbolizing the foundation for abundance and prosperity.

Place the handful of coins or gemstones on the soil, visualizing them as a representation of wealth and prosperity. Feel the energy of abundance flowing into the coins or gemstones.

Take the sprig of fresh mint and hold it in your hands. Inhale its aroma, which is associated with abundance and good fortune in both ancient Egyptian and Celtic traditions.

On the piece of paper or parchment, write down your intention for abundance and prosperity. Be specific and affirmative, such as "I attract financial abundance and prosperity into my life with ease and joy."

Roll up the paper or parchment and tie it with the sprig of mint, symbolizing the binding of your intention with the energy of abundance.

Hold the rolled-up paper and sprig of mint over the flame of the green candle, visualizing the intention being infused with the transformative power of the fire.

Place the rolled-up paper and mint bundle in the bowl of coins or gemstones. As you do so, imagine the energy of abundance being absorbed by the intention.

Keep the bowl in a prominent place in your home or workspace, where you can see it daily. Allow the coins or gemstones to serve as a reminder of abundance and prosperity.

Each time you pass by the bowl, take a moment to visualize and affirm your intention for abundance and prosperity.

As the spell concludes, express your gratitude to the energies and deities associated with abundance and prosperity, such as the Egyptian god Osiris or the Celtic goddess Brigid.

Interpretation and Significance

The incorporation of foreign gods and religious practices into ancient Egyptian prayers, hymns, chants, and spells during the Late Period holds great cultural and religious significance. It represents a period of cultural exchange, interaction, and adaptation between the Egyptians and various foreign cultures, such as the Greeks, Persians, and Romans. This syncretism demonstrates the openness and flexibility of Egyptian religious traditions, as well as their ability to assimilate and integrate new beliefs and practices.

By incorporating elements from foreign traditions, these syncretic texts served as a bridge between different cultures and religions. They allowed for the expression of shared beliefs and the formation of a shared religious language, fostering understanding and cooperation among diverse communities. Additionally, syncretism provided a means for individuals to navigate the complexities of religious identity and affiliation in a multicultural society.

Analysis of the theological implications and worldview conveyed through these texts:

The syncretic prayers, hymns, chants, and spells reflect a blending of religious concepts, symbolism, and rituals from different cultures. They convey a worldview that acknowledges the interconnectedness of religious traditions and the universality of spiritual experiences. The combination of Egyptian and foreign deities, symbols, and rituals in these texts implies a recognition of the underlying unity of divine forces, despite their different cultural expressions.

Furthermore, these syncretic texts often convey a sense of harmony and balance between different aspects of existence. They may emphasize the harmonious relationship between the human and divine realms, the balance between order and chaos, or the interconnectedness of nature and spirituality. Through these theological implications, syncretic texts invite individuals to embrace a holistic understanding of the world and their place within it.

Reflection on the impact of syncretism on the evolution of ancient Egyptian religious beliefs and practices:

The practice of syncretism played a significant role in the evolution of ancient Egyptian religious beliefs and practices during the Late Period. It brought about a transformation and enrichment of the religious landscape, expanding the pantheon of deities, introducing new rituals and ceremonies, and influencing the overall religious worldview.

Syncretism allowed for the preservation of ancient Egyptian religious traditions in the face of foreign domination. By incorporating elements from foreign cultures, Egyptians were able to adapt and maintain their religious identity while also accommodating new beliefs and practices. This adaptive nature of Egyptian religion contributed to its resilience and longevity over several centuries.

Moreover, syncretism fostered cultural exchange and mutual influence between Egypt and other civilizations. It facilitated the spread of Egyptian religious ideas and practices to foreign lands, while also absorbing and integrating aspects of foreign religions into Egyptian beliefs. This dynamic process of cultural exchange and adaptation shaped the religious landscape of not only ancient Egypt but also neighboring regions, leaving a lasting impact on the development of religious traditions in the wider Mediterranean world.

In conclusion, the syncretic prayers, hymns, chants, and spells of ancient Egypt offer valuable insights into the cultural and religious dynamics of the Late Period. They highlight the significance of syncretism as a means of cultural exchange and adaptation, the theological implications of blending diverse religious traditions, and the transformative impact of syncretism on ancient Egyptian religious beliefs and practices. By studying and reflecting upon these texts, we gain a deeper understanding of the complex and ever-evolving nature of religious expression in ancient Egypt.

Part 7: Ptolemaic and Roman Periods (332 BCE - 395 CE)

The Ptolemaic and Roman Periods mark a significant era in the history of ancient Egypt, spanning from the conquest of Egypt by Alexander the Great in 332 BCE to the fall of the Western Roman Empire in 395 CE. This period is characterized by the rule of the Ptolemaic dynasty, founded by one of Alexander's generals, Ptolemy I, and later followed by the Roman conquest and subsequent Roman rule over Egypt.

Political and Cultural Transformations

The Ptolemaic Dynasty: With the establishment of the Ptolemaic dynasty, Egypt witnessed a fusion of Greek and Egyptian cultures. The Ptolemaic rulers, eager to legitimize their reign, adopted Egyptian royal traditions and integrated themselves into the religious and administrative systems of ancient Egypt. This blending of Greek and Egyptian elements resulted in a unique cultural and religious landscape.

Roman Influence: The Roman conquest of Egypt in 30 BCE brought about significant changes in the political, social, and religious spheres. Roman rulers, such as Augustus, sought to establish their authority by adopting the trappings of Egyptian kingship and incorporating Egyptian deities into the Roman pantheon. This syncretism between Roman and Egyptian religious traditions had a profound impact on the religious practices of the time.

Continuity and Transformation of Religious Practices

Temple Worship: Despite the political changes, temple worship remained a central aspect of religious life during the Ptolemaic and Roman Periods. Temples continued to serve as important centers of religious and civic activities, where rituals, processions, and festivals were conducted to honor the gods.

Integration of Greek and Egyptian Traditions: The Ptolemaic and Roman Periods witnessed a blending of Greek and Egyptian religious traditions. Greek deities were equated with their Egyptian counterparts, resulting in the emergence of hybrid deities like Serapis and Isis-Sothis. This syncretism reflects the cultural exchange and religious adaptation that occurred during this time.

Transformation of Magic and Ritual Practices: Magic and ritual practices in ancient Egypt underwent significant transformations during the Ptolemaic and Roman Periods. Influenced by Greek magical traditions and Hellenistic astrology, Egyptian magical texts and rituals incorporated new elements and concepts. Additionally, the rise of Christianity in the later Roman period introduced new religious practices and beliefs.

Aim of Part 7: Exploring the Ptolemaic and Roman Periods

The aim of Part 7 is to provide an in-depth exploration of the Ptolemaic and Roman Periods and their impact on ancient Egyptian religious practices. By examining the political, cultural, and religious dynamics of this era, we gain insights into the continuity and transformation of ancient Egyptian religion under foreign influence. Through the analysis of historical sources, archaeological evidence, and textual materials, we aim to unravel the complexities of religious syncretism, the integration of foreign deities, and the evolution of magical and ritual practices during this period.

As we delve into this chapter, we will encounter various examples, problems, and exercises to illustrate the topics and engage students in critical thinking and discussion. By examining diverse perspectives and analyzing primary sources, students will develop a comprehensive understanding of the Ptolemaic and Roman Periods and their impact on ancient Egyptian religious beliefs and practices.

Ruler	Spouse(s)	Children	Notable Accomplishments	Years Ruled
Ptolemy I	Berenice I, Eurydice	Ptolemy II, Arsinoe II, etc.	Founded the Ptolemaic Dynasty	305 BCE - 283 BCE
Ptolemy II	Arsinoe I, Arsinoe II, etc.	Ptolemy III, Berenice, etc.	Construction of the Pharos Lighthouse	283 BCE - 246 BCE
Ptolemy III	Berenice II	Ptolemy IV, Arsinoe III, etc.	Expanding the Ptolemaic Empire	246 BCE - 222 BCE
Ptolemy IV	Arsinoe III	Ptolemy V, Cleopatra I	Defeat of the Seleucid Empire	222 BCE - 204 BCE
Ptolemy V	Cleopatra I	Ptolemy VI, Cleopatra II	Rosetta Stone and Memphis Decree	204 BCE - 180 BCE

Cleopatra II	Ptolemy VI, Ptolemy VIII	Ptolemy VII, Cleopatra III	Struggles for power within the dynasty	180 BCE - 145 BCE
Ptolemy VIII	Cleopatra II, Cleopatra III	Cleopatra II, Cleopatra III	Civil wars and conflicts with siblings	170 BCE - 163 BCE
Cleopatra III	Ptolemy VIII	Ptolemy IX, Cleopatra IV	Reign marked by political instability	142 BCE - 101 BCE
Cleopatra IV	Ptolemy IX	None	Short-lived reign	116 BCE - 115 BCE
Ptolemy IX	Cleopatra IV, Cleopatra Selene II	Ptolemy X, Cleopatra Selene I	Fought against rival claimants to power	116 BCE - 107 BCE, 88 BCE
Cleopatra Selene	Antiochus VIII, Juba of Numidia	None	Last ruler of the Ptolemaic dynasty	47 BCE - 30 BCE
Julius Caesar	Cleopatra VII	Caesarion (with Cleopatra)	Relationship with Cleopatra, Roman ally	48 BCE - 44 BCE
Mark Antony	Cleopatra VII	Alexander Helios, Cleopatra Selene II, Ptolemy Philadelphus	Defeat by Octavian, suicide with Cleopatra	44 BCE - 30 BCE
Octavian (Augustus)		None	Annexation of Egypt, establishment of Roman rule	30 BCE - 14 CE
Roman Emperors	Various wives and consorts		Romanization of Egypt, spread of Christianity	14 CE - 395 CE

Chapter 19: Integration of Egyptian Religious Beliefs with Greek and Roman Influences

The Ptolemaic and Roman Periods in ancient Egypt marked a significant era of cultural and religious transformation. Following Alexander the Great's conquest of Egypt in 332 BCE, Greek and later Roman influences began to permeate Egyptian society, including its religious landscape. This chapter aims to explore the integration of Egyptian religious beliefs with Greek and Roman influences, examining the factors that facilitated this syncretism and its impact on the ancient Egyptian worldview.

Cultural Exchange and Syncretism

The integration of Egyptian religious beliefs with Greek and Roman influences was not a sudden occurrence but rather a gradual process that unfolded over several centuries. It was driven by the cultural exchange between the indigenous Egyptian population and the Greek and Roman conquerors and settlers. This exchange fostered a rich interplay of ideas, beliefs, and practices, resulting in the emergence of a syncretic religious framework.

The syncretism of Egyptian religious beliefs with Greek and Roman influences was facilitated by several factors. Firstly, the conquest of Egypt by Alexander the Great and the establishment of the Ptolemaic dynasty led to the coexistence of Greek and Egyptian cultures. Greek rulers and officials encouraged the assimilation of Greek culture and religion into Egyptian society, leading to the introduction of Greek gods and cults alongside the traditional Egyptian deities. This syncretism was further reinforced during the Roman period when Egypt became a province of the Roman Empire.

Blending of Deities and Cults

One of the most significant aspects of the integration of Egyptian religious beliefs with Greek and Roman influences was the blending of deities and cults. The Egyptian pantheon, with its rich tapestry of gods and goddesses, saw the inclusion of Greek and Roman deities, resulting in the emergence of hybrid divine figures. For example, the Egyptian goddess Isis became associated with the Greek goddess Demeter and the Roman goddess Ceres, forming a syncretic deity known as Isis-Demeter or Isis-Ceres.

The syncretism of deities also extended to their respective cults and worship practices. Temples dedicated to Egyptian deities began to incorporate Greek and Roman architectural elements, such as the use of columns and capitals, while still maintaining their distinct Egyptian character. Similarly, Greek and Roman religious practices, such as the offering of animal sacrifices and the use of processions, became integrated into Egyptian religious rituals.

Philosophical and Theological Synthesis

The integration of Egyptian religious beliefs with Greek and Roman influences also entailed a philosophical and theological synthesis. Greek philosophy, particularly Neoplatonism, played a significant role in shaping the intellectual landscape of the Greco-Roman world, including Egypt. Neoplatonist philosophers sought to reconcile Greek philosophical concepts with Egyptian religious beliefs, creating a hybrid philosophical system that incorporated elements of both traditions.

This synthesis resulted in the development of philosophical concepts such as the existence of a supreme divine principle, the immortality of the soul, and the idea of spiritual purification and ascent. These ideas found their way into Egyptian religious thought, enriching the understanding of the divine and the afterlife. The blending of Greek philosophy with Egyptian religious beliefs also influenced the practices of divination, magic, and the pursuit of spiritual enlightenment.

Conclusion

The integration of Egyptian religious beliefs with Greek and Roman influences during the Ptolemaic and Roman Periods marked a significant chapter in the history of ancient Egypt. This syncretism led to the blending of deities, cults, and philosophical ideas, creating a unique religious landscape that incorporated elements from various traditions. The cultural exchange and interaction between the Greek, Roman, and Egyptian populations facilitated this syncretism, allowing for the emergence of a diverse and inclusive religious worldview.

The exploration of the integration of Egyptian religious beliefs with Greek and Roman influences opens the door to a deeper understanding of the complex interplay between different cultures and the evolution of religious thought. Through the examination of various examples, problems, and exercises, students will engage in critical thinking and discussion, delving into the nuances of syncretism and its impact on ancient Egyptian society.

Cultural Exchange and Syncretism

The integration of Egyptian religious beliefs with Greek and Roman influences was a gradual and complex process that occurred over centuries. As a result of conquest, colonization, and cultural interactions, the boundaries between these civilizations became porous, leading to a blending of religious traditions, practices, and beliefs. This syncretism allowed for the coexistence and mutual influence of Egyptian, Greek, and Roman cultural elements within the religious landscape of ancient Egypt.

Influence of the conquest of Egypt by Alexander the Great and the establishment of the Ptolemaic dynasty

The conquest of Egypt by Alexander the Great in 332 BCE marked a significant turning point in the cultural exchange between Egypt and Greece. The establishment of the Ptolemaic dynasty, which ruled Egypt for nearly three centuries, further facilitated the interaction and integration of Greek and Egyptian cultures. The Ptolemies, particularly Ptolemy I and his successors, encouraged the fusion of Greek and Egyptian traditions, resulting in a syncretic religious landscape that incorporated both Greek and Egyptian deities and practices.

Coexistence of Greek and Egyptian cultures and the assimilation of Greek practices and beliefs

During the Ptolemaic period, Greek settlers and officials coexisted with the Egyptian population, leading to a mingling of cultures and the adoption of Greek practices and beliefs by the Egyptians. Greek language, literature, philosophy, and religious ideas permeated Egyptian society, influencing various aspects of life, including religion. The assimilation of Greek practices and beliefs into Egyptian religious traditions contributed to the syncretic nature of the religious landscape, as Egyptian deities began to be identified with their Greek counterparts and new hybrid divine figures emerged.

Impact of Roman rule and the further integration of Roman influences

With the conquest of Egypt by the Romans in 30 BCE, the cultural exchange and syncretism continued and intensified. Roman rulers, such as the Emperor Augustus, sought to maintain the stability of the region by respecting Egyptian religious traditions and integrating them into the wider Roman pantheon. This led to the inclusion of Egyptian deities in the Roman religious system and the development of syncretic cults that blended Egyptian and Roman beliefs and practices. The influence of Roman culture extended beyond religion and affected various aspects of Egyptian society, including art, architecture, language, and social customs.

The cultural exchange and syncretism between Egyptian, Greek, and Roman cultures during the Ptolemaic and Roman periods played a significant role in shaping the religious landscape of ancient Egypt. The gradual assimilation of Greek and Roman practices and beliefs into Egyptian religious traditions resulted in a syncretic fusion that reflected the complex and interconnected nature of the ancient world. This chapter aims to explore this process of integration, examining its implications for religious beliefs, practices, and cultural dynamics.

Blending of Deities and Cults

The integration of Greek and Roman deities into the Egyptian pantheon was a key aspect of the syncretic religious landscape of the Ptolemaic and Roman periods. Egyptian deities were often identified with their Greek and Roman counterparts, resulting in a blending of their characteristics and attributes. For example, the Egyptian goddess Isis became associated with the Greek goddess Demeter, and the Egyptian god Amun merged with the Greek god Zeus. This process of identification allowed for the coexistence and worship of both Egyptian and foreign deities within the same religious framework.

Emergence of hybrid divine figures through syncretism

Syncretism also gave rise to the emergence of hybrid divine figures that combined attributes and characteristics from both Egyptian and Greek or Roman traditions. One notable example is the deity Serapis, who was a fusion of the Egyptian gods Osiris and Apis with Greek influences. Serapis embodied qualities of fertility, resurrection, and ruler of the underworld, appealing to both Egyptian and Greek religious sensibilities. The creation of such hybrid divine figures reflected the syncretic nature of the religious beliefs and the desire to bridge the cultural divide between the different civilizations.

Incorporation of Greek and Roman architectural elements in Egyptian temples

The syncretic nature of the religious landscape is evident not only in the deities but also in the architectural elements of Egyptian temples. As Greek and Roman influences permeated Egyptian society, temples began to incorporate architectural features associated with Greek and Roman temples. This included the use of colonnades, porticos, and decorative elements such as capitals, friezes, and pediments. These architectural elements reflected the fusion of Greek, Roman, and Egyptian styles, creating a distinct hybrid architectural form that embodied the syncretism of the period.

Integration of Greek and Roman religious practices into Egyptian rituals

The integration of Greek and Roman religious practices into Egyptian rituals was another significant aspect of the syncretic religious landscape. Egyptian rituals and festivals began to incorporate elements of Greek and Roman customs, such as processions, libations, and offerings, which were familiar to the foreign populations. This blending of practices allowed for a shared religious experience that appealed to both Egyptians and the Greek and Roman communities. Additionally, new rituals and ceremonies emerged that combined elements from all three traditions, emphasizing the syncretic nature of religious practices during this period.

The blending of deities and cults in the Ptolemaic and Roman periods resulted in a dynamic and diverse religious landscape. The inclusion of Greek and Roman deities, the emergence of hybrid divine figures, the incorporation of architectural elements, and the integration of religious practices from different cultures all contributed to the syncretism that defined this era. Understanding the interplay between Egyptian, Greek, and Roman religious beliefs and practices is crucial for comprehending the complexity and richness of the ancient Egyptian religious experience during these periods.

Philosophical and Theological Synthesis

Greek philosophy, and in particular Neoplatonism, played a significant role in shaping the intellectual landscape during the Ptolemaic and Roman periods in Egypt. Neoplatonism, a philosophical school that sought to reconcile various philosophical and religious traditions, had a profound impact on the synthesis of Greek and Egyptian religious beliefs. Neoplatonic philosophers, such as Plotinus and Proclus, sought to find common ground between Egyptian and Greek cosmologies, metaphysics, and spiritual practices. Their writings and teachings influenced the religious and philosophical discourse of the time, fostering a climate of intellectual exchange and syncretism.

Reconciliation of Greek philosophical concepts with Egyptian religious beliefs

The syncretic religious landscape of the Ptolemaic and Roman periods saw a concerted effort to reconcile Greek philosophical concepts with Egyptian religious beliefs. Greek philosophical ideas, such as the concept of the soul, the nature of the divine, and the pursuit of virtue and wisdom, were integrated into the existing Egyptian religious framework. This synthesis allowed for the exploration of profound metaphysical and ethical questions within an Egyptian religious context, blending the wisdom of both cultures and creating a unique philosophical and theological synthesis.

Influence of philosophical ideas on the understanding of the divine and the afterlife

The philosophical ideas that emerged during this period had a significant impact on the understanding of the divine and the afterlife in ancient Egyptian religion. Greek philosophical concepts, such as the existence of a supreme being or a cosmic order, influenced Egyptian notions of the divine hierarchy and the role of gods in the universe. Moreover, philosophical ideas regarding the immortality of the soul and the nature of the afterlife influenced Egyptian beliefs in the journey of the deceased through the realms of the afterlife. This philosophical lens provided a deeper intellectual understanding and exploration of these religious concepts.

Impact on divination, magic, and the pursuit of spiritual enlightenment

The philosophical and theological synthesis of Greek and Egyptian beliefs also had implications for divination, magic, and the pursuit of spiritual enlightenment. Greek philosophical schools, such as theurgy, explored the use of rituals, symbols, and divine invocations to commune with the gods and achieve spiritual union. These ideas merged with Egyptian magical practices, rituals, and divinatory methods, resulting in a rich blend of magical and mystical traditions. The pursuit of spiritual enlightenment and mystical experiences, influenced by Greek philosophical ideas, became intertwined with Egyptian religious and magical practices, further enriching the spiritual landscape of the time.

In conclusion, the philosophical and theological synthesis of Greek and Egyptian beliefs during the Ptolemaic and Roman periods in Egypt had a profound impact on the intellectual, philosophical, and religious landscape of the time. The reconciliation of Greek philosophical concepts with Egyptian religious beliefs, the influence of Neoplatonism, the understanding of the divine and the afterlife, and the impact on divination, magic, and the pursuit of spiritual enlightenment all contributed to the vibrant syncretism and intellectual flourishing of this era. Understanding the interplay between philosophical and theological ideas is essential for comprehending the complexity and depth of religious and intellectual thought in ancient Egypt during these periods.

Case Studies and Examples

One approach to understanding the integration of Greek and Roman influences in Egyptian religious beliefs is to examine specific deities and their syncretic associations. For example, the Egyptian god Amun, associated with kingship and fertility, became merged with the Greek god Zeus, resulting in the deity Amun-Zeus. This syncretic deity combined the attributes and characteristics of both Egyptian and Greek gods, symbolizing the blending of religious traditions. Another example is the goddess Isis, who gained popularity in the Greco-Roman period and became associated with various Greek and Roman goddesses, such as Aphrodite and Demeter. These syncretic associations not only reflected cultural exchange but also allowed devotees to connect with multiple traditions and pantheons.

Analysis of temples and architectural features reflecting the integration of Greek and Roman influences

The architectural features of temples provide valuable insights into the integration of Greek and Roman influences in Egyptian religious practices. The temple of Philae, for instance, showcases a combination of Egyptian and Hellenistic architectural styles. The use of classical Greek columns alongside Egyptian elements, such as pylons and hypostyle halls, exemplifies the syncretic nature of temple design during this period. Similarly, the temple of Kom Ombo demonstrates the blending of Egyptian and Roman architectural features, including Roman-style courts and Roman gods depicted alongside traditional Egyptian deities on temple walls. These examples highlight the physical manifestations of syncretism and the adaptation of architectural styles to accommodate the religious syncretism of the time.

Exploration of philosophical concepts and their presence in religious texts and practices

The integration of Greek and Roman influences in Egyptian religious beliefs is also evident in the presence of philosophical concepts within religious texts and practices. The Corpus Hermeticum, a collection of philosophical and religious texts attributed to the mythical figure Hermes Trismegistus, fuses Greek philosophical ideas with Egyptian religious and magical practices. These texts explore concepts such as the nature of the divine, the immortality of the soul, and the pursuit of spiritual enlightenment. They represent an attempt to synthesize philosophical and religious thought, providing a philosophical framework within an Egyptian religious context.

Study of syncretic rituals, festivals, and worship practices

The syncretism of Greek and Roman influences in Egyptian religious beliefs is further evident in the study of syncretic rituals, festivals, and worship practices. The worship of Serapis, a syncretic deity combining aspects of Egyptian and Greek gods, became popular during the Ptolemaic and Roman periods. Serapis had a dedicated temple in Alexandria, where Egyptians and Greeks alike could worship this syncretic god. The festival of the Mysteries of Isis and Osiris, celebrated throughout the Greco-Roman world, combined Egyptian rituals with Greek theatrical performances and processions, demonstrating the fusion of religious practices from both cultures. These examples highlight the dynamic nature of religious rituals and the willingness of devotees to embrace syncretism in their worship practices.

In conclusion, the integration of Greek and Roman influences in Egyptian religious beliefs during the Ptolemaic and Roman periods is evident in the examination of specific deities and their syncretic associations, the analysis of temple architecture, the exploration of philosophical concepts in religious texts, and the study of syncretic rituals, festivals, and worship practices. These case studies and examples shed light on the complex interplay between different cultural and religious traditions, revealing the multifaceted nature of syncretism and the enduring influence of Greek and Roman cultures on the religious landscape of ancient Egypt.

Impact and Legacy

The integration of Greek and Roman influences in ancient Egyptian religious beliefs marked a significant evolution in the religious landscape of the region. The syncretism of deities, rituals, and philosophical concepts resulted in the emergence of new religious syntheses that combined elements from both Egyptian and Greco-Roman traditions. This integration led to the reinterpretation and reimagining of traditional Egyptian religious beliefs, as well as the adoption of new practices and ideas.

For example, the syncretic deity Serapis, who combined attributes of Egyptian and Greek gods, became one of the most prominent gods in the Ptolemaic and Roman periods. Serapis represented the fusion of Egyptian fertility and afterlife beliefs with Greek concepts of healing and salvation. This evolution in religious beliefs and practices reflected the cultural exchange and adaptation that occurred during this period.

Influence on subsequent religious traditions and cultural developments

The syncretism of Egyptian religious beliefs with Greek and Roman influences had a lasting impact on subsequent religious traditions and cultural developments. The blending of religious ideas and practices set a precedent for later syncretic movements and contributed to the development of new religious systems.

For example, the worship of Isis, a syncretic goddess who gained popularity during the Greco-Roman period, continued to influence religious practices in the Mediterranean region and beyond. The spread of Isis worship, along with the adoption of syncretic elements, can be seen in the rise of the cult of the Magna Mater (Great Mother) in the Roman Empire, which drew inspiration from Egyptian and Anatolian religious traditions.

Reflection on the significance of syncretism in shaping religious worldviews

The syncretism of Egyptian religious beliefs with Greek and Roman influences offers valuable insights into the dynamics of religious syncretism and its impact on religious worldviews. It demonstrates the adaptability and flexibility of religious systems in incorporating new ideas and practices while maintaining core beliefs.

Syncretism served as a bridge between different cultures, facilitating dialogue, exchange, and the exploration of new spiritual possibilities. It allowed individuals to navigate between different religious traditions and find common ground, leading to a more inclusive and interconnected religious worldview. Syncretism also provided a means for individuals to express their cultural identities and forge connections between diverse communities.

Consideration of the challenges and controversies surrounding syncretism in ancient Egypt

While syncretism in ancient Egypt brought about significant cultural and religious developments, it was not without challenges and controversies. The assimilation of foreign deities and practices into Egyptian religious beliefs and the resulting syncretic worship could be met with resistance from traditionalists who sought to preserve the purity of Egyptian religious traditions.

Critics argued that syncretism diluted the authenticity of Egyptian religious practices and compromised the integrity of the pantheon. They raised concerns about the merging of deities and the potential loss of distinctive cultural and religious identities.

Furthermore, syncretism also raised questions about cultural appropriation and power dynamics, as the adoption of Greek and Roman religious elements could be seen as a form of cultural domination by foreign powers.

The challenges and controversies surrounding syncretism highlight the complex nature of cultural and religious exchange and the tension between tradition and innovation. They prompt us to critically examine the motivations, consequences, and ethical implications of syncretism in ancient Egypt and its broader significance in the study of religious and cultural history.

Chapter 20: Temples, Festivals, and Tools used 332 BCE - 395 CE

The Ptolemaic and Roman periods mark a significant phase in the history of ancient Egypt, characterized by the rule of foreign powers and the interplay between Egyptian religious traditions and Greek and Roman influences. Following the conquest of Egypt by Alexander the Great in 332 BCE, the Ptolemaic dynasty, founded by one of Alexander's generals, ruled over Egypt until the Roman annexation in 30 BCE. The Roman period then witnessed the integration of Egyptian culture into the broader Roman Empire, leading to further transformations in religious practices.

Significance of temples, festivals, and tools in religious practices during this period

Temples, festivals, and tools held immense significance in the religious practices of ancient Egypt during the Ptolemaic and Roman periods. Temples were not only sacred spaces but also served as centers of religious, economic, and administrative activities. They were believed to be the dwelling places of deities, where rituals, offerings, and prayers were conducted to maintain cosmic order and seek divine favor.

Festivals played a vital role in the religious calendar, marking important occasions and honoring specific deities. These festive gatherings brought communities together, fostering a sense of shared identity and reinforcing religious devotion. Rituals, processions, and various activities were carried out during festivals to honor and interact with the gods, ensuring the continued prosperity and well-being of individuals and society as a whole.

Tools and implements used in religious rituals were essential for facilitating communication with the divine and performing sacred acts. These objects, such as statues, altars, and offering tables, held symbolic and practical significance. They represented the presence of deities, provided a platform for making offerings, and facilitated the transmission of prayers and petitions.

Aim of the chapter to explore the continuity and transformation of these religious practices

The aim of this chapter is to delve into the rich tapestry of religious practices during the Ptolemaic and Roman periods, focusing specifically on temples, festivals, and tools. Through a thorough examination of archaeological evidence, textual sources, and scholarly research, we will explore how these practices evolved, adapted, and assimilated Greek and Roman influences.

By studying the continuity and transformation of religious practices, we aim to gain a deeper understanding of the complex interplay between Egyptian, Greek, and Roman cultures. We will analyze the impact of foreign rule and cultural exchange on temple architecture, festival traditions, and the use of tools in religious rituals. Furthermore, we will consider the implications of these transformations on religious beliefs, social dynamics, and the broader religious landscape of ancient Egypt during this period.

Throughout the chapter, examples, problems, and exercises will be provided to illustrate and engage students in critical thinking and discussion. By exploring the intricacies of temples, festivals, and tools, we will unravel the religious fabric of the Ptolemaic and Roman periods, shedding light on the intermingling of diverse cultural influences and the enduring legacy of ancient Egyptian religious practices.

Temples in the Ptolemaic and Roman Periods

During the Ptolemaic and Roman periods, temple architecture in Egypt underwent significant changes influenced by both Greek and Roman styles. The temples of this period displayed a fusion of Egyptian, Greek, and Roman architectural elements, resulting in a unique syncretic style.

Greek architectural influences can be seen in the use of columns, particularly the Corinthian order, which became prevalent in temple construction. Greek decorative motifs, such as acanthus leaves and friezes depicting mythological scenes, were also incorporated into the temple designs. Roman architectural influences introduced features like larger and more elaborate temple complexes, monumental gateways, and open courtyards.

The integration of these different architectural styles reflected the cultural exchange and syncretism that occurred during this period. It was an expression of the coexistence and intermingling of Egyptian, Greek, and Roman traditions, creating a distinct architectural identity for the temples of the Ptolemaic and Roman periods.

Role of temples as centers of religious, economic, and administrative activities

Temples held a central role in the socio-religious life of ancient Egypt during the Ptolemaic and Roman periods. They served as not only places of worship but also as centers of economic and administrative activities.

Religiously, temples were considered the dwelling places of deities, where divine rituals were conducted to maintain cosmic order and ensure the well-being of the community. Priests and priestesses played a crucial role in overseeing temple rituals, offerings, and maintaining the sacred spaces.

Economically, temples owned vast lands and received offerings from devotees, including agricultural produce, livestock, and precious goods. These offerings provided sustenance for the temple personnel and were often redistributed to support the local community. Temples also served as banks, offering loans and acting as intermediaries in commercial transactions.

Administratively, temples played a significant role in local governance and law enforcement. They had their own hierarchies and administrative structures, with high-ranking priests holding positions of authority. Temples were involved in the regulation of religious and social matters, including the collection of taxes and the resolution of disputes.

Functions and symbolism of different areas within temple complexes

Temple complexes were divided into distinct areas, each serving a specific function and carrying symbolic significance. These areas included the sanctuary, offering halls, and courtyards.

The sanctuary, also known as the naos, was the most sacred part of the temple. It housed the cult statue of the deity to whom the temple was dedicated. The sanctuary was accessible only to the high-ranking priests and was considered the dwelling place of the deity. It represented the divine presence and served as the focal point of worship and communication with the gods.

Offering halls were spaces within the temple complex where various rituals and offerings took place. They were often adorned with reliefs and inscriptions depicting religious scenes and were used for making offerings to the deities. Offerings included food, drink, incense, and symbolic representations of wealth and fertility. These halls symbolized the reciprocity between humans and the divine, with offerings given as acts of devotion and gratitude.

Courtyards were open spaces within the temple complex where processions, festivals, and communal gatherings took place. They provided an area for public worship, where devotees could participate in rituals and witness religious performances. Courtyards were often adorned with statues, stelae, and other decorative elements, reinforcing the sacredness of the space. They served as communal spaces, fostering a sense of unity and shared religious experience among the worshippers.

Understanding the functions and symbolism of different areas within temple complexes provides insights into the religious practices, social dynamics, and symbolic worldview of the Ptolemaic and Roman periods. By studying the architecture and design of temples, as well as the activities that took place within them, we can gain a deeper appreciation for the multifaceted role of temples in ancient Egyptian society during this transformative era.

Festivals and Celebrations

Festivals held immense significance in the religious calendar of ancient Egypt during the Ptolemaic and Roman periods. They served as key moments of religious observance and communal celebration, marking important events in the mythological narratives and honoring the deities. Festivals provided a structured framework for the expression of religious devotion and the reaffirmation of the cosmic order.

Overview of major festivals and their associated deities

Numerous festivals were celebrated throughout the Ptolemaic and Roman periods, each dedicated to specific deities and their mythological narratives. Some of the major festivals include:

Opet Festival: Held in honor of the Theban triad—Amun, Mut, and Khonsu. The festival involved a grand procession where the cult statues of the deities were carried from the temple of Karnak to the temple of Luxor.

Festival of Bastet: Devoted to the goddess Bastet, the festival celebrated her protective and nurturing aspects. It included music, dancing, and processions with the statue of Bastet, as well as the offering of food and drink.

Heb-Sed Festival: A jubilee festival celebrated by the pharaoh to renew his kingship. It involved elaborate rituals, including the pharaoh's participation in athletic competitions and the symbolic reenactment of his coronation.

Festival of Isis: Dedicated to the goddess Isis, this festival celebrated her role as a divine mother and protector. It involved processions, music, and dramatic performances depicting the resurrection of Osiris.

Rituals, processions, and activities during festivals

Festivals were characterized by a variety of rituals, processions, and activities that aimed to honor the deities, engage the community, and ensure the continued divine favor. These included:

Offering ceremonies: Devotees presented offerings of food, drink, incense, and symbolic objects to the deities as acts of devotion and gratitude. These offerings were believed to nourish the gods and establish a reciprocal relationship between humans and the divine.

Processions: Festivals often featured grand processions where the cult statues of the deities were paraded through the streets or within the temple complex. These processions allowed the deities to interact with their worshippers, while the participants demonstrated their devotion and sought blessings.

Ritual performances: Ritual performances, including music, dancing, and theatrical reenactments of mythological stories, were integral to many festivals. These performances served to invoke the presence of the deities, communicate their mythic narratives, and engage the audience in a shared religious experience.

Significance of festivals in community cohesion and religious devotion

Festivals played a vital role in fostering community cohesion and strengthening religious devotion among the ancient Egyptian population. These communal celebrations provided a sense of belonging and shared identity, as people from different social strata came together to honor the deities.

Participating in festivals allowed individuals to express their religious beliefs, reaffirm their cultural values, and connect with the divine. The rituals and activities during festivals were seen as opportunities to seek blessings, protection, and divine favor for themselves, their families, and the community as a whole.

Furthermore, festivals provided a platform for the dissemination of religious teachings, mythological narratives, and moral values. Through the theatrical performances and symbolic rituals, individuals were not only entertained but also educated about the religious and ethical principles upheld by their society.

In conclusion, festivals held immense importance in the religious and social fabric of ancient Egypt during the Ptolemaic and Roman periods. They served as key moments of religious observance, community cohesion, and spiritual rejuvenation. By actively participating in festivals, individuals reaffirmed their connection to the divine, celebrated their cultural heritage, and sought spiritual fulfillment.

Tools and Implements in Rituals

Religious rituals often involve the use of various tools and implements that hold symbolic and functional significance. These objects assist in creating a sacred space, facilitating communication with the divine, and carrying out specific religious practices. Understanding the role and significance of these tools is essential to comprehending the religious beliefs and practices of a given culture or tradition.

Ritual objects, such as statues, altars, and offering tables

Statues, altars, and offering tables are among the most prominent ritual objects found in religious practices across different cultures. Statues, often representing deities or revered figures, serve as physical embodiments or focal points of divine presence. They can be made of various materials such as stone, wood, or metal.

Altars and offering tables provide dedicated spaces for rituals and offerings. They are often adorned with symbols and imagery associated with the particular deity or religious tradition. These objects serve as platforms for making offerings, conducting ceremonies, and establishing a connection between the human and divine realms.

Symbols and symbolism in religious artifacts

Symbols play a crucial role in religious artifacts and tools, as they convey deeper meanings and represent abstract concepts. Symbols can be found in various forms, such as engravings, carvings, or painted representations on objects.

They may include sacred images, geometric patterns, or specific motifs associated with the religious tradition.

Symbolism in religious artifacts helps to communicate and evoke specific religious ideas, principles, or narratives. For example, a symbol of a lotus flower in ancient Egyptian religious artifacts could represent rebirth and the cycle of life, while a cross in Christian religious artifacts signifies sacrifice and redemption.

Materials and techniques used in crafting religious tools

The materials and techniques used in crafting religious tools depend on the cultural and historical context. Ancient civilizations often utilized materials that were readily available in their surroundings, such as stone, wood, clay, or precious metals.

Craftsmen and artisans employed various techniques, including carving, sculpting, painting, and metalworking, to create intricate and visually striking religious tools. The craftsmanship and attention to detail in these objects reflected the reverence and importance placed on religious rituals and practices.

In conclusion, tools and implements used in religious rituals are essential elements in expressing and facilitating religious beliefs and practices. Statues, altars, offering tables, and other objects possess both practical and symbolic significance, providing a tangible connection between the human and divine realms. Symbols and materials used in religious artifacts further enhance the religious experience, conveying deeper meanings and invoking spiritual connections.

Integration of Greek and Roman Influences

During the Ptolemaic and Roman periods in ancient Egypt, the influence of Greek and Roman cultures had a significant impact on temple architecture and design. As a result of the conquest of Egypt by Alexander the Great and the subsequent rule of the Ptolemaic dynasty, Greek architectural styles and design principles became intertwined with traditional Egyptian temple structures.

Greek architectural elements, such as the use of columns, porticos, and pediments, were incorporated into Egyptian temple designs, blending with the existing Egyptian architectural features. This fusion of styles created a unique architectural synthesis that showcased the cultural exchange and syncretism between Greek and Egyptian traditions.

Incorporation of Greek and Roman deities and practices into Egyptian festivals

With the establishment of Greek and Roman rule, the religious landscape of ancient Egypt underwent significant changes. Greek and Roman deities were integrated into the Egyptian pantheon, and their associated practices and rituals became a part of Egyptian religious festivals.

For example, the worship of Greek deities like Isis, Serapis, and Dionysus became popular in Egypt. Festivals honoring these deities incorporated Greek rituals and processions alongside traditional Egyptian practices. This syncretic approach allowed for the coexistence and blending of religious beliefs and practices from different cultural backgrounds.

Shifts in religious symbolism and the use of tools and implements

The integration of Greek and Roman influences in Egyptian religious practices led to shifts in religious symbolism and the use of tools and implements. Greek and Roman symbolism and iconography became intertwined with traditional Egyptian symbols, creating a rich and complex tapestry of religious imagery.

Tools and implements used in rituals also underwent changes as a result of syncretism. Egyptian religious tools and objects, such as statues, amulets, and ritual vessels, began to incorporate Greek and Roman design elements and motifs. These syncretic objects reflected the blended religious beliefs and practices of the time and served as tangible expressions of the cultural exchange between different civilizations.

Impact of syncretism on the overall religious landscape

The process of syncretism, influenced by the integration of Greek and Roman cultures, had a profound impact on the overall religious landscape of ancient Egypt during the Ptolemaic and Roman periods. Syncretism resulted in the coexistence and blending of different religious traditions, creating a diverse and pluralistic religious environment.

The integration of Greek and Roman deities, rituals, and practices into Egyptian religious life brought about a new understanding of the divine and expanded the religious worldview of the ancient Egyptians. This syncretic approach allowed for the adaptation and evolution of religious beliefs, accommodating diverse cultural influences and promoting cultural exchange and tolerance.

However, syncretism was not without its challenges and controversies. The blending of different religious traditions sometimes resulted in conflicts and tensions between different groups. Some individuals and factions resisted the assimilation of foreign influences and advocated for the preservation of traditional Egyptian religious practices. These debates and disagreements added further complexity to the religious landscape and demonstrate the ongoing dialogue and negotiation between different religious perspectives.

In conclusion, the integration of Greek and Roman influences in ancient Egypt had a profound impact on temple architecture, religious festivals, symbolism, and religious practices. Syncretism allowed for the coexistence and blending of different cultural and religious traditions, shaping the religious landscape and expanding the religious worldview of ancient Egyptians during the Ptolemaic and Roman periods.

Preservation and Destruction

During the Ptolemaic and Roman periods in ancient Egypt, there were concerted efforts to preserve and maintain temples and religious sites. Temples held significant religious, cultural, and economic importance, and their upkeep was seen as crucial for the well-being of the community and the continuity of religious practices.

The priests and temple staff played a vital role in the maintenance of temples. They were responsible for conducting rituals, ensuring the cleanliness of the temple grounds, and overseeing repairs and renovations. The pharaohs and elite members of society also made substantial contributions to the upkeep of temples through patronage and donations.

Various rituals and ceremonies were performed regularly to honor the deities and maintain the sanctity of the temples. These rituals involved offerings, purification rites, and processions, all aimed at fostering a connection between the human and divine realms. The temples were considered sacred spaces, and their preservation was seen as essential for maintaining divine favor and cosmic order.

Instances of temple destruction and repurposing under foreign rule

Despite efforts to preserve temples, there were instances of temple destruction and repurposing under foreign rule. Throughout history, Egypt came under the control of various foreign powers, including the Persians, Greeks, and Romans. These conquerors often brought their own religious beliefs and practices, which sometimes led to the alteration or destruction of existing temples.

For example, during the reign of Akhenaten in the 14th century BCE, the temples dedicated to traditional Egyptian gods were dismantled and abandoned in favor of the worship of the Aten, the sun disc. Similarly, when Egypt came under Roman rule, some temples were repurposed or converted into Christian churches, as Christianity became the dominant religion in the later Roman period.

The destruction and repurposing of temples were often driven by political, religious, or cultural motivations. Conquerors sought to assert their authority, erase the symbols of previous rulers, or impose their own religious beliefs. These actions not only altered the physical landscape but also had profound implications for the religious practices and cultural identity of the Egyptian people.

Rediscovery and archaeological study of temples and religious artifacts from this period

In modern times, there has been a resurgence of interest in ancient Egypt, leading to the rediscovery and archaeological study of temples and religious artifacts from the Ptolemaic and Roman periods. Archaeological expeditions and excavations have uncovered numerous temples, statues, inscriptions, and religious objects, shedding light on the religious practices and beliefs of the time.

The study of these artifacts has provided valuable insights into the architectural styles, construction techniques, and artistic representations of temples. They have also revealed the complex interplay between Egyptian, Greek, and Roman influences in temple design and religious iconography.

Archaeologists and historians have pieced together the history of temple destruction and repurposing through the analysis of inscriptions, historical records, and architectural evidence. By studying the remains of temples, researchers have gained a deeper understanding of the religious rituals, ceremonies, and festivals that took place within these sacred spaces.

The rediscovery and ongoing archaeological study of temples and religious artifacts have not only contributed to our knowledge of ancient Egypt but have also raised awareness about the need for their preservation and protection. These efforts ensure that these invaluable cultural and religious treasures are conserved for future generations to study, appreciate, and learn from.

Conclusion

In conclusion, the study of temples, festivals, and tools used during the Ptolemaic and Roman periods in ancient Egypt provides us with a wealth of knowledge about the religious practices and beliefs of this time. Throughout this chapter, we have explored various aspects of these religious practices and their integration with Greek and Roman influences. Let us recapitulate the key findings and insights that have emerged from our exploration.

Firstly, we have seen that temples played a central role in the religious, economic, and administrative life of ancient Egypt. They were not merely places of worship but also served as centers of community activity and cultural expression. The architectural styles and design influences in temple construction reflected the blending of Egyptian, Greek, and Roman cultures, showcasing the syncretism and cultural exchange that characterized this period.

Festivals held great importance in the religious calendar, serving as occasions for communal celebration and devotion. Major festivals were associated with specific deities and involved elaborate rituals, processions, and activities that reinforced social cohesion and expressed religious fervor. The festivals provided opportunities for the community to come together, interact with the divine, and reaffirm their religious identities.

The tools and implements used in religious rituals were not only practical objects but also held symbolic significance. Statues, altars, offering tables, and other ritual objects were crafted with precision and adorned with symbols that conveyed religious meaning. The materials and techniques used in their creation further reflected the cultural exchange and syncretism that permeated the religious landscape.

The integration of Greek and Roman influences had a profound impact on Egyptian religious practices during this period. Greek and Roman deities found their place within the Egyptian pantheon, leading to the emergence of hybrid divine figures through syncretism. Greek philosophical ideas, particularly Neoplatonism, influenced the intellectual landscape and contributed to the theological synthesis between Greek philosophy and Egyptian religious beliefs.

Exploring the Rituals, Beliefs, and Syncretism of Ancient Egyptian Religion

This integration extended to rituals, festivals, and the pursuit of spiritual enlightenment, creating a unique blend of traditions.

The enduring legacy of temples, festivals, and tools in ancient Egyptian religious practices is significant. These practices shaped the religious worldview of the people and left a lasting impact on subsequent religious traditions and cultural developments. The syncretism and cultural exchange that characterized this period continue to be areas of study and research, deepening our understanding of ancient Egyptian religion and its broader influence.

Looking ahead, further research and study in the field of ancient Egyptian religion during the Ptolemaic and Roman periods hold great promise. Exploring specific case studies, analyzing primary sources, and conducting archaeological investigations can provide more nuanced insights into the religious practices, beliefs, and cultural dynamics of this time. Additionally, interdisciplinary approaches, drawing from fields such as archaeology, anthropology, and religious studies, can offer new perspectives and shed light on previously unexplored aspects of this rich and complex era.

In conclusion, the examination of temples, festivals, and tools used during the Ptolemaic and Roman periods offers a window into the religious practices, cultural interactions, and historical developments of ancient Egypt. Through the lens of syncretism, we have gained a deeper appreciation for the blending of Egyptian, Greek, and Roman influences and the enduring legacy they have left on ancient Egyptian religion. Further research and study in this field will undoubtedly continue to enrich our understanding of this fascinating period in Egyptian history.

Chapter 21: Prayers, Hymns, Chants, and Spells Blending Egyptian and Hellenistic-Roman Religious Traditions

The Hellenistic-Roman period in Egypt, spanning from 332 BCE to 395 CE, marked a significant phase in the country's history, characterized by the blending of Egyptian and Hellenistic-Roman cultural and religious traditions. This period was shaped by the conquest of Egypt by Alexander the Great and the subsequent establishment of the Ptolemaic dynasty, followed by the Roman conquest and the integration of Egypt into the Roman Empire. These historical events brought forth a dynamic cultural exchange and syncretism between Egyptian, Greek, and Roman beliefs, practices, and religious systems.

Religious texts, such as prayers, hymns, chants, and spells, played a crucial role in this syncretic landscape, acting as bridges between the ancient Egyptian religious heritage and the influences from the Hellenistic and Roman cultures. These texts provide valuable insights into the evolving religious practices and the intermingling of Egyptian and Hellenistic-Roman religious beliefs and concepts. By studying these texts, we can gain a deeper understanding of the complex and nuanced nature of religious syncretism during this period.

Prayers, as expressions of devotion and communication with the divine, were an integral part of religious life in both ancient Egypt and the Hellenistic-Roman world. During the Hellenistic-Roman period, prayers underwent a transformation as Egyptian religious traditions merged with Greek and Roman influences. Syncretic prayers emerged, incorporating elements and language from both Egyptian and Hellenistic-Roman religious traditions. These prayers reflected the attempts to reconcile and blend the deities, cosmologies, and theological concepts of the different cultures.

Hymns, on the other hand, were poetic compositions that extolled the virtues and qualities of deities. They served as a means to honor and worship the gods, as well as to express spiritual and emotional sentiments. In the Hellenistic-Roman period, hymns witnessed a fascinating fusion of Egyptian and Hellenistic-Roman religious themes, symbolism, and imagery. They showcased the adaptation of Egyptian deities into the Hellenistic and Roman pantheons, resulting in the creation of hybrid divine figures and the incorporation of Greek and Roman poetic techniques and literary styles.

Chants, with their repetitive and rhythmic nature, played a significant role in religious rituals and communal worship. These vocal expressions created a sense of unity and heightened spiritual experience among the participants. In the Hellenistic-Roman context, chants underwent a process of syncretism, incorporating elements from Egyptian, Greek, and Roman religious practices. The rhythmic patterns, vocal techniques, and musical elements in syncretic chants reflected the blending of diverse cultural traditions, creating a unique and harmonious expression of worship.

Spells, or magical incantations, were an integral part of ancient Egyptian religious practices and played a prominent role in the Hellenistic-Roman period as well. These spells were believed to have the power to invoke divine forces, protect against evil, or bring about desired outcomes. Syncretic spells emerged during this period, combining elements from Egyptian magical traditions with Hellenistic and Roman magical practices. They reflected the fusion of beliefs, rituals, and magical techniques, serving as a testament to the integration and exchange of magical knowledge and practices between the cultures.

In conclusion, the Hellenistic-Roman period in Egypt witnessed a remarkable blending of Egyptian and Hellenistic-Roman religious traditions, as reflected in the prayers, hymns, chants, and spells of the time. These religious texts offer a window into the syncretic nature of the period, where Egyptian, Greek, and Roman beliefs and practices merged, adapted, and transformed. Through the study of these texts, we can gain a deeper understanding of the cultural exchange, theological developments, and the rich tapestry of religious beliefs and practices that characterized this period. By exploring the intricacies of prayers, hymns, chants, and spells, we can unravel the complexities of religious syncretism and its enduring influence on the religious landscape of ancient Egypt.

Syncretism in Religious Practices

Syncretism, in the context of religious practices, refers to the blending or amalgamation of different religious beliefs, rituals, and traditions. It occurs when cultures come into contact with one another and mutually influence each other, resulting in the integration and transformation of religious ideas and practices. During the Hellenistic-Roman period in Egypt, syncretism played a significant role in shaping the religious landscape, as Egyptian, Greek, and Roman cultures interacted and merged.

Exploring the Rituals, Beliefs, and Syncretism of Ancient Egyptian Religion

The influence of Hellenistic and Roman religious beliefs and practices on Egyptian traditions during this period cannot be overstated. With the conquest of Egypt by Alexander the Great and the subsequent establishment of the Ptolemaic dynasty, Greek culture and religion began to exert a profound influence on Egyptian society. Greek deities were assimilated into the Egyptian pantheon, and Egyptian deities were often identified with their Greek counterparts, resulting in the creation of hybrid divine figures. This syncretic approach allowed for a harmonious coexistence of both Egyptian and Greek religious beliefs.

Similarly, the Roman conquest of Egypt further impacted the religious landscape by introducing Roman deities and religious practices. Roman religious festivals and rituals were integrated into Egyptian religious calendar, and temples dedicated to Roman deities were constructed alongside Egyptian temples. The assimilation of Roman religious influences added another layer of syncretism to the already blended Egyptian-Greek religious traditions.

Syncretic texts, such as prayers, hymns, chants, and spells, served as tangible evidence of the blending of Egyptian, Greek, and Roman religious traditions. These texts reflected the syncretic nature of religious beliefs and practices during the Hellenistic-Roman period. They incorporated elements, language, and symbolism from all three cultures, showcasing the attempts to reconcile and merge diverse religious concepts.

For instance, prayers from this period often invoked both Egyptian and Hellenistic-Roman deities, demonstrating the integration of pantheons and the acknowledgment of multiple religious traditions. Hymns combined Egyptian and Hellenistic-Roman poetic styles, praising deities from both cultures. Chants, with their rhythmic patterns and musical elements, incorporated techniques and motifs from all three cultures, creating a syncretic expression of worship. Spells, with their magical incantations, blended Egyptian magical practices with Hellenistic and Roman influences, showcasing the fusion of magical knowledge and techniques.

These syncretic texts not only provide insight into the religious beliefs and practices of the time but also reflect the cultural and social dynamics of the Hellenistic-Roman period in Egypt. They highlight the ongoing dialogue and exchange between Egyptian, Greek, and Roman religious systems, as well as the evolving religious worldview that emerged as a result.

In conclusion, syncretism played a pivotal role in the religious practices of the Hellenistic-Roman period in Egypt. The influence of Greek and Roman cultures resulted in the blending and integration of Egyptian religious traditions, giving rise to a syncretic religious landscape. Syncretic texts, such as prayers, hymns, chants, and spells, served as valuable sources that reflect the blending of these traditions. They provide a tangible representation of the cultural exchange, theological developments, and the ongoing dialogue between Egyptian, Greek, and Roman religious beliefs and practices during this transformative period in ancient Egypt.

Prayers Reflecting Syncretism

Prayers reflecting syncretism during the Hellenistic-Roman period in Egypt offer a fascinating glimpse into the blending of Egyptian and Hellenistic-Roman religious traditions. These prayers demonstrate the syncretic nature of religious beliefs and provide valuable insights into the cultural and theological dynamics of the time.

One of the key aspects of syncretic prayers is the incorporation of elements from both Egyptian and Hellenistic-Roman religious traditions. They often invoke deities from both pantheons, highlighting the assimilation and integration of different divine figures. For example, prayers may address Egyptian gods such as Amun or Isis alongside Greek or Roman gods like Zeus or Jupiter. By including deities from multiple traditions, syncretic prayers reflect the attempts to unify and harmonize various religious beliefs.

Common themes and motifs can be identified in these syncretic prayers. They often express universal human concerns such as protection, guidance, and blessings. Additionally, they emphasize concepts of divine power, wisdom, and benevolence, which are shared across different religious systems. The prayers may also address specific needs or challenges faced by individuals or the community, seeking divine intervention and assistance.

The language and structure of syncretic prayers exhibit a fusion of Egyptian and Hellenistic-Roman influences. Egyptian prayers often had a formulaic structure, with specific invocations and praises for the gods. Greek and Roman poetic styles and rhetorical devices, such as metaphors and vivid imagery, were integrated into the prayers. This blending of linguistic and structural elements reflects the syncretic nature of the religious practices and the attempts to reconcile different cultural and religious traditions.

The purpose of syncretic prayers in the context of syncretism was multi-faceted. They served as a means of communication with the divine, seeking blessings, protection, and guidance from the gods. Prayers were also performed as part of rituals and religious ceremonies, reinforcing communal bonds and fostering a sense of religious identity. Moreover, they played a role in expressing devotion, gratitude, and reverence towards the gods, enhancing the spiritual connection between the individual and the divine.

In the context of syncretism, syncretic prayers demonstrate the fluidity and adaptability of religious beliefs and practices. They reflect the cultural exchange and dialogue between Egyptian, Greek, and Roman religious traditions, as well as the efforts to integrate and harmonize diverse theological concepts. These prayers provide evidence of the dynamic and evolving religious landscape during the Hellenistic-Roman period, highlighting the cultural and theological transformation that occurred as a result of syncretism.

In conclusion, the analysis of prayers reflecting syncretism reveals the blending of Egyptian and Hellenistic-Roman religious traditions. These prayers incorporate elements from both pantheons, address common themes and concerns, and exhibit a fusion of linguistic and structural influences. They serve as a means of communication with the divine, express devotion and gratitude, and play a role in communal worship and ritual practices. The study of syncretic prayers provides valuable insights into the cultural, theological, and social dynamics of the Hellenistic-Roman period in Egypt and the impact of syncretism on ancient Egyptian religious beliefs and practices.

Hymns Reflecting Syncretism

Hymns reflecting syncretism during the Hellenistic-Roman period in Egypt serve as remarkable examples of the blending of Egyptian and Hellenistic-Roman religious traditions. These hymns offer valuable insights into the cultural and theological dynamics of the time, showcasing the interplay between different religious systems and the creative synthesis that resulted.

The examination of syncretic hymns reveals the fusion of Egyptian and Hellenistic-Roman religious themes and symbolism. These hymns often incorporate elements from both traditions, intertwining the imagery and symbolism associated with Egyptian deities and their Hellenistic-Roman counterparts. For instance, a syncretic hymn might combine references to the Egyptian god Horus with the Greek god Apollo, presenting them as intertwined aspects of a unified divine entity. Through this blending, syncretic hymns reflect the syncretism that took place during this period and the attempt to harmonize diverse religious beliefs.

Poetic elements, metaphors, and imagery are important components of syncretic hymns. These hymns employ poetic language, employing literary devices such as similes, metaphors, and alliteration to create vivid and evocative descriptions. They draw upon the rich symbolism and mythological narratives of both Egyptian and Hellenistic-Roman traditions, using them to convey complex theological concepts and profound spiritual experiences. By weaving together diverse poetic elements, syncretic hymns create a unique artistic expression that transcends the boundaries of individual religious systems.

Syncretic hymns play a crucial role in expressing devotion and establishing a connection with the divine. Through the recitation or singing of these hymns, worshippers express their reverence and adoration for the gods, seeking to establish a profound spiritual connection. The hymns serve as a means of praising and glorifying the divine, expressing gratitude, and seeking divine favor. They provide a channel for worshippers to convey their deepest emotions and aspirations, fostering a sense of spiritual communion and unity with the divine presence.

Furthermore, syncretic hymns serve as a bridge between different religious traditions, facilitating a sense of religious harmony and inclusivity. They demonstrate the recognition and acknowledgment of shared spiritual values and the interconnectedness of various divine entities. By blending the religious themes and symbolism of different traditions, syncretic hymns promote a sense of interfaith dialogue and reconciliation, encouraging worshippers to transcend the boundaries of their respective religious backgrounds and engage in a more holistic and inclusive spiritual experience.

In conclusion, the analysis of hymns reflecting syncretism reveals the blending of Egyptian and Hellenistic-Roman religious themes and symbolism. These hymns incorporate elements from both traditions and employ poetic language, metaphors, and imagery to convey complex theological concepts. They serve as a means of expressing devotion, establishing a connection with the divine, and fostering a sense of religious harmony and inclusivity. The study of syncretic hymns provides valuable insights into the cultural, artistic, and spiritual dynamics of the Hellenistic-Roman period in Egypt and the role of syncretism in shaping religious beliefs and practices.

Chants Reflecting Syncretism

Chants reflecting syncretism during the Hellenistic-Roman period in Egypt offer intriguing glimpses into the blending of Hellenistic-Roman and Egyptian religious practices and beliefs. These chants provide valuable evidence of the cultural exchange and integration that took place during this time, as well as the evolution of religious rituals and worship.

The identification of chants that incorporate elements of Hellenistic-Roman religious practices and beliefs is a key aspect of understanding syncretism in the context of chant traditions. These syncretic chants often combine elements from both Egyptian and Hellenistic-Roman traditions, weaving together prayers, invocations, and ritualistic phrases from different religious systems. For example, a syncretic chant may incorporate Greek hymns dedicated to a particular deity alongside Egyptian invocations invoking the same or related deity. By merging these elements, syncretic chants reflect the coexistence and blending of diverse religious practices.

The analysis of syncretic chants involves the exploration of their rhythmic patterns, vocal techniques, and musical elements. These chants often exhibit unique rhythmic patterns, influenced by the traditions of both Egyptian and Hellenistic-Roman music. They may incorporate elements such as repetitive melodic phrases, vocal ornamentation, and call-and-response structures. By studying the rhythmic and musical characteristics of these chants, scholars can gain insights into the performative aspects of syncretic worship and the ways in which different musical traditions were integrated.

Furthermore, an exploration of the performative aspects of syncretic chants reveals their role in communal worship and ritual practices. Chants were integral to religious ceremonies and played a significant role in creating a sense of collective identity and shared spiritual experience. Syncretic chants were often performed in group settings, allowing worshippers from different religious backgrounds to come together and participate in a unified worship experience. The communal aspect of these chants fostered a sense of cohesion and solidarity among the worshippers, transcending individual religious boundaries and emphasizing shared spiritual values.

In addition to their performative role, syncretic chants served as powerful tools for invoking divine presence and facilitating spiritual transformation. Through the repetition of sacred phrases and the rhythmic chanting, worshippers aimed to establish a direct connection with the divine realm and evoke a sense of sacredness in the ritual space. The melodic and rhythmic elements of the chants, combined with the emotive power of the human voice, created an atmosphere conducive to spiritual contemplation and communion with the divine.

In conclusion, the study of chants reflecting syncretism in the Hellenistic-Roman period provides valuable insights into the blending of Hellenistic-Roman and Egyptian religious practices and beliefs. These chants incorporate elements from both traditions and exhibit unique rhythmic patterns, vocal techniques, and musical elements. They play a crucial role in communal worship and ritual practices, fostering a sense of unity and shared spiritual experience. By exploring the performative aspects of these chants, scholars can gain a deeper understanding of the cultural and religious dynamics of the Hellenistic-Roman period in Egypt and the ways in which syncretism shaped religious rituals and communal worship.

Spells Reflecting Syncretism

Spells reflecting syncretism during the Hellenistic-Roman period in Egypt provide fascinating insights into the merging of Egyptian and Hellenistic-Roman magical traditions and practices. These syncretic spells offer a rich tapestry of linguistic, structural, and symbolic elements that showcase the interplay between different magical systems and the evolution of magical beliefs and practices.

To begin with, the examination of syncretic spells involves a detailed analysis of the ways in which Egyptian and Hellenistic-Roman magical traditions were combined. These spells often incorporate elements such as invocations, rituals, and symbols from both traditions, creating a unique amalgamation of magical practices. For example, a syncretic spell may invoke Egyptian deities alongside Greek or Roman magical formulas, drawing on the perceived powers and influences of multiple divine beings. By examining the specific elements and techniques used in these spells, scholars can unravel the intricate web of syncretism and trace the influences of different magical traditions.

The analysis of the language, structure, and symbols used in syncretic spells offers valuable insights into the syncretic mindset and the ways in which practitioners navigated the complexities of merging diverse magical systems. Language plays a significant role in spellcasting, and syncretic spells often employ a combination of Egyptian, Greek, and Latin words and phrases. This linguistic blending reflects the linguistic landscape of the time and highlights the fluidity of magical traditions in a multicultural context. Additionally, the structure of syncretic spells may draw upon established spellcasting formats from both Egyptian and Hellenistic-Roman traditions, incorporating elements such as invocations, ritual actions, and symbolic gestures. Symbols, both visual and textual, are essential components of syncretic spells, representing the intermingling of deities, magical concepts, and cosmological forces.

The intended purposes and effects of syncretic spells within the context of syncretism are multifaceted. These spells were designed to address a range of needs and desires, including protection, healing, love, divination, and spiritual empowerment. Syncretic spells often aimed to harness the combined powers and influences of Egyptian and Hellenistic-Roman deities, creating a potent blend of magical energies. They were used to access the divine realms, seek favor from specific gods or goddesses, and manipulate cosmic forces for desired outcomes. The effects of these spells were believed to manifest in the physical, emotional, and spiritual realms, influencing the course of events and the well-being of individuals.

Furthermore, syncretic spells served as expressions of personal and communal religious devotion, reflecting the syncretic religious worldview of the time. They provided a means for individuals to engage with multiple cultural and religious traditions, bridging the gap between different belief systems and seeking spiritual empowerment and protection. Syncretic spells were also employed by professional magicians, healers, and diviners who catered to the magical and spiritual needs of the community. These practitioners played a crucial role in mediating between different religious and magical traditions, facilitating the integration and adaptation of diverse practices.

In conclusion, the study of spells reflecting syncretism in the Hellenistic-Roman period reveals the intricate interplay between Egyptian and Hellenistic-Roman magical traditions. These spells combine elements of language, structure, and symbols from both traditions, showcasing the fusion of diverse magical systems. They were designed to address various needs and desires, harnessing the powers of multiple deities and cosmic forces. Syncretic spells serve as testament to the syncretic mindset and the dynamic nature of magical beliefs and practices in a multicultural context. By examining these spells, scholars can gain a deeper understanding of the intermingling of magical traditions and the ways in which syncretism shaped the landscape of ancient Egyptian magic during the Hellenistic-Roman period.

Title: Spell of Harmonious Protection

Ingredients:

A small figurine representing the Egyptian goddess Isis
A piece of parchment paper
A quill or fine-tipped pen
A small vial of sacred oil, infused with herbs representing protection (such as lavender and rosemary)

Exploring the Rituals, Beliefs, and Syncretism of Ancient Egyptian Religion

A white candle
A small offering of bread or fruit
Procedure:

Begin by creating a sacred space for the spellcasting. Cleanse the area and yourself using a ritual purifying technique, such as smudging with herbs or sprinkling consecrated water.

Light the white candle, symbolizing purity and divine presence. Allow its warm glow to fill the space with a tranquil atmosphere.

Take the piece of parchment paper and write the following incantation in a flowing, deliberate manner:

"Isis, great and mighty goddess,
Divine protector of all who seek your aid,
I call upon your sacred presence to be with me now.
In this syncretic blend of traditions,
May your power and wisdom intertwine with the divine forces of [name of chosen Hellenistic-Roman deity],
Creating a harmonious shield of protection around me."

Hold the figurine of Isis in your hands and visualize her divine energy enveloping you with a radiant shield of light. Feel the presence of the chosen Hellenistic-Roman deity merging with Isis, their energies intertwining in perfect harmony.

Anoint the figurine of Isis with a few drops of the sacred oil, symbolizing the infusion of protective energies. As you do so, recite the incantation again, focusing on the combined powers of Isis and the chosen deity.

Place the anointed figurine on the piece of parchment paper, folding it carefully to create a small packet. This packet represents the harmonious shield of protection.

Hold the packet in your hands and speak your intentions aloud, stating your desire for divine protection from all negative influences and harm. Ask the blended energies of Isis and the chosen deity to surround you with their loving and powerful shield.

Place the packet near the lit white candle and let it burn in a safe and controlled manner. As the flame consumes the parchment, envision your intentions being released into the universe and manifesting as a potent shield of protection.

Once the flame has extinguished, take a moment to express gratitude to Isis, the chosen deity, and any other divine forces you feel connected to. Offer a small portion of bread or fruit as a token of appreciation for their assistance.

Close the ritual by expressing your gratitude once again and extinguishing the white candle. Keep the figurine of Isis in a special place as a reminder of the harmonious blend of traditions and the protective energies invoked.

Title: Spell of Divine Guidance

Ingredients:

A small bowl or chalice
Dried herbs representing wisdom and clarity (such as sage and bay leaves)
A small piece of parchment paper
A quill or fine-tipped pen
Red ink or paint
A small amulet or talisman symbolizing divine guidance
A white or yellow candle
Sandalwood incense
Procedure:

Begin by preparing your sacred space. Clear the area of any distractions and ensure you have a quiet and peaceful environment for your spellwork. Light the sandalwood incense to purify the space and create a tranquil atmosphere.

Take the small bowl or chalice and fill it with water. This water represents the divine flow of wisdom and guidance.

Arrange the dried herbs around the bowl, creating a circular pattern. As you place each herb, focus on its symbolic significance in providing clarity and insight.

Write the following incantation on the piece of parchment paper using the red ink or paint:

"Great goddess Isis, embodiment of ancient Egyptian wisdom,
And [name of chosen Hellenistic-Roman deity], guardian of knowledge,
I invoke your combined powers to guide my path.
Grant me clarity of mind, insight, and divine inspiration.
May your wisdom flow through me like the sacred waters,
Leading me towards the answers I seek."

Hold the amulet or talisman in your hands and visualize the energies of Isis and the chosen deity intertwining within it. Envision a radiant light emanating from the amulet, symbolizing divine guidance and illumination.

Place the amulet on top of the parchment paper, allowing it to absorb the written incantation. As you do this, recite the incantation once more, infusing the amulet with your intentions and the blended energies of the deities.

Light the white or yellow candle, representing the divine spark of inspiration and enlightenment. Hold the amulet over the candle flame, allowing it to be cleansed and charged by the fire's transformative energy. Visualize the amulet absorbing the flame's energy, becoming a conduit for divine guidance.

Immerse the amulet into the bowl of water, allowing it to rest on the surface. As it touches the water, envision ripples of wisdom spreading throughout the liquid, infusing it with divine guidance.

Take a moment to gaze into the bowl of water, allowing your mind to become receptive to messages and insights from the deities. Ask for their guidance and clarity on a specific issue or question you seek answers for.

When you feel ready, remove the amulet from the water and gently pat it dry. Hold it in your hands and express your gratitude to Isis, the chosen deity, and any other divine forces you feel connected to. Thank them for their wisdom and guidance.

Close the ritual by extinguishing the candle and thanking the divine energies once again. Keep the amulet with you or wear it as a symbol of the blended wisdom and guidance you have invoked.

Interpretation and Significance

The cultural and religious significance of syncretic prayers, hymns, chants, and spells during the Hellenistic-Roman period in Egypt cannot be understated. These texts represent a blending of Egyptian and Hellenistic-Roman religious traditions, reflecting the complex interplay between different cultural and spiritual influences.

The theological implications of syncretic texts are multifaceted. They demonstrate the interconnectedness of religious beliefs and practices, highlighting the human tendency to seek common ground and merge diverse spiritual ideas. Syncretism allows for the integration of new concepts and deities into existing religious frameworks, resulting in a theological landscape that is dynamic and ever-evolving.

The syncretic texts also provide insights into the worldview of the people during this period. They reveal a willingness to embrace and incorporate foreign elements into their religious practices, demonstrating a certain openness and adaptability in their spiritual outlook. The blending of Egyptian and Hellenistic-Roman traditions suggests a desire to find commonalities and shared values across different cultures, emphasizing unity and harmony in the realm of religious belief.

The impact of syncretism on shaping religious beliefs and practices cannot be underestimated. It fostered a cultural exchange that enriched and diversified religious experiences. By incorporating elements from different traditions, syncretism provided individuals with a broader spiritual repertoire, allowing them to draw from a wider range of practices and beliefs to meet their religious needs. This integration of diverse influences contributed to the development of a rich and complex religious tapestry during the Hellenistic-Roman period in Egypt.

However, syncretism also raises important questions and challenges. Critics argue that it dilutes the authenticity of religious traditions and erodes the distinctiveness of individual cultures. They contend that syncretism can lead to the loss of cultural identity and a superficial blending of beliefs without a deep understanding of their origins and meanings.

By examining the cultural and religious significance of syncretic texts, analyzing their theological implications, and reflecting on the impact of syncretism on religious beliefs and practices, we gain a deeper understanding of the complexities of religious syncretism during the Hellenistic-Roman period in Egypt. This exploration invites us to consider the ways in which different cultures and belief systems can influence and interact with one another, shaping the religious landscape and the worldviews of those who embrace syncretic practices.

Conclusion

In conclusion, the study of syncretism in ancient Egyptian and Hellenistic-Roman religious traditions reveals a fascinating interplay of cultural influences and the blending of beliefs and practices. Throughout this chapter, we have explored the cultural, theological, and ritual aspects of syncretic prayers, hymns, chants, and spells, shedding light on their significance and impact during the Hellenistic-Roman period in Egypt.

Exploring the Rituals, Beliefs, and Syncretism of Ancient Egyptian Religion

One of the key findings of this chapter is the gradual integration of Egyptian and Hellenistic-Roman religious traditions through syncretism. We have seen how these syncretic texts served as bridges between different cultural and religious systems, showcasing the willingness of individuals and communities to adapt and incorporate diverse spiritual elements. The syncretic nature of these texts reflects the dynamic nature of religious beliefs and practices, highlighting the human capacity for cultural exchange and the formation of new spiritual identities.

The enduring legacy and influence of syncretism in ancient Egyptian and Hellenistic-Roman religious traditions cannot be overlooked. The syncretic texts we have examined serve as important artifacts that bear witness to the blending of beliefs, the evolution of religious practices, and the complex interplay of cultural influences. They continue to shape our understanding of the religious landscape of the time and provide valuable insights into the beliefs and aspirations of ancient Egyptian and Hellenistic-Roman societies.

Further research in the field of ancient Egyptian religion during the Hellenistic-Roman period holds great potential for expanding our knowledge and deepening our understanding. Future studies could focus on the examination of additional syncretic texts and the analysis of their linguistic and symbolic elements. Exploring the social and cultural contexts in which these texts were produced and used would provide valuable insights into the motivations and experiences of the individuals who embraced syncretic practices.

Additionally, interdisciplinary approaches that draw on fields such as anthropology, archaeology, and comparative religion can shed further light on the complexities of syncretism and its impact on religious belief systems. Comparative studies between different syncretic traditions across time and space would offer a broader perspective on the phenomenon and its significance in the wider context of human spiritual experiences.

In conclusion, the study of syncretic prayers, hymns, chants, and spells blending Egyptian and Hellenistic-Roman religious traditions provides a window into the rich tapestry of religious beliefs and practices during the Hellenistic-Roman period in Egypt. It underscores the dynamic and transformative nature of religious syncretism and invites us to explore further the interplay between cultures, beliefs, and spiritual experiences in ancient civilizations.

Temple of Isis at Pompeii

The Temple of Isis at Pompeii is a remarkable archaeological site that offers valuable insights into the religious practices and beliefs of the ancient Romans, particularly their fascination with Egyptian deities and syncretism between Egyptian and Roman religious traditions. Located in the ancient city of Pompeii, which was buried by the eruption of Mount Vesuvius in 79 CE, the Temple of Isis stands as a testament to the cultural exchange and religious syncretism that occurred during the Hellenistic-Roman period.

The Temple of Isis was dedicated to the Egyptian goddess Isis, who was worshipped as a powerful deity associated with magic, healing, and protection. Isis, with her Egyptian origins, gained popularity throughout the Roman Empire, and her worship became increasingly prominent during the Hellenistic period. The construction of the temple in Pompeii reflects the Romans' fascination with Egyptian culture and their eagerness to incorporate foreign deities into their religious practices.

The architectural design of the Temple of Isis exhibits a fusion of Egyptian and Roman elements, reflecting the syncretism of religious traditions. The temple's entrance, known as the propylaeum, features Egyptian-inspired motifs, such as lotus flower decorations and hieroglyphs. The interior of the temple comprises a central nave and side aisles, reminiscent of Roman architectural styles, while the sanctuary area, known as the adyton, contains an altar dedicated to the goddess Isis.

The presence of the Temple of Isis in Pompeii speaks to the cultural and religious diversity that existed in the ancient world. It served as a center of worship and a focal point for religious rituals and ceremonies. Devotees of Isis would gather at the temple to offer prayers, perform rituals, and seek the blessings and protection of the goddess. The temple complex likely included spaces for religious processions, musical performances, and other communal activities associated with religious worship.

The excavation and preservation of the Temple of Isis have provided archaeologists and historians with valuable insights into the religious practices and syncretism of the Hellenistic-Roman period. The discovery of statues, inscriptions, and other artifacts within the temple complex has helped to reconstruct the rituals and beliefs associated with the worship of Isis. These findings contribute to our understanding of how the ancient Romans embraced and adapted foreign religious traditions, blending them with their own spiritual practices.

Exploring the Rituals, Beliefs, and Syncretism of Ancient Egyptian Religion

The Temple of Isis at Pompeii stands as a testament to the cultural exchange and religious syncretism that occurred during the Hellenistic-Roman period. It serves as a reminder of the diverse religious landscape of ancient Rome and the fascination with foreign deities and rituals. The site offers a window into the beliefs, practices, and religious experiences of the people of Pompeii and provides valuable insights into the broader cultural and religious dynamics of the time.

Mysteries of Osiris-Dionysus

The mysteries of Osiris-Dionysus represent a fascinating and complex religious phenomenon that emerged from the blending of Egyptian and Greek religious traditions. This syncretic deity, combining elements of the Egyptian god Osiris and the Greek god Dionysus, embodies the convergence of two distinct cultural and religious systems.

Osiris, the ancient Egyptian god of the afterlife, death, and resurrection, was associated with fertility, renewal, and the cycle of life. Dionysus, on the other hand, was the Greek god of wine, ecstasy, and revelry, representing the transformative power of intoxication and the celebration of life. The merging of these two deities highlights the shared themes of death and rebirth, divine kingship, and the transformative potential of ritual practices.

The mysteries of Osiris-Dionysus were secretive religious rituals and ceremonies that aimed to initiate participants into the deeper mysteries of life, death, and the divine. These mysteries were characterized by ecstatic experiences, symbolic reenactments, and profound spiritual transformation. They offered a path to transcendence, connecting individuals with the divine and providing insights into the nature of existence and the afterlife.

The central myth of Osiris-Dionysus revolves around the death and resurrection of the god. Osiris, in Egyptian mythology, was murdered by his brother Set and subsequently resurrected by his wife Isis. In the Greek tradition, Dionysus experienced dismemberment and rebirth, symbolizing the cyclical nature of life and the transformative power of death and renewal. These myths formed the narrative framework for the mysteries, guiding initiates through a symbolic journey of death, descent into the underworld, and ultimate resurrection or spiritual rebirth.

The mysteries of Osiris-Dionysus involved various rituals, performances, and communal celebrations. These included processions, dramatic performances, music, dance, and symbolic acts such as the consumption of sacred substances or the wearing of ritual masks. Initiates underwent a series of trials and revelations, gradually gaining deeper insights into the mysteries and their personal connection to the divine.

The significance of the mysteries of Osiris-Dionysus extends beyond their religious and spiritual aspects. They served as a means of social cohesion, bringing individuals together in shared rituals and communal experiences. The mysteries provided a sense of belonging and identity within the larger religious and cultural context. They also offered individuals a transformative and cathartic experience, allowing them to confront their own mortality, experience transcendence, and seek personal liberation.

Despite the secrecy surrounding the mysteries, they left traces in the form of artistic depictions, inscriptions, and testimonies from ancient writers. These sources provide glimpses into the profound impact and enduring legacy of the Osiris-Dionysus mysteries. Their influence can be seen in various aspects of ancient culture, including art, literature, philosophy, and religious practices.

The mysteries of Osiris-Dionysus continue to captivate scholars and researchers, inspiring ongoing study and interpretation. They invite us to explore the depths of human spirituality, the transformative power of ritual, and the interconnectedness of diverse religious traditions. The mysteries remind us of the universal human longing for meaning, transcendence, and a deeper understanding of the mysteries of life and death.

Exploring the Rituals, Beliefs, and Syncretism of Ancient Egyptian Religion

Conclusion

In conclusion, this book has delved into the rich and intricate world of ancient Egyptian religion, focusing specifically on the blending of Egyptian and Hellenistic-Roman religious traditions during the Ptolemaic and Roman periods. We have explored various aspects of this cultural and religious exchange, including the integration of Greek and Roman influences in temples, festivals, tools, prayers, hymns, chants, and spells.

Throughout the book, we have examined the significance of these religious practices and texts in understanding the continuity and transformation of ancient Egyptian religious beliefs and practices. We have seen how syncretism played a crucial role in shaping the religious landscape of the time, as Egyptian and Hellenistic-Roman traditions merged, resulting in a unique and complex religious syncretism.

The chapters on temples, festivals, and tools have shed light on the architectural styles, functions, and symbolism of temple complexes, as well as the importance of festivals in religious calendars and community cohesion. We have explored the integration of Greek and Roman influences in temple design, the inclusion of foreign deities in the Egyptian pantheon, and the adaptation of Greek and Roman religious practices in Egyptian rituals.

Furthermore, the chapters on prayers, hymns, chants, and spells have highlighted the blending of Egyptian and Hellenistic-Roman religious concepts, themes, and symbolism. We have analyzed the language, structure, and purpose of these texts, uncovering their theological implications and the worldview they conveyed. Through the examination of syncretic prayers, hymns, chants, and spells, we have gained insights into the complex religious syncretism of the time.

The enduring legacy of these religious practices and texts is significant. They not only provide valuable insights into the ancient Egyptian culture and religious beliefs during the Ptolemaic and Roman periods but also serve as a testament to the dynamic nature of religion and its ability to adapt and evolve in response to cultural and historical contexts. The syncretism evident in these practices and texts reflects the interconnectedness of different religious traditions and the human inclination to seek spiritual meaning and connection.

In conclusion, this book has offered a comprehensive exploration of ancient Egyptian religion during the Ptolemaic and Roman periods, focusing on the integration of Greek and Roman influences. By examining temples, festivals, tools, prayers, hymns, chants, and spells, we have gained a deeper understanding of the complexities and intricacies of religious syncretism. The significance and enduring legacy of these ancient Egyptian practices and texts continue to inspire further research and study, inviting us to engage in critical thinking, discussion, and appreciation of the diverse religious heritage of ancient Egypt.

Appendix

Chants: Repetitive vocalizations or rhythmic utterances performed in a religious context, often accompanied by music or dance.

Continuity and Transformation: The simultaneous preservation of certain religious elements and the adaptation and evolution of others over time.

Cultural Context: The social, political, and historical circumstances in which a culture and its religious practices exist.

Cultural Exchange: The exchange of ideas, beliefs, and practices between different cultures, leading to mutual influence and adaptation.

Festival: Ceremonial events celebrated in honor of specific deities, involving rituals, processions, and communal activities.

Hymns: Poetic compositions praising and glorifying deities, often sung or recited during religious rituals and ceremonies.

Interconnectedness: The interconnected nature of religious traditions, as different cultures and belief systems influence and interact with one another.

Legacy: The lasting impact or influence of a particular historical period, culture, or religious practice on subsequent generations and traditions.

Prayers: Verbal or written expressions of devotion, supplication, and communication with the divine.

Ptolemaic Period: The period of ancient Egyptian history from 332 BCE to 30 BCE, characterized by the rule of the Ptolemaic dynasty of Greek origin.

Religious Syncretism: The merging of religious traditions and beliefs, resulting in the creation of new syncretic forms.

Roman Period: The period of ancient Egyptian history from 30 BCE to 395 CE, during which Egypt was under Roman rule.

Spells: Ritualized incantations or magical formulas used to invoke supernatural powers, protect against harm, or achieve desired outcomes.

Exploring the Rituals, Beliefs, and Syncretism of Ancient Egyptian Religion

Symbolism: The use of symbols to convey abstract concepts, emotions, or spiritual meanings.

Syncretism: The blending or fusion of different religious traditions, beliefs, and practices.

Syncretic Prayers, Hymns, Chants, and Spells: Religious texts and practices that combine elements of both Egyptian and Hellenistic-Roman traditions, reflecting the blending of religious beliefs and practices.

Temple: Sacred structures dedicated to deities, serving as places of worship, religious rituals, and community gathering.

Theological Implications: The philosophical and doctrinal consequences of religious beliefs and practices.

Tools: Objects and implements used in religious rituals and ceremonies, such as statues, altars, offering tables, and sacred instruments.

Worldview: A comprehensive framework of beliefs, values, and perspectives that shapes an individual or a society's understanding of the world and their place in it.

www.ingramcontent.com/pod-product-compliance
Lightning Source LLC
Chambersburg PA
CBHW082139120626
46553CB00010B/2712

* 9 7 9 8 8 8 9 9 0 0 3 4 4 *